Practical Spanish Grammar

Wiley Self-Teaching Guides teach practical skills from accounting to astronomy, management to mathematics. Look for them at your local bookstore.

Languages

French: A Self-Teaching Guide, by Suzanne A. Hershfield

German: A Self-Teaching Guide, by Heimy Taylor

Italian: A Self-Teaching Guide, by Edoardo A. Lebano

Advanced Spanish Grammar: A Self-Teaching Guide, by Marcial Prado

Business Skills

Making Successful Presentations: A Self-Teaching Guide, by Terry C. Smith

Managing Assertively: A Self-Teaching Guide, by Madelyn Burley-Allen

Managing Behavior on the Job: A Self-Teaching Guide, by Paul L. Brown

Teleselling: A Self-Teaching Guide, by James Porterfield

Successful Time Management: A Self-Teaching Guide, by Jack D. Ferner

Science

Astronomy: A Self-Teaching Guide, by Dinah L. Moche

Basic Physics: A Self-Teaching Guide, by Karl F. Kuhn

Chemistry: A Self-Teaching Guide, by Clifford C. Houk and Richard Post

Biology: A Self-Teaching Guide, by Steven D. Garber

Other Skills

How Grammar Works: A Self-Teaching Guide, by Patricia Osborn

Listening: The Forgotten Skill, A Self-Teaching Guide, by Madelyn Burley-Allen

Quick Vocabulary Power: A Self-Teaching Guide, by Jack S. Romine and Henry Ehrlich

Study Skills: A Student's Guide for Survival, A Self-Teaching Guide, by Robert A. Carman

Practical Spanish Grammar

A Self-Teaching Guide

Second Edition

Marcial Prado

John Wiley & Sons, Inc.
New York • Chichester • Weinheim • Brisbane • Singapore • Toronto

Copyright © 1983, 1997 by John Wiley & Sons, Inc.

Library of Congress Cataloging-in-Publication Data

Prado, Marcial
    Practical Spanish grammar / Marcial Prado. —2nd ed.
      p.   cm. — (A self-teaching guide)
    Includes index.
    ISBN 0-471-13446-5 (pbk. : alk. paper)
    1. Spanish language—Self-instruction.   2. Spanish language—
Grammar.   I. Title.   II. Series.
PC4112.5.P7   1997
468.2'421—dc21   96-39865

Printed in the United States of America

10 9 8 7 6 5 4 3 2 1

Contents

Preface

Practical Spanish Grammar: A Self-Teaching Guide aims at teaching the essentials of the Spanish language at the beginning level in a practical and pleasant manner. This programmed text-/workbook is designed for your use as a self-teaching guide; and it allows you to progress at your own pace as you practice, master, and test yourself on the points covered in each lesson. *Practical Spanish Grammar* may also be used in beginning college courses. The core content is that of the average textbook intended for a year of college Spanish—about 70 percent of the grammatical structures of the language and about one thousand of the most frequently used Spanish words. A typical textbook for first-year Spanish has thousands of colorful pictures, hundreds of short and long stories, many optional activities and exercises; and some of them have extended the vocabulary to about twenty-five hundred words, far beyond a realistic scope of a typical first-year Spanish grammar. Obviously we have omitted all of those things for practical reasons.

This book uses a linguistic approach in treating grammatical structures. Concise and down-to-earth explanations are followed by completion exercises for testing and reinforcing comprehension of the grammar—a unique feature not found in any other textbook. A variety of practical exercises completes each grammar section. As always, new words have to be memorized. To help you in this, a variety of exercises reinforces your memorization, and it expands your vocabulary. Furthermore, the new words are used in the grammar sections, both in the examples and in the exercises.

Features Contained in the Fifteen Lessons
- A vocabulary list of the words used in the lesson, with some cultural notes and several practical drills for the new words.
- A dialogue using the key words of the previous vocabulary—some with cultural notes—followed by exercises in comprehension and vocabulary.
- Three grammar sections, each with a corresponding completion practice, followed by one or more exercises.
- Answers for all of the exercises for self-correction.
- In addition, the book has a preliminary lesson on Spanish sounds and a 100-question exam with answer key after each group of five lessons for self-testing (90–100 is an *A*, 80–89 is a *B*, and so on).

Some Helpful Pointers for Using This Book
In taking the responsibility for your own progress, you will notice your knowledge of Spanish increasing quickly. The programmed format affords both a challenge and a means of self-evaluation. The following tips should help you make the best use of this book.

1. Do the exercises one at a time and check your answers right away. The faster you correct yourself, the faster you learn. Immediate feedback is a very important feature of this approach to learning.

2. Use common sense in correcting your answers. Although the answer key gives you all the correct answers as such, in some cases there are several possible answers. Also, word order is more flexible in Spanish than it is in English; so do not let this surprise or trouble you.

3. Master all material before going on. If you missed more than two or three answers in one exercise, go back and review the vocabulary or the grammatical explanations. Then try your answers again. Language learning, like mathematics, is cumulative; you cannot multiply without learning first how to add.

4. Watch the spelling all the time, including the written accents. Some of the questions in the exercises may look too easy and too repetitive, but 80 percent of our knowledge comes through our eyes; and the best way to "see" the words is by writing them. This is the secret of the people who write the new words on cards to memorize them.

5. Review the preceding five lessons before taking each exam. The longer it takes you to cover the five lessons, the more you need to give them a review. Fifty percent of the exam is on vocabulary and 50 percent on grammar. You don't want this long test to be a surprise. You don't need to score more than 90 percent, but you don't want to score less than 80 percent either! Remember, you are taking a course by your own will and you are judging yourself about the progress you are making.

To the Instructor

If you are a first-year college instructor, you can use this programmed text-/workbook effectively in four ways.

1. *As a self-teaching guide for individualized learning.* The student studies and completes every lesson; this gives you practically the whole class time to practice conversation on the materials covered in the lesson. Obviously you will have to prepare some guidelines and activities for this oral work. Then you give students a test on the material covered. After completion of each group of five lessons, you give the review exam, or you can prepare your own exam. The number of credits should be proportionate to credit given for work in regular courses in your college.

2. *As an intensive review.* This course is ideal for students who have had one or two years of high school Spanish, or for students who have learned some Spanish at home. You will have a lot of time to practice conversation on the materials completed and presented by the students. You will want to supplement your course with a graded reader in Spanish.

3. *As a supplement workbook to the main Spanish text.* The grammatical explanations and exercises should be helpful to the students who need further practice.

4. *As a mandatory or recommended review text for second-year Spanish.* For example, if you teach a conversation class and feel that the students need some grammar review, *Practical Spanish Grammar* is the ideal book, because the students can use it by themselves as a self-teaching guide.

What's New in This Second Edition?

There are no drastic changes in this new edition of *Practical Spanish Grammar.* There are two reasons for this: 1) The grammar of a language does not change in ten or twenty years; 2) the first edition has been doing so well in the maketplace, with sales increasing with the years, that the reason for change was not there. However, if the grammar does not change in a decade or two, the vocabulary of the language, the topics of interest to the public, and the approaches to language learning do. Here, then, are the three kinds of changes we have made in this second edition.

1. *Word Lists.* Word lists have been made more relevant—uncommon words have been replaced by more common ones—and situational exercises to practice the new words and grammar, added.

2. *Dialogues.* The dialogues have been updated with more realistic situations to capture more details of Hispanic culture. While the emphasis is still on Latin America, there are also three dialogues that deal strictly with Spain.

3. *Culture.* We have added more cultural notes, and this is the strongest asset to this second edition. Nowadays there is a strong emphasis on a cultural approach to language learning, because international corporations are invading Spain and Latin America. Besides, Americans are traveling more and more to Hispanic countries for pleasure and for business. You will want to be bilingual and bicultural!

Acknowledgments

I wish to thank the late Dr. Walter Kline as well as Mrs. Ann Kline for their good criticism and suggestions. I am greatly thankful to my wife Rita for her continuous support and her practical and valuable insights into the Spanish language. After teaching beginning Spanish students most of her life, she has something that is rarely found in textbooks: experience. I also would like to express my appreciation to the editors of John Wiley & Sons for their valuable suggestions and to Generosa Gina Protano, of GGP Publishing, Inc., and staff for their hard work and perseverance in developing and producing the book.

M. Prado

Spanish Sounds

There are a few sounds in Spanish that do not exist in English, and vice versa. Some sounds are the same in both languages. An important fact to keep in mind is that in Spanish we run several words together to form what is called a "breath group"; in other words, we link together all the words between pauses. As a result, we omit one of two identical vowels or consonants, and we soften certain consonants (such as *b, d, g*) within the breath group.

EX: **Ella va a ver a mi hijo.** (Pronounced as **éyabábéramíjo.**)

Guidelines on how to pronounce letters of the Spanish alphabet are given below using English words with corresponding sounds.

A. **Vowels.** There are five vowels in Spanish: **a, e, i, o, u.** Whether stressed or unstressed, the sounds of these vowels are clear, tense, and short. The stress doesn't change a vowel in Spanish the way it does in English. For example, the three *a's* of *Panamá* have the same sound.

1. In Spanish the letter *a* is pronounced with the mouth open as in the *a* of English *far.*

   EXS: **mañana, banana, Canadá**

2. *E* is pronounced with the lips stretched and the tongue higher than when pronouncing *a,* as in the vowel sound of English *pet.*

   EXS: **este, desde, ese, perro**

3. *I* and *y* are pronounced with the lips very stretched and the tongue nearly touching the roof of the mouth, as in English *see,* but shorter. When *y* is by itself, it means *and; y* may also appear at the end of a word after another vowel.

   EXS: **cita, sí; Juan y María, soy, rey,**

4. *O* is pronounced with the lips rounded as in the *o* of English *for.*

   EXS: **profesor, tonto, solo**

5. *U* is pronounced in a very rounded way and its pronunciation formed in the back of the mouth, as in English *boot,* but shorter.

   EXS: **tú, Cuba, luna, zulú**

6. **Semivowels.** Spanish semivowels *i, u,* are pronounced shorter than *i, u,* whenever they are unstressed and are directly preceded or followed by another vowel. They are the "weak" part of the two-vowel combination we call diphthong.

   EXS: **bien [ie], patio [io], aire [ai], veinte [ei], hay [ai], puente [ue], causa [au], muy [ui]**

B. **Consonants.** In general, Spanish consonants are pronounced with less strength and friction than English consonants, especially *b, d, g.* The following consonants are used in standard Latin American Spanish. There is an extra consonant sound in Spain, which we will mention at the end.

1. The letters *b* and *v* in Spanish are pronounced like the letter *b* in English when they occur at the beginning of a breath group, after a pause, or after a nasal sound. In other cases, they are pronounced softly, with a slight friction between the lower and upper lips. The sound of *v* in English does not exist in Spanish.

   EXS: labio, vaca, vamos a ver

2. The letter *c* + *a, o, u, l,* or *r* and the letter combination *qu* (with silent *u*) + *e* or *i* are pronounced like the English letter *k,* but they are never followed by the puff of air heard in the English initial *k.*

   EXS: casa, cosa, cuando, clase, crema; que, Quito, Quijote

   The spelling with *k* is used in a few foreign words such as **kilómetro, kiosko, kimono;** but even these words can be spelled with **qu.**

3. The *ch* letter combination in Spanish is pronounced in the same way as the *ch* letter combination in English words like *church.*

   EXS: muchacho, chico, mucho

4. The letter *d* is pronounced with the tip of the tongue against the upper teeth at the beginning of a breath group and after an *n.* Within the breath group, it is pronounced in the same way as the *th* letter combination in English, as in *father* and *there,* but with even less friction.

   EX: dámelo, dedo

5. The letter *f* is pronounced in the same way as the letter *f* in English. Unlike English, however, this sound in Spanish is never written as *ph* or *ff.*

   EXS: teléfono, oficina

6. The letter *g* + *a, o, u, r,* or *l* and the letter combination *gu* + *e* or *i* are pronounced like the *g* in *get* at the beginning of a breath group or after an *n.* Otherwise, they are pronounced in a similar way as the sound of *g* in *sugar*—softly, and with only a slight friction.

   EX: gato, lago, gloria; agua, guerra, guitarra

   The *u* of *gu* is silent. When it is pronounced, it is written with a diaresis (two dots), as the **gü** in **pingüino** and **vergüenza.**

7. The letter *h* in Spanish is never pronounced.

   EXS: hablar [aßlár], prohibir [proißír], alcohol [alkól]

8. In Spanish the letter *j* + *a, e, i, o,* or *u* and the letter *g* + *e* or *i* are pronounced like the *h* in *hat,* but with more friction in the back of the mouth.

   EXS: jamón, jerez, viaje, Juan; gente, gitano

   The *x* of **México** and **Texas** is pronounced in the same way as the *j* or *g.*

9. The letter *l* is pronounced like the *l* in English in words like *let.* The sound of the *l* at the end of a syllable or word in English is very soft,

dark, and relaxed. The sound of the *l* in Spanish is always clear, high, and tense, with the tip of the tongue touching the roof of the mouth. This sound more than any other will readily betray an English accent.

EXS: **los, hotel, mil, tal, alto**

10. The double *l* (*ll*) and the *y* are pronounced in the same way as the *y* in English, but usually with more friction, depending on the country.

EXS: **mayo, bello**

In Argentina this sound has a lot of friction, similar to English *s* in words like *pleasure* and *lesion*.

11. The letter *m* is pronounced like the letter *m* in English. However, this sound in Spanish is never written as *mm*.

EXS: **madre, gramática, inmediato**

12. The letter *n* is pronounced the same way as the letter *n* in English.

EXS: **nada, mono, antes, hablan**

13. The letter *ñ* in Spanish is pronounced in the same way as the letters *ny* and *ni* in English in words like *canyon* and *onion*.

EXS: **mañana, España**

14. The letter *p* in Spanish is pronounced like the English *p* in *spy*, and it is never followed by the puff of air heard in the English initial *p* of *pie*. You would have a strong English-language accent if you pronounced that puff of air in Spanish words with initial *p*.

EXS: **papa, Pedro, papel**

15. The *r* is pronounced like the *d* or *t* in English in words like *ladder* and *matter*.

EXS: **pero, para, árbol, comer**

16. The double *r* (*rr*) has no comparable sound in English. The tip of the tongue moves quickly five to eight time against the gum ridge. It is a trilled sound.

EXS: **perro, arroz**

The single *r* at the beginning of a word and after *n, l,* or *s* is pronounced in the same way as the double *r* in Spanish.

EXS: **rosa [rrosa], rojo [rrójo]; honra [ónrra], alrededor [alreðeðór], Israel [Isrraél]**

17. Four different letters in Spanish have the same sound as the *s* in English. They are: 1) the *s* in front of any vowel or final syllable (*soy, caras, estoy*). 2) in the Americas, the *z* in front of *a, o, u,* and at the end of a word (*zapato, feliz, vez*). 3) in the Americas, the *c* and the letter combination *sc* in front of *e* or *i* (*felices, felicidades, ascensor*). 4) the second half of the sound of the letter *x* (*examen* [eksámen], *sexo* [sékso]). Avoid the sound of the letter *z* in English in words like *zapato, visita, presidente*.

18. The letter *t* is pronounced with the tip of the tongue against the upper teeth, never followed by the puff of air heard in English initial *t*. There is no double *t* (*tt*) or *th* in Spanish orthography.

    EXS: tú, total

19. In Spain there is a sound not heard in Spanish America. It is the sound of the letter *z* and the letter *c* in front of *e* or *i*. It is exactly like the sound for the *th* letter combination in English in words like *thought* and *thing*.

    EXS: zapato, feliz, decir, hacer

NOTES

1. There is no letter *w* in the Spanish alphabet except as it occurs in a few foreign words, such as **Washington, sandwich,** which is also spelled **sángüiche.** Spanish has the same sound as the English *w* for the letter *u* preceded by *h* and followed by *e* or *i*.

    EXS: huevo [wéßo], hueso [wéso], huir [wír]

2. Identical vowels between two words are pronounced as just one vowel. The same is true for two identical consonants within the breath group.

    EXS: va a casa [bákása], le encanta [lenkánta], el lado [eláðo]

Summary

1. The five vowels *a, e, i, o, u,* are short, tense, and clear, with or without stress.

2. Avoid the English sound of *a* as in *Ann*. There is no such sound in Spanish, which uses instead the sound of *a* as in *far*.

3. Avoid the lengthening of final vowels as is done in English; for example, *no* is much shorter in Spanish than it is in English where the glide is added to the *o*.

4. A diphthong occurs whenever *i* or *u* is directly preceded or followed by another vowel: *aire, piano, causa, puerta.*

5. Consonants *b, d, g,* within a breath group are very soft in Spanish : lado [láðo].

6. Consonants *c, p, t,* at the beginning of words are never followed by the puff of air heard in English initial consonants *c, p, t.*

7. The *h* is always silent. The *u* is silent in *qu* and *gue, gui,* but not in *güe, güi.*

8. Strengthen the sound of *h* in English for the Spanish *j* and *g*: **Juan, gente, jirafa.**

9. Keep your tongue high to pronounce final *l,* or you will betray a strong English accent: *tal.*

10. In words written with the letter *z,* pronounce the *z* as if it were the English letter *s.*

11. Avoid the sound of the English *z* for the single *s* between vowels in words like *visita* and *presente.*

12. Link the words together within a breath group as if they were one long word.

13. Don't make the stressed syllable too long to avoid the *uh* sound of English in the unstressed syllable that follows the stressed vowel.

14. The Spanish speech rhythm is machine-gun-like; all the syllables are almost even.

1 Basic Expressions

Buenos días, señor.	Good morning, sir.
Buenas tardes, señora.	Good afternoon, madam.
Buenas noches, señorita.	Good evening, miss.
¡Hola! ¿Cómo está usted?	Hi! How are you?
Muy bien, gracias. ¿Y usted?	Very well, thank you. And you?
Bastante bien, gracias.	Fairly well, thank you.
Regular. No muy bien.	So-so. Not too well.
¿Cómo se llama usted?	What's your name?
Me llamo Roberto.	My name is Robert.
¿Dónde vive usted?	Where do you live?
Vivo en California.	I live in California.
¿En qué puedo servirle?	How can I help you?
¿Dónde está el baño, por favor?	Where is the bathroom, please?
Allí, a la derecha.	Over there, to the right.
¿Cómo se dice *left* en español?	How do you say *left* in Spanish?
Se dice *izquierda*.	You say *izquierda*.
Hasta luego.	So long.
Hasta mañana.	See you tomorrow.
Adiós.	Good-bye

PRACTICE THE BASIC EXPRESSIONS

ANSWERS p. 78

1. How do you say *Good morning* in Spanish? _____.

2. After 12:00 P.M. we don't say **Buenos días** but _____.

3. After dark we don't say **Buenas tardes** but _____.

4. How do you say *madam* and *miss* in Spanish? _____.

5. How would you reply to ¿**Cómo está usted?** _____.

6. How would you reply to ¿**Cómo se llama usted?** _____.

7. In English we write the question and exclamation mark at the end of the sentence, whereas in Spanish we write it both at the _____ and at the end of the sentence.

8. How would you reply to ¿**Dónde vive usted?** _____.

9. If you were looking for the bathroom, how would you ask for directions? ¿_____? A possible reply is _____.

10. If you wanted to know the word for *left* in Spanish, how would you ask? ¿_____? A good reply is _____.

11. *Good-bye* is _____ in Spanish, and *So long* is _____.

12. How do you say *please* in Spanish? _____.

13. How do you say *How can I help you* in Spanish? _____?

14. How do you say *So-so. Not too well* in Spanish? _____.

PALABRAS NUEVAS *(New Words)*

You will find these words in the grammar explanations and in exercises in this lesson, and also in later lessons. Try to memorize them, and pay attention to the spelling, including the written accents.

la acción	action	el inglés[1]	English	la pluma	pen
el agua (*f.*)	water	el lápiz	pencil	la policía	police
el águila (*f.*)	eagle	la lección	lesson		department
el árbol	tree	el libro[2]	book	el policía	policeman
el autobús	bus	el lunes	Monday	la mujer	policewoman
el avión	airplane	la luz	light	policía	
el calor	heat	la mano	hand	el porcentaje	percentage
la casa	house	la mañana	morning	el problema	problem
la clase	class	el mar[2]	sea	el sabor	taste, flavor
el color	color	la mesa	table	el sol	sun
la confusión	confusion	la mujer	woman	el sur	south
el día	day	la nariz	nose	la tarde	afternoon
la estación	station;	la noche	night	el/la taxista	taxi driver
	season	el nombre	name	el tema	theme
el garaje	garage	nuevo(a)	new	el tren	train
el gato	cat	la palabra	word	la verdad	truth
el hambre (*f.*)	hunger	el papel	paper	la vez	time (*in a*
el hombre	man	el paraguas	umbrella		*series*)
el hotel	hotel	la pared	wall		

NOTAS

1. Notice that adjectives related to countries are not capitalized in Spanish: **inglés, americano, español.** The days of the week and the months of the year are not capitalized either: **lunes, mayo, diciembre.**

2. To memorize the new words, try to associate every word with something you know. For example, *mar* means *sea*; so it follows that it should be related to English *marine* and *marina*. *Libro* may not look like *book*, but it does look like *library*. *Sol* may look different from *sun*, but it does not look so different from the word *solar* in *solar energy*. It is said that as many as 53 percent of English terms are related to Spanish terms.

3. You may have noticed that many words look alike in Spanish and English, some of them even have the very same spelling. These words are called *cognates*. Cognates may or may not have the same meaning in both languages. When they have different meanings, they are known as *false cognates*, and they can be deceptive. You will find some false cognates later in this book.

PRACTIQUE LAS PALABRAS NUEVAS (*Practice the New Words*)

ANSWERS p. 78

A. Write the Spanish cognate for each of the following words.

1. action _____
2. bus _____
3. class _____
4. color _____
5. station _____
6. paper _____
7. percentage _____
8. south _____
9. train _____
10. confusion _____
11. garage _____
12. hotel _____
13. English _____
14. lesson _____
15. police _____
16. tourist _____
17. theme _____
18. eagle _____

ANSWERS p. 78

B. Did you memorize the new words? Can you write the Spanish equivalent for each of the following words?

1. water _____
2. cat _____
3. taste _____
4. woman _____
5. time _____
6. Monday _____
7. truth _____
8. pen _____
9. nose _____
10. umbrella _____

11. wall _____   15. word _____

12. name _____   16. pencil _____

13. table _____   17. heat _____

14. light _____   18. hunger _____

GRAMMAR I Indefinite Articles • Gender of Nouns

A. There are two indefinite articles in English: *a* and *an,* as in *a book, an apple.* In Spanish the indefinite articles are *un,* which is masculine, and *una,* which is feminine, as in *un* señor, *una* señora.

B. Nouns referring to males are masculine, and nouns referring to females are feminine, as in *un* hombre, *una* mujer, *un* gato, *una* gata. The article tells a male from a female when the noun has the same spelling for males and females.

   EX: *un* taxista (*a male taxi driver*); *una* taxista (*a female taxi driver*)

C. Nouns referring to *things* are neuter in English (= *it*). In Spanish, they are either masculine or feminine, and they take either *un* or *una*. In this case, the gender of the noun—that is, whether it is masculine or feminine—has nothing to do with the idea of males or females; grammatical gender is merely a characteristic of all nouns in Spanish.

   EX: *una* casa, *un* patio, *un* árbol, *una* pared

D. The only way to predict the gender of an inanimate noun in Spanish is by looking at the final letter(s) of the word.

   1. Nouns ending in *l, o, n, e, r,* and *s* (*L-O-N-E-R-S*) are almost always masculine (97 percent).

   2. Nouns ending in *d, ión, z,* and *a* (*D-IÓN-Z-A*) are almost always feminine (98 percent).

   EXS: *un* papel, *un* libro, *un* tren, *un* garaje, *un* color, *un* lunes, *un* paraguas
   una pared, *una* lección, *una* luz, *una* vez, *una* nariz, *una* mesa

E. There are important exceptions to these two rules, and they should be memorized when you learn new words.

   1. Some nouns ending in *-ma* are masculine rather than feminine.

   EXS: *un* proble*ma*, *un* te*ma*, un progra*ma*, *un* dile*ma*, *un* dra*ma*, *un* poe*ma*

   2. The following nouns are other important exceptions.

una calle (*a street*)	una muerte (*a death*)	un avión
una clase	una noche	un camión (*a truck*)
una llave (*a key*)	una suerte (*a destiny*)	un día
una mano	una tarde	un lápiz

PRACTIQUE LOS ARTÍCULOS (*Practice the Articles*)

ANSWERS p. 78

1. The two indefinite articles in Spanish are _____ and _____. Their English translation is _____ or _____.

2. The difference between *un* and *una* is what we call gender: *un* is _____, whereas *una* is _____.

3. All the nouns referring to males are _____, and all the nouns referring to females are _____.

4. We can say that there are three genders in the English pronoun system: a) masculine (males: *he/him*); b) feminine (females: *she/her*); and c) neuter: (*it*), which refers to _____—that is, inanimate nouns, such as *book, melon, patience.*

5. In Spanish we don't have neuter nouns: they are either _____ or _____—that is, they take *un* or *una.*

6. Is there any significance to the gender of nouns referring to things? _____. Actually, the only way to tell whether the noun referring to a thing is masculine or feminine is by the last _____ of the noun.

7. The article may serve to distinguish a male from a _____ when the same word is used for both of them. For example, *un* **taxista** means _____, and *una* **taxista** means _____.

8. You can predict the gender of an inanimate noun by the last _____ of the word. A word ending in *-o* is masculine and a word ending in *-a* is _____.

9. How about the other final letters that predict the gender of a noun? Most nouns ending in _____ are masculine, and most nouns ending in _____ are feminine.

10. Therefore, you can predict that the word *tacón* (*heel*) is _____, a word like *mes* (*month*) is _____, and a word like *bondad* (*goodness*) is _____.

11. About 10 percent of the nouns ending in *-e* are feminine and 90 percent are _____. For example, _____ **tarde** (*an afternoon*), _____ **noche** (*a night*).

12. An important exception to these rules are nouns ending in *-ma* that are _____ rather than feminine—for example, _____ **poema** (*a poem*).

13. Other exceptions are **mano** and **día**: we say _____ **mano** (*a hand*) and _____ **día** (*a day*). For the same reason, you did not learn **Buenas días** but _____ for *Good morning.*

14. Do we say **una lápiz** or **un lápiz**? _____ **Una tarde** or **un tarde**? _____.

EXERCISE

ANSWERS
p. 79

Write the article *un* or *una*.

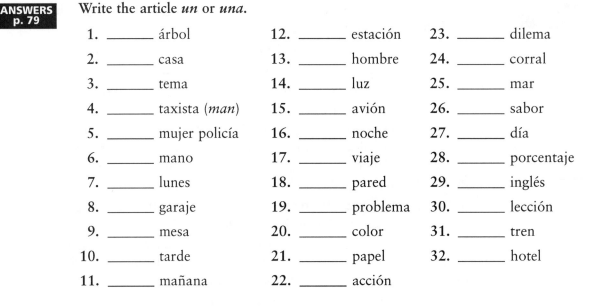

1. _____ árbol
2. _____ casa
3. _____ tema
4. _____ taxista (*man*)
5. _____ mujer policía
6. _____ mano
7. _____ lunes
8. _____ garaje
9. _____ mesa
10. _____ tarde
11. _____ mañana

12. _____ estación
13. _____ hombre
14. _____ luz
15. _____ avión
16. _____ noche
17. _____ viaje
18. _____ pared
19. _____ problema
20. _____ color
21. _____ papel
22. _____ acción

23. _____ dilema
24. _____ corral
25. _____ mar
26. _____ sabor
27. _____ día
28. _____ porcentaje
29. _____ inglés
30. _____ lección
31. _____ tren
32. _____ hotel

GRAMMAR II   Definite Articles and Contractions

A. In English there is only one definite article: *the.* In Spanish there are four: el / la (masculine / feminine singular) and **los / las** (masculine, feminine plural). These articles agree in gender and number with the nouns they precede.

B. We use *el / los* with masculine nouns and *la / las* with feminine nouns. Remember that nouns referring to males are always masculine and nouns referring to females are always feminine. Things are either masculine or feminine, according to the last letter(s) of the word.

   1. Nouns ending in *l, o, n, e, r,* and *s* (*L-O-N-E-R-S*) are generally *masculine* (97 percent).

   2. Nouns ending in *d, ión, z,* and *a* (*D-IÓN-Z-A*) are generally *feminine* (98 percent).

   EXS: *el* tren, *el* nombre, *el* papel, *el* lunes
           la lección, *la* luz, *la* verdad

C. Remember that there are important exceptions to these rules. Review them:

   1. Nouns ending in *-ma* are masculine rather than feminine: *el* proble*ma*, *el* te*ma*.

2. Nouns like *la* **mano,** *el* **día,** *la* **clase,** *la* **noche,** *la* **tarde,** *el* **lápiz, el avión,** and *el* **camión** are other exceptions.

D. The article *la* precedes feminine nouns, but if the feminine noun begins with a stressed *a, el* is used instead of *la.* Actually, the noun may begin with *a* or *ha* because the *h* is silent in Spanish.

EXS: *el* **agua,** *el* **águila.** PLURAL: *las* **aguas,** *las* **águilas**
el **hambre** (pronounced [elámbre]). PLURAL: *las* **hambres**

But we say *la* **americana,** *la* **alfalfa,** because the initial **a** of each word is unstressed.

E. This same rule applies to the indefinite article ***una,*** which precedes all feminine nouns, except the ones beginning with stressed *a.*

EXS: ***un*** **águila** rather than ***una*** **águila,** ***un*** **hambre** rather than ***una*** **hambre**

But ***una*** **americana,** ***una*** **alfalfa,** because the initial *a* of each word is unstressed.

F. We have only two contractions in Spanish—that is, two words combine into one. The prepositions *de* (*of, from*) and *a* (*to*) are combined with the article *el.*

1. **de + el** becomes **del** (*of the*)

2. **a + el** becomes **al** (*to the*)

EXS: **el árbol** *del* **patio** (*the tree <u>in the</u> yard*), **la luz** *del* **día** (*the light <u>of</u> <u>the</u> day*)
Voy *al* **patio.** (*I am going <u>to the</u> yard.*) BUT **Voy** *a la* **casa.** (*I am going <u>to the</u> house.*)

PRACTIQUE LOS ARTÍCULOS DEFINIDOS (*the Definite Articles*)

1. The definite article *the* has four possible translations in Spanish: _____.

2. Inanimate nouns (things) are usually masculine in Spanish when they end in _____, and they are feminine when they end in _____.

3. According to these rules, you can predict the gender of most nouns; for example, *nariz* is _____, *sol* is _____, *paraguas* is _____.

4. There are exceptions to these rules; for example, nouns ending in *-ma* are _____, such as _____ **problema** (*the problem*), and _____ **programa** (*the program*).

5. A few nouns ending in *-z* are masculine rather than _____, such as _____ **lápiz** (*the pencil*); but _____ **luz** (*the light*), _____ **vez** (*the time*), _____ **nariz** (*the nose*).

6. The preposition *de* (*of*) followed by the article *el* becomes one word: _____. The preposition *a* (*to*) followed by the article *el* becomes one word: _____.

7. Not every feminine noun takes the feminine article *la* or *una;* the masculine article *el* or *un* is used instead if the noun begins with a _____ *a* [á], such as _____ agua (*the water*), and _____ águila (*an eagle*). The plural forms require *las:* las aguas, las águilas.

8. Which letter is always silent in Spanish? _____. This means that if a feminine noun starts with *ha* [á], it will take the definite article _____ rather than _____. For example, _____ hambre ([*the*] *hunger*).

9. Is it correct Spanish to say **el americana**? _____. Here we don't use *el* because the first *a* is not _____: phonetically, [amerikána].

10. We say **la casa** _____ **presidente,** because *de* + *el* contracts into _____.

11. Is *la casa de la señora* correct? _____. There is no contraction formed with *de* and the feminine article _____. There are no contractions formed with the plural articles either: **a los, de los, a las, de las.**

EXERCICE

Write the definite article *el* or *la.*

1. _____ árbol
2. _____ casa
3. _____ tema
4. _____ taxista (*man*)
5. _____ mujer policía
6. _____ mano
7. _____ lunes
8. _____ garaje
9. _____ mesa
10. _____ hambre
11. _____ alfalfa

12. _____ estación
13. _____ hombre
14. _____ luz
15. _____ avión
16. _____ águila
17. _____ viaje
18. _____ pared
19. _____ problema
20. _____ agua
21. _____ papel
22. _____ acción

23. _____ dilema
24. _____ corral
25. _____ mar
26. _____ sabor
27. _____ día
28. _____ porcentaje
29. _____ inglés
30. _____ americana
31. _____ tren
32. _____ hotel

GRAMMAR III   Subject Pronouns

A. Memorize the subject pronouns in the chart.

Singular	(English)	Plural	(English)
yo	I	nosotros(as)	we
tú	you (*familiar*)	vosotros(as)	you (*familiar*)
usted (Ud.)	you (*formal*)	ustedes (Uds.)	you (*formal*)
él/ella	he / she	ellos/ellas	they (*males / females*)

Note that:

1. *I* is always capitalized, *yo* is not. Each refers to the speaker in the sentence.

2. *Nosotros* becomes *nosotras* if the speakers in the sentence are all females. If the speakers are males and females, the masculine *nosotros* is used instead.

3. *Tú* is the familiar form for singular *you;* it is used among friends and within the family. Its frequency of usage as compared to the formal *usted* may vary from country to country.

4. *Vosotros(as)* is the plural of *tú;* it is used only in Spain. In Latin America the plural of *tú* is *ustedes.* Since this text is oriented toward Latin American Spanish, *vosotros(as)* will not be used in the exercises.

5. *Usted* and the plural *ustedes* are more formal than *tú;* they are used with persons we don't know well. In Latin America *ustedes* is the plural both of *tú* and of *usted,* since *vosotros(as)* is not used.

6. *Ellas* refers only to females, whereas *ellos* may refer only to males or to combinations of males and females.

7. There are two pronouns with a written accent (**acento escrito**): tú and él.

B. There is *no subject pronoun* for the English neuter *it.* The subject pronoun is usually omitted with inanimate nouns (things) in Spanish.

EXS: *¿La mujer es americana? —Sí, ella es americana.* (*Yes, <u>she</u> is American.*)
        ¿La mesa es americana? —Sí, es americana. (*Yes, it is American.*)

The same rule applies in the plural: *ellos* and *ellas* refer to persons or animals, never to things.

NOTES

1. *Usted* is abbreviated into *Ud.* or *Vd.* and *ustedes* into *Uds.* or *Vds.* The reason for the *V* in *Vd.* and in *Vds.* is that historically the origin of *usted* is *Vuestra Merced* (*Your Highness*).

2. In Argentina and Uruguay *vos* is used instead of *tú* as a familiar pronoun.

3. Although traditionally *nosotras* has been used when two or more females are talking, it is common in modern Spanish to hear *nosotros* even when two or more females refer to themselves.

PRACTIQUE LOS PRONOMBRES (*the Pronouns*)

1. Which pronoun is always capitalized in English but not in Spanish? _____ = _____.

2. The pronoun *we* has two possible words in Spanish: _____ / _____.

3. *Vosotros* is the plural of _____ in Spain, but it is not used in Latin America. In its place, Latin Americans use _____. In other words, Latin Americans do not differentiate between familiarity and formality in the plural.

4. Which one is more familiar, *tú* or *usted*? _____.

5. *Nosotras* is used when two or more _____ are speaking, but *nosotros* can be all males or a combination of males and _____.

6. If Mr. Pérez is talking for himself and his wife, which pronoun is he going to use? _____

7. In Spanish *you* can be either *tú* or *usted* depending on the relationship with the speaker. *Usted* shows respect, whereas *tú* is more intimate. A Spanish-speaking student would address his teacher as _____, and the teacher would reply with _____. The same principle applies to parents and children.

8. The mark (´) on a vowel in Spanish is called **acento**, and later you will learn the rules for its use. Which are the two pronouns with **acento**? _____ and _____.

9. *He* always refers to a person (or an animal—especially a pet) as subject of a sentence. The Spanish word for *he* is _____, for *she* is _____, and for *it* is _____.

10. If we talk to Mary and Jane, we refer to them as *they*; the Spanish pronoun is _____. If we talk to Mary and Joe, we refer to them as *they*; the pronoun is _____.

11. If we talk about the *tables,* we refer to them as *they* as the subject of a sentence; the Spanish equivalent for *they* in this case is _____.

12. How do you know when to use *tú* and when to use *usted*? When you call a person by his or her first name (John, Mary, and so on), you use *tú*. When you use last names (Mr. Martínez, Miss García), you use _____.

13. *Usted* is abbreviated in two ways: _____ and _____; and *ustedes* is abbreviated in two ways, too: _____ and _____.

EXERCISE

ANSWERS
p. 79

Write the Spanish pronouns.

1. we (*all females*) _____

2. you (*familiar singular*) _____

3. you (*familiar plural, Spain*) _____

4. they (*all females*) _____

5. they (*things, inanimate nouns*) _____

6. you (*formal singular*) _____

7. they (*all males*) _____

8. we (*males and females*) _____

9. they (*males and females*) _____

10. you (*formal plural*) _____

11. he / she / it _____ / _____ / _____

2 En un restaurante
(In a Restaurant)

el almuerzo[1]	lunch	la langosta	lobster
el/la amigo(a)	friend	la lechuga	lettuce
el/la azúcar[2]	sugar	los legumbres	vegetables
el bisté, el bistec	beefsteak	el menú[6]	menu
la caja	cash register	el/la mesero(a)	waiter, waitress
el/la camarero(a)[3]	waiter, waitress	el/la mozo(a)	waiter, waitress
la carta	menu	la nieve (*México*)	ice cream (*Mexico*)
a la carta	à la carte	la nievería	ice cream store
la cerveza	beer	(*México*)	(*Mexico*)
la comida	food, meal	las papas fritas	French fries
la crema	cream	la patata[7]	potato
la cuenta	bill	el postre[8]	dessert
la ensalada	salad	el sabor	taste, flavor
el filete,[4] el bisté	steak, fillet	la salsa	sauce
el flan	custard	la sopa	soup
la fruta	fruit	el tomate	tomato
la heladería	ice cream store	los vegetales[9]	vegetables
el helado[5]	ice cream	las verduras	greens, (green)
el jamón	ham		vegetables

aprender	to learn	leer	to read
beber[10]	to drink	ordenar	to order
bebido(a)	drunk	pagar	to pay
comer	to eat	pasar	to pass
completar	to complete	salir	to leave, go out
creer	to believe	ser	to be
desear	to want, wish	subir	to go up, climb
disfrutar de	to enjoy	tomar	to take, drink
escribir	to write	tomado(a)	drunk
estar	to be	trabajar	to work
estudiar	to study	usar	to use
hablar	to speak	vivir	to live

algo	something	excelente	excellent
allí	there, over there	fresco(a)	fresh
aquí	here	también	also
blando(a)[11]	tender, soft	tarde	late
¡cómo no!	of course!	la tarde	afternoon
delicioso(a)	delicious	verde	green
dos	two		

NOTAS

1. *Almuerzo* (*lunch*) is the main meal of the day in Spanish-speaking countries. It is served between one and three o'clock in the afternoon depending on the country and the time of the year. This meal is more commonly called **comida,** a word that also means *food* in general.

2. *Azúcar* is one of a few nouns that is masculine in some countries and feminine in others. So **el azúcar** is as correct as **la azúcar.**

3. *Camarero(a)* is the traditional word for *waiter* (*waitress*); but in some countries people use *mesero(a),* and in others *mozo(a).* For many years in a typical restaurant in a Spanish-speaking country there were only **camareros,** but in the last ten years or so, women have been admitted to this kind of work.

4. *Filete* is the traditional word for *steak,* but *bistec,* from the English *beefsteak,* has been used for years. The Real Academia de la Lengua prefers the spelling **bisté.**

5. *Helado* is the international Spanish word for *ice cream.* In Mexico people say **nieve** (*snow*) instead. *Nievería* or *heladería* is the place where ice cream is sold.

6. *Menú* is the modern term for *menu.* Some countries use *carta,* which gave rise to the expression *a la carta* (*à la carte*).

7. In Spain, people say **patata** for *potato.* In Latin-American countries, they say **papas.**

8. *Postre* means *dessert* in English. In Spanish-speaking countries, where a lot of fruit is consumed, dessert traditionally consists of fruit.

9. *Vegetales* is the Spanish word for *vegetables* in general. In some countries people use **legumbres** (*legumes,* like peas or beans) or **verduras** (*greens,* like escarole or chicory) to mean all vegetables.

10. *Beber* is the general word for *to drink.* In some countries, people use **beber** for alcoholic drinks and **toma**r for non-alcoholic ones. In some other countries people use the words the other way around. Consequently, **bebido** and **tomado** both mean *drunk.*

11. *Blando* is an example of a false cognate. It does not mean *bland* but *tender, soft.* The word for *bland* is **insípido.**

PRACTIQUE LAS PALABRAS NUEVAS

ANSWERS
p. 80

A. Write the Spanish cognate for each English word that follows.

1. cream _____   10. salad _____

2. beefsteak _____   11. fruit _____

3. menu _____   12. sauce _____

4. soup _____   13. tomato _____

5. vegetables _____   14. to complete _____

6. to study _____   15. to order _____

7. to pass _____   16. to use _____

8. delicious _____   17. excellent _____

9. fillet _____   18. fresh _____

ANSWERS
p. 80

B. Write the article *el* or *la* in front of each noun. Remember that *L-O-N-E-R-S* is masculine and *D-IÓN-Z-A* is feminine.

1. ___ salsa   6. ___ postre   11. ___ bisté   16. ___ cuenta

2. ___ filete   7. ___ crema   12. ___ tomate   17. ___ lechuga

3. ___ jamón   8. ___ menú   13. ___ comida

4. ___ caja   9. ___ flan   14. ___ fruta

5. ___ azúcar   10. ___ almuerzo   15. ___ vegetal

ANSWERS
p. 80

C. Match the columns by writing the appropriate letter.

1. _D_ flan
2. _F_ cuenta
3. _I_ algo
4. _A_ cerveza
5. _K_ almuerzo
6. _B_ pagar
7. _N_ beber
8. _L_ salir
9. _G_ leer
10. _E_ helado

11. _M_ filete
12. _Q_ caja
13. _R_ también
14. _C_ aquí
15. _O_ verde
16. _P_ blando
17. _H_ camarero

A. beer
B. to pay
C. here
D. custard
E. ice cream
F. check (*restaurant*)
G. to read
H. waiter
I. something
J. fried

K. lunch
L. to leave
M. steak
N. to drink
O. green
P. tender, soft
Q. cash register
R. also

DIÁLOGO   En un restaurante

Roberto y Antonio son dos amigos y están en un restaurante para disfrutar de una buena comida. Hablan con el camarero.

CAMARERO: Buenas tardes, señores. Aquí está el menú. ¿Desean ustedes beber algo?

ROBERTO: Sí, dos cervezas, por favor.

ANTONIO: También deseamos ordenar la comida.

CAMARERO: Sí, ¡cómo no!

ROBERTO: Yo deseo un filete con papas fritas, ensalada de lechuga y tomate, y de postre —helado de chocolate.

CAMARERO: Y usted, señor, ¿qué desea?

ANTONIO: Sopa de vegetales, langosta en salsa verde con verduras y fruta fresca —de postre.

CAMARERO: ¿Toman ustedes café con la comida?

ROBERTO: Sí, pero sólo con el postre.

* * *

CAMARERO: ¿Cómo está la comida, señores?

ROBERTO: Excelente. Mi filete está muy blando, y la ensalada, muy fresca.

ANTONIO: Sí, la langosta tiene un sabor delicioso, y también las verduras.

* * *

ROBERTO: Ya es tarde. ¡Camarero, la cuenta, por favor!

CAMARERO: Aquí está. Ustedes pagan allí en la caja. Adiós y gracias.

ANTONIO: Adiós. Hasta luego.

DIALOGUE   In a Restaurant

Robert and Anthony are two friends and are in a restaurant to enjoy a good meal. They are talking with the waiter.

WAITER: Good afternoon, gentlemen. Here's the menu. Would you care for anything to drink?

ROBERT: Yes, two beers, please.

ANTHONY: We also want to order dinner.

WAITER: Yes, of course!

ROBERT: I want a steak with french fries, a lettuce and tomato salad, and chocolate ice cream for dessert.

WAITER: And you, sir, what would you like?

ANTHONY: Vegetable soup, lobster in green sauce with vegetables, and fresh fruit for dessert.

WAITER: Do you take coffee with your meals?

ROBERT: Yes, but only with the dessert.

                              * * *

WAITER: How is the food, gentlemen?

ROBERT: Excellent. My steak is very tender, and the salad is really fresh.

ANTHONY: Yes, the lobster has a delicious flavor, and so do the vegetables.

                              * * *

ROBERT: It's late. Waiter, the check please!

WAITER: Here it is. You pay over there at the cash register. Good-bye and thank you.

ANTHONY: Good-bye. So long.

EXERCISES

ANSWERS p. 80

A. Complete the sentences using the information from the dialogue.

1. Roberto y Antonio son dos _____ y van a comer juntos (*together*).

2. Ellos desean beber dos _____ con la comida.

3. Los dos amigos hablan con el _____ del restaurante.

4. Ellos ordenan el _____ por el menú.

5. Roberto desea comer un filete con _____.

6. Roberto también desea una ensalada de _____ y tomate.

7. Antonio desea tomar una _____ de vegetales.

8. Antonio también desea una _____ en salsa verde.

9. Roberto ordena _____ de postre.

10. Antonio no ordena helado; él desea _____ de postre.

11. La comida del restaurante está _____.

12. El filete de Roberto está _____, y la ensalada, _____.

13. La langosta tiene un sabor _____ y también las _____.

14. Los dos amigos toman café con _____.

15. Ellos pagan la cuenta de la comida en la _____.

B. **Underline the word that makes sense.**

1. Ordenamos el almuerzo por (la caja, el postre, el menú, la cerveza).

2. Usamos azúcar y crema en (las papas, el café, la sopa, el helado).

3. El camarero trabaja en (el jamón, la caja, el restaurante, el aeropuerto).

4. Roberto desea beber (un helado de chocolate, una cerveza, un flan, una langosta).

5. La ensalada es de (filete, crema con azúcar, lechuga y tomate, salsa verde).

6. Roberto toma el café con (crema y azúcar, salsa verde, legumbres frescas, ensalada).

7. (El filete, El flan, La verdura, La cuenta) es una clase de postre.

8. (El tomate, El azúcar, La carta, La nieve) es una clase de legumbre.

9. Generalmente usamos el azúcar en (el bisté, la sopa, las verduras, el café).

10. El bisté de Roberto está muy (blando, helado, frito, en salsa verde).

11. Los dos amigos leen (el filete, la cerveza, el menú, la lechuga).

12. Una clase popular de helado es (de chocolate, de jamón, de papas, de verduras).

13. Antonio come langosta con (tomate, fruta, salsa verde, crema y azúcar).

14. La ensalada de Roberto está (fresca, deliciosa, frita, blanda).

GRAMMAR I   The Three Conjugations • Present Indicative of Regular -*ar* Verbs

A. **The three conjugations**

There are three kinds of verbs in Spanish, each classified according to the ending of the infinitive. The form of the verb listed in dictionaries is the infinitive. Its equivalent in English is the form that starts with *to: to speak.* The three kinds of verbs are said to be of the first, second, or third conjugation.

1. *FIRST CONJUGATION:* Verbs ending in -**ar,** such as **hablar** (*to speak*)

2. *SECOND CONJUGATION:* Verbs ending in -**er,** such as **comer** (*to eat*)

3. *THIRD CONJUGATION:* Verbs ending in -**ir,** such as **vivir** (*to live*)

Every verb form is divided into two parts: *stem + ending.* The stem carries the meaning, and it is the same in all persons and tenses. The *ending* is the part that changes to signal the different persons (like *I, you, he, she*) and tenses (past, present, future).

EXS: **habl + ar.** The stem is **habl-** (*speak*), the ending is -**ar** (infinitive).
habl + as. The stem is **habl-** (*speak*), the ending is -**as** (*you,* present indicative).

B. **Present indicative of regular -*ar* verbs**

Look at the present indicative of *hablar* (*to speak*), given in the chart that follows.

	habl ar			to speak
yo	habl o	I		speak, am speaking, do speak
tú	habl as		you	speak, are speaking, do speak
él/ella ⎫	habl a	⎧ he/she		speaks, is speaking, does speak
Ud. ⎭		⎩ you		speak, are speaking, do speak
nosotros(as)	habl amos	we		speak, are speaking, do speak
ellos/ellas/Uds.	habl an	they/you		speak, are speaking, do speak

Note that:

1. The stem **habl-** is the same for all the persons, and it doesn't change for the different tenses. This is why we call *hablar* a regular verb.

2. The endings identify the persons and tense: -**o** means *yo* (*I*); -**amos** means *nosotros(as)* (*we*); -**as** means *tú* (familiar *you*); -**a** means *él, ella, usted,* (*he, she, you*) and -**an** means *ellos, ellas, ustedes,* (*they, you*).These endings are not the same in all the tenses.

3. Since the subject pronoun information is given by the verb ending, we omit the subject pronouns unless we want to add emphasis to the subject.

For example, *Tú hablas español* means <u>You</u> *speak Spanish* (giving emphasis by raising the voice on *you*).

C. **Uses of the present indicative**

1. The present indicative is used to indicate *an action in progress* at the time of speaking. Notice that the progressive form is *mandatory* in English in this case.

   EX: *Hablo* **español ahora.** (<u>*I am speaking*</u> *Spanish now.*)

2. The present indicative is used to show a *habit,* something we continue doing. In this case, to show a *habit* or *custom,* we use the simple present in English.

   EX: *Hablo* **español siempre.** (<u>*I speak*</u> *Spanish all the time.*)

3. The present indicative can be used for *an action in the future,* but an adverb or a context to differentiate it from the present is needed. This use is very common in Spanish.

   EX: **Mañana** *hablo* **con usted.** (<u>*I will speak*</u> *with you tomorrow.*)

4. The present indicative also translates the emphatic *I do speak* by raising the voice on the verb or by adding an adverb such as *sí* (*indeed*), *ciertamente* (*certainly*), and so on.

   EX: **Elena** *sí habla* **inglés.** (*Helen* <u>*does speak*</u> *English.*)

PRACTIQUE EL PRESENTE DE INDICATIVO

**ANSWERS
p. 81**

1. The three kinds of Spanish verbs are identified by the endings of the _____. The first conjugation ends in _____; the second, in _____; and the third in _____. Actually, we can say that the vowels **a, e, i,** identify these verbs, just as the *r* identifies the infinitives and *to* precedes all the infinitives in English.

2. The *stem* of a verb carries the basic _____, and it is repeated in all the persons and tenses. What is the stem of *hablar?* _____ And the stem of *vivir?* _____ And the stem of *comer?* _____.

3. The ending -**amos** gives the subject pronoun information for _____. The ending -**as** signals the subject _____, and the ending -**o** repeats the subject _____.

4. Any noun takes the same third-person verb ending as *él, ella, ellos,* or *ellas.* Now complete the sentence **Roberto** _____ **mucho.** (*Robert* <u>*talks*</u> *a lot.*)

5. *We* is a combination of *somebody else* and *I;* therefore, to say in Spanish *She and I speak Spanish,* you would say **Ella y yo** _____ **español.**

6. Notice that the stem of *estudiar* ends in an *i* after you drop the ending **-ar.** This means that we must keep that *i* in all the persons, moods, and tenses. Write how you would say *We study.* _____.

7. Since the verb endings repeat the information carried by the subject pronouns, we don't use the subject pronouns unless we want to add _____ to the subject.

8. The present indicative is used for an action in _____ at the time of speaking. For example, *She is studying now* is translated as **Ella** _____ **ahora.**

9. The verb *usar* has a short stem: _____. Write how you would say *We are using the book.* _____. Write how you would say *They are using the book.* _____.

10. A *habit* is an action we repeat many times. How would you say *I speak Spanish at home all the time?* **Siempre** _____ **español en casa.**

11. We can use the present indicative for a future action with the help of an adverb or a context. How would you say *I will study the lesson tomorrow?* _____ **la lección mañana.**

12. In Spanish we don't have an emphatic auxiliary like *do* in the sentence *You do speak well.* We use the ordinary present tense form **hablas;** and we either emphasize it with the voice, or we add an adverb like *sí* (*indeed, sure*) in front of it. Using this last method, write how you would say *Mary does study a lot.* **María** _____ **mucho.**

EXERCISE

ANSWERS p. 81 Complete the sentence with the correct form of the verb in parentheses.

1. Ustedes _____ español. (*estudiar*)

2. Roberto y Antonio _____ la comida. (*ordenar*)

3. Ellos _____ la cuenta en la caja. (*pagar*)

4. (Tú) _____ el café con crema y azúcar. (*tomar*)

5. El camarero _____ en un restaurante excelente. (*trabajar*)

6. En Estados Unidos (nosotros) _____ mucha gasolina. (*usar*)

7. María y yo _____ en la clase de español. (*estar*)

8. (Yo) _____ comer una ensalada de lechuga y tomate. (*desear*)

9. Señores, ¿_____ ustedes leer el menú? (*desear*)

10. La camarera _____ el menú a Roberto. (*pasar*)

11. El postre _____ una comida deliciosa. (*completar*)

12. (Tú) _____ beber una cerveza mexicana. (*desear*)

13. Ella y él _____ el autobús por la noche. (*tomar*)

14. Roberto y Antonio _____ de una comida excelente. (*disfrutar*)

15. Los camareros _____ en el restaurante. (*trabajar*)

16. ¿Dónde _____ (nosotros) la cuenta? (*pagar*)

17. Trescientos cincuenta millones de personas _____ el español. (*hablar*)

18. El taxista _____ un taxi excelente, un Mercedes Benz. (*usar*)

19. José _____ muy tarde los lunes. (*trabajar*)

20. Antonio _____ de la langosta y de las verduras. (*disfrutar*)

GRAMMAR II   Regular Verbs Ending in -*er* and -*ir*

A. **The present indicative of *comer* and *vivir***

The regular verb **comer** (*to eat*) is a second conjugation verb, ending in -er in the infinitive. The regular verb **vivir** (*to live*) is a third conjugation verb ending in -ir. These two kinds of verbs share the same endings in almost all the tenses. Memorize their present indicatives.

	com er (*to eat*)	*viv ir* (*to live*)
yo	com o	viv o
tú	com es	viv es
él/ella/Ud.	com e	viv e
nosotros(as)	com emos	viv imos
ellos/ellas/Uds.	com en	viv en

Note that:

1. The stem of *comer* is **com-**, and the stem of *vivir* is **viv-**. The stem carries the meaning of the verb. Both stems stay the same in all the persons and tenses: present, past, future.

2. The endings are very similar to those of the first conjugation: -o means *yo;* -emos and -imos mean *nosotros(as);* -es means *tú;* -e means *él/ella/Ud.;* and -en means *ellos/ellas/Uds.*

3. The endings of *comer* and *vivir* are the same in all the persons except the first person plural: **com emos** *vs.* **viv imos**. The difference is the same as in the infinitive: e *vs.* i.

B. Uses of the present indicative
The uses of the present indicative are the same for second- (**comer**) and third-conjugation (**vivir**) verbs as they are for first-conjugation (**hablar**) ones. In fact, they are the same for all the verbs in the language, including the ones that are just being coined, like **faxear** (*to fax*). Let's review these uses:

1. An action *in progress.*

   EX: *Ella come* **ahora mismo.** (<u>*She's eating*</u> *right now.*)

2. An action as a *habit.*

   EX: *Ella* **siempre** *come* **mucho.** (<u>*She always eats*</u> *a lot.*)

3. An action *in the future.*

   EX: ¿Dónde *comes* **mañana?** (*Where <u>will you eat</u> tomorrow?*)

4. The present indicative translates the English emphatic form *do* + (verb) by raising the voice on the verb or by adding an adverb such as *sí* (*sure, indeed*), *ciertamente* (*certainly*), and so on.

   EX: *Ud. sí come* **muchas verduras.** (<u>*You do eat*</u> *lots of vegetables.*)

PRACTIQUE EL PRESENTE DE INDICATIVO

ANSWERS
p. 81

1. The second kind of verb is characterized by the _____ ending of the infinitive, and the third kind by the _____ ending

2. The stem carries the _____ of the verb. What is the stem of *escribir?* _____ And the stem of *leer?* _____

3. The subject pronouns are usually omitted in Spanish because the _____ of the verb carries the same *information.* For example, the ending -o means _____.

4. You may have noticed that the difference between *habl amos* and *com emos* is the ending -**amos** *vs.* -**emos,** or better yet, the vowels **a** and **e.** What is the **nosotros** form of **vivir?** _____. You can see the vowel **i** in contrast with the vowels **a** and **e.**

5. *Comer* and *vivir* have the same endings in all the persons of the present indicative except in the _____. Note that it is the same vowels that differentiate the second from the third conjugation: -**er** *vs.* -**ir.**

6. The present indicative of any verb is used for an action *in progress.* For example, *Where are you living now?* is translated as ¿Dónde _____ Ud. ahora?

7. A *habit* is an action we repeat many times. If the habit still exists now, we express that action in the _____. For example, *You drink milk all the time* is translated as **Usted siempre** _____ **leche.** (*beber*)

8. The present tense is often used instead of the *future* tense for an action still to come. For example, **Mañana (yo)** _____ **la novela *Don Quijote de la Mancha.*** (*leer*)

9. *Escribir* means *to write*. Can you write in English the four meanings of *escribimos?*

   a) An action in progress: _____.

   b) An action as a habit: _____.

   c) An action in the future: _____.

   d) An action with emphasis: _____.

EXERCISE

ANSWERS
p. 81

Complete each sentence with the correct form(s) of the verb(s). (Remember that the pronouns can be omitted but that they are given in parentheses as clues for the persons you have to use in your answers.)

1. (Nosotros) _____ español en este libro. (*aprender*)

2. El policía _____ el reporte en la estación. (*leer*)

3. ¿Dónde _____ (tú) la cuenta de la comida? (*pagar*)

4. (Yo) _____ el tren en la estación de Chamartín. (*tomar*)

5. Los alemanes (Germans) _____ mucha cerveza. (*beber*)

6. Antonio y yo _____ la Sierra Nevada. (*subir*)

7. El avión no _____ muy tarde de Nueva York. (*salir*)

8. Ellas _____ un postre delicioso. (*comer*)

9. Ustedes no _____ la verdad. (*creer*)

10. Los lunes mi familia y yo _____ en un restaurante. (*comer*)

11. (Nosotros) _____ del tema del hambre en la clase. (*hablar*)

12–13. (Ud.) _____ el menú y luego _____ la comida. (*leer/ ordenar*)

14. (Yo) _____ las palabras nuevas para aprenderlas. (*escribir*)

15. José _____ mañana para San Francisco. (*salir*)

16. El agua del mar _____ con la marea (*tide*). (*subir*)

17. Mañana (yo) no _____ porque es domingo (*Sunday*). (*trabajar*)

18-19. ¡Cómo no! Los mexicanos _____ en México y _____ español. (*vivir/hablar*)

20. El gato _____ muy bien a los árboles. (*subir*)

21. Roberto _____ del filete y la ensalada. (*disfrutar*)

22. El tren no _____ por San Clemente sino (*but*) por San Diego. (*pasar*)

23. Los dos amigos _____ juntos en el restaurante. (*comer*)

GRAMMAR III   Forms and Usage of *ser* and *estar*

A. *Ser* and *estar* (*to be*) **in the present indicative**

	s er (to be)	est ar (to be)	
yo	s oy	est oy	I am
tú	er es	est ás	you are
él/ella Ud. }	es	est á	{ he/she/it is you are
nosotros (as)	s omos	est amos	we are
ellos/ellas/Uds.	s on	est án	they/you are

Note that:

1. These two verbs are irregular because they don't follow the conjugations of regular -**ar,** and -**er** verbs. They have changes in the stems and in the endings.

2. Like *to be, ser* and *estar* are irregular in more ways than other verbs are. However, you will learn all these irregular forms easily, because you will use them often.

3. The first person ending for both verbs is -**oy** instead of -**o** as in **hablo, vivo, leo.**

4. *Estar* has three forms with a written accent: **estás, está, están.**

   (NOTE: If you pay attention to the words with written accents as you go along, you will find it easier to learn the rules about the accent when you study them later.)

B. Uses of *ser* and *estar*

1. *Ser* is used to identify a person, an animal, a concept, a thing, or any noun.

    EXS: **Esto *es* un lápiz.** (*This is a pencil.*)
    Juan *es* maestro. (*John is a teacher.*) (There is no equivalent for the English *a* in the Spanish sentence.)

2. *Estar* is used to show the location of a person, animal, or thing. (Compare this use of *estar* with *to stay* in English.)

    EXS: **El lápiz *está* aquí.** (*The pencil is here.*)
    Juan *está* en casa. (*John is at home.*)

3. *Ser* is used with an adjective to show that a characteristic is the *norm* for the noun. For example, it is the norm for snow to be white, soft, cold, and so on.

    EXS: **La nieve *es* blanca.** (*Snow is white.*)
    Roberto *es* mexicano. (*Robert is Mexican.*)

4. *Estar* is used with an adjective to show that the characteristic is a *change* or a *condition*.

    EXS: **Esta nieve *está* roja.** (*This snow is red* [because of red paint or blood].)
    Esta hierba *está* verde. (*This grass is green* [because of fertilizers or watering].)

5. *Ser* is used with the preposition **de** to indicate:

    a) ORIGIN: **Esta langosta *es* de Chile.** (*This lobster is from Chile.*)

    b) MATERIAL: **La mesa *es* de plástico.** (*The table is made of plastic.*)

    c) POSSESSION: **La casa *es* de mi amigo.** (*The house belongs to my friend.*)

PRACTIQUE *SER* Y *ESTAR*

**ANSWERS
P. 81**

1. There are two verbs in Spanish for English *to be:* _____.

2. *Ser* is an -er verb and *estar* is an -ar verb, but they don't follow the patterns of *comer* and *hablar.* For this reason we say that they are _____ verbs.

3. The first persons of *hablar* and *comer* end with the vowel o; the first persons of *ser* and *estar* don't end with o but with _____.

4. *Estar* has three forms, each with a written accent (**acento escrito**):

    _____.

5. Which verb is used to show the *place* where a person, an animal, or a thing *is, ser* or *estar*? _____ For example, **El gato** _____ **en el patio.**

6. Which verb is used to *identify* something, *ser* or *estar*? _____. For example, **Washington** _____ **la capital federal de Estados Unidos.**

7. When Shakespeare wrote *to be or not to be,* perhaps he was thinking that a person should identify himself or herself the way he or she is. How would you translate that saying in Spanish? _____.

8. An adjective shows a characteristic of a noun: *red, big, good, roomy,* and so on. If that characteristic is a *norm* for the noun, we use the verb _____ in Spanish. If that characteristic is a *change* for the noun, we use _____.

9. Grass is usually green; that seems to be the *norm* for grass. In Spanish you say **La hierba** _____ **verde.**

10. It is a *norm* for coffee to be brown when roasted, but not to be hot or cold. You heat it to make it hot. That's a *change:* **El café** _____ **caliente.**

11. To indicate the *origin* of a person, a product, and so on, we use the verb _____ in Spanish. For example, **El taxista** _____ **de Chicago.** After all, giving the origin of a person or product is a way of identifying that person or product.

12. To indicate the *material* something is made of, we use the verb _____. For example, **La sopa** _____ **de vegetales.** It's another way of identifying something.

13. To show *possession* in Spanish, we use the verb _____. For example, **La cuenta** _____ **de Roberto y Antonio.**

EXERCISE

ANSWERS
p. 82

Complete each sentence with the correct form of *ser* and/or *estar.*

1. Yo __soy__ de España. ¿De dónde __son__ ustedes?

2. Ella __es__ americana, pero __está__ en Madrid.

3. El café bueno __es__ de Colombia o de Costa Rica.

4. Los policías __están son__ en la estación de policía.

5. La langosta buena __es__ de Maine, dicen los expertos.

6. ¿Quién (*who*) _____ *es* _____ el Presidente de Estados Unidos ahora?

7. Las camareras _____ *están* _____ en el restaurante.

8. Pepe y yo no _____ *somos* _____ mexicanos sino (*but*) chilenos.

9. Ustedes _____ *están* _____ muy buenos con las camareras.

10. ¿Cómo _____ *está* _____ usted hoy? —(Yo) _____ *estoy* _____ muy bien, gracias.

11. No deseo el café; _____ *está* _____ muy frío (*cold*).

12. La nieve _____ *es* _____ blanca; la hierba (*grass*) _____ *es* _____ verde.

13. El filete de Roberto _____ *está* _____ blando y caliente.

14. Mi amigo _____ *es* _____ taxista; trabaja en Nueva York.

15. La ensalada _____ *es* _____ de lechuga y tomate; _____ *está* *es* _____ verde y roja.

16. El jamón _____ *es* _____ un producto del puerco o cerdo (*pig*).

17. El helado _____ *es* _____ dulce (*sweet*); la cerveza no _____ *es* _____ dulce.

18. La langosta de Antonio _____ *está* _____ deliciosa y las verduras también.

19. Una ensalada buena _____ *está* _____ fresca y también los vegetales.

20. La cerveza _____ *está* _____ muy fría (*cold*); _____ *está* _____ en el refrigerador.

21. El libro no _____ *es* _____ de inglés; _____ *es* _____ de español.

22. El agua mineral _____ *es* _____ buena para la salud (*health*).

3 En un restaurante de mariscos
(In a Seafood Restaurant)

el aperitivo	aperitif	la paella[2]	paella
la boca	mouth	el pan	bread
la botella	bottle	la pareja	pair
el camarón[1]	shrimp	el plato	dish, plate
la cena	supper	la ración	order, serving
el cheque	check	la tarjeta	(credit) card
la ciudad	city, town	el tiempo	time
la idea	idea	el vaso	(drinking) glass
la mantequilla	butter	el vermut,[3]	vermouth
la margarina	margarine	el vermú	
el marisco	seafood	el/la viajero(a)	traveler
el mundo	world	el vino	wine

aceptar	to accept	mirar	to look at
acompañar	to accompany	necesitar	to need
cenar	to have supper	pedir	to ask for
dar	to give	preparar	to prepare
decir	to say, tell	saber	to know
especializar	to specialize	servir	to serve, help
hacer	to do, make	ver[4]	to see, look at
ir	to go		

amarillo(a)	yellow	malo(a)[5]	bad, sick
barato(a)	cheap	mejor	better, best
blanco(a)	white	mucho(a)	much, a lot
bueno(a)	good, healthy	negro(a)	black
caliente	hot	pequeño(a)	small
caro(a)	expensive	rojo(a)	red
dulce	sweet	rosado(a)	pink, rosé
frío(a)	cold	seco(a)	dry
grande	large, big	todo(a)	all

además	besides	**hacer la boca agua**	to make one's
ahora	now		mouth water
a la plancha	on the grill,	**para**	to, in order to; for
	grilled	**por supuesto**	of course
este (*m.*)	this	**primero**	first

NOTAS

1. *Camarón* is *shrimp* in Latin America. In Spain shrimp is called **gamba**.

2. **Paella** is a popular dish in Spain and Latin America. It is originally from Valencia, where Catalan is spoken, and *paella* means *pot* in Catalan. This dish is prepared with chicken, pork, sausage, rice, saffron, and all kinds of seafood, such as shrimp, clams, lobster, crab, and mussels.

3. *Vermut* is masculine, and it doesn't change in the plural: **un vermut / dos vermut**. However, most people say **vermú** in the singular and **vermús** in the plural. The Real Academia Española (a group of experts in the Spanish language) has admitted *vermú* to its dictionary (*Diccionario de la lengua epañola*).

4. *Ver* means both *to see* and *to look at, watch.* In this second sense, *ver* overlaps with the meaning of *mirar* (*to watch*). Actually, people in some countries use only *ver,* and *mirar* has disappeared, while in other regions it is the opposite: they use only *mirar.*

5. *Malo* means *bad,* but when it is used with people and the verb *estar* (*to be*), it means *sick,* as in **María está mala** (*Mary is sick*). In the same way, *bueno* means *good,* but also *healthy* when used with *estar* and applied to people. **El muchacho está bueno** (*The boy is healthy*).

PRACTIQUE LAS PALABRAS NUEVAS

ANSWERS p. 82

A. Write the article *el* or *la* before each noun. Remember that *el* is used before nouns ending in *L-O-N-E-R-S* and *la* before those ending in *D-IÓN-Z-A.*

1. _____ paella   5. _____ ración   9. _____ tarjeta   13. _____ mundo

2. _____ marisco   6. _____ cheque   10. _____ camarón   14. _____ plancha

3. _____ pan   7. _____ viajero   11. _____ pareja   15. _____ viajera

4. _____ idea   8. _____ ciudad   12. _____ vino   16. _____ gamba

ANSWERS p. 82

B. Complete the sentences with words from the chapter vocabulary.

1. La langosta y el *camarón* son dos clases de mariscos.

2. Dos personas (o animales) es una *pareja*.

3. Usamos un _____vaso_____ para beber el vino.

4. La _____paella_____ es un plato con muchos mariscos.

5. Este vino no es dulce; es _____seco_____.

6. El color del vino es blanco, rojo o _____amarillo rosado_____

7. La langosta y el camarón no son baratos; son _____caros_____.

8. Los camarones se llaman _____los gambas_____ en España.

9. El hambre es el mejor _____aperitivo_____.

10. En este restaurante aceptamos _____tarjetas_____ de crédito (*credit*).

11. Pagamos la cuenta con un _____cheques_____ de viajeros.

12. Nueva York es una _____ciudad_____ muy grande.

13. Comemos el pan con margarina o _____mantequilla_____.

14. ¿Cómo se dice *to ask for* en español? _____pedir_____.

15. ¿Cómo se dice *a la plancha* en inglés? _____on the plan_____.

ANSWERS
p. 82

C. **Fill in the correct word.**

1. El antónimo de *blanco* es _____.

2. El antónimo de *caro* es _____.

3. El antónimo de *frío* es _____.

4. El antónimo de *dulce* (*talking about wines*) es _____.

5. El antónimo de *grande* es _____.

6. El antónimo de *bueno* es _____.

7. El antónimo de *postre* es _____.

8. El antónimo de *hombre* es _____.

9. La forma femenina de *camarero* es _____.

10. La forma femenina de *viajero* es _____.

11. El antónimo de *un turista* es _____.

12. La forma femenina de *un policía* es _____.

13. El antónimo de *allí* es _____.

14. El antónimo de *día* es _____.

15. El antónimo de *norte* (*north*) es _____.

DIÁLOGO   En un restaurante de mariscos

Una pareja cena en un restaurante que se especializa en mariscos.

CAMARERA: Buenas noches. ¿En qué puedo servirles?

ANTONIO: ¿Es verdad que este restaurante prepara los mejores mariscos de la ciudad?

CAMARERA: Sí, aquí servimos la mejor paella del mundo.

CECILIA: ¡Qué bueno! ¡La boca se me hace agua!

CAMARERA: Aquí está el menú. ¿Desean un aperitivo primero?

ANTONIO: Sí, dos vermús dulces, por favor...

CECILIA: ... y dos raciones de camarones a la plancha.

CAMARERA: Muy bien. ¿Desean pedir la comida ahora? La paella necesita tiempo.

CECILIA: Sí, vamos a ordenar una paella para dos, ¡con muchos mariscos!

ANTONIO: Además, pan con mantequilla. Y de postre, dos flanes.

CAMARERA: ¿Algo de beber con la cena?

CECILIA: Una botella de vino blanco para acompañar la paella.

ANTONIO: ¿Aceptan ustedes tarjetas de crédito?

CAMARERA: Por supuesto. Y cheques de viajero también.

DIALOGUE   In a Seafood Restaurant

A couple is going to eat in a restaurant that specializes in seafood.

WAITRESS: Good evening. How can I help you?

ANTHONY: Is it true that this restaurant prepares the best seafood in town?

WAITRESS: Yes, here we serve the best paella in the world.

CECILIA: That sounds good! It makes my mouth water!

WAITRESS: Here's the menu. Do you want an aperitif first?

ANTHONY: Yes, two sweet vermouths, please . . .

CECILIA: . . . and two orders of grilled shrimp.

WAITRESS: Very well. Do you want to order your dinner now? The paella takes time.

CECILIA: Yes, we're going to order a paella for two, with plenty of seafood!

ANTHONY: And bread and butter. And two custards for dessert.

WAITRESS: Anything to drink with your supper?

CECILIA: A bottle of white wine to accompany the paella.

ANTHONY: Do you take credit cards?

WAITRESS: Of course. And traveler's checks, too.

EXERCISES

ANSWERS
p. 82 **A. Complete the story using the information from the dialogue.**

Antonio y Cecilia son una pareja que cena en un restaurante de
(1) _____. La camarera habla con la (2) _____. En este
restaurante sirven la mejor paella del (3) _____. La pareja desea
tomar primero un (4) _____. Antonio y Cecilia toman dos vermús
(5) _____. Cecilia ordena dos (6) _____ de camarones a
la (7) _____. La camarera da el (8) _____ a la pareja.
Cecilia ordena una paella (9) _____, con muchos mariscos. Además,
Antonio desea pan con (10) _____. Ellos van a comer flan
(11) _____. Para beber Cecilia ordena una (12) _____
de vino (13) _____. En este restaurante aceptan (14) _____
de crédito, y también aceptan cheques de (15) _____.

ANSWERS
p. 82 **B. Match the two columns. (One of the letters in the column on the right
matches two numbers.)**

1. _____ Deseo camarones...

2. _____ ¡Cómo no!

3. _____ Comemos pan...

4. _____ El restaurante se especializa...

5. _____ El amarillo es...

6. _____ La boca...

7. _____ Aquí aceptamos...

8. _____ Comemos flan...

9. _____ Ahora la langosta...

10. _____ VISA es una tarjeta...

11. _____ Necesito cheques...

12. _____ Una ración de camarones...

13. _____ Deseamos dos vermús...

A. de crédito

B. de postre

C. de viajero

D. a la plancha

E. de aperitivo

F. con mantequilla

G. ¡Por supuesto!

H. un color muy popular

I. en mariscos

J. se hace agua

K. tarjetas de crédito

L. es muy cara

GRAMMAR I   Adjective-Noun Agreement • Plural of Nouns and Adjectives

A. An adjective describes a noun with such characteristics as color, shape, size, quality, nationality, and so on. The adjective agrees with its noun in *gender* (masculine / feminine) and *number* (singular / plural) in Spanish. In English adjectives never change; there is no agreement.

EXS: un libro bueno (*a good book*): masculine singular
una mesa buena (*a good table*): feminine singular
unos libros buenos (*some good books*): masculine plural
unas mesas buenas (*some good tables*): feminine plural

B. Adjectives ending in *o* change to *a* in the feminine: **bueno / buena.** If the adjective ends in any other letter, the feminine is the same as the masculine (there is no gender change).

EXS: libro verde / salsa verde, mejor libro / mejor paella

C. Adjectives ending in *L-N-R-S* (part of *L-O-N-E-R-S*) and *referring to nationalities* add an *a* to the last consonant to form the feminine. They are also used as nouns.

EXS: un profesor español / una profesora española, un español / una española
un camarero inglés / una camarera inglesa, un inglés / una inglesa
un libro alemán / una universidad alemana, un alemán / una alemana

D. *Plural* means two or more. Nouns and adjectives follow the same rules to form the plural.

1. If a word ends in a vowel, we add an *s:* **libro bueno / libros buenos.**

2. If a word ends in a consonant, we add *es:* **papel azul** (*blue paper*) / **papeles azules.**

3. If a word ends in a *z,* we change *z* to *c* and add *es:* **lápiz / lápices.**

4. If a word ends in an *s,* there are two rules for the plural.

   a) If the *s* is preceded by a *stressed vowel,* we add *es:* **inglés / ingleses.**

   b) If the *s* is preceded by an *unstressed vowel,* there is no change.

      EXS: *un* lunes / *dos* lunes, *una* crisis / *dos* crisis

5. There are a few words ending in *stressed í* or *stressed ú,* that have two plural forms, one in *es* and the other in *s.*

   a) The *es* plural form is traditional, formal usage now: **rubí / rubíes, hindú / hindúes** (*Hindu*), **champú / champúes.**

   b) The *s* plural form is colloquial and very common today: **rubí / rubís, hindú / hindús, champú / champús.**

E. The position of the adjective is often different in Spanish than in English. In Spanish, descriptive adjectives usually follow the noun. Adjectives of quantity, however, precede the noun, as in English.

EX: **un vino blanco** BUT **muchos platos**

PRACTIQUE LA GRAMÁTICA

ANSWERS
p. 82

1. An adjective describes a _____. In Spanish the adjective changes with the noun for gender and _____.

2. Remember that nouns ending in **L-O-N-E-R-S** are _____. This means that these six endings will match adjectives ending in the letter _____.

3. Nouns ending in **D-IÓN-Z-A** are _____. These endings will match adjectives ending in the letter _____.

4. Do adjectives ending in *e* change from masculine to feminine? _____ For example, **libro verde** (*green*), **tarjeta** _____.

5. Which is correct, **pared blanco** or **pared blanca?** _____.

6. Which is correct, **papel amarillo** or **papel amarilla?** _____.

7. Remember that nouns ending in *ma* are *not* feminine. Would you say **programa americano** or **programa americana?** _____.

8. Which is correct, **luz rojo** or **luz roja?** _____.

9. Would an adjective ending in *e,* such as **grande,** change from masculine to feminine? _____.

    EXS: **un libro grande, una casa** _____

10. The plural of *bueno* is _____. We add an *s* because the last letter is a _____.

11. The plural of *camarón* is _____. We add *es* because the last letter is a _____.

12. The plural of *luz* is _____. We add *es* because the last letter is a consonant, but we change the *z* to _____ because in Spanish there is rarely a *z* before an *e* or an *i*.

13. The plural of *lunes* is _____. The last letter is an *s,* and the preceding vowel, *e,* carries no _____; so there is no change.

14. The plural of *inglés* is _____. The last letter is an *s,* but it is preceded by a _____ vowel, *é.* Therefore we add *es*.

15. There are two plurals for words ending in stressed *i* or *ú: s* and _____.
The traditional plural of the precious stone **rubí** is _____,
whereas the modern plural is _____.

EXERCISES

**ANSWERS
p. 83**

A. **Write the plural form.**

1. el aperitivo pequeño _____

2. el camarón caro _____

3. la mejor paella _____

4. el cheque amarillo _____

5. la cena grande _____

6. la idea mala _____

7. la ración deliciosa _____

8. el café caliente _____

9. el mejor papel _____

10. el vino seco _____

11. el rubí caro (*traditional form*) _____

12. la luz verde _____

13. el champú americano (*modern form*) _____

14. el lunes pasado (*past*) _____

15. el agua caliente _____

16. la crisis económica _____

**ANSWERS
p. 83**

B. **Underline the adjective that agrees with the noun. Two answers are possible
in two cases. (Remember the rules for masculine/feminine gender.)**

1. programa (bueno, buena, buenos, buenas)

2. papeles (rojo, roja, rojos, rojas)

3. vermú (seco, seca, secos, secas)

4. vinos (dulce, dulza, dulces, dulzas)

5. mano (pequeño, pequeña, pequeños, pequeñas)

6. hambre (grande, granda, grandes, grandas)

7. luces (mejor, mejora, mejores, mejoras)

8. lunes (pasado, pasada, pasados, pasadas)

9. libros (inglés, inglesa, ingleses, inglesas)

10. rubís (caro, cara, caros, caras)

11. dos ciudades (hindú, hindús, indúes, hindúes)

GRAMMAR II   Present Indicative of *ir, dar, ver, saber,* and *decir*

Memorize the present indicative of the verbs in the chart.

	ir (to go)	*d ar* (to give)	*v er* (to see)	*sab er* (to know)	*dec ir* (to say)
yo	v oy	d oy	ve o	sé	dig o
tú	v as	d as	v es	sab es	dic es
él/ella/Ud.	v a	d a	v e	sab e	dic e
nosotros(as)	v amos	d amos	v emos	sab emos	dec imos
ellos/ellas/Uds.	v an	d an	v en	sab en	dic en

Note that:

1. *Ir* and *dar* are irregular because they add *y* to the *o* in the first person singular, just like *ser* (*soy*) and *estar* (*estoy*).

2. *Ver* is irregular in the first person singular because it adds an *e* to the stem *v:* (yo) **veo.**

3. *Saber* is very irregular in the first person singular. The *yo* form is *sé*.4.

4. *Decir* is the most irregular verb in this group. As a stem-changing verb (see page 54), it changes *e* to *i* in **digo, dices, dice, dicen.** It also changes *c* to *g* in **digo.**

5. The person and number correspondence between the ending of a verb and its subject is the same for all these verbs.

   -o (-oy) → yo, -mos → nosotros, -s → tú, -n → ellos/ellas/ustedes

   The only exception is the *-é* of *sé*.

NOTE

Quite frequently we use *ir* + *a* + (infinitive) to indicate an action in the future, parallel to the English *to be* + *going* + (infinitive). In this case *ir* is used in the present indicative.

EX: Ellos *van a estudiar* mañana. (*They are going to study tomorrow.*)

PRACTIQUE LOS VERBOS

ANSWERS
p. 83

1. The basic meaning of a verb is carried by the _____ of the verb. For example, the part of *saber* with the meaning *to know* is _____.

2. *Dar* is an **-ar** verb; its stem is very short: _____. *Ver* is an **-er** verb, and its stem is also very short: _____. Remember that the stem is the part of the verb that is repeated in all the tenses if the verb is regular. If the verb is irregular, the stem changes.

3. The letter that is repeated in all present indicative forms of the verb *ir* is

   _____.

4. Most verbs have an *-o* for *yo* in the present indicative, but a few have *-oy* instead. For example, from *ir* we get yo _____, and from *dar*, yo _____.

5. For *saber* we don't say **yo sabo,** but yo _____. For *decir* we don't say **yo deco,** but yo _____.

6. For *ver* (*v er*) we don't say **yo vo,** but yo _____. Notice the difference in spelling between *van* and *ven*: *van* means *they* _____; *ven* means *they* _____.

7. The person and number correspondence between the ending of a verb and its subject is the same for all verbs: **-mos** means _____; **-s** means _____, and **-n** means _____.

8. We can use the simple present indicative for an action in the future, for example, **Voy a clase mañana** (*I will go to class tomorrow*). We can also use the verb *ir* followed by the preposition *a* and the main verb: **Voy a verte mañana.** (*I am going to see you tomorrow*). How would you say *He is going to eat?* _____.

9. The present tense can be used for an action that is a habit. How would you say *I always tell the truth* in Spanish? **Yo siempre** _____.

EXERCISE

ANSWERS
p. 83

Complete each sentence with the correct present indicative form of the verb in parentheses.

1. Jorge y yo _____ a clase todos los días. (*to go*)

2. Ustedes _____ cheques de viajero. (*to need*)

3. Todas las noches tú _____ la televisión. (*to watch*)

4. La camarera _____ el menú a la pareja. (*to give*)

5. María _____ a su mamá. (*to accompany*)

6. Este restaurante se _____ en mariscos. (*to specialize*)

7. Este restaurante no _____ tarjetas de crédito. (*to accept*)

8. Ellos _____ hablar español y francés. (*to know* [*how*])

9. La camarera _____ el café. (*to be going to serve*)

10. Usted _____ unos platos deliciosos. (*to prepare*)

11. Cecilia y yo _____ toda la verdad. (*to tell*)

12. En casa de María (ellos) _____ muy tarde. (*to have supper*)

13. Yo no _____ preparar una paella. (*to know* [*how*])

14. (Tú) _____ a cenar a mi (*my*) casa. (*to be going to go*)

15. Nosotras _____ dos vasos de vermut. (*to ask for*)

16. ¡Con tanta (*so much*) comida, la boca se me _____ agua! (*to make*)

17. El banco (*bank*) _____ cheques de viajero. (*to give*)

18. (Yo) _____ un plato muy grande para la paella. (*to need*)

19. Antonio no _____ vino seco sino (*but*) dulce. (*to drink*)

20. El camarero y la camarera _____ español. (*to know*)

GRAMMAR III   Question Words • Numbers in Spanish

A. Memorize the following question words. Notice that all of them have a written accent (**acento**).

¿Adónde? *Where to?*	**¿De quién?** *Whose?*
¿Cómo? *How?*	**¿Dónde?** *Where?*
¿Cuál? *Which?*	**¿Qué?** *What?*
¿Cuándo? *When?*	**¿Quién?** *Who?*
¿Cuánto(a)? *How much?*	**¿Para qué?** *What for?*
¿Cuántos(as)? *How many?*	**¿Por qué?** *Why?*

¿Adónde? can be spelled as two words: **¿A dónde?**

Notice the question mark (**¿**) at the beginning of a question.

EX: **¿Cuándo comen ustedes?** (*When do you eat?*)

In questions beginning with question words, the subject (**ustedes** in this case) *follows* the verb rather than preceding it.

B. Question words carry a written accent (´) when used in *direct* questions as well as in *indirect* ones.

EX: **Deseo saber** *cómo* **estás.** (*I want to know <u>how</u> you are.*)

C. Memorize the numbers in Spanish.

0	cero	17	diecisiete	60	sesenta
1	un/uno/una	18	dieciocho	70	setenta
2	dos	19	diecinueve	80	ochenta
3	tres	20	veinte	90	noventa
4	cuatro	21	veintiuno(a)	100	cien, ciento
5	cinco	22	veintidós	101	ciento uno (un, una)
6	seis	23	veintitrés	200	doscientos(as)
7	siete	24	veinticuatro	300	trescientos(as)
8	ocho	25	veinticinco	400	cuatrocientos(as)
9	nueve	26	veintiséis	500	quinientos(as)
10	diez	27	veintisiete	600	seiscientos(as)
11	once	28	veintiocho	700	setecientos(as)
12	doce	29	veintinueve	800	ochocientos(as)
13	trece	30	treinta	900	novecientos(as)
14	catorce	31	treinta y uno	1.000	mil
15	quince	40	cuarenta	2.000	dos mil
16	dieciséis	50	cincuenta	1.000.000	un millón

D. Notice the following facts about numbers.

1. The numbers from 16 to 29 are written as only one word and pronounced with only one phonetic stress. (In English compound numbers carry two stresses.)

   EXS: **dieciséis** (*síxtéen*), **veintidós, veintitrés, veintiséis.**

2. Some people write checks with three words for the numbers 16 to 29, such as **diez y seis** (16), **veinte y dos** (22). Books and newspapers print only one word.

3. For *one* we use *un* before a masculine noun, *una* before a feminine noun, *uno* when the masculine noun is omitted, and *una* when the feminine noun is omitted.

   EXS: *un* libro, *una* novela. ¿Lee usted *un* libro? —Sí, leo *uno.*

   This same rule applies to compounds: **veintiún** libros, **veintiuna** mesas.

4. **Cien** is used before nouns. **Ciento** is used when counting (99, 100, 101, and so on) and in compound numbers.

   The expression *one hundred percent* is *cien por cien,* or *ciento por ciento,* according to the country and region.

5. In the hundreds (**doscientos, trescientos, cuatrocientos**), we use *doscientas, trescientas, cuatrocientas* when we talk about feminine nouns, as in **quinientas mesas.**

6. *Mil* doesn't change: **mil, dos mil, tres mil,** and so on. Notice that we don't say **un mil** for *one thousand;* simply **mil.** We use the plural **miles** to refer to a large but inexact amount. English uses *hundreds* or *tons* in this case.

   EX: **Tengo *miles* de amigos.** (*I have* <u>hundreds</u> *[tons] of friends*).

7. Notice the spelling of *million:* **millón** (not **-llion**). The plural is *millones,* and like *millón,* it is always followed by *de* before the noun we are counting.

   EX: **un millón de dólares** (*a million dollars*)

NOTE

In Spanish we use a period (.) to indicate thousand and million, and a comma (,) to indicate decimals. In English it is the other way around. However, stores in Spain are using cash registers imported from the United States more and more, and these machines use the period and the comma the same way as in the United States. Actually, Mexico changed to the American system many years ago.

PRACTIQUE LAS PALABRAS INTERROGATIVAS Y LOS NÚMEROS

ANSWERS
p. 83

1. Question words in Spanish carry a written _____. For example, ¿*Cuando?* is incorrect; it should be ¿_____?.

2. ¿*Adónde?* can also be spelled ¿_____?

3. Is *donde* correct in *No sé donde vive Ud.?* _____; it should be _____.

4. In Spanish, *zero* is not spelled with a *z* but a _____. Notice that *diez* (10) has a *z,* but *dieziséis* is incorrect; it should be _____. Remember that this same change occurs in the plural of nouns and adjectives ending in *z:* **lápiz / lápices.**

5. How many stresses does a compound number have in Spanish? _____. For example, **veinticinco** has the stress in the second number: _____.

6. There are two words for 100 in Spanish: _____ and _____. Before a noun such as **pesos,** we say _____ **pesos.**

7. Do we use *cien* or *ciento* in numbers over one hundred? _____
   For example, on a Spanish bank check 105 is spelled like this:
   _____.

8. The indefinite article *un/una* is exactly like the number *one* in Spanish: *un*
   is used before a _____ noun, and *una* before a _____
   noun.

9. *Uno* is used when a _____ noun is omitted, that is, when it's
   alone. For example, ¿Desea Ud. un lápiz? —Sí, deseo _____.

10. *Dos cientos* (200) is not correct; it should be _____. All
    multiples of one hundred change from *masculine* to *feminine* just like any
    other adjective. How do you say *three hundred bottles?* _____
    botellas.

11. How do you say *one thousand* in Spanish? _____ (Notice that
    we don't translate *one!*) How do you say *two thousand?* _____.

12. *Millión* is not correct in Spanish; it should be _____. The plural
    of *millón* is _____ (no written accent! You'll understand why
    later).

13. We use the preposition _____ between *millón* or *millones* and
    the noun being counted. For example, *two million dollars* is **dos**
    _____ **dólares.**

14. To indicate **mil** and **millón** in Spanish, do we use a comma or a period?
    _____. How do we indicate decimals, with a comma or a
    period? _____. Write how this figure would appear in Spanish:
    2,200,300.50: _____.

EXERCISE

ANSWERS p. 84

Complete sentences 1 to 9 with the translation of the word in parentheses.

1. ¿_____ vas a San Francisco? (*when*)

2. ¿_____ es este lápiz amarillo? (*whose*)

3. ¿_____ ves la televisión todos los días? (*why*)

4. ¿_____ cheques de viajero necesita Ud.? (*how many*)

5. ¿_____ clase de vino desea tomar? (*what*)

6. Marcos necesita saber _____ vive usted. (*where*)

7. María va a decir _____ es el mejor de todos. (*which*)

8. ¿_____ va usted con la botella? (*where to*)

9. ¿_____ café desea usted, señora? (*how much*)

Complete sentences 10 to 20 by writing out the number(s) in parentheses in Spanish.

10. Elena sabe _____ lenguas (*languages*); yo sólo sé _____. (*3, 1*)

11. Jorge necesita _____ vaso, y yo también necesito _____. (*1, 1*)

12. Mañana es el día _____ de junio (*June*). (*16*)

13. ¿Tú vas a comer _____ tacos? ¡Es imposible! (*22*)

14. Necesito _____ dólares para la comida. (*32*)

15. Este cheque es de _____ pesos. (*500*)

16. Esta cuenta del gas es de _____ pesos. (*110*)

17. ¿Quién va a pagar los _____ dólares? (*2,000*)

18. Aquí cenan todos los días _____ personas. (*500*)

19. ¿Deseas leer _____ libros? ¡Imposible! (*2,000,000*)

20. Estás correcto _____. (*100 percent*)

4 En el aeropuerto de Sevilla
(At Seville's Airport)

la aduana	customs	la maleta	suitcase
la aerolínea[1]	airline	el maletín	briefcase
el aeropuerto	airport	el pasaje	ticket
el asiento	seat	el/la pasajero(a)	passenger
el avión	airplane	el pasaporte	passport
la azafata[2]	stewardess	el piloto	pilot
el billete	ticket	la puerta	door, gate
el cigarrillo	cigarette	la reservación	reservation
el cinturón[3]	seat belt	la salida	departure, exit
el/la empleado(a)	employee	la ventana	window
el equipaje	luggage	la ventanilla[4]	small window
la hora	hour	el viaje	travel, trip
la llegada	arrival	el vuelo	flight
la luz roja	red light, traffic light		

abrochar	to fasten	pensar[6] (ie)	to think
ayudar	to help	poder (ue)	to be able to
bajar (de)	to get off, go down	poner	to put
comprar	to buy	querer (ie)	to wish, want
deshacer	to undo, melt	salir	to leave
detener	to stop, detain	seguir (i)	to follow
	(people)	sentarse (ie)	to sit down
facturar	to check in	servir (i)	to serve, help
fumar	to smoke	subir	to go up, climb
hacer	to do, make	tener	to have
inspeccionar	to inspect	venir	to come
llegar	to arrive	viajar	to travel
mostrar (ue)[5]	to show	volar (ue)	to fly
pedir (i)	to ask for	volver (ue)	to come back

alto(a)	high, tall	**medio(a)**	half
bajo(a)	low, short	**rápido(a)**	fast, quick
corto(a)	short	**sencillo(a)**[7]	single (*room*), one way
estupendo(a)	terrific		(*ticket*)
largo(a)	long	**simpático(a)**	nice, pleasant

antes (de)	beforehand, before	**más o menos**	more or less
a tiempo	on time	**o**	or
después (de)	after, afterwards	**tener que +**	to have to + (infinitive)
en punto	sharp (*exact time*)	**(infinitivo)**	
ida y vuelta	round-trip	**salir de + (lugar)**	to leave (a place)

NOTAS

1. *Aerolínea* is also called **línea aérea**.

2. *Azafata* is used in some countries for *stewardess*; other countries use **aeromoza** and even *camarera*. Lately the word *sobrecargo* is used for both men and women working on the airplane. Another word used nowadays is **asistente** (*assistant*).

3. *Cinturón de seguridad* (*safety belt, seat belt*), or simply *cinturón*, is used for the belt people wear on airplanes or cars. The belt people wear as part of clothing is called **cinto**; *cinta* is *ribbon*.

4. *Ventanilla* means *small window*; and it is used to refer to the *teller's window* in the bank and to the *small window* in an airplane, a car, at the post office, and so on.

5. The letters in parentheses following some verbs — (*i*), (*ie*), (*ue*) — are explained later in the grammar of this lesson.

6. *Pensar* + (infinitive) means *to plan, to intend to do something* + (verb).

   EX: *Pienso ir* a México = <u>I plan to go</u> to Mexico.

7. *Sencillo(a)* means *simple* referring to people, problems, and so on. It means *single* or *one way* when talking about hotel room reservations or transportation tickets. The opposite is *ida y vuelta,* that is, *round trip.* However, in Mexico *viaje redondo* is used for *round trip.*

8. *Antes* and *después* require *de* when a noun or an infinitive follows.

   EXS: **Voy** *antes de* **comer.** (*I'll go <u>before</u> eating.*)
   Voy *después de* **la comida.** (*I'll go <u>after</u> dinner.*)

PRACTIQUE LAS PALABRAS NUEVAS

ANSWERS p. 84

A. Write the article *el* or *la* before the noun. Remember that *avión* and *camión* (*truck*) are masculine. All other *-IÓN* nouns are feminine.

1. ___ avión   4. ___ vuelo   7. ___ cinturón   10. ___ pasaporte

2. ___ azafata   5. ___ reservación   8. ___ pasaje   11. ___ billete

3. ___ maletín   6. ___ equipaje   9. ___ ventanilla   12. ___ maleta

ANSWERS
p. 84
B. Underline the word that makes sense in each group.

1. El pasajero llega (al pasaje, a la llegada, al cigarrillo, al aeropuerto).

2. La azafata sirve (el vuelo, la comida, la maleta, el pasaporte).

3. En el aeropuerto facturamos (la llegada, el cinturón, el billete, el equipaje).

4. En el avión nos abrochamos (la maleta, el cinturón, la puerta, el pasaje).

5. En el aeropuerto compramos (el pasaje, el pasaporte, el vuelo, la maleta).

6. Yo siempre me siento (a la ventanilla, a la azafata, al equipaje, al cigarrillo).

7. En el aeropuerto hablo con (el piloto, el empleado, la azafata, el maletín).

8. Decimos adiós a los amigos antes de (subir, servir, deshacer, comprar) al avión.

9. Pensamos hacer (un asiento, una salida, un vuelo, una aduana) a Chicago.

10. ¿Quién ayuda (a los cinturones, a los pasajeros, al avión, al asiento)?

11. Salimos por la puerta de (aerolínea, aduana, equipaje, salida).

12. Vamos a comer después de (llegar, poder, poner, seguir).

13. Ellos inspeccionan el equipaje en (el pasaje, la aduana, la maleta, el pasaporte).

14. El avión sale (a tiempo, a la ventanilla, al asiento, al empleado).

15. Necesito un pasaje (corto, de ida y vuelta, más o menos, a tiempo).

16. Señor Martínez, ¿en qué puedo (comprarle, seguirle, servirle, deshacerle)?

ANSWERS
p. 84
C. Match the two columns.

1. ___ abrocharse	A. aeropuerto de Madrid
2. ___ llegar	B. en avión a Barcelona
3. ___ facturar	C. el pasaporte para viajar a Portugal
4. ___ volar	D. cigarrillos o pipa
5. ___ mostrar	E. sencillo o de ida y vuelta
6. ___ sentarse	F. volver
7. ___ fumar	G. la comida en el restaurante, en el avión
8. ___ servir	H. viajar a Argentina
9. ___ comprar un pasaje	I. el cinturón (de seguridad)
10. ___ hacer una reservación	J. la aduana de Bogotá
11. ___ salir del	K. el equipaje: maletas, maletín
12. ___ pensar	L. para el vuelo en avión
13. ___ inspeccionar el equipaje en	M. a la ventanilla, en el asiento
14. ___ ir y (*the opposite*)	N. a tiempo, tarde

DIÁLOGO   En el aeropuerto de Sevilla

Carlos llega al aeropuerto de Sevilla a las dos y diez de la tarde y habla con una empleada de Iberia, Aerolíneas Españolas.

EMPLEADA: Buenas tardes, señor. ¿En qué puedo servirle?

CARLOS: Quiero hacer una reservación para un vuelo a Lisboa. Pienso viajar por Portugal quince días.

EMPLEADA: Llega usted a tiempo. El vuelo 400 para Lisboa sale en cincuenta minutos, a las tres en punto.

CARLOS: ¡Estupendo! Es un viaje corto, ¿no?

EMPLEADA: Sí, una hora de vuelo más o menos. ¿Quiere un pasaje de ida y vuelta?

CARLOS: No, sencillo. ¿Puede darme un asiento con ventanilla?

EMPLEADA: ¿En la sección de fumar?

CARLOS: No, por favor; no fumo.

EMPLEADA: En este caso, sí puedo darle ventanilla. ¿Tiene Ud. su pasaporte?

CARLOS: Aquí está. ¿Algo más?

EMPLEADA: No… Aquí está el pasaje. Su asiento es el número 20A, con ventanilla.

CARLOS: ¡Qué bueno! ¡Es usted muy simpática!

EMPLEADA: Gracias. ¿Dónde está su equipaje?

CARLOS: Quiero facturar esta maleta.

EMPLEADA: Muy bien. Puede llevar el maletín con Ud. en el avión.

CARLOS: ¿Cuál es la puerta de salida para el vuelo 400?

EMPLEADA: Es el número 7. ¡Buen viaje!

CARLOS: Muchas gracias. Adiós.

DIALOGUE   At Seville's Airport

Charles arrives at Seville's airport at 2:10 P.M. and talks to an employee of Iberia, Airline of Spain.

EMPLOYEE: Good afternoon, sir. How may I help you?

CHARLES: I want to make a reservation for a flight to Lisbon. I plan to travel through Portugal for fifteen days.

EMPLOYEE: You got here just in time. Flight 400 for Lisbon leaves in fifty minutes, at three o'clock sharp.

CHARLES: Terrific! It's a short trip, isn't it?

EMPLOYEE: Yes, a one-hour flight, more or less. Do you want a round-trip ticket?

CHARLES: No, one-way. Can you give me a seat by the window?

EMPLOYEE:	In the smoking section?
CHARLES:	No, please, I don't smoke.
EMPLOYEE:	In that case, I can give you a window seat. Do you have your passport?
CHARLES:	Here it is. Anything else?
EMPLOYEE:	No. . . . Here is your ticket. Your seat number is 20A, by the window.
CHARLES:	Great! You're very nice!
EMPLOYEE:	Thanks. Where is your luggage?
CHARLES:	I want to check this suitcase.
EMPLOYEE:	Fine. You can take the briefcase with you on the plane.
CHARLES:	What is the departure gate for Flight 400?
EMPLOYEE:	It's number 7. Have a nice trip!
CHARLES:	Thank you. Good-bye.

NOTE

Actually, citizens of any European Common Market country can travel to other European Common Market countries without a passport. All they need is some form of identification, such as a driver's license. A Spaniard, for example, doesn't need a passport to travel to Portugal and vice versa.

EXERCISES

ANSWERS
p. 84

A. *En el aeropuerto de Sevilla.* **Complete the story using the information from the dialogue.**

Carlos (1) _____ al aeropuerto de Sevilla a las 2:10 de la
(2) _____ y habla con una (3) _____ de Iberia. Carlos quiere
una (4) _____ para un vuelo a Lisboa, la capital de Portugal. Él piensa
(5) _____ por Portugal quince días. El avión sale a las tres
(6) _____, pero es un vuelo corto, de una hora más o (7) _____.
Carlos no desea un pasaje de ida y vuelta sino (*but*) (8) _____, pero
quiere un asiento (9) _____ en la sección de (10) _____ porque
no fuma. Carlos tiene que mostrar el (11) _____ a la empleada porque
es un vuelo internacional. Él le dice a la empleada que es muy (12) _____
porque le da un buen (13) _____, exactamente el número 20A, con
ventanilla. Carlos no tiene mucho equipaje: una (14) _____ y un
maletín. Tiene que (15) _____ la maleta, pero puede subir el
(16) _____ al avión. La (17) _____ de salida para el vuelo 400
es el número 7. La empleada le desea buen (18) _____ a Carlos.

ANSWERS
p. 84

B. Match the two columns.

1. _____ El avión llega a las dos...
2. _____ La azafata es una camarera...
3. _____ El pasajero compra...
4. _____ Las maletas son parte...
5. _____ Para viajar de España a Portugal, Ud. necesita...
6. _____ Quiero un asiento...
7. _____ Esta aerolínea tiene empleadas...
8. _____ Una maleta pequeña es...
9. _____ Tengo dos reservaciones...
10. _____ Los pasajeros se abrochan...
11. _____ Las asistentes del avión ayudan...
12. _____ El piloto es responsable...
13. _____ El avión sale en treinta minutos. Ud. llega...
14. _____ Quiero reservar...
15. _____ No quiero un pasaje sencillo, sino...
16. _____ Las personas que trabajan en el avión son...
17. _____ Este viaje no es largo; al contrario, es...

A. con ventanilla
B. muy simpáticas
C. el cinturón de seguridad
D. empleados de la aerolínea
E. en el avión
F. en punto
G. a los pasajeros
H. de ida y vuelta
I. el billete (pasaje)
J. un asiento
K. a tiempo
L. corto
M. para el vuelo 400
N. un maletín
O. del vuelo
P. tener pasaporte
Q. del equipaje

GRAMMAR I Present Indicative of *tener, venir, poner, salir,* and *hacer*

A. Memorize the present indicative of the verbs in the chart.

	ten er (*to have*)	ven ir (*to come*)	pon er (*to put*)	sal ir (*to leave*)	hac er (*to do*)
yo	teng o	veng o	pong o	salg o	hag o
tú	tien es	vien es	pon es	sal es	hac es
él/ella/Ud.	tien e	vien e	pon e	sal e	hac e
nosotros(as)	ten emos	ven imos	pon emos	sal imos	hac emos
ellos/ellas/Uds.	tien en	vien en	pon en	sal en	hac en

Note that:

1. These five verbs add a *g* to the stem in the first person singular. Actually, *hacer* changes *c* to *g*: *hac-* changes to *hag-* in *yo hago*.

2. *Poner, salir,* and *hacer* are regular in all forms except the subject **yo**. All persons except **yo** have the same stem as the infinitive: **pon-, sal-,** and **hac-**.

3. *Tener* and *venir* change *e* to *ie* in the second and third persons: **tienes, tiene, tienen.** They belong to a large group of stem-changing verbs. These verbs are presented in Grammar III Section of this lesson. (See p. 54.)

4. There are many compounds of these five verbs. The compounds have the same changes as the original verbs. There are two of them in this lesson: **detener** (de + tener) meaning to *stop, arrest* and **deshacer** (des + hacer) meaning *to undo, unpack, melt.*

   EXS: **Ella *se detiene* en la luz roja.** (*She <u>stops</u> at the red light.*)
   Yo *deshago* la maleta. (*I <u>am unpacking</u> the suitcase.*)

B. Here are some uses of ***tener, salir,*** and ***venir.***

1. *Tener* means *to have, possess.*

   EX: ***Tengo*** un carro azul. (*<u>I have</u> a blue car.*)

   Tener que + (infinitive) indicates obligation; it is equivalent to the English *to have to* + (verb).

   EX: ¿Cuándo ***tienes que ir*** a Lisboa? (*When do you <u>have to go</u> to Lisbon?*)

2. *Salir* means *to go away, leave;* and it requires *de* when the point of departure is mentioned in the sentence. *To leave* is followed by the place *without* a preposition.

   EX: **Carlos *sale de* Sevilla en avión.** (*Charles <u>leaves</u> Seville by plane.*)

3. *Venir* means *to come,* and it is the opposite of *ir. Venir* is to move from anywhere to where the speaker is, and *ir* is to move from the speaker to somewhere else. Note that both *ir* and *venir* can mean *to come,* depending on the context.

   EX: ¿Cuándo ***vienes*** a verme? —**Voy** mañana. (*When <u>are you coming</u> to see me? — I <u>am coming</u> tomorrow.*)

PRACTIQUE LOS VERBOS

ANSWERS
p. 85

1. *Tener* has three different stem changes in the present: _____, _____, _____, and all three share the same basic meaning of possession; in English, *tener* means _____.

2. *Vengo, tengo, pongo,* and *salgo* are irregular because they add the letter _____ to their stems: **ven-, ten-, pon-, sal-**. *Hacer* changes the *c* to _____ in **yo** _____.

3. *Vienes* and *tienes* change the original *e* from **ven-** and **ten-** to _____. Are *venimos* and *tenemos* irregular? _____.

4. In order to translate the idea of obligation involved in *to have to* + (verb), Spanish adds _____ to *tener*. How do you say *I have to leave*? _____.

5. *Salir* means *to leave*. If we mention the place we are leaving, we need the preposition _____ before the place. For example, *I'm leaving home* is _____.

6. *Venir* means _____. In English *to come* can mean to move toward the speaker or away from the speaker, whereas in Spanish *venir* only means to move from somewhere to where the _____ is.

7. A child who replies *I'm coming, Mom* is moving toward her. How would you say in Spanish *I'm coming now, Mom*? **Ahora** _____, **mamá.**

8. Compound verbs follow the same changes as the original verbs. If *deshacer* is *to undo, unpack*, how would you say *I am unpacking my suitcase*? **Yo** _____ **mi maleta.**

9. If *detener* is *to stop, detain (people)*, how do you say *They are stopping at the light*? **Ellos se** _____ **en el semáforo (luz).**

EXERCISE

ANSWERS
p. 85

Complete each sentence with the correct form of the verb in the present indicative. (Before starting this excercise, review the new verbs in the vocabulary at the beginning of this lesson.)

1. Este avión _____ de Madrid. (*to come*)

2. Mañana (yo) _____ comprar un libro. (*to have to*)

3. La azafata _____ a los pasajeros. (*to help*)

4. ¿Cuándo _____ tú para Argentina? (*to leave*)

5. Carmen _____ la comida todos los lunes. (*to prepare*)

6. Los pasajeros se _____ los cinturones. (*to fasten*)

7. ¿_____ usted reservación en este vuelo? (*to have*)

8. (Yo) _____ el maletín en el avión. (*to put*)

9. ¿Cuándo _____ el vuelo 304 de Nueva York? (*to arrive*)

10. El policía _____ al criminal. (*to stop, detain*)

11. Paco _____ todo el equipaje. (*to check*)

12. Yo no _____ en la clase de español. (*to smoke*)

13. Carmen y yo _____ a tiempo a la fiesta. (*to come*)

14. Los pasajeros _____ ahora del avión. (*to get off*)

15. El turista _____ la maleta antes del viaje, y después del viaje
    tiene que _____ la misma (*same*) maleta. (*to pack/to unpack*)

16. Los funcionarios (*officers*) _____ las maletas en la aduana. (*to inspect*)

17. ¿_____ usted un asiento reservado para Lisboa? (*to have*)

18. El niño le dice a su mamá: *I'm coming now, Mom:* **Ahora** _____,
    mamá.

19. Nosotros _____ el pasaje en el aeropuerto. (*to buy*)

GRAMMAR II   ¿Qué hora es? (*What time is it?*)

A. Memorize the following expressions for telling time.

1.	*Exact time:*	**Es** la una.	(*It's one o'clock.*)
	(**Hora exacta**)	**Son** las doce.	(*It's two o'clock.*)
		Son las diez.	(*It's ten o'clock.*)
2.	*After the hour:*	Es la una **y diez.**	(*It's 1:10.*)
	(+) = **y**	Son las dos **y cuarto.**	(*It's 2:15.*)
		Son las dos **y quince.**	(*It's 2:15.*)
		Son las dos **y media.**	(*It's 2:30.*)
		Son las dos **y treinta.**	(*It's 2:30.*)
3.	*Before the hour:*	Es la una *menos* **diez.**	(*It's 12:50.*)
	(–) = **menos**	Son las dos *menos* **cuarto**	(*It's 1:45.*)
		Son las dos *menos* **quince.**	(*It's 1:45.*)
		Son las dos *menos* **veinte.**	(*It's 1:40.*)

B. *De la mañana/de la tarde/de la noche:* A.M. and P.M.

  1. A.M. = **de la mañana** (from midnight to noon)

  2. P.M. = **de la tarde** (from noon to dark—officially, 6:00 P.M.)

     = **de la noche** (from dark to midnight—officially, 6:00 P.M. to
     midnight)

C. Notice that we say **Es la una** (*hora*); the word *hora* is understood. The verb **es** changes to the plural **son** from two to twelve: the hours are more than *one*.

D. To express *sharp* when referring to time, we say **en punto** or **exactamente**. To express *about*, we can say **más o menos** (*more or less*) and **como**. To say *at*, we use the preposition **a** followed by the article **la** or **las**.

> EXS: **Son las dos** *más o menos*. (*It's about two o'clock*.)
> **Son** *como* **las dos.** (*It's about two o'clock*.)
> **Llegamos** *a la* **una.** (*We arrive at one o'clock*.)

E. *De la tarde/de la noche* will change with the season of the year, just like the greetings **Buenas tardes/Buenas noches**. On programs, schedules, and so on, after 6:00 P.M. is considered evening.

F. To ask for the time in Mexico they say **¿Qué horas son?** instead of **¿Qué hora es?** Languages are not logical but systematic. Mexican Spanish seems more logical since there are *eleven* **horas** and only *one* **hora**.

G. Official time expressed in newscasts, newspapers, plane and train schedules, TV programs, and so on, uses the 24-hour clock and the words *hora* or *horas*. Expressions such as *de la mañana, de la tarde,* are omitted. For example, **El accidente ocurrió** *a las 14* (*catorce*) *horas* in colloquial Spanish would be **El accidente ocurrió** *a las dos de la tarde*. (*The accident occurred at 2:00 P.M.*)

PRACTIQUE LA HORA Y LOS NÚMEROS

ANSWERS p. 85

1. *Son* and *es* are forms of *ser,* the verb used for identification. To tell time we use the singular form **es** with the number _____, and the plural **son** with the numbers _____.

2. In telling time, *fifteen minutes* has two possible words in Spanish: _____ and _____.

3. In telling time, *thirty minutes* also has two possible words in Spanish: _____ and _____.

4. To tell the minutes *after* the hour, we add the minutes with the conjunction _____. To subtract minutes *before* the next hour, we use the word _____.

5. How do you translate *sharp* when talking about time? _____. How do you say *about* when talking about time? _____ or _____.

6. There is only one translation for A.M.: _____.

7. There are two translations for *P.M.*: _____ and _____ .

8. Is it correct to say **Salgo a una** (*I'm leaving at one o'clock*)? _____ The article _____ is missing before ***una.***

9. When telling time, we say **a las dos, a la una,** with the articles **la** and **las** because the feminine word _____ is understood.

10. To ask for the time, Mexicans don't say **¿Qué hora es?** but _____ .

11. In newscasts, newspapers, plane schedules, TV programs, and so on, the _____-hour clock is used. The word _____ precedes the number *one*; the word _____ precedes the numbers *two* to *twenty-four*. The words _____ and _____ are always used in time expressions with the 24-hour clock. The expressions ***de la mañana*** and ***de la tarde*** are omitted.

EXERCISE

ANSWERS p. 85

Translate the following time expressions.

1. *It's 3:10 P.M.* _____

2. *It's 2:15 A.M.* _____

3. *It's 1:30 P.M.* _____

4. *It's 5:50 A.M.* _____

5. *It's 11:00 P.M.* _____

6. *It's 11:20 A.M.* _____

7. *It's 12:45 P.M.* _____

8. *It's 1:05 A.M.* _____

9. El avión sale _____ . (*at 2:00 sharp*)

10. En mi casa cenamos todos los días _____ . (*at 8:30*)

11. Todos los días salgo de casa _____ . (*at 7:00 A.M.*)

12. Lolita mira la televisión _____ . (*at 10:00 P.M.*)

13. El vuelo llega a Madrid _____ . (*at about 2:00*)

Official Time. (**Remember! Twenty-four hours are used along with the words** *hora/horas.*)

14. El avión sale _____ . (*at 3:00 P.M.*)

15. El avión llega _____ . (*at 1:00 A.M.*)

16. El presidente habla _____ . (*at 6:00 P.M.*)

GRAMMAR III   Present Indicative of Stem-Changing Verbs

A. Memorize the present indicative of the verbs in the chart.

	pens ar (to think)	*volv er* (to return)	*ped ir* (to ask for)	*segu ir* (to follow)
yo	piens o	vuelv o	pid o	sig o
tú	piens as	vuelv es	pid es	sigu es
él/ella/Ud.	piens a	vuelv e	pid e	sigu e
nosotros(as)	pens amos	volv emos	ped imos	segu imos
ellos/ellas/Uds.	piens an	vuelv en	pid en	sigu en

Note that:

1. All these verbs are called stem-changing verbs because they change a vowel in the stem; there are about six hundred common verbs in Spanish with this same feature.

2. The stem of *pensar* is **pens-**, but the *e* changes to *ie* in all the persons except **pensamos**, which is regular.

3. *Volver* changes *o* to *ue* in all the persons except **volvemos**.

4. *Pedir* and *seguir* have the same stem change: *e* changes to *i* in all the persons except the first person plural: **pedimos** and **seguimos**.

5. *Seguir* has the stem **segu-**, with a silent *u,* when it is followed by *i* or *e:* seguir, sigues, sigue, seguimos, siguen. However, the *u* is dropped in front of *o:* sigo.

B. Here is a partial list of stem-changing verbs. Notice that on vocabulary lists and in most dictionaries, (*ie*), (*ue*), or (*i*) appears after certain verbs. This is to remind you that it's a stem-changing verb. These are the stem-changing verbs you have encountered so far:

e → ie	o → ue	e → i
pensar to think, plan	**mostrar** to show	**pedir** to ask for
querer to wish; to love	**poder** to be able to, can	**seguir** to follow
sentarse to sit down	**volar** to fly	**servir** to serve
tener to have, possess	**volver** to return	**decir** to say, tell

C. Following are uses of *pedir, querer,* and *volver.*

1. *Pedir* means *to ask for.* Notice that *for* is not translated in Spanish.

   EX: Voy a *pedir* café. (*I'm going <u>to ask for</u> coffee.*)

2. *Querer* means *to wish, want,* when used with things and actions; but it means *to love* when referring to people, and it is used with the preposition **a** linking the verb with the noun.

EXS:　*Quiero* una casa grande. (*I want a big house.*)
　　　　¿*Quieres a* tu mamá? (*Do you love your mother?*)

3. *Volver* means *to return, come back*. *Volver a* + (infinitive) means that an action is being repeated. It means *to do again*.

EXS:　¿Cuándo *vuelves* a clase? (*When are you returning to class?*)
　　　　Ella *vuelve a viajar* a Chile. (*She is traveling again to Chile.*)

PRACTIQUE LOS VERBOS

ANSWERS p. 86

1. The stem of *querer* is _____, and the stem of *quieres* is _____. This means that the vowel **e** in the infinitive has changed to _____.

2. The stem of *decir* is _____, and the stem of *dices* is _____. This means that the vowel **e** in the infinitive has changed to _____.

3. The stem of *poder* is _____, and the stem of *puedo* is _____. In this case, the vowel **o** has changed to _____.

4. Is the stem of *pedimos* the same as the stem of *pedir?* _____. Then *pedimos* is regular because the stem doesn't change.

5. *Querer* means *to wish, want* when it's used with things, but it means *to love* when it's used with _____; for example, **José** _____ **a su esposa.**

6. In the expression *to ask for,* the word _____ is not translated in Spanish. How do you say *we ask for?* _____. And *they ask for?* _____.

7. *Servir* (*i*) is a stem-changing verb like *pedir.* How do you say *I'm serving dinner?* _____ **la comida.** And *they are serving?* _____.

8. *Volar* (*ue*) is a stem-changing verb, like *volver.* How do you complete this sentence? **El avión** _____ **de San Francisco a Chicago.**

9. *Mostrar* is an irregular verb, like *volver.* Remember that we can use the present with future meaning. How do you say *I'll show it to you?* **Yo te lo** _____.

10. There is no special auxiliary in Spanish for the emphatic *do* in expressions like *We do work hard.* We replace *do* with an emphatic adverb such as **sí, ciertamente.** How do you say *I do love you?* (**Yo**) _____.

11. The stem of *seguir* is _____, and the stem of *sigues* is _____; but the letter _____ is silent, and it is dropped before an *o*. How do you say *I follow you?* (**Yo**) **te** _____.

12. *Volver* is *to return*, but *volver a* + (infinitive) means *to do* _____.
    For example, **Volvemos a viajar** means _____.

13. The spelling change from *e* to *ie* also occurs in adjectives and nouns. For
    example, you remember the numbers **setenta** and _____ (7).
    Notice the change from *o* to *ue* from **noventa** to _____ (9).

EXERCISE

ANSWERS
p. 86

Complete each sentence with the correct form of the verb in parentheses.

1. Usted no _____ fumar en esta sección del avión. (*can*)

2. Sí, ellos _____ mañana de Miami a Nueva York. (*to fly*)

3. ¿Cuándo _____ ustedes a México? (*to return*)

4. Nosotros _____ hacer un viaje a Perú. (*to plan*)

5. ¿Por qué _____ (tú) comer en este restaurante? (*to want*)

6–7. Ella _____ a la derecha, y yo _____ a la izquierda. (*to follow*)

8. ¿Para qué _____ (tú) doscientos dólares a tu papá? (*to ask for*)

9. (Yo) me _____ a la ventanilla derecha. (*to sit*)

10. El turista _____ el pasaporte en la aduana. (*to show*)

11. Las aeromozas _____ la comida en el avión. (*to serve*)

12. ¿A dónde _____ viajar usted? (*to want*)

13. ¿Qué día _____ Carlitos a clase? (*to return*)

14. Sí, yo sí _____ estudiar más español. (*to plan*)

15. El águila _____ muy rápido y muy alto en el cielo (*sky*). (*to fly*)

16. No, yo no _____ ir el lunes a clase. (*to be able to*)

17. Paquito _____ a su mamá. (*to love*)

18. Por favor, ¿_____ darme un cigarrillo? (*can*)

19. ¿Cómo se _____ *to ask for* en español? (*to say*)

20. ¿Quién _____? (*to be next, follow*)

21. ¿Quiénes (plural *who*) _____ el billete de ida y vuelta? (*to have*)

22. Mañana nosotros no _____ venir aquí. (*can*)

23. Mis amigos _____ a las cuatro más o menos. (*to come*)

24. Ustedes _____ los pasajes al sobrecargo del avión. (*to show*)

25. (Yo) no _____ fumar más. La nicotina da cáncer. (*to want*)

5 La familia hispana y la casa
(The Hispanic Family and the House)

el / la abuelo(a)[1]	grandfather, grandmother	la mamá	mom
el baño[2]	bathroom	el mueble[7]	furniture
la cama	bed	el / la nieto(a)	grandson, granddaughter
el carro,[3] el coche	car	el / la niño(a)	boy, son
la chimenea	fireplace	el / la novio(a)	fiancé, fiancée
la cocina	kitchen	el padre	father
el / la cocinero(a)	cook	los padres	parents
el comedor	dining room	el papá	father, dad
el cuarto	room	el pariente	relative
el dormitorio[4]	bedroom	el piso	floor
la ducha[5]	shower	el / la primo(a)	cousin
el / la esposo(a)	spouse	el reloj	clock, watch
la familia	family	la silla	chair
la flor[6]	flower	el sillón	armchair
el / la hermano(a)	brother, sister	el / la sobrino(a)	nephew, niece
el / la hijo(a)	son, daughter	el / la suegro(a)	father-in-law, mother-in-law
la invitación	invitation		
el jardín	garden	el tejado	roof
el lavaplatos	dishwasher	el / la tío(a)	uncle, aunt
la madre	mother		

aparecer	to appear	invitar	to invite
apreciar	to appreciate	lavar	to wash
bañarse	to bathe	morir (ue)	to die
caer	to fall	nacer	to be born
concluir	to conclude	ofrecer	to offer
conducir[8]	to drive	oír[9]	to hear
conocer	to know, meet	parecer	to seem
construir	to build	presentar	to present
creer	to believe	producir	to produce
deber	must, should	reconocer	to recognize
destruir	to destroy	recordar (ue)	to remember
dormir (ue)	to sleep	traducir	to translate
huir	to flee	traer	to bring
importar	to matter		

alegre	happy, glad	joven	young
amable	kind, nice	lindo(a)	pretty
bonito(a)	pretty	pobre	poor
casado(a)	married	poco(a)	little
corto(a)	short	rico(a)	rich
fantástico(a)	fantastic	soltero(a)[10]	single
feliz	happy	terrible	terrible
feo(a)	ugly	triste	sad
futuro(a)	future	viejo(a)	old
guapo(a)	handsome		

ayer	yesterday	sobre	about
desde	from	solamente	only
entonces	then	su, sus	his/her (s. & pl.)
hasta	until, to	temprano	early
hoy	today	tener... años	to be . . . years old
mi, mis[11]	my	todavía	still, yet
pero	but	tu, tus	your
que	that		

NOTAS

1. *Abuelos* has two different meanings, according to the context: *grandfathers* or *grandparents* (grandmother[s] and grandfather[s]). The same thing happens with all the pairs in family words, such as **hermanos, hijos, padres,** and so on.

   EXS: hermanos (*brothers/brother[s] and sister[s]*)
   tíos (*uncles/aunt[s] and uncle[s]*)

2. *Baño* is the word for *bathroom* in some countries, but there are many other words for this room: **servicio, inodoro, váter, aseo, retrete, excusado.**

3. *Carro* is used in Latin America for *car, automobile,* whereas *coche* is used in Spain. *Automóvil* is used in all the countries.

4. *Dormitorio* is not *dormitory* but *bedroom.* Other words used for *bedroom* in different regions are **alcoba, recámara, cuarto,** and **habitación,** which usually applies to a *hotel room.* The word for *dormitory* is **residencia.**

5. *Ducha* is not *douche* but the *shower* in the bathroom. A *rain shower* is **aguacero.**

6. *Flor* is an exception to the gender rules; it is feminine: **la flor.** *Reloj* is the only word in Spanish ending in **j,** and it's masculine: **el reloj.**

7. *Mueble* is a count noun in Spanish; that is, unlike *furniture,* **mueble** is used both in the singular and plural.

   EX: **La silla y la mesa son *dos muebles.*** (*The chair and the table are <u>two pieces of furniture</u>.*)

8. *Conducir* means *to drive* in Spain, *to conduct* in all the other countries. In Latin America *to drive* is **manejar.**

9. *Oír* can mean both *to hear* and *to listen,* just like **ver** can mean *to see* and *to watch.* The verb *escuchar* also means *to listen,* but it is used less frequently than *oír.*

10. *Soltero* means *single* in the sense of *not married.* Remember that *single* referring to a *one-way* (*trip*) is **sencillo.** *Solterona* means *old maid.*

11. We will study the possessive adjectives in Lesson 7. In the meantime notice that *mi* (*my*) changes to the plural *mis* if the thing possessed is plural. The same goes for *tu* (*your*) and **tus,** and *su* (*his, her, their*) and **sus.**

PRACTIQUE LAS PALABRAS NUEVAS

ANSWERS p. 86

A. Write *el* or *la* in front of the noun.

1. ___ mueble	5. ___ garaje	9. ___ comedor	13. ___ chimenea
2. ___ pariente	6. ___ reloj	10. ___ papá	14. ___ tejado
3. ___ invitación	7. ___ silla	11. ___ sillón	15. ___ madre
4. ___ flor	8. ___ coche	12. ___ lavaplatos	16. ___ jardín

ANSWERS p. 86

B. Complete the following sentences about the family.

1. El padre de mi padre es mi _____.

2. El hermano de mi padre es mi _____.

3. Los hijos de mi hermana son mis _____.

4. Los hijos de mi hija son mis _____.

5. La hija de mi tío es mi _____.

6. Las hermanas de mi papá son mis _____.

7. Mis abuelos son los padres de mis _____.

8. Los hijos de mis tíos son mis _____.

9. La madre de mi esposa es mi _____.

10. Los hijos de mis padres son mis _____.

11. El papá de mi esposo es mi _____.

12. Mi abuela es la mamá de mi _____.

ANSWERS p. 86

C. Write the opposite word.

1. alegre _____
2. bonito _____
3. joven _____
4. soltero _____
5. largo _____

6. pobre _____
7. lindo _____
8. mucho _____
9. nacer _____
10. desde _____

11. construir _____
12. terrible _____
13. tarde _____
14. día _____

ANSWERS p. 86

D. Match the two columns.

1. _____ Conducimos o manejamos...
2. _____ Oímos o escuchamos...
3. _____ Construimos...
4. _____ Traducimos...
5. _____ Dormimos...
6. _____ Nacemos... y morimos
7. _____ Ofrecemos...
8. _____ Nos bañamos...
9. _____ Queremos...
10. _____ Nos sentamos...

A. del inglés al español
B. una casa, un hotel
C. en una silla o un sillón
D. a los amigos y a los parientes
E. en la ducha, en el mar
F. la radio, la música
G. el coche, el carro, el avión
H. una cerveza, un aperitivo
I. en la cama por la noche
J. en un hospital, generalmente

ANSWERS p. 86

E. Underline the word that makes sense.

1. El cocinero trabaja en (el piso, el jardín, el reloj, la cocina).

2. Ponemos los coches en (el garaje, el tejado, la ducha, el cuarto).

3. Hacemos el fuego (*fire*) en (el jardín, el lavaplatos, la chimenea, la flor).

4. Mi jardín es bonito; tiene muchos(as) (cuartos, flores, camas, muebles).

5. Mi casa es grande; tiene cinco (muebles, relojes, dormitorios, lavaplatos).

6. Un mueble de la cocina es (el lavaplatos, la cama, el sillón, el comedor).

7. Un mueble del comedor es (la ducha, la mesa, la chimenea, el baño).

8. Un mueble del dormitorio es (el piso, el tejado, la cama, el baño).

9. Nos bañamos en (el jardín, la ducha, las flores, el lavaplatos).

10. *Coche* también se dice (sobrino, reloj, carro, sillón).

11. Sabemos la hora por (el lavaplatos, el tejado, el mueble, el reloj).

12. *Hijos* también se dice en español (nieto, sobrinos, niños, tíos).

13. La parte alta de la casa es (el tejado, el cuarto, el comedor, la cama).

14. La rosa y el geranio son dos (muebles, flores, sillones, baños).

15. La cama y el sillón son dos (muebles, baños, relojes, tejados).

16. Toda la familia cena en (el cuarto, el comedor, el sillón, el garaje).

17. Ella y él no son esposos todavía. Son (padres, sobrinos, novios, nietos).

18. José no tiene hijos; es (abuelo, rico, soltero, pariente).

19. No tengo muchos dólares; soy (casado, viejo, triste, pobre).

20. Los abuelos no son muy (jóvenes, casados, solteros, cortos).

21. Mi tía es vieja y no es casada; es (joven, solterona, novia, pobre).

DIÁLOGO   La familia de Carlos

Carlos es mexicano y Debbie es una joven americana que estudia en México; los dos son muy buenos amigos. Se conocieron (they met) *en la universidad.*

CARLOS: ¿Por qué no vienes a comer a mi casa hoy?

DEBBIE: Pero no conozco bien a tus padres todavía.

CARLOS: No importa. Ellos quieren conocerte mejor también.

DEBBIE: Está bien. Acepto tu invitación. ¿Cuántos hermanos tienes?

CARLOS: Somos dos hermanos y una hermana.

DEBBIE: ¿Viven los abuelos con ustedes?

CARLOS: Solamente mi abuela materna, y también mi tía Carlota; es hermana de mi padre.

DEBBIE: Entonces deben tener una casa grande.

CARLOS: Sí, tiene cinco dormitorios, un garaje grande y un patio con jardín con muchos árboles y flores. También tenemos tres baños.

DEBBIE: Quiero conocer a tu abuelita. ¿Es muy vieja?

CARLOS: Tiene setenta y seis años, pero está joven todavía. Trabaja en la casa desde temprano hasta la noche.

DEBBIE: Ustedes los latinos saben apreciar a la familia mejor que nosotros los americanos.

CARLOS: Bueno… ¡pero las suegras son terribles!

DEBBIE: No lo creo. Conozco un poco a mi «futura suegra» y sé que es ¡fantástica!

DIALOGUE Carlos's Family

Carlos is Mexican and Debbie is an American student in Mexico; they are very good friends; they met at the university.

CARLOS: Why don't you come to eat at my house today?

DEBBIE: But I don't know your parents very well yet.

CARLOS: It doesn't matter. They want to to get to know you better, too.

DEBBIE: Okay. I accept your invitation. How many brothers and sisters do you have?

CARLOS: We're two brothers and one sister.

DEBBIE: Do your grandparents live with you?

CARLOS: Just my maternal grandmother and my aunt Carlota; she's my father's sister.

DEBBIE: Then you must have a big house.

CARLOS: Yes, it has five bedrooms, a large garage, and a yard with a garden with many trees and flowers. We also have three bathrooms.

DEBBIE: I want to meet your grandma. Is she very old?

CARLOS: She's seventy-six years old, but she still looks young. She works in the house from morning 'til night.

DEBBIE: You *Latinos* know how to appreciate your families better than we Americans do.

CARLOS: Yeah . . . but mothers-in-law are terrible!

DEBBIE: I don't believe so. I know my "future mother-in-law" a little bit, and I know that she's fantastic!

EXERCISES

ANSWERS p. 87

A. *La familia de Carlos.* **Complete the story using the information from the dialogue.**

Debbie es una (1) _____ americana que estudia en la universidad en México. Carlos y Debbie son muy buenos (2) _____ desde que se conocieron (*met*) en las clases. Carlos (3) _____ a Debbie a comer en su casa hoy. Debbie dice que no (4) _____ bien a sus (5) _____ todavía, pero Carlos le dice que ellos (6) _____ conocerla (7) _____ también. Debbie (8) _____ la invitación muy contenta. Carlos tiene un hermano y una (9) _____, y también viven con ellos su (10) _____ materna y una (11) _____ que es hermana de su padre. La casa de Carlos es grande: tiene cinco (12) _____, o como dicen en México, recámaras, tres (13) _____, un garaje grande, un patio con (14) _____ que tiene muchos (15) _____ y flores. Debbie quiere (16) _____ a la abuelita que tiene sententa y seis (17) _____, pero está (18) _____ todavía y trabaja todo el día en la casa. Debbie le dice a Carlos que los latinos saben (19) _____ a su familia mejor que los (20) _____. Carlos dice que todas las (21) _____ son terribles, pero Debbie le asegura (*assures him*) que su futura suegra es (22) _____. Esto (*this*) muestra que Debbie ya (*already*) se considera la (23) _____ de Carlos.

B. Match the two columns.

1.	_____ La casa de Carlos tiene un jardín con...	**A.**	joven
2.	_____ Preparamos la comida...	**B.**	sillón
3.	_____ La parte más alta de la casa es...	**C.**	en el garaje
4.	_____ Para saber la hora leemos...	**D.**	árboles y flores
5.	_____ Una silla grande y cómoda es un...	**E.**	vieja
6.	_____ Toda la familia cena...	**F.**	en el dormitorio
7.	_____ Dejamos los carros o coches...	**G.**	en la cocina
8.	_____ Una persona de noventa años sí es...	**H.**	en un hospital
9.	_____ Los novios todavía no son...	**I.**	el tejado
10.	_____ Si Ud. tiene veinte años es muy...	**J.**	el reloj
11.	_____ Dormimos la siesta...	**K.**	en el comedor
12.	_____ Generalmente nacemos...	**L.**	casados

GRAMMAR I Present Indicative of *oír, traer, conocer,* and *huir* • Contrasting *saber* and *conocer*

A. Memorize the present indicative of the verbs in the chart.

	o ír (to hear)	tra er (to bring)	conoc er (to know)	hu ir (to flee)
yo	oig o	traig o	conozc o	huy o
tú	oy es	tra es	conoc es	huy es
él/ella/Ud.	oy e	tra e	conoc e	huy e
nosotros(as)	o ímos	tra emos	conoc emos	hu imos
ellos/ellas/Uds.	oy en	tra en	conoc en	huy en

Note that:

1. *Oír* has a short stem: **o-**. It expands to **oig-** for the first person singular, and to **oy-** for all the other persons except **oímos,** which is regular.

2. The stem of *traer* is **tra-**, and it is expanded to **traig-** in *traigo.* The other persons are regular: **traes, trae,** and so on.

3. *Conocer* has the stem **conoc-**. In the first-person singular the final *c* changes to *z* and adds the letter *c* with the [k] sound: **conozco.** Remember that *c* followed by *e* or *i* is pronounced *s* in Latin America.

4. *Huir* has the stem **hu-**, which is expanded to **huy-** in all the forms except **huimos,** which is regular.

B. **Verbs conjugated like *conocer* and *huir***

Most verbs ending in -cer and -cir add *c* in the yo form, like *conocer.* Verbs ending in -uir add *y* in all the forms except **nosotros,** just like *huir.*

-cer	*-cir*	*-uir*
aparecer to appear	**conducir** to drive	**concluir** to conclude
nacer to be born	**producir** to produce	**construir** to build
ofrecer to offer	**reducir** to reduce	**destruir** to destroy
parecer to seem, look like	**traducir** to translate	**huir** to flee, escape
reconocer to recognize		**instruir** to instruct

C. **Differences between *saber* and *conocer***

1. *Conocer* is *to be acquainted with, to meet people.*

2. *Conocer* is *to know places, countries,* and *people,* in the sense of being familiar with them.

> EXS: ¿**Conoces** a mi tío? (*Are you <u>acquainted with</u> my uncle?*)
> ¿**Conoces** (*a*) Cuba? (*Do you <u>know</u> Cuba?*)

Some regions use the preposition **a** before cities and countries following *conocer.* Other regions omit it.

> EX: *Conozco* Chile. / *Conozco a* Chile. (*I <u>know</u> Chile.*)

3. *Saber* is *to know facts.*

> EX: *Sé* que México es grande. (*I <u>know</u> that Mexico is large.*)

4. *Saber* is *to know by heart,* like numbers.

> EX: ¿*Sabes* mi teléfono? (*Do you <u>know</u> my telephone number?*)

5. *Saber* is *to know how,* but we don't translate the word *how.*

> EX: **Pablo** *sabe* hacer paella. (*Paul <u>knows how</u> to make paella.*)

PRACTIQUE LOS VERBOS

ANSWERS p. 87

1. *Oír* has three different stems in the present: _____, _____, _____. The only regular form is (**nosotros**) _____ (with a written accent!).

2. *Traer* and *caer* are irregular in the first person only: _____/ _____. Both add these two letters to the stem: _____.

3. *Conocer* changes to **yo** _____. The *c* has changed to *z* because of a spelling rule, but it has added the sound [**k**], which is the letter _____.

4. Most of the verbs ending in **-cer** and **-cir** are irregular like *conocer*. For example, from *ofrecer,* **yo** _____; and from *conducir,* **yo** _____.

5. The stem of *huir* is **hu-**, but it adds the letter _____ in **huyo, huyes,** and so on. The only regular form is (**nosotros**) _____.

6. All the verbs ending in **-uir** add the *y* to the stem like *huir.*

   EXS: **construir, yo** _____; **concluir, ellos** _____.

7. *Nacer* is a passive verb in English, *to be born.* We use this verb in the past more often than in the present: *I was born in* . . . But it is possible to say *I am born,* at least in poetry. The translation in Spanish is _____.

8. *Saber* and *conocer* mean *to know.* Which one do you use for *to know* or *meet people?* _____. And *to know facts?* _____.

9. *To know how* implies knowledge and practice. Do you use *saber* or *conocer?* _____. Do you translate *how* in *to know how?* _____.

10. If you *know a city* or *a state,* do you use *saber* or *conocer?* _____. For example, **Nosotros** _____ **a Nueva York.**

11. If you *know* my telephone number and my address, it means that you have memorized numbers and names. How would you say *I know your telephone number?* _____ **tu teléfono.**

12. How do you say *I know how to cook?* _____.

EXERCISE

ANSWERS p. 87

Complete each sentence with the correct form(s) of the verb(s) in parentheses.

1. Venezuela y México _____ mucho petróleo. (*to produce*)

2. Yo no _____ este coche: es demasiado (*too*) viejo. (*to drive*)

3. Mis padres _____ la radio todos los días. (*to listen*)

4. Los criminales _____ de los policías. (*to flee, go away*)

5. ¿Por qué (tú) no _____ en tu casa? (*to sleep*)

6. Los empleados _____ un hospital grande. (*to build*)

7. Muchos niños _____ de hambre (*hunger, starvation*). (*to die*)

8. (Yo) no _____ el carro a la universidad todos los días. (*to bring*)

9. Tu novio _____ que es muy simpático. (*to seem*)

10. Mi suegra no _____ sus errores. (*to recognize*)

11. Mi abuela _____ a todos sus parientes. (*to remember*)

12. Ellos _____ las palabras del inglés al japonés. (*to translate*)

13. Esta clase _____ a las doce menos diez. (*to conclude, end*)

14. Cuando voy al trabajo, siempre _____ la radio del coche. (*to listen*)

15. Mi amiga _____ bien la ciudad de Nueva York. (*to know*)

16-17. Cuando bebo demasiado (*too much*) vino, me _____ en la cama y me _____ rápidamente. (*to fall, sleep*)

18. (Yo) no _____ preparar paella, pero sí café. (*to know how*)

19. La camarera _____ el menú a los invitados. (*to offer, give*)

20. Las guerras (*wars*) _____ a muchas personas inocentes. (*to destroy*)

GRAMMAR II   The Written Accent

A. Spanish words carry *one* and *only one* phonetic stress. This stress is marked with the a written accent (´) according to the following fixed rules. In order for these rules to be effective, you should be able to "hear" the stress, and the other way around: these rules will help you to place the stress when you read if you don't know the word.

B. The following three rules show you when to add an accent mark.

1. Words with stress on the *last syllable* need an accent if the last letter is a vowel or the consonant **n** or **s**. Also, the word must have two or more syllables: **estás, está, están, aquí, menú, champú, jardín, dieciséis** (but **seis**), **veintidós** (but **dos**), **también** (but **bien**).

2. Words with stress on the *next-to-last syllable* need an accent if the last letter is any consonant *except* **n** or **s**: **árbol, lápiz, estándar, azúcar, fácil** (*easy*).

3. Words with stress *two syllables before the last* need an accent. Here the last letter has nothing to do with the accent: **número(s), fantástico(s), águila(s), línea, aéreo.**

C. The exceptions to these three rules are for reasons other than the stress. There are two additional rules:

1. We write an accent on the vowel **í** or **ú** to break a diphthong—that is, when the **í** or the **ú** carries the stress and is before or after any of the other three vowels: **a, e, o.**

   EXS: **oír, día, tío, rubíes, hindúes, María, maíz** (*corn*)

2. Pairs of words with the same spelling but different meanings need an accent; the only way to tell them apart is the accent on one of them. Try to memorize them.

aún (*yet*)/**aun** (*even*)	**más** (*more*)/**mas** (*but*)	**sí** (*yes*)/**si** (*if*)
dé (*give*)/**de** (*of*)	**mí** (*me*)/**mi** (*my*)	**sólo** (*only*)/**solo** (*alone*)
él (*he*)/**el** (*the*)	**sé** (*I know*)/**se** (*himself*)	**tú** (*you*)/**tu** (*your*)

D. Remember that question words always have an accent, even though the above rules may not apply. This is also true for question words used in indirect questions.

   EX: **María sabe *cuándo* vamos a llegar.** (*Mary knows <u>when</u> we're going to arrive.*)

No spelling rules, including rules for the accent, are as good as a "visual memory." Try to pay attention to the spelling of words as you learn them. *Be a good word-watcher!*

PRACTIQUE EL ACENTO

ANSWERS p. 87

1. How many stresses does a Spanish word carry? _____. For example, compound words such as ***diecinueve*** lose the stress of the first word. *Diecinueve* has no stress on *diec-* but on _____.

2. *Café* has an accent because the stress is on _____ syllable, and the last letter is a _____, as in **menú, está, bambú.**

3. *Avión* and *menús* need an accent because the stress is on the _____ syllable, and the last letters are the consonants _____ and _____.

4. *Pared, verdad,* and *comer* don't carry an accent because the stress is on the _____ syllable, but the last letter in neither a _____ nor the consonants _____ or _____.

5. *Lápiz* and *árbol* carry an accent because the stress is one syllable before the last and the last letter is a _____ but not *n* or *s*.

6. *Lápices, número,* and *águila* carry an accent because the stress is _____ syllables before the last. The _____ letter doesn't matter at all.

7. A diphthong is formed with two vowels in one syllable, one of which is either *i* or *u*. Both *María* and *oír* carry an accent for the same reason: to mark the break in the _____ between the í and the vowels _____ and _____.

8. In English *lead* can mean two different things (*an action* or a *metal*), altough the spelling is the same. In Spanish we indicate such differences with an accent. For example, *él* means _____, whereas *el* means _____.

9. The word *tú* means _____, whereas *tu* means _____.

10. The word *sí* means _____, whereas *si* means _____.

11. The word *más* means _____, whereas *mas* means _____.

12. Words with just one syllable don't need an accent: **dos, va, ve, tres, son,** and so on. However, if these words appear in compound words, they will need one; for example, *él prevé* (*he foresees*). How do you spell twenty-two in Spanish? _____.

EXERCISE

Be a good word-watcher and a good listener! **All the following words are in previous lessons. Write the accent when needed.**

1. amarillo	8. lapices	15. feliz	22. papeles	29. veintiun
2. luz	9. mama	16. avion	23. dieciseis	30. el (*the*)
3. aguila	10. tu (*you*)	17. camarera	24. dia	31. se (*I know*)
4. rubi	11. traemos	18. champu	25. novio	32. arbol
5. creer	12. huimos	19. el (*he*)	26. estudio	33. rubis
6. oir	13. oimos	20. arboles	27. seis	34. diecisiete
7. numero	14. estan	21. flores	28. ingles	35. veintitres

GRAMMAR III   Negative Constructions

A. Memorize the following negative and affirmative words.

jamás / siempre never / always
nada / algo nothing / something
nadie / alguien nobody / somebody
ninguno / alguno no one, none / some

no / sí no / yes
nunca / siempre never / always
sin / con without / with
tampoco / también neither, either / also

B. Notice the following rules about the words in the list above.

1. *Jamás* and *nunca* mean *never,* but *jamás* is more emphatic. Actually the two words can be used in the same sentence to make the negation even stronger.

    EX: Carlos *nunca jamás* estudia. (*Charles <u>never never</u> studies.*)

2. *Nadie* and *alguien* refer to people only, whereas *nada* and *algo* refer to things.

    EXS: ¿*Alguien* sabe esta palabra? (*Does <u>anybody</u> know this word?*)
          Nadie dice eso. (<u>*Nobody*</u> *says that.*)

3. *Alguno* and *ninguno* refer to people or things. They change to *alguna/ ninguna* for the feminine. *Algunos(as)* is the plural of *alguno(a),* **but** *ninguno(a)* has no plural. *Alguno* and *ninguno* become *algún/ningún* in front of a masculine noun: *algún* libro.

    EX: ¿Conoces a *algún* francés en París? —No, no conzco a *ninguno.*
         (*Do you know <u>any</u> French people in Paris? —No, I don't know <u>any</u>.*)

4. *Alguno* is used only before a noun, or as a pronoun when the noun has already been mentioned, whereas *alguien* is always used without a noun. The same rule applies to *ninguno* versus *nadie.*

    EXS: ¿Cuántos niños vienen? — No viene *ninguno.*
          (*How many boys are coming? —<u>None</u> are coming.*)
          ¿Conoces esos libros? — Sí, conozco *algunos.*
          (*Do you know those books? —Yes, I know <u>some</u>.*)

C. **Double negative in Spanish**
    If a sentence starts with a negative word, an affirmative word cannot be used after the verb. Another negative word must be used. For example, it's incorrect to say **No viene alguien;** it must be **No viene nadie.** The double negative is summarized in the following chart. Notice that it is possible to have a triple negative.

Negative word	Verb	Negative word	Negative word
(Ella) No	dice	nada	nunca

EXS: Juan *no* habla español *tampoco.* (*John <u>doesn't</u> speak Spanish <u>either</u>.*)
      Juan *no* fuma *nada nunca.* (*John <u>doesn't</u> smoke <u>anything ever</u>.*)

D. **Simple negative and double negative**
    A simple or double negative can often be used to carry the same message. The double negative is more emphatic.

    EXS: *Nadie* habla español aquí. = *No* habla *nadie* español aquí. (<u>*Nobody*</u> *speaks Spanish here.*)
          Ella *tampoco* habla español. = Ella *no* habla español *tampoco.* (*She <u>doesn't</u> speak Spanish <u>either</u>.*)

PRACTIQUE LAS PALABRAS NEGATIVAS

1. Lo contrario de (*the opposite of*) *alguno* es _____, y lo contrario de *algo* es _____.

2. Lo contrario de *también* es _____, y lo contrario de *con* es _____.

3. Which is more emphatic, **Nadie habla** or **No habla nadie?** _____.

4. ¿Cuál es correcto, **Él es no bueno** or **Él no es bueno?** _____.

5. ¿Cuál es correcto, **Él está no aquí** or **Él no está aquí?** _____.

6. *Alguno/ninguno* become _____ / _____ in front of a masculine noun.

7. When we say **nadie** in Spanish, we mean **ninguna** _____, and when we say **nada,** we mean **ninguna** _____.

8. **Tú no sabes inglés también** is incorrect; it should be: **Tú no sabes inglés** _____.

EXERCISE

ANSWERS p. 88

Complete each sentence.

1. Lo contrario de (*the opposite of*) *nadie* es _____.

2. Lo contrario de *tampoco* es _____.

3. Lo contrario de *alguno* es _____.

4. Lo contrario de *siempre* es _____.

5. Lo contrario de *algo* es _____.

6. Lo contrario de *sin* es _____.

7. Lo contrario de *ningún* es _____.

8. ¿Cómo traduce usted *I know nothing?* _____.

9. ¿Como traduce usted *I don't know anything?* _____.

10. **No digo algo** es incorrecto. Debe ser _____.

11. **No habla alguien** es incorrecto. Debe ser _____.

12. **Nunca digo algo** es incorrecto. Debe ser _____.

13. **No trabaja también** es incorrecto. Debe ser _____.

14. **No tengo algún** libro es incorrecto. Debe ser _____.

15. **Ella es no cubana** es incorrecto. Debe ser _____.

16. **Ella está no bien** es incorrecto. Debe ser _____.

17. There are two words for *anything* in Spanish: _____.

18. There are two words for *also* in Spanish: _____.

19. There are two words in Spanish for *never*: _____.

EXAM 1   LESSONS 1–5

Part I.   Practique las palabras nuevas (50 puntos)

ANSWERS
p. 88
A. Match the two columns.

1. ___ Camarón	**A.**	Es un mueble para dormir.
2. ___ Almuerzo	**B.**	Es la maleta, el maletín, para viajar.
3. ___ Postre	**C.**	Es el hijo de mi hermana.
4. ___ Sillón	**D.**	Es el padre de mi esposa.
5. ___ Cinturón	**E.**	Es lo contrario de *triste.*
6. ___ Cama	**F.**	Es la camarera o camarero del avión.
7. ___ Reloj	**G.**	Es comida o bebida antes de la comida.
8. ___ Equipaje	**H.**	Es la comida entre las 12:00 y las 2:00 P.M.
9. ___ Cocina	**I.**	Es llegar a la hora exacta.
10. ___ Vaso	**J.**	Es el flan, el helado, la fruta.
11. ___ Primo	**K.**	Es un grupo de dos personas o animales.
12. ___ Aperitivo	**L.**	Es para comer con pan y vegetales.
13. ___ Suegro	**M.**	Es un marisco caro, pero delicioso.
14. ___ En punto	**N.**	Es para abrocharse en el avión, el coche.
15. ___ Sobrino	**O.**	Es lo contrario de *salida.*
16. ___ Alegre	**P.**	Es el hijo de mis tíos.
17. ___ Sobrecargo	**Q.**	Es un mueble para sentarse.
18. ___ Mantequilla	**R.**	Es para servir vino, cerveza.
19. ___ Pareja	**S.**	Es para saber la hora.
20. ___ Llegada	**T.**	Es donde preparamos la comida.

ANSWERS
p. 88
B. Complete each sentence with an appropriate word.

21. Normalmente una _____ es una futura esposa.

22. Pago la cuenta con una _____ de crédito.

23. Quiero un _____ con ventanilla para el vuelo 400.

24. La parte más alta de la casa es el _____.

25. Para decir treinta minutos con la hora también decimos _____.

26. Para decir quince minutos con la hora también decimos _____.

27. Quiero la langosta en _____ verde.

28. Lo contrario de *caro* es _____.

29. La comida española de la noche (9:00 P.M.) se llama _____.

30. Los hijos de mis hijos son mis _____.

31. Mi jardín tiene muchos árboles y _____.

32. Lo contrario de *casado* es _____.

33. Nueva York y Los Ángeles son dos _____ muy grandes.

34. Tenemos dos manos: la derecha y la _____.

35. Usted puede pagar la cuenta con cheques de _____.

ANSWERS p. 88

C. Underline the expression that best completes the sentence.

36. La cocinera prepara (la ducha, la nariz, el filete, el águila).

37. La maleta es parte (del carro, del equipaje, de la pared, de la lechuga).

38. Necesito comprar (un pasaje, un calor, una aduana, un lavaplatos) para viajar.

39. Deseo una ensalada de tomate y (botella, lechuga, luz, mantequilla).

40. Tenemos vino de color blanco, rosado y (verde, amarillo, excelente, rojo).

41. El criminal (trae, huye, cree, nace) de la policía.

42. José conduce muy bien (el sabor, la luz, el postre, el coche).

43. Cuando conduzco siempre me detengo en (el tejado, la aduana, el maletín, la luz roja).

44. Queremos dos (parejas, raciones, clases, manos) de camarones a la plancha.

45. El vuelo 400 tiene (salida, puerta, pilota, hora) de Miami a las tres en punto.

ANSWERS p. 88

D. Write the letter of the best response in the space provided.

46. ___ Jorge tiene que lavar el coche esta tarde; no puede ir con nosotros.

   A. ¡Por supuesto! ¡Hoy es lunes, las veinticuatro horas del día!

   B. No importa. Mi cocina tiene lavaplatos.

   C. ¡Por supuesto! Tiene que facturar la maleta.

   D. No importa. Nosotros podemos ayudarle (*him*).

47. ___ En esta sección del autobús nadie puede fumar.

    A. Está bien. Los pasajeros también fuman.

    B. Está bien. Yo tampoco voy a fumar.

    C. Está bien. Los cigarrillos son baratos.

    D. Está bien. Vamos a fumar un cigarrillo.

48. ___ El jamón, el filete, la ensalada, todo está delicioso.

    A. Es verdad. Este restaurante se especializa en mariscos.

    B. Es verdad. Mi sopa de vegetales está excelente también.

    C. Es verdad. Todas las camareras son muy simpáticas.

    D. Es verdad. La cocinera inspecciona bien el equipaje.

49. ___ De aperitivo deseamos dos vermús y una ración de camarones a la plancha.

    A. ¡Cómo no! Aquí servimos la mejor paella del mundo.

    B. Muy bien. Los mariscos siempre son caros.

    C. Por supuesto. Los camarones viven en el mar.

    D. Muy bien. Voy a traer la orden ahora mismo (*right now*).

50. ___ ¿Quién va a pagar la cuenta? Aquí no aceptan tarjetas de crédito.

    A. No sé. Yo no puedo pagar. Sólo traigo un dólar.

    B. Está bien. Los mariscos de aquí son fantásticos.

    C. No importa. La caja está a la derecha de la puerta.

    D. Muy bien. Pasamos la cuenta a una de las camareras.

Part II.   Practique la gramática (50 puntos)

**ANSWERS
p. 89**

A. Complete each sentence with the correct form of the present indicative.

    1. ¿Quién _____ tu futura suegra? (*to be*)

    2. Iberia _____ de Madrid a Nueva York todos los días. (*to fly*)

    3. ¿Cuándo _____ (tú) venir a verme? (*to be able to*)

    4. Mis hijos _____ nueve horas todas las noches. (*to sleep*)

    5. ¿Por qué _____ (tú) ese programa de televisión? (*to watch*)

    6. Usted _____ por la derecha hasta la luz roja. (*to continue*)

    7. Yo siempre _____ vino rosado con la cena. (*to ask for*)

    8. Mis padres no _____ que digo la verdad. (*to believe*)

    9. Este cigarrillo _____ de Panamá. (*to be*)

   10. Mi abuela tiene setenta años, pero _____ joven todavía. (*to be*)

   11. ¿Cuándo _____ ustedes a Perú? (*to return*)

12. ¿Dónde _____ usted pasar la noche? (*to plan*)

13. Los camareros _____ la comida en el restaurante. (*to serve*)

14. ¿A dónde _____ (tú) a viajar en el futuro? (*to go*)

15. ¿Cuántas cervezas _____ ustedes? (*to want*)

16. Yo no _____ nada en casa los lunes. (*to do*)

17. Nosotras _____ bien el nombre de él. (*to remember*)

18. El vuelo de Washington a Nueva York _____ muy corto. (*to be*)

19. Carlos dice que él _____ un libro todos los días. (*to read*)

20. Yo siempre _____ a mis amigos. (*to recognize*)

21. Después del viaje la aeromoza _____ la maleta. (*to unpack*)

22. Después de tres cervezas, Juan no _____ nada. (*to remember*)

23. (Yo) siempre _____ dos dólares a la iglesia (church). (*to give*)

24. Nosotros _____ casa muy temprano. (*to leave*)

25. Mi padre _____ pagar la cuenta hoy. (*to have to*)

ANSWERS p. 89

B. **Only one of the choices correctly completes the sentence. First try to complete the sentence on your own; then look at the four choices, and write the letter of the correct answer in the space provided.**

26. ____ Veinte menos cuatro son...
   A. diez y seis   C. dieciséis
   B. dieziséis   D. deceséis

27. ____ En el Caribe... camarones son grandes.
   A. el   C. las
   B. la   D. los

28. ____ El plural de *lunes feliz* es...
   A. lunes felices   C. lúneses felices
   B. lunes felizes   D. lúneses felizes

29. ____ El plural de *papel inglés* es...
   A. papels ingleses   C. papeles ingléses
   B. papeles ingleses   D. papeles inglés

30. ____ ¿Cómo se dice en español *It's 1:30 P.M.*?
   A. Es la una y media de la mañana.
   B. Son la una y media de la tarde.
   C. Es la una y treinta de la tarde.
   D. Son la una y treinta de la mañana.

31. ___ ¿Cómo se dice en español *It's 2:45 A.M.?*
  A. Son las dos y cuarto de la mañana.
  B. Son quince para las tres de la tarde.
  C. Son las tres menos quince de la tarde.
  D. Son las tres menos cuarto de la mañana.

32. ___ Treinta menos siete son...
  A. veinte y tres   C. ventitrés
  B. veintitrés   D. veintitres

33. ___ ¿Cómo se escribe y se dice *Two million dollars?*
  A. Dos millón de dólares.   C. Dos millones de dólares.
  B. Dos millones dólares.   D. Dos milliones de dólares.

34. ___ ¿Cómo se escribe en un cheque 110 en español?
  A. Un ciento y diez.   C. Cien y diez.
  B. Ciento diez.   D. Ciento y diez.

35. ___ Ustedes... la clase a las dos menos diez. (*to conclude*)
  A. concluyen   C. concluen
  B. conclúen   D. concluyan

36. ___ Yo siempre me ... antes de llegar la luz roja. (*to stop*)
  A. detieno   C. detengo
  B. deteno   D. detiengo

37. ___ **José nunca llama** también se dice **José no llama...**
  A. alguna vez   C. siempre
  B. jamás   D. tampoco

38. ___ Yo no... radio por la tarde sino por la mañana. (*to listen to*)
  A. oyo   C. oi
  B. ogo   D. oigo

39. ___ Yo voy por la derecha, y tú... por la izquierda. (*to follow*)
  A. siges   C. sigues
  B. seges   D. segues

40. ___ El nido (*nest*)... está en una montaña alta.
  A. del águila   C. de el águila
  B. de la águila   D. dela águila

41. ___ Yo no... hablar italiano. (*to know how*)
  A. sago   C. se
  B. sabo   D. sé

42. ___ Este hotel tiene... camas.

    A. trescientos   C. trescientas
    B. tres cientos   D. tres cientas

43. ___ El oxígeno y el hidrógeno son los dos elementos...

    A. dela agua   C. del agua
    B. de la agua   D. del el agua

44. ___ José nunca estudia...

    A. algo   C. alguno
    B. también   D. nada

45. ___ Yo siempre... la mano a mis amigos. (*to shake, offer*)

    A. ofrezo   C. ofreso
    B. ofrezco   D. ofreco

46. ___ Para ir allí no necesitas tomar... (*any bus*)

    A. ninguna autobús   C. algún autobús
    B. alguna autobús   D. ningún autobús

47. ___ Ustedes nunca tienen... en su casa. (*any problem*)

    A. ningún problema   C. algún problema
    B. ninguna problema   D. alguna problema

48. ___ Después del viaje (yo)... las maletas. (*to unpack, undo*)

    A. deshaco   C. deshago
    B. deshazo   D. deshaso

49. ___ Mi sobrino... malo desde el lunes pasado. (*to be*)

    A. es   C. soy
    B. estoy   D. está

50. ___ Todos mis abuelos... de Colombia.

    A. están   C. son
    B. estan   D. són

(The grading scale is on page 89.)

ANSWERS LESSONS 1–5 AND EXAM 1

Lesson 1

Practice the Basic Expressions

1. Buenos días
2. Buenas tardes
3. Buenas noches
4. Señora / señorita
5. Estoy bien, gracias
   Bastante bien, gracias
   Regular. No muy bien

6. Me llamo…
7. beginning
8. Vivo en…
9. Dónde está el baño
   —Allí, a la derecha

10. Cómo se dice *left* en español
    —Se dice **izquierda**
11. Adiós / Hasta luego
12. por favor
13. En qué puedo servirle
14. Regular. No muy bien

Practique las palabras nuevas (*Practice the New Words*)

A.
1. acción
2. autobús
3. clase
4. color

5. estación
6. papel
7. porcentaje
8. sur

9. tren
10. confusión
11. garaje
12. hotel

13. inglés
14. lección
15. policía
16. turista

17. tema
18. águila

B.
1. agua
2. gato
3. gusto
4. mujer

5. vez / tiempo
6. lunes
7. verdad
8. pluma

9. nariz
10. paraguas
11. pared
12. nombre

13. mesa
14. luz
15. palabra
16. lápiz

17. calor
18. hambre

Practique los artículos (*Practice the Articles*)

1. un / una / a / an
2. masculine / feminine
3. masculine / feminine
4. things
5. masculine / feminine
6. No / letter(s)
7. female / a male taxi driver /
   a female taxi driver

8. letter(s) / feminine
9. *L-O-N-E-R-S / D-IÓN-Z-A*
10. masculine / masculine / feminine
11. masculine / un / una
12. masculine / un
13. una / un / Buenos días
14. un lápiz / una tarde

Exercise

1. un	6. una	11. una	16. una	21. un	26. un	31. un
2. una	7. un	12. una	17. un	22. una	27. un	32. un
3. un	8. un	13. un	18. una	23. un	28. un	
4. un	9. una	14. una	19. un	24. un	29. un	
5. una	10. una	15. un	20. un	25. un	30. una	

Practique los artículos definidos (*the Definite Articles*)

1. el/la, los/las
2. *L-O-N-E-R-S/D-IÓN-Z-A*
3. feminine/masculine/masculine
4. masculine/el/el
5. feminine/el/la/la/la
6. del/al
7. stressed/el/el
8. h/el/la/el
9. No/stressed
10. del/del
11. Yes/la

Exercise

1. el	6. la	11. la	16. el	21. el	26. el	31. el
2. la	7. el	12. la	17. el	22. la	27. el	32. el
3. el	8. el	13. el	18. la	23. el	28. el	
4. el	9. la	14. la	19. el	24. el	29. el	
5. la	10. el	15. el	20. el	25. el	30. la	

Practique los pronombres (*the Pronouns*)

1. I/yo
2. nosotros/nosotras
3. tú/ustedes
4. tú
5. females/females
6. nosotros
7. usted/tú
8. tú/él
9. él/ella/nothing
10. ellas/ellos
11. nothing
12. usted
13. Ud./Vd., Uds./Vds.

Exercise

1. nosotras	4. ellas	7. ellos	10. ustedes
2. tú	5. nothing	8. nosotros	11. él/ella/nothing
3. vosotros	6. usted	9. ellos	

Lesson 2

Practique las palabras nuevas

A. 1. crema
   2. bisté/bistec
   3. menú
   4. sopa
   5. vegetales/legumbres/verduras
   6. estudiar
   7. pasar
   8. delicioso
   9. filete
   10. ensalada
   11. fruta
   12. salsa
   13. tomate
   14. completar
   15. ordenar
   16. usar
   17. excelente
   18. fresco

B. 1. la
   2. el
   3. el
   4. la
   5. el/la
   6. el
   7. la
   8. el
   9. el
   10. el
   11. el
   12. el
   13. la
   14. la
   15. el
   16. la
   17. la

C. 1. D
   2. F
   3. I
   4. A
   5. K
   6. B
   7. N
   8. L
   9. G
   10. E
   11. M
   12. Q
   13. R
   14. C
   15. O
   16. P
   17. H

Exercises

A. 1. amigos
   2. cervezas
   3. camarero
   4. almuerzo
   5. papas fritas
   6. lechuga
   7. sopa
   8. langosta
   9. helado de chocolate
   10. fruta
   11. excelente
   12. blando/fresca
   13. delicioso/verduras
   14. el postre
   15. caja

B. 1. el menú
   2. el café
   3. el restaurante
   4. una cerveza
   5. lechuga y tomate
   6. crema y azúcar
   7. El flan
   8. El tomate
   9. el café
   10. blando
   11. el menú
   12. de chocolate
   13. salsa verde
   14. fresca

Practique el presente de indicativo

1. infinitive / ar / er / ir
2. meaning / habl- / viv- / com-
3. nosotros / tú / yo
4. habla
5. hablamos
6. Estudiamos
7. emphasis
8. progress / estudia
9. us- / usamos / usan
10. hablo
11. Estudio
12. sí estudia

Exercise

1. estudian
2. ordenan
3. pagan
4. tomas
5. trabaja
6. usamos
7. estamos
8. deseo
9. desean
10. pasa
11. completa
12. deseas
13. toman
14. disfrutan
15. trabajan
16. pagamos
17. hablan
18. usa
19. trabaja
20. disfruta

Practique el presente de indicativo

1. -er / -ir
2. meaning / Escrib- / Le-
3. ending / yo
4. Vivimos
5. first person plural
6. vive
7. present indicative / bebe
8. leo
9. We are writing / We write / We will write / We do write

Exercise

1. aprendemos
2. lee
3. pagas
4. tomo
5. beben
6. subimos
7. sale
8. comen
9. creen
10. comemos
11. hablamos
12. lee
13. ordena
14. escribo
15. sale
16. sube
17. trabajo
18. viven
19. hablan
20. sube
21. disfruta
22. pasa
23. comen

Practique *ser* y *estar*

1. ser / estar
2. irregular
3. oy
4. estás / está / están
5. estar / está
6. ser / es
7. Ser / o no ser
8. ser / estar
9. es
10. está
11. ser / es
12. ser / es
13. ser / es

Exercise

1. soy/son	6. es	11. está	16. es	21. es/es
2. es/está	7. están	12. es/es	17. es/es	22. es
3. es	8. somos	13. está	18. está	
4. están	9. son	14. es	19. está	
5. es	10. está/estoy	15. es/es	20. está/está	

Lesson 3

Practique las palabras nuevas

A. 1. la   3. el   5. la   7. el   9. la   11. la   13. el   15. la
   2. el   4. la   6. el   8. la   10. el   12. el   14. la   16. la

B. 1. camarón   4. paella   7. caros   10. tarjetas   13. mantequilla
   2. pareja   5. seco   8. gambas   11. cheque   14. pedir
   3. vaso   6. rosado   9. aperitivo   12. ciudad   15. on the grill

C. 1. negro   4. seco   7. aperitivo   10. viajera   13. aquí
   2. barato   5. pequeño   8. mujer   11. una turista   14. noche
   3. caliente   6. malo   9. camarera   12. una policía   15. sur

Exercises

A. 1. mariscos   4. aperitivo   7. plancha   10. mantequilla   13. blanco
   2. pareja   5. dulces   8. menú   11. de postre   14. tarjetas
   3. mundo   6. raciones   9. para dos   12. botella   15. viajero

B. 1. D   3. F   5. H   7. K   9. L   11. C   13. E
   2. G   4. I   6. J   8. B   10. A   12. D

Practique la gramática

1. noun/number
2. masculine/o
3. feminine/a
4. No/verde
5. Pared blanca
6. Papel amarillo
7. Programa americano
8. Luz roja
9. No/grande
10. buenos/vowel
11. camarones/consonant
12. luces/c
13. lunes/stress
14. ingleses/stressed
15. es/rubíes/rubís

Exercises

A.
1. los aperitivos pequeños
2. los camarones caros
3. las mejores paellas
4. los cheques amarillos
5. las cenas grandes
6. las ideas malas
7. las raciones deliciosas
8. los cafés calientes
9. los mejores papeles
10. los vinos secos
11. los rubíes caros
12. las luces verdes
13. los champús americanos
14. los lunes pasados
15. las aguas calientes
16. las crisis económicas

B.
1. bueno
2. rojos
3. seco
4. dulces
5. pequeña
6. grande
7. mejores
8. pasado/pasados
9. ingleses
10. caros
11. hindús/hindúes

Practique los verbos

1. stem/sab-
2. d-/v-
3. v
4. voy/doy
5. sé/digo
6. veo/go/see
7. nosotros/tú/ellos, ellas, ustedes
8. (Él) va a comer
9. digo la verdad

Exercise

1. vamos
2. necesitan
3. ves (miras)
4. da
5. acompaña
6. especializa
7. acepta
8. saben
9. va a servir
10. prepara
11. decimos
12. cenan
13. sé
14. vas a ir
15. pedimos
16. hace
17. da
18. necesito
19. bebe (toma)
20. saben

Practique las palabras interrogativas y los números

1. accent/Cuándo
2. A dónde
3. No/dónde
4. c/dieciséis
5. One/cinco
6. cien, ciento/cien
7. Ciento/ciento cinco
8. masculine/feminine
9. masculine/uno
10. doscientos/Trescientas
11. Mil/Dos mil
12. millón/millones
13. de/millones de
14. A period/A comma/ 2.200.300,50

Exercise

1. Cuándo	6. dónde	11. un/uno	16. ciento diez
2. De quién	7. cuál	12. dieceséis	17. dos mil
3. Por qué	8. Adónde (A dónde)	13. veintidós	18. quinientas
4. Cuántos	9. Cuánto	14. treinta y dos	19. dos millones de
5. Qué (cuál)	10. tres/una	15. quinientos	20. cien por cien (ciento por ciento)

Lesson 4

Practique las palabras nuevas

A. 1. el   3. el   5. la   7. el   9. la   11. el
    2. la   4. el   6. el   8. el   10. el   12. la

B. 1. al aeropuerto   5. el pasaje   9. un vuelo   13. la aduana
    2. la comida   6. a la ventanilla   10. a los pasajeros   14. a tiempo
    3. el equipaje   7. el empleado   11. salida   15. de ida y vuelta
    4. el cinturón   8. subir   12. llegar   16. servirle

C. 1. I   4. B   7. D   10. L   13. J
    2. N   5. C   8. G   11. A   14. F
    3. K   6. M   9. E   12. H

Exercises

A. 1. llega   6. en punto   11. pasaporte   16. maletín
    2. tarde   7. menos   12. simpática   17. puerta
    3. empleada   8. sencillo   13. asiento   18. viaje
    4. reservación   9. con ventanilla   14. maleta
    5. viajar   10. no fumar   15. facturar

B. 1. F   4. Q   7. B   10. C   13. K   16. D
    2. E   5. P   8. N   11. G   14. J   17. L
    3. I   6. A   9. M   12. O   15. H

Practique los verbos

1. ten/tien/teng/to have
2. g/g/hago
3. ie/no
4. que/Tengo que salir
5. de/Salgo de casa
6. to come/speaker
7. voy
8. deshago
9. detienen

Exercise

1. viene
2. tengo que
3. ayuda
4. sales
5. prepara
6. abrochan
7. Tiene
8. Pongo
9. llega
10. detiene
11. factura
12. fumo
13. venimos
14. bajan
15. hace/deshacer
16. inspeccionan
17. Tiene
18. voy
19. compramos

Practique la hora y los números

1. una (singular)/2–12 (plural)
2. quince/cuarto
3. treinta/media
4. y/menos
5. en punto/más o menos/como
6. de la mañana
7. de la tarde/de la noche
8. no/la
9. hora
10. ¿Qué horas son?
11. 24/la/las/hora/horas

Exercise

1. Son las tres y diez de la tarde.
2. Son las dos y quince (cuarto) de la mañana.
3. Es la una y treinta (media) de la tarde.
4. Son las seis menos diez de la mañana.
5. Son las once de la noche.
6. Son las once y veinte de la mañana.
7. Es la una menos quince (cuarto) de la tarde.
8. Es la una y cinco de la mañana.
9. a las dos en punto
10. a las ocho y media
11. a las siete de la mañana
12. a las diez de la noche
13. como a las dos (más o menos)
14. a las quince (15) horas
15. a la una hora
16. a las dieciocho (18) horas

Practique los verbos

1. quer-/quier-/ie
2. dec-/dic-/i
3. pod-/pued-/ue
4. yes

5. people/quiere
6. for/Pedimos/Piden
7. Sirvo/Sirven
8. vuela

9. muestro
10. Sí te quiero
11. segu-/sigu-/u/sigo
12. again/We are flying again

13. siete/nueve

Exercise

1. puede
2. vuelan
3. vuelven
4. pensamos
5. quieres

6. sigue
7. sigo
8. pides
9. siento
10. muestra

11. sirven
12. quiere
13. vuelve
14. pienso
15. vuela

16. puedo
17. quiere
18. puede
19. dice
20. sigue

21. tienen
22. podemos
23. vienen
24. muestran
25. quiero

Lesson 5

Practique las palabras nuevas

A. 1. el
2. el
3. la

4. la
5. el
6. el

7. la
8. el
9. el

10. el
11. el
12. el

13. la
14. el
15. la

16. el

B. 1. abuelo
2. tío
3. sobrinos

4. nietos
5. prima
6. tías

7. padres
8. primos
9. suegra

10. hermanos
11. suegro
12. mamá (madre)/papá (padre)

C. 1. triste
2. feo
3. viejo

4. casado
5. corto
6. rico

7. feo
8. poco
9. morir

10. hasta
11. destruir
12. fantástico

13. temprano
14. noche

D. 1. G
2. F

3. B
4. A

5. I
6. J

7. H
8. E

9. D
10. C

E. 1. la cocina
2. el garaje
3. la chimenea
4. muchas flores
5. dormitorios
6. el lavaplatos

7. la mesa
8. la cama
9. la ducha
10. carro
11. el reloj
12. niños

13. el tejado
14. flores
15. muebles
16. el comedor
17. novios
18. soltero

19. pobre
20. jóvenes
21. solterona

Exercises

A.

1. joven	6. quieren	11. tía	16. conocer	21. suegras
2. amigos	7. mejor	12. dormitorios	17. años	22. fantástica
3. invita	8. acepta	13. baños	18. joven	23. novia
4. conoce	9. hermana	14. jardín	19. apreciar	
5. padres	10. abuela	15. árboles	20. americanos	

B.

1. D	3. I	5. B	7. C	9. L	11. F
2. G	4. J	6. K	8. E	10. A	12. H

Practique los verbos

1. o-/oig-/oy-/oímos
2. traigo/caigo/ig
3. conozco/c
4. ofrezco/conduzco
5. y/huimos
6. construyo/concluyen
7. nazco
8. conocer/saber
9. saber/no
10. conocer/conocemos
11. Sé
12. Sé cocinar

Exercise

1. producen	6. construyen	11. recuerda	16. caigo
2. conduzco	7. mueren	12. traducen	17. duermo
3. oyen (escuchan)	8. traigo	13. concluye	18. sé
4. huyen	9. parece	14. oigo (escucho)	19. ofrece
5. duermes	10. reconoce	15. conoce	20. destruyen

Practique el acento

1. One/nueve
2. the last/vowel
3. last/n and s
4. last/vowel/n or s
5. consonant
6. two/last
7. diphthong/o, a
8. he/the
9. you/your
10. yes/if
11. more/but
12. Veintidós

Exercise

1. amarillo	8. lápices	15. feliz	22. papeles	29. veintiún
2. luz	9. mamá	16. avión	23. dieciséis	30. el
3. águila	10. tú	17. camarera	24. día	31. sé
4. rubí	11. traemos	18. champú	25. novio	32. árbol
5. creer	12. huimos	19. él	26. estudio	33. rubís
6. oír	13. oímos	20. árboles	27. seis	34. diecisiete
7. número	14. están	21. flores	28. inglés	35. veintitrés

Practique las palabras negativas

1. ninguno/nada	3. No habla nadie	5. Él no está aquí	7. persona/cosa
2. tampoco/sin	4. Él no es bueno	6. algún/ningún	8. tampoco

Exercise

1. alguien	8. No sé nada	15. Ella no es cubana
2. también	9. No sé nada	16. Ella no está bien
3. ninguno	10. No digo nada	17. algo/nada
4. nunca (jamás)	11. No habla nadie	18. también/tampoco
5. nada	12. Nunca digo nada	19. nunca/jamás
6. con	13. No trabaja tampoco	
7. algún	14. No tengo ningún libro	

Exam 1

Part I.   Practique las palabras nuevas (50 puntos)

1. M	11. P	21. novia	31. flores (frutas)	41. huye
2. H	12. G	22. tarjeta	32. soltero	42. el coche
3. J	13. D	23. asiento	33. ciudades	43. la luz
4. Q	14. I	24. tejado	34. izquierda	44. raciones
5. N	15. C	25. media (hora)	35. viajero	45. salida
6. A	16. E	26. cuarto (de hora)	36. el filete	46. D
7. S	17. F	27. salsa	37. del equipaje	47. B
8. B	18. L	28. barato	38. un pasaje	48. B
9. T	19. K	29. cena	39. lechuga	49. D
10. R	20. 0	30. nietos	40. rojo	50. A

Part II.   Practique la gramática (50 puntos)

1. es	11. vuelven	21. deshace	31. D	41. D
2. vuela	12. piensa	22. recuerda	32. B	42. C
3. puedes	13. sirven	23. doy	33. C	43. C
4. duermen	14. vas	24. salimos de	34. B	44. D
5. ves (miras)	15. quieren (desean)	25. tiene que	35. A	45. B
6. sigue	16. hago	26. C	36. C	46. D
7. pido	17. recordamos	27. D	37. B	47. A
8. creen	18. es	28. A	38. D	48. C
9. es	19. lee	29. B	39. C	49. D
10. está	20. reconozco	30. C	40. A	50. C

Scale for grading the exam:

94–100 points   A   73–83 points   C
84–93 points   B   62–72 points   D

6 En un hotel en México
(At a Hotel in Mexico)

el ascensor[1]	elevator	el mozo[4]	bellboy
el banco	bank	la nieve	snow
el botón[2]	button	la nube	cloud
el botones	bellboy	la pensión	boardinghouse
el desayuno	breakfast	el peso[5]	peso
el dinero	money	el piso	floor, story
la divisa	foreign money	la plaza	square
la época	season, epoch	el precio	price
la escalera[3]	staircase	la recepción	front desk
el estacionamento	parking	la recepcionista	receptionist
la fecha	date	el servicio a los cuartos	room service
la habitación	room		
el hotel	hotel	la telenovela[6]	soap opera
el jabón	soap	la toalla	towel
la llave	key	la vista	sight, view
la lluvia	rain		

abrir	to open	interesar	to interest
cambiar	to change	llover (ue)	to rain
cerrar (ie)	to close	nevar (ie)	to snow
cobrar[7]	to charge, get paid	perdonar	to pardon
decidir	to decide	permitir	to allow
divertirse (ie)	to have fun	preferir (ie)	to prefer
entrar a[8] (en)	to enter	registrarse[9]	to register
estacionar, parquear	to park	reservar	to reserve
		subir	to go up
firmar	to sign	tratar de[10]	to try to
incluir (y)	to include	visitar	to visit

ancho(a)	wide	**estrecho(a)**	narrow
animado(a)	lively	**nublado(a)**	cloudy
antiguo(a)	ancient, former	**nuevo(a)**	new
bastante	enough	**razonable**	reasonable
disponible	available	**sencillo(a)**	single; simple
doble	double	**tercero(a)**[11]	third

¿A cómo está... ?	What's the price of . . . ?	**estar nublado**	to be cloudy
		lejos	far away
Aquí tiene la llave.	Here is the key.	**por día**	per day
cerca	near	**por eso**	because of that
dar a + (a place)	to face + (a place)	**porque**	because
enseguida, en seguida	right away		

hacer + (noun)

¿Qué tiempo hace? *What's the weather?*

hacer buen tiempo ⎫
hacer bueno ⎭ *to be good weather*

hacer mal tiempo ⎫
hacer malo ⎭ *to be bad weather*

hacer ⎧ **calor** — hot
⎪ **fresco** — cool
⎨ **frío** to be cold
⎪ **sol** — sunny
⎩ **viento** — windy

tener + (noun)

tener ⎧ **calor** — (feel) hot
⎪ **frío** — (feel) cold
⎪ **hambre** — hungry
⎪ **sed** — thirsty
⎨ **éxito** to be successful
⎪ **razón** — right
⎪ **sueño** — sleepy
⎪ **suerte** — lucky
⎩ **(diez) años.** — (ten) years old

tener ⎧ **ansias de** ⎫ to feel like, want
⎩ **ganas de** ⎭

NOTAS

1. *Ascensor* is used in Spain for *elevator.* The term in Latin America is *elevador,* and this word is as old as the first elevator installed in Latin American hotels.

2. Notice that the plural of **botón** is **botones** (*buttons*), but this plural form becomes singular to designate the name of a person "with many buttons": *a bellboy.* We say **un botones, dos botones** (*one bellboy, two bellboys*).

3. *Escalera* means *staircase* and can also mean *ladder.*

4. *Mozo* means literally *young man,* but in some countries it is used in place of **camarero** (*waiter*) and **botones** (*bellboy*). It can also refer to a porter at the airport. *Moza* has a similar use for women.

5. *Peso* is the currency of Mexico, Argentina, Chile, Cuba, Colombia, and Uruguay. *Peseta* is the currency of Spain.

6. *Telenovela* means *soap opera.* **Telenovelas** became popular almost from the first days of TV in Latin America. They are shown at prime time and the leading actors of the country compete for the best roles. Spain has no **telenovelas** of its own, but

culebrones (as they are called in Spain) from Latin America and from the United States are shown.

7. *Cobrar* has several meanings: *to charge* (for a product); *to get paid; to cash* (checks).

8. *Entrar a* is used in Latin America and *entrar en* in Spain for *to enter, come in.*

9. *Registrarse* is used to register at a hotel, at city hall, and to register a car at the motor vehicle bureau. These places have a *registro*. We use *matricular* or *inscribir* for *to register* a student in a school.

10. *Tratar de* + (infinitive) is translated as *to try to* + (infinitive).

    EX: **Juan *trata de terminar* su carrera para graduarse.** (*John is trying to finish* his career to graduate.)

11. *Tercero* (*third*) becomes *tercer* in front of a masculine noun, just as *bueno* becomes *buen* and *malo* becomes *mal*—for example, **el tercer piso,** but **la tercera puerta.**

PRACTIQUE LAS PALABRAS NUEVAS

ANSWERS p. 188

A. Write *el, la, los,* or *las* before each noun.

1. ___ ascensor	5. ___ precio	9. ___ divisas	13. ___ lluvia
2. ___ hotel	6. ___ recepción	10. ___ jabón	14. ___ pensión
3. ___ botones	7. ___ botón	11. ___ nube	15. ___ llaves
4. ___ elevador	8. ___ pesos	12. ___ hambre	16. ___ calor

ANSWERS p. 188

B. *Word families.* The dictionary of a language has many words that are related to each other. The meaningful *roots* are fewer in number than the dictionary entries. Try to relate new words to the ones you know, as if they were grouped in families. For example, if you know **comer,** you can associate **comedor** and **comida** with it. If you know **beber,** then it's easy to see that *bebida* (*drink*) and *bebedor* (*drinker*) are of the same family. **The following list includes words you studied before and are associated with others you know. Write one word related to each one given here.**

1. servicio _____   9. reservación _____

2. baño _____   10. turista _____

3. desayuno _____   11. caliente _____

4. fumador _____   12. oído (*ear*) _____

5. perdón _____   13. vista _____

6. registro _____   14. viajar _____

7. lluvia _____   15. pasajero _____

8. nieve (la) _____   16. rosa _____

17. lavar _____

18. invitar _____

19. dormir _____

20. asiento _____

21. casado _____

23. nube _____

24. cocinero _____

25. señora _____

26. cena _____

27. llegar _____

28. mar _____

29. salir _____

30. volar _____

C. Write the opposite word.

1. ancho _____

2. moderno _____

3. calor _____

4. hambre _____

5. doble _____

6. cerca _____

7. abrir _____.

8. buen tiempo _____.

9. salir _____.

10. bajar _____.

11. joven _____.

12. prohibir _____.

D. Write an appropriate word to complete each sentence.

1. La comida que comemos por la mañana temprano es el _____.

2. El dinero de México no es el dólar sino el _____.

3. Subimos al tercer piso por la escalera o por el _____.

4. El agua que cae cuando llueve es la _____.

5. Una pareja duerme mejor en una cama _____.

6. Para cambiar divisas vamos a un _____.

7. Todas las ciudades antiguas de España y Latinoamérica tienen una _____ central en medio de la ciudad.

8. Mi casa no está cerca de aquí; al contrario, está _____.

9. Para bañarnos usamos agua y _____.

10. La persona del hotel que lleva las maletas es el _____.

11. Un precio que no es caro ni (*nor*) barato, es _____.

12. Los cuartos del hotel también se llaman _____.

13. Cuando hace _____, me pongo botas (*boots*) y abrigo (*overcoat*).

14. Cuando tengo _____, voy a tomar agua fría o una Coca-Cola.

15. Cuando está _____, llevo el paraguas por si (*just in case*) llueve.

16. *General Hospital* es una _____ de Estados Unidos.

ANSWERS
p. 188

E. **Match the two columns.**

1. _____ Nos bañamos...   A. dólares a pesos

2. _____ Firmamos...   B. aprender español muy rápido

3. _____ Abrimos...   C. un error en un amigo

4. _____ Subimos...   D. la comida en el precio

5. _____ Cobramos...   E. el nombre en el registro del hotel

6. _____ Estacionamos...   F. en una fiesta, en un viaje

7. _____ Cambiamos...   G. con agua y jabón en la ducha

8. _____ Tratamos de...   H. el coche (carro) en el garaje

9. _____ Nos divertimos...   I. el equipaje a la habitación

10. _____ Perdonamos...   J. la puerta con la llave

11. _____ Incluimos...   K. cuatrocientos pesos por día

ANSWERS
p. 189

F. **Practice the new verbs by filling in the present indicative forms of the verbs given.** (The verb is the core of the Spanish language. Once you master the verb system, you master the language. Notice the irregular verbs on page 90, indicated with [ie], [ue], [y]).

1. En Arizona y California _____ muy poco. (*to rain*)

2. En Colorado _____ mucho todos los años. (*to snow*)

3. Cuando voy a una fiesta, siempre me _____. (*to have fun*)

4. Todos los años mi esposa y yo _____ Las Vegas. (*to visit*)

5. Esta habitación _____ un patio antiguo. (*to face*)

6. José _____ doscientos dólares en su trabajo. (*to get paid, earn*)

7. ¿_____ ustedes un cuarto con cama doble? (*to prefer*)

8. Los señores Roy se _____ en el hotel. (*to register*)

9. El inspector o agente de la aduana _____ las maletas. (*to open*)

10. El mozo del aeropuerto _____ las maletas al autobús. (*to take up*)

11. Todos los pasajeros _____ avión. (*to enter*)

12. Las puertas del hotel se _____ a las 12:00 P.M. (*to close*)

13. ¿A cómo _____ el cambio (*exchange*) del dólar hoy? (*to be*)

14. El precio de la pensión _____ también el desayuno. (*to include*)

15. ¿Por qué no _____ Ud. _____ hablar siempre español? (*to try to*)

16. Los libros de Cervantes me _____ mucho. (*to interest*)

17. Ella _____ estudiar español para visitar México. (*to decide*)

18. Mi padre no nos _____ fumar en casa. (*to allow, permit*)

19. Cuando voy a México, _____ dólares a pesos. (*to exchange*)

20. ¿Dónde _____ ustedes el hotel? (*to reserve*)

21. Mi esposa y yo nos _____ en el viaje. (*to have fun*)

22. Hoy hace mucho calor; yo _____ ir a la playa (*beach*). (*to prefer*)

23. Esta escalera _____ antigua; por eso _____ muy estrecha. (*to be/to be*)

DIÁLOGO   En un hotel en México

Los señores González llegan a la ciudad de México para visitar la capital. Deciden pasar tres días en un hotel de tercera clase porque no tienen mucho dinero. Hablan con el recepcionista del hotel.

RECEPCIONISTA: Buenas tardes, señores. ¿En qué puedo servirles?

SR. GONZALEZ: Queremos una recámara con cama doble para tres días.

RECEPCIONISTA: ¿Tienen ustedes reservación?

SRA. GONZALEZ: Pues no, pero no es época de turismo ahora.

RECEPCIONISTA: Tiene usted razón, señora. Tenemos un cuarto disponible en el tercer piso. Tiene una ventana que da a la plaza central.

SR. GONZALEZ: ¿Cuánto cobran ustedes por día?

RECEPCIONISTA: Ciento ochenta pesos, sin incluir la comida. La recámara también tiene televisor.

SRA. GONZALEZ: ¡Qué bueno!… porque yo no puedo perderme (*miss*) la telenovela de las nueve.

SR. GONZALEZ: No es tan barato como una pensión, pero me parece razonable.

SRA. GONZALEZ: ¿Tiene agua caliente el baño?

RECEPCIONISTA: Por supuesto. Y toallas… y jabón.

SR. GONZALEZ: ¿A qué hora abren el comedor por la mañana?

RECEPCIONISTA: El desayuno se sirve desde las ocho hasta las once. Por la noche cerramos el comedor a las once y el bar a las dos de la mañana.

SR. GONZALEZ: Está bien. Tomamos la recámara por tres días.

RECEPCIONISTA: ¿Quiere firmar el registro, por favor? Aquí tienen la llave. El botones sube el equipaje enseguida.

SRA. GONZALEZ: Muchas gracias. Muy amable.

DIALOGUE   At a Hotel in Mexico

Mr. and Mrs. Gonzalez arrive in Mexico City to visit the capital. They decide to spend three days in a third-class hotel because they don't have much money. They talk to the hotel receptionist

RECEPTIONIST:	Good afternoon. How may I help you?
MR. GONZALEZ:	We want a room with a double bed for three days.
RECEPTIONIST:	Do you have a reservation?
MRS. GONZALEZ:	Well, no, but this isn't the tourist season.
RECEPTIONIST:	You're right, madam. We have a room available on the third floor. It has a window facing the central square.
MR. GONZALEZ:	How much do you charge a day?
RECEPTIONIST:	One hundred eighty pesos, without meals. There is a TV set in the room, too.
MRS. GONZALEZ:	Terrific! . . . because I cannot miss my soap opera at nine in the evening.
MR. GONZALEZ:	It's not as cheap as a boardinghouse, but the price seems reasonable.
MRS. GONZALEZ:	Does the bathroom have hot water?
RECEPTIONIST:	Of course. And towels . . . and soap.
MR. GONZALEZ:	At what time does the dining room open in the morning?
RECEPTIONIST:	Breakfast is served from eight to eleven. We close the dining room at eleven in the evening and the bar at two in the morning.
MR. GONZALEZ:	Okay. We'll take the room for three days.
RECEPTIONIST:	Sign the register, please. Here's the key. The bellboy will take your luggage up right away.
MRS. GONZALEZ:	Thank you. You're very kind.

NOTE

Hotels in Hispanic countries are classified in five categories. In some countries they use the word *estrella* (*star*) instead of *clase*. The hotel with five stars is the most elegant and expensive. Notice that in Mexico they use the word *recámara* instead of *habitación* (*room*).

EXERCISES

ANSWERS p. 189

A. *En un hotel de México.* **Complete the story using the information from the dialogue.**

Los señores González llegan a la ciudad de México para (1) _____ la capital. Ellos deciden pasar tres días en un (2) _____ de tercera

clase (de tres estrellas) porque no tienen mucho (3) _____. Hablan
con el recepcionista y le piden una (4) _____ con cama
(5) _____. Los González no tienen reservación, pero no es
(6) _____ de turismo y por eso tienen un cuarto (7) _____
en el tercer (8) _____. La recámara tiene una ventana que
(9) _____ la plaza central. Este hotel no es caro; solamente
(10) _____ 180 pesos por día sin incluir la (11) _____. El
cuarto tiene agua fría y (12) _____ en el baño, con toallas y
(13) _____ para ducharse. También tiene un televisor para ver las
(14) _____ que la Sra. González no se pierde (*misses*) nunca. El
(15) _____ se sirve entre las ocho y las once todos los días, y el
comedor se (16) _____ a las once de la noche, pero el (17) _____
se cierra a las dos de la mañana. El Sr. González (18) _____ el
registro, y la Sra. González recibe la (19) _____ de la recámara para
(20) _____ la puerta. El (21) _____ sube el equipaje al
cuarto (22) _____ (*right away*).

ANSWERS
p. 189

B. **Underline the correct answer.**

1. Subimos en el ascensor o por (la toalla, el dinero, la escalera, la llave).

2. Cuando el cielo (*sky*) está muy nublado, nieva o (firma, incluye, cambia, llueve).

3. Para pedir comida o bebida en mi habitación pido (servicio, toalla, fecha, jabón) a los cuartos.

4. Esta ventana (cobra, baja, sube, da) a la plaza central.

5. El precio de la recámara es (doble, razonable, disponible, estrecho).

6. Para cambiar (desayunos, divisas, cuartos, visitas) vamos a un banco.

7. Cuando hablamos de (sencillo, bastante, doble, nuevo) pensamos en una pareja.

8. Subimos a un piso alto en (el dinero, la plaza, el servicio, el ascensor).

9. Cuando hace buen tiempo, no tenemos (nubes, elevadores, épocas, toallas).

10. Tomo una cerveza cuando tengo (hambre, suerte, frío, sed).

11. Cuando firmamos, escribimos nuestro(a) (*our*) (vista, nombre, precio, dinero).

12. Comemos cuando tenemos (éxito, sed, suerte, hambre).

13. Voy a la fiesta para (perdonar, reservar, divertirme, permitir).

14. En el trabajo cobramos (un servicio, un cheque, una divisa, una toalla) cada semana.

15. José prefiere (el hotel, la vista, la plaza, la fecha) a la pensión.

GRAMMAR I   Idiomatic Expressions with *hacer* and *tener*

A. **¿Qué tiempo hace?** (*How's the weather?*) To talk about the weather in Spanish, the verb *hacer* (*to make*) is used with nouns such as **calor** (*heat*), **sol** (*sun*), and **viento** (*wind*). Note that these are idiomatic expressions and different from English. Memorize the following expressions.

Hace bueno. It's good weather.	**Hace (mucho) fresco.** It's (very) cool.
Hace malo. It's bad weather.	**Hace (mucho) sol.** It's (very) sunny.
Hace (mucho) calor. It's (very) hot.	**Hace (mucho) viento.** It's (very) windy.
Hace (mucho) frío. It's (very) cold.	

B. The adjectives *mucho* (*much*) and *poco* (*little*) are used with nouns to express that it is, for example, *very hot* or *not very sunny*. As adjectives, *mucho* and *poco* must agree with the noun.

   EX: **Hoy hace *mucho viento* y *poco sol*.** (*Today it's <u>very windy</u> and <u>not very sunny.</u>*)

   Note that *nublado* is an exception.

   EX: **Está nublado.** (*It is cloudy.*)

C. To say that you are *feeling* hot, cold, hungry, thirsty, and so on, there is another idiomatic expression in Spanish. In this expression, the verb *tener* (*to have*) is used with nouns such as **calor** (*heat*), **frío** (*cold*), **hambre** (*hunger*), **sed** (*thirst*), and so on.

   Memorize the following expressions.

Tengo frío. I'm cold.	**Tengo suerte.** I'm lucky.
Tengo calor. I'm hot.	**Tengo sueño.** I'm sleepy.
Tengo hambre. I'm hungry.	**Tengo cuidado.** I'm careful.
Tengo sed. I'm thirsty.	**Tengo éxito.** I'm successful.
Tengo razón. I'm right.	**No tengo razón.** I'm wrong.

D. Adjectives such as **mucho** (*much*) and **poco** (*little*) are used with the nouns and must agree with them.

   EXS: **Tengo *poca hambre*.** (*I am <u>not very hungry.</u>*)
   Ella tiene *mucho sueño*. (*She is <u>very sleepy.</u>*)

E. The verb *tener* is also used in two other idiomatic expressions that are different from English.

   1. To express age, *tener* + (**años** [*years*]) is used.

      EXS: **Ella tiene trece años.** (*She is thirteen years old.*)
      Los abuelos tienen muchos años. (*The grandparents are very old.*)

2. To express desire or inclination, *tener* + (ganas de) or *tener* + (ansias de) are used.

   EXS: *¿Tienes ganas de tomar una cerveza?* (*Do you want a beer?*)
   No tenemos ansias de ir a clase. (*We don't feel like going to class.*)

   Note that **tener ganas** and **tener ansias** both require the preposition *de*.

F. Remember that the above expressions are used in the contexts mentioned. The verbs *estar* and *ser* are used with nouns and adjectives. *Estar* is used with qualities that could possibly change.

   EX: **El agua no *está* fría; *está* caliente.** (*The water is not cold; it is hot.*)

   (Water can be cold or hot. This indicates a change in the state of the water.)

   Ser is used with adjectives that describe the norm for the particular noun. These qualities are unlikely to change—the size, shape, texture, or color of an object, for example, or such things as personal characteristics when referring to people.

   EX: **La nieve *es* blanca; no *es* dulce ni verde.** (*The snow is white; it is not sweet nor green.*)

PRACTIQUE LAS EXPRESIONES

**ANSWERS
p. 189**

1. In the expression *hace frío,* is *frío* an adjective or a noun? _____.
   To say *It is very cold* we use the expression *Hace* _____.

2. *Hace muy sol* is not correct. It should be _____.

3. In Spanish people and animals "have" hunger or cold; whereas in English they "are" hungry or cold. How would you say *I'm hungry* in Spanish? _____.

4. *Tenemos muy hambre* is not correct because *hambre* is a noun. *Mucho hambre* is not correct either because *hambre* is feminine. It must be *Tenemos* _____.

5. *To be wrong* is the opposite of *to be right*. In Spanish the opposite of *tener razón* is _____.

6. How would you translate literally **tengo sed?** _____.

7. *Tener ganas* (or *ansias*) always needs the preposition _____ before the noun or the infinitive. How would you say *I feel like sleeping*? **Tengo** _____.

8. Remember that *ser* identifies a noun with a characteristic that is the _____ for that noun. For example, **La escalera** _____ estrecha. (*is*)

9. *Estar* indicates the result of a _____; it doesn't indicate the norm for a noun. For example, *This room is very cold* translates into **Esta recámara** _____ **muy fría.**

EXERCISE

ANSWERS
p. 189
Complete each sentence with the correct form of *ser, estar, hacer,* or *tener.*

1. En Alaska _____ más frío que en California.

2. En Arizona y en la Florida _____ mucho sol.

3. Creo que el director del banco _____ sesenta años.

4. Mi profesora _____ furiosa hoy, no sé por qué.

5. Mi cuenta del banco _____ muy baja ahora.

6. El piso de esta clase _____ muy sucio (*dirty*).

7. Vamos a comer algo porque (yo) _____ mucha hambre.

8. ¿Qué hora _____? —Creo que _____ las cinco más o menos.

9. Quiero saber cómo _____ mis padres; voy a llamar por teléfono.

10. ¿Es verdad que en Chicago siempre _____ mucho viento?

11. No puedo tomar este café porque _____ muy frío.

12. Voy a dormir porque _____. (*I'm sleepy*)

13. Yucatán está en México. Usted _____. (*You're right.*)

14. Creo que va a llover porque _____. (*it's bad weather*)

15. Ésta es la antigua casa de George Washington: _____ muy vieja, pero _____ bien conservada (*well preserved*).

16. Siempre que vas a Las Vegas, _____. (*you're lucky*)

17. Prefiero mayo (*May*) y junio porque _____. (*it's cool*)

18. El niño llora (*is crying*) porque _____. (*he's hungry*)

19. Cuando manejo el carro siempre _____. (*I'm careful*)

20. Josefina _____ viajar a Madrid. (*feels like*)

GRAMMAR II   Demonstrative Adjectives and Pronouns

A. Memorize the demonstrative adjectives and pronouns in the chart.

Distance	Masculine	Feminine	(English)
Near speaker	**este** (libro) **estos** (libros)	**esta** (casa) **estas** (casas)	this (book, house) these (books, houses)
Near listener	**ese** (libro) **esos** (libros)	**esa** (casa) **esas** (casas)	that (book, house) }(near you, the those (books, houses) } listener)
Far both from speaker and listener	**aquel** (niño) **aquellos** (niños)	**aquella** (nube) **aquellas** (nubes)	that (boy, cloud) }([way] over there) those (boys, clouds) }

Note that:

1. Demonstrative adjectives show the *distance* a noun is from the speaker, the listener, or from both of them. When the speaker talks about a noun nearby, she will use *este/estos, estas/estas.*

    EXS: *este* **libro,** *esta* **casa** (<u>this</u> book, <u>this</u> house)

2. When the speaker is talking about a noun *near the listener,* he will use *ese/esos, esa/esas.*

    EX: **¿Cómo** *se* **llama ese libro que** *tú* **lees?** (*What is the name of <u>that</u> book <u>you</u>'re reading?*)

3. When the speaker refers to a noun *far both from her and the listener,* she will use **aquel/aquellos, aquella/aquellas.**

    EX: **¿Quién es** *aquel* **niño** *allí lejos?* (*Who is <u>that</u> boy <u>way over there?</u>*)

B. The neuter forms *esto/eso/aquello* are used to refer to a noun when we don't specify which noun we're talking about. There are no neuter nouns in Spanish. We use *esto/eso/aquello* to refer to a statement, a speech, or an idea.

    EXS: **¿Qué es** *eso* **que tienes en la mano?** (*What's <u>that</u> you have in your hand?*)
    ¿Quieres tener éxito? Para *eso* **tienes que estudiar mucho.**
    (*Do you want to be successful? For <u>that</u> you have to study a lot.*)

C. Demonstratives can be used in two ways: (1) as adjectives in front of a noun, as in the examples under B above; (2) as pronouns, that is, when a noun is omitted because it is understood. In this case the demonstratives carry a written accent.

    EXS: **¿Quieres** *este* **libro? —No, quiero** *ése.* (*Do you want <u>this</u> book? —No, I want <u>that</u> one.*)
    ¿Vas a comprar *ese* **carro? —No, voy a comprar** *aquél.* (*Are you going to buy <u>that</u> car? —No, I'm going to buy <u>that</u> one over there.*)

Notice that in English you add *one* to *this* and *that* when the noun is omitted.

PRACTIQUE LOS DEMONSTRATIVOS

ANSWERS p. 190

1. If I'm talking about things or people *near me*, I use any of these four demonstratives: _____ .

2. If I'm talking about things or people *near you* (the listener), I use any of these four demonstratives: _____ .

3. Demonstrative adjectives must agree with the noun in gender (masculine/feminine) and _____, just like other adjectives or articles.

4. Notice that in English *that* and *those* are used for something near the listener or far from the listener; you would have to add *over there* to specify that something is far from both the listener and the speaker. In Spanish we have two different demonstratives for *that* and *those*: **ese** *vs.* _____, **esos** *vs.* _____, **esa** *vs.* _____, and **esas** *vs.* _____.

5. Which word don't we translate in the expression *this one?* _____.

6. *Éste, ése, ésa,* etc., take an accent when they are _____, because the noun has been omitted. The idea of nearness and distance does not change.

7. *No quiero este libro; prefiero ese* is not correct. The accent is missing on _____.

8. The neuter demonstratives **esto, eso,** and **aquello** are never used in front of a _____. In other words, they are like pronouns; they replace statements, speeches, or ideas. Do they take an accent? _____.

9. Have you noticed that the *masculine* form of the demonstratives doesn't end in *o* like that of many other adjectives? Actually, it ends in the vowel _____, except for **aquel.**

10. The difference in distance between *ese* and *aquel* (what is *near* or *far* from the listener) is relative. The tendency today is to use *ese* more than *aquel;* the same is true for their neuter counterparts: _____ .

EXERCISE

ANSWERS p. 190

Complete each sentence with the correct demonstratives. Pay attention to number and gender.

1. ¿Conoces a _____ hombre que está allí con Elena? (*that*)

2. _____ (*this*) café está frío ; _____ (*that one*) está caliente.

3. ¿Qué es _____ que llevas en la maleta? (*that*)

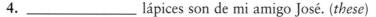

4. _____ lápices son de mi amigo José. (*these*)

5. _____ (*this*) libro que (yo) leo es más interesante que _____
   (*that one*) que tú lees.

6. ¿Qué es _____ que vemos allí lejos? (*that over there*)

7. Puedes lavarte las manos con _____ jabón. (*this*)

8. No quiero _____ (*this*) llave; prefiero _____. (*that one*)

9. No puedo aceptar _____ que usted dice. (*that*)

10. _____ es un día muy importante para los novios. (*this*)

11. Voy a comprar _____ reloj que está allí en la pared. (*that*)

12. El taxista se detiene en _____ luz cuando está roja. (*this*)

13. No sé qué es _____ que llevas en la mano. (*that*)

14. _____ (*this*) pensión es más barata que _____ (*that*) hotel.

15. Jorge cree que siempre tiene razón; _____ no me parece bien. (*that*)

GRAMMAR III   Possessive Adjectives and Pronouns

A. Memorize the possessive adjectives and pronouns in the chart.

	Short Forms	Long Forms		(English)	
Persons	**Masc. & Fem.**	**Masculine**	**Feminine**	**Adjectives**	**Pronouns**
First Second Third	mi/mis tu/tus su/sus	mío/míos tuyo/tuyos suyo/suyos	mía/mías tuya/tuyas suya/suyas	my your his/hers/its their	mine yours his/hers/its theirs
First plural		nuestro/nuestros	nuestra/nuestras	our	ours

Note that:

1. The short forms are used only before nouns and agree in number with those nouns: **mi libro/mis libros.**

2. *Nuestro/nuestros, nuestra/nuestras,* do not have short forms. They always agree with the nouns they modify in gender and number: **nuestro libro/nuestra casa/nuestras llaves.**

3. Usually the short forms such as **mi/tu/su** are unstressed. They are pronounced as if they belonged to the next word, just like the articles **el/los, la/las.** Some native speakers do stress *mi/tu/su* and their plurals for emphasis.

B. The long forms are used after the noun or alone as pronouns. They carry stress, and we can emphasize them in our intonation. Notice that in English the pronouns have different forms than the adjectives: *my* vs. *mine, your* vs. *yours,* and so on. In Spanish they are the same.

> EX: **El libro *mío* está aquí; el *tuyo* está en casa.** (<u>My</u> *book is here;* <u>yours</u> *is at home.*)

C. English pronouns *mine, yours,* and so on never take an article, whereas Spanish *mío/tuyo,* and so on always need the article when they are pronouns, except after *ser.*

> EX: **Este libro *es mío:* ¿dónde *está el tuyo?* ** (*This book is* <u>mine</u>; *where's* <u>yours</u>?)

We use *el mío/el tuyo* with *ser* if the noun is being differentiated from other nouns:

> EX: **¿Los libros? No sé cuál es *el tuyo,* pero éste es *el mío.* ** (*The books? I don't know which one is* <u>yours</u>, *but this one is* <u>mine</u>.)

D. In English the third person has more forms than others, because there are three different subjects to refer to: *he* → *his, she* → *her, it* → *its,* and the plural *they* → *their.* In Spanish there is only one form for all of them: **su/sus.** This means that *su/sus* can be very ambiguous. To make the meaning clear, the preposition *de* plus the pronoun (**de + él, de + ella, de + usted,** and so on) is sometimes used after the noun (instead of *su/sus* before the noun).

> EXS: **Conozco a tus abuelos; *su casa* (*la casa de ellos*) es grande.** (*I know your grandparents;* <u>their house</u> *is large.*)
> **Aquí están Carlos y María; *el carro de él* es éste.** (*Here are Carlos and María;* <u>his</u> *car is this one.*)

E. With parts of the body and clothes we are wearing, we use definite articles (**el/los, la/las**) in Spanish, since ownership is obvious. In English we use possessive adjectives instead.

> EX: **Lávese *las* manos.** (*Wash* <u>your</u> *hands.*)

PRACTIQUE LOS POSESIVOS

ANSWERS
p. 190

1. There are three short forms of the possessives in the singular: _____, _____, _____, and three in the plural: _____, _____, _____.

2. Do you usually stress *mi/tu/su?* _____, though some native speakers do stress these forms for _____.

3. *Su* can be translated five different ways in English, including the possessive referring to *Ud./Uds.* Possible translations are: _____.

4. *Tu hijos* is incorrect because *hijos* is plural; it should be _____.

5. Are the long forms **mío / tuyo / suyo** used before or after the noun? _____.

6. *Mine / yours,* and so on stand alone (without a noun). Which forms stand alone in Spanish, **mi / tu / su** or **mío / tuyo / suyo**? _____.

7. The plural of *mi* is _____, and the plural of *tu* is _____.

8. Remember that *tu* has two different meanings, depending on whether it's spelled with an accent (**acento**) or without it. **Tú** (with an accent) means _____, and **tu** (without an accent) means _____.

9. *Yo uso mi libro y tú usas tuyo* is incorrect. What's missing before *tuyo*? _____.

10. If we want to talk about *Mary's house* we can say **su casa** in Spanish, without repeating **María**. However, **su casa** can be confusing; we can clarify it by saying _____.

11. Spanish possessives agree with the _____ that follows in gender and number.

12. Which form is correct, **nuestra jabón** or **nuestro jabón**? _____.

EXERCISE

Translate the possessives in parentheses.

1. Te doy _____ reloj por un día solamente, pero debes tener cuidado con él porque no es _____. (*my / yours*).

2. _____ habitación está en el tercer piso. (*our*)

3. Este lápiz es _____; _____ está en la mesa. (*mine / yours*)

4. Jorge y Elena tienen una casa en la montaña. _____ casa no es grande, pero es muy agradable. (*their*)

5. Tengo la toalla _____ en la maleta. José me va dar _____. (*my / his*)

6. Este hotel es de tres estrellas; _____ precios son razonables. (*its*)

7. Debemos bajar por la escalera del hotel. _____ ascensor está roto (*broken*) (*its*) .

8. _____ pensión tiene solamente ocho habitaciones. (*our*)

9. _____ padres viven en España. _____ casa es muy antigua. (*my/their*)

10. Las luces de _____ comedor son amarillas. (*our*)

11. Carlos y Sonia tienen _____ propios carros: el _____ es un Toyota, y el _____ es un Chevy (*their/his/hers*) .

12. Ud. siempre me invita a _____ fiestas, y yo siempre le invito a Ud. a _____ . (*your/mine*)

7 Una fiesta de cumpleaños
(A Birthday Party)

el arroz	rice	la pachanga	party
la bebida	drink	(*México*)	(*Mexico*)
la botana (*México*)[1]	snack (*Mexico*)	el país	country
el champán	champagne	el piano	piano
el chocolate	chocolate	el pollo	chicken
el/la compañero(a)	schoolmate,	el rato[4]	a while
	fellow student	el recado	message, errand
la copa	glass	el refresco	refreshment, cold
el cumpleaños	birthday		drink (*nonalcoholic*)
el domingo[2]	Sunday	el resfriado	cold
el entremés	appetizer	la residencia	residence
la felicidad	happiness	el ritmo	rhythm
la fiesta	party	el sábado	Saturday
la guitarra	guitar	la sangría[5]	wine cooler
el jueves	Thursday	la semana	week
la limonada	lemonade	el sueño	dream, sleep
el lunes	Monday	el teléfono	telephone
el mariachi[3]	mariachi	el tocadiscos	record player
el martes	Tuesday	la torta	cake
el mes	month	la vela	candle
el miércoles	Wednesday	el viernes	Friday
la música	music		

apagar	to turn off	encargarse de	to take charge of
avisar	to warn, inform	encender[8] (ie)	to light
bailar	to dance	entender (ie)	to understand
celebrar	to celebrate	felicitar	to congratulate
cocinar	to cook	merecer (c)	to deserve
comenzar (ie)	to start	molestar[9]	to bother
comprender	to understand	prometer	to promise
cumplir[6]	to fulfill	sonar (ue)	to ring, sound
dejar[7]	to leave	soñar (ue)	to dream
dejar de	to stop	tocar[10]	to play, touch
encantar	to charm, like		

aburrido(a)[11]	boring, bored	oscuro(a)	dark
alegre	cheerful	próximo(a)	next, coming
antipático(a)	unpleasant	puntual	punctual
atrasado(a)	late	sabroso(a)	tasty, delicious
claro(a)	clear	simpático(a)	nice, pleasant
feliz	happy	típico(a)	typical
gracioso(a)	funny	varios(as)	several, various
moderno(a)	modern		

¡Aló!, dígame[12]	Hello!	esta noche	tonight
así que	so	felicidades	congratulations
a veces	sometimes	hágame el favor	please, do me a favor
casi	almost		
con mucho gusto	it's a pleasure	junto a	close to, near
		por casualidad	by chance

NOTAS

1. *Botana* and *antojitos* are words used by Mexicans for *aperitivo* (*appetizer*). In Spain there are different words, such as **entremés, tapa, pincho.** The international expression *hors d'oeuvre* is used in formal Spanish.

2. Days of the week are capitalized in English but not in Spanish. This is also true for the months of the year.

3. *Mariachi* refers to the typical Mexican street band as well as to each individual in the band. **Mariachis** are very popular in California, Texas, Arizona, and other states with heavy Mexican-American populations.

4. *Rato* means *a while*, but in Spanish *rato* is always a short period of time. In English *a while* can be days and even weeks, whereas *rato* is no more than a few hours.

5. *Sangría* is a wine cooler, originally from Andalucía in southern Spain. It is made with red or rosé wine mixed with fruits and soda water or lemonade. It is served cold. The name **sangría** comes from *sangre* (*blood*), because of its red color.

6. *Cumplir* is to *fulfill a duty, obey a law.* **Cumplir años** is to *reach an age.* From this verb we get the noun **cumpleaños** (*birthday*).

7. *Dejar* is *to leave something, someplace, somebody.* When *dejar de* is followed by an infinitive, it means *to stop.*

    EX: **Quiero *dejar de* fumar.** (*I want <u>to stop</u> smoking.*)

8. *Encender* (*ie*) means *to light a fire or cigarette,* and also *to turn on the light, radio, TV,* and so on. The letters in parentheses (**ie**) remind you that the present is **enciendo, enciendes,** and so on.

9. *Molestar* does not mean *to molest,* as the spelling suggests. It is simply *to bother,* whereas *to molest* is **abusar sexualmente.**

    EX: **Me *molesta* el cigarrillo.** (*The cigarette <u>bothers</u> me.*)

10. *Tocar* means to *touch something or somebody,* and also *to play music or a musical instrument*: **tocar la guitarra** (*to play the guitar*). From this verb we get *tocadiscos* for *record player.* Today we talk about *stereos,* in Spanish **estéreo.**

11. *Aburrido* has the meaning of *boring* with **ser** and the meaning of *bored* with **estar.**

    EX: **Este libro *es aburrido.*** VS. **Jorge *está aburrido.***
    (*This book <u>is boring</u>.*) VS. (*George <u>is bored</u>.*)

12. Different Hispanic countries use different expressions to answer the phone. Here are some of them: **diga** (*tell*), **dígame** (*tell me*), **oigo** (*I'm listening*), **bueno, ¡hola!, ¡aló!.**

PRACTIQUE LAS PALABRAS NUEVAS

ANSWERS p. 190

A. Write *el* or *la* before each noun.

1. _____ champán	6. _____ estéreo	11. _____ chocolate
2. _____ mes	7. _____ viernes	12. _____ sangría
3. _____ felicidad	8. _____ tocadiscos	13. _____ arroz
4. _____ martes	9. _____ entremés	14. _____ país
5. _____ cumpleaños	10. _____ mariachi	15. _____ miércoles

ANSWERS p. 190

B. Write the plural forms.

1. mes _____	6. alegre _____
2. feliz _____	7. mariachi _____
3. viernes _____	8. tocadiscos _____
4. país _____	9. entremés _____
5. puntual _____	10. miércoles _____

ANSWERS
p. 191

C. Match the two columns. (Some answers require the plural form.)

1. ___ champán

2. ___ vela

3. ___ torta

4. ___ teléfono

5. ___ país

6. ___ compañeros

7. ___ recados

8. ___ semana

9. ___ mariachis

10. ___ sangría

11. ___ entremeses

12. ___ tocadiscos

13. ___ domingos

14. ___ sueño

15. ___ pollo

16. ___ refresco

17. ___ rato

18. ___ felicidad

19. ___ copa

20. ___ con mucho gusto

21. ___ guitarra

22. ___ resfriado

23. ___ piano

24. ___ esta noche

25. ___ sabroso/ -a / -s

A. Colombia es un... diferente de Venezuela.

B. Si ponemos frutas y refresco con vino rojo tenemos una...

C. No tengo mucho tiempo; sólo voy a pasar un... a su casa.

D. Vamos a comer algunos... antes de la cena.

E. La música de los... es muy popular en México y Texas.

F. Margarita va a preparar una... para tu cumpleaños.

G. Muchos celebran el Año Nuevo con una copa de...

H. Generalmente trabajamos los lunes, pero no los...

I. Cuando cumplimos doce años encendemos doce... en la torta.

J. La camarera me sirve una... de champán bien frío.

K. Tengo que hacer muchos... para la fiesta de mi amiga.

L. Un plato típico de Cuba es arroz con...

M. ¿Quieres prepararme el tocadiscos? —Sí,...

N. Tengo que llamar por... a mis amigos de Miami.

O. Te deseo mucha... en tu cumpleaños.

P. Roberto y Sofía son... de universidad, pero no de cuarto.

Q. Necesitamos un... para poner música en la fiesta.

R. Las botanas de la fiesta están muy...

S. Andrés Segovia fue (*was*) un gran maestro de... clásica.

T. ¿Por qué no vamos al teatro...?

U. Cuando hablamos de ocho días queremos decir una...

V. El «... americano» puede convertirse en realidad para ti.

W. Mi amigo no viene a la fiesta porque tiene...

X. No tomo sangría ni (*nor*) vino; prefiero un...

Y. No toco bien la guitarra, pero sí el...

ANSWERS
p. 191

D. Write the opposite of the words given.

1. claro _____   6. aburrido _____

2. apagar _____   7. moderno _____

3. antipático _____   8. nadie _____

4. atrasado _____   9. triste _____

5. comida _____   10. comenzar _____

ANSWERS
p. 191

E. You have a list of new verbs in the vocabulary of this lesson. Review them and pay attention to the irregular ones: they are marked with *ie, ue,* and *c.* Complete the sentences with the present indicative form of the verb given in parentheses.

1. ¿A qué hora _____ usted a trabajar? (*to start*)

2. En Chile (nosotros) _____ el Año Nuevo. (*to celebrate*)

3. Tu hermana _____ muy bien. (*to dance*)

4. ¿Usted _____ bien el italiano? (*to understand*)

5. Ellos _____ a viajar el miércoles? (*to start*)

6. Creo que mi teléfono _____ en este momento. (*to ring*)

7. Cuando salgo del baño, yo siempre _____ la luz. (*to turn off*)

8. Si bebes agua antes de dormir, _____ mucho. (*to dream*)

9. Mis hijos siempre me _____ con sus problemas. (*to bother*)

10. ¿Por qué (tú) no _____ el piano en la fiesta? (*to play*)

11. María Elena se _____ de las bebidas. (*to take charge of*)

12. Yo sé un poco de francés, pero no lo _____ bien. (*to understand*)

13. Creo que yo no _____ este honor. (*to deserve*)

14. La secretaria _____ a su jefe (*boss*). (*to warn, inform*)

15. ¿Dónde _____ Ud. el carro todos los días? (*to leave, park*)

16. Los niños siempre _____ ser buenos. (*to promise*)

17. Esos esposos siempre _____ con el deber. (*to fulfill*)

18. ¿Quién _____ las velas de la torta? (*to light*)

19. Roberto _____ veintitrés años el próximo sábado. (*to reach the age of*)

20. Mi despertador (*alarm clock*) es puntual; siempre _____ a las siete en punto. (*to ring*)

DIÁLOGO   El cumpleaños de Roberto

Jorge quiere organizar la fiesta de cumpleaños de su amigo Roberto. Llama por teléfono a Lola para invitarla. Son compañeros de universidad.

LOLA: ¡Aló!... dígame.

JORGE: ¡Hola! ¿Cómo estás, Lola?

LOLA: ¡Ah! ¿Eres tú, Jorge? Yo, bastante bien, pero tu amiga Elena tiene un resfriado terrible.

JORGE: Sí, ya me dijo (*she told me*), y no va a poder venir a la fiesta. Te llamo para invitarte a la fiesta de cumpleaños de Roberto el viernes próximo.

LOLA: ¿Así que el viernes es su cumpleaños? ¿Quién va a preparar la fiesta?

JORGE: Bueno, todos un poco. Josefina trae los entremeses; Luisa va a cocinar un arroz con pollo muy sabroso; Marcos hace una buena ensalada...

LOLA: ¿Y tú, qué? ¿Vas a ser el inspector de operaciones?

JORGE: Yo me encargo de las bebidas, del estéreo y de la música. Tú puedes encargarte de la torta, ¿no?

LOLA: Sí, claro. Por eso la invitación, ¿no es verdad?

JORGE: Ya sabes que la fiesta es para todos, y tú te diviertes más que nadie en la pachanga.

* * *

Ya están todos disfrutando de la fiesta y llega Lola con la torta.

JORGE: ¡Qué torta tan linda, Lola! ¡Y de chocolate! ¡Mmmm... !¿Quieres tomar algo? ¿Cerveza, sangría, vino, champán?

LOLA: Una sangría o un refresco bien frío, por favor.

JORGE: ¿Un cigarrillo?

LOLA: Gracias. Tú sabes que no fumo.

JORGE: Entonces yo tampoco. ¿Bailamos?

LOLA: Con mucho gusto. Todos los ritmos modernos me encantan.

DIALOGUE   Robert's Birthday Party

Jorge wants to organize a birthday party for his friend Robert. Jorge calls Lola to invite her to the party. They are fellow students at the university.

LOLA: Hello!

GEORGE: Hi! How are you, Lola?

LOLA: Oh! Is that you, George? I'm pretty well, but your friend Ellen has a
            terrible cold.

GEORGE: Yeah, she told me already, and she won't be able to come. I'm calling
            to invite you to Robert's birthday party next Friday.

LOLA: So his birthday is Friday? Who's giving the party?

GEORGE: Well, everybody is going to pitch in. Josephine is bringing the snacks,
            Louise is going to cook a delicious chicken and rice, Mark is making
            a good salad. . . .

LOLA: What about you? Are you going to be the supervisor?

GEORGE: I'm in charge of the beverages, the stereo, and the music. You can
            take care of the cake, can't you?

LOLA: Yes, sure. That's the reason for the invitation, isn't it?

GEORGE: You know the party is for everybody, and you have more fun than
            anybody else at a party.

* * *

Everybody is enjoying the party. Lola arrives with the cake.

GEORGE: What a beautiful cake, Lola! And it is made of chocolate! Mmm. . . .
            Do you want anything to drink? Beer, sangría, wine, champagne?

LOLA: Sangría or soda, very cold, please.

GEORGE: A cigarette?

LOLA: No thanks. You know I don't smoke.

GEORGE: Then I won't either. Shall we dance?

LOLA: It's a pleasure. I love all the modern rhythms.

EXERCISES

ANSWERS p. 191

A. *La fiesta del cumpleaños de Roberto.* **Complete the story using the
    information from the dialogue.**

    Jorge organiza una fiesta de (1) _____ para su amigo Roberto,
    y llama por (2) _____ a su amiga Lola para (3) _____
    la (her) a la fiesta que van a tener el (4) _____ próximo. Ellos
    son amigos de (5) _____. Lola le informa a Jorge que su amiga
    Elena tiene un (6) _____ terrible, y Jorge le dice que ya lo sabe y
    que por eso ella no va a poder (7) _____ a la fiesta. Jorge quiere
    que Lola prepare la torta de cumpleaños. Todos van a (8) _____

algo para la fiesta: Josefina va a traer los (9) _____, Luisa va a cocinar un (10) _____ muy sabroso, y Marcos va a hacer la (11) _____.

Lola promete que va a hacer la (12) _____ de cumpleaños después de informarse que Jorge no es el (13) _____ de operaciones, sino que se va a encargar de las (14) _____, del estéreo y de la música. Lola se (15) _____ en las fiestas más que nadie.

Todos disfrutan de la fiesta cuando Lola (16) _____ con la torta. Jorge dice que la torta de chocolate es (17) _____, y la invita a (18) _____ sangría, cerveza, vino o (19) _____. Lola le pide sangría o un (20) _____ bien frío, pero no acepta el (21) _____ porque no fuma. Entonces Jorge tampoco fuma y la invita a (22) _____, y ella dice que le encantan todos los (23) _____ modernos. ¡Viva la pachanga!

ANSWERS p. 191

B. **Circle the answer that best completes the sentence.**

1. En una fiesta de cumpleaños encendemos (botanas, velas, recados, cigarrillos).

2. Si hoy es martes, mañana es (lunes, sábado, jueves, miércoles).

3. Bebemos el champán en (una copa, una vela, un vaso, una torta).

4. De aperitivo comemos entremeses o (platos, sangría, botanas, mariachis).

5. Muchas personas no trabajan los (domingos, martes, jueves, viernes).

6. Carlos no toca el piano sino (*but*) (el ritmo, la guitarra, el recado, el teléfono).

7. ¿Por qué (enciendes, entiendes, comienzas, cocinas) el cigarrillo en la clase?

8. Elena no puede ir a la fiesta porque tiene (sueño, cumpleaños, resfriado, refresco).

9. Ocho días es (un mes, un rato, un año, una semana).

10. Muchas personas (sueñan, avisan, suenan, molestan) cuando duermen.

11. Jorge (merece, comienza, prepara, avisa) a Lola del cumpleaños de Roberto.

12. Luisa no entiende inglés porque no es de (esta residencia, esta semana, este país, este ritmo).

13. Roberto (promete, sueña, enciende, cumple) veintitrés años el viernes.

14. Antes de entrar al ascensor, debes (encender, comenzar, encargar, apagar) el cigarrillo.

15. Para oír la música necesitamos (el recado, el champán, el estéreo, la guitarra).

ANSWERS p. 191

C. Circle the adjective that best completes the sentence.

1. Juanito llega (moderno, típico, atrasado, claro).

2. Por la noche no vemos nada porque está (simpático, próximo, oscuro, alegre).

3. El pollo frito está (aburrido, sabroso, gracioso, puntual).

4. María vive junto a mi casa; ella está muy (graciosa, aburrida, típica, próxima).

5. Ese libro no es interesante; es muy (feliz, gracioso, aburrido, moderno).

6. Hoy hace muy mal tiempo; el día está (claro, oscuro, atrasado, sabroso).

ANSWERS p. 192

D. Form sentences with the following words. Use the present indicative. Watch out for the agreement between nouns and adjectives as well as articles. You will have to add prepositions and articles, the plural form of nouns, and so on. The words are given in the right order.

1. José / tener ganas / leer / libro *Hawaii* /.

   _____

2. ¿por qué / tú / no dejar / fumar / hoy /?

   _____

3. fiesta / mi cumpleaños / ser / sábado / próximo /.

   _____

4. torta / cumpleaños / Roberto / tener / veintitrés / vela /.

   _____

5. María / querer / bailar / ritmo / moderno /.

   _____

6. ustedes / llegar / atrasado / fiesta /.

   _____

7. este / entremeses / estar / muy / sabroso /.

   _____

8. tu / sobrinos / ser / bastante / gracioso /.

   _____

GRAMMAR I Direct Object Nouns and Pronouns • Personal *a*

A. The direct object is the noun or pronoun that completes the meaning of a transitive verb. For example, *to buy* makes no sense without someone (the subject of the sentence) buying something. In the sentence **Compramos el champán**, *champán* is the direct object.

B. In Spanish, if the direct object is a person rather than a thing, the preposition *a* precedes it. This distinction is not made in English.

   EXS: Veo *la casa*. (*I see the house*.)
   Veo *a la niña*. (*I see the girl*.)

   If the person is indefinite, *a* is omitted, and the person becomes "depersonalized," as if he or she were a thing.

   EXS: Veo *al** médico. (*I see the doctor*.)
   Necesito médico. (*I need medical help*.)

   *Remember the contraction *a + el = al.*

C. Memorize the direct object pronouns in the chart.

Subject Pronoun	Direct Object Pronoun	(English)
yo	me	me
tú	te	you (*familiar*)
él	lo/le (Spain)	him, it/him
ella	la	her, it
ellos	los/les (Spain)	them
ellas	las	them
usted	lo/le (Spain)/la	you (*formal*)
ustedes	los/les (Spain)/las	you (*formal plural*)
nosotros(as)	nos	us

Note that:

1. *Lo/los* are used in Latin America to refer to masculine nouns, either people or things. In Spain *le/les* is used if the direct object is a person and *lo/los* if it is a thing. Following the policy of this book, we will use the Latin American pronouns.

   EXS: SPAIN: ¿Ve usted *a Juan?* —Sí, *le* veo.
   LATIN AMERICA: ¿Ve usted *a Juan?* —Sí, *lo* veo.
   (*Do you see John? —Yes, I see him*.)

2. The direct object pronouns are unstressed in Spanish, and we pronounce them as if they were part of the verb; they cannot be emphasized phonetically. In English they are usually stressed.

3. In Spanish, the direct object pronoun precedes the conjugated verb. In English it always follows the verb.

    EX: **Usted *me* entiende.** (*You understand me.*)

4. If the direct object pronoun is the object of an infinitive, it may either precede the conjugated verb or follow the infinitive. When it follows the infinitive, it is attached to it, forming one word. The meaning is the same in both cases.

    EX: **Quiero vert*e* = *Te* quiero ver.** (*I want to see <u>you</u>.*)

    The direct object pronoun may also be attached to an affirmative command.

    EX: **¡Dígame!** (*Tell <u>me</u>!*)

PRACTIQUE LOS PRONOMBRES

**ANSWERS
p. 192**

1. A transitive verb completes its meaning in the _____ of the sentence. For this reason we sometimes call it direct complement.

2. **Yo *conozco tu tía*** is incorrect because *tía* is a person. It should be **Yo conozco** _____. For this reason this preposition is called the "personal _____."

3. Remember that ***nadie*** is the negative of ***alguien,*** and that both refer to persons. Is it correct to say **Conozco alguien aquí?** _____. The preposition _____ is required in front of _____.

4. The direct object pronouns in Spanish never carry phonetic _____. That's why they are always pronounced as if they were part of the

    _____.

5. The third-person direct object pronouns are almost identical to the definite articles. There are four in Latin America: _____.

6. In Spain people would say **¿Juan? No le veo,** whereas in Latin America they would say **¿Juan? No** _____. The same is true in the plural: *les* becomes _____.

7. Do the direct object pronouns precede or follow the conjugated verb in the indicative? _____. Do the same pronouns precede or follow the infinitive? _____.

8. An infinitive usually follows a verb form in the indicative. In this case the pronoun may follow the _____ or precede the _____.

9. Which sentence is correct **Quiero ayudarte** or **Te quiero ayudar?** _____.

10. If the person who is the direct object is indefinite, we treat him or her as a "thing" by omitting the preposition _____. For example, *We need waitresses* would be in Spanish **Necesitamos** _____.

EXERCISES

A. Answer the questions by replacing the direct object noun with the pronoun. Pay attention to the verb. This is a good review of verbs you have learned in previous lessons.

1. ¿Trae usted *las plumas?* —Sí, _____.

2. ¿Oye usted *la radio?* —Sí, _____.

3. ¿Hace usted *su trabajo?* —Sí, _____.

4. ¿Conoce Ud. *a mi tía?* —Sí, _____.

5. ¿Quiere Ud. *más café?* —No, no _____.

6. ¿Habla Ud. *japonés?* —No, no _____.

7. ¿Fuma usted *cigarrillos?* —No, no _____.

8. ¿Ve usted *a su amiga?* —No, no _____.

9. ¿Quiere Ud. leer *este libro?* —Sí, _____.

10. (*Answer Number 9 differently.*) —Sí, _____.

11. ¿Tiene que oír *la radio?* —Sí, _____.

12. (*answer Number 11 differently.*) —Sí, _____.

B. Fill in the blank with the "personal *a*" if required. Remember the contraction *a + el = al.*

1. ¿Por qué no invitas _____ mi novia a la fiesta?

2. No pienso invitar _____ nadie.

3. Josefina no entiende bien _____ esta lección.

4. En este restaurante necesitan _____ camareros.

5. Voy a llamar _____ camarero porque quiero pagar la cuenta.

6. ¿ _____ quién piensas invitar a la fiesta? ¿_____ José?

C. Answer the questions with direct object pronouns *me, te, nos,* and so on.

1. ¿Quien me llama? ¿José? —Sí, José _____. (*familiar*)

2. ¿Quién nos felicita? ¿Marcos? —Sí, _____.

3. ¿Puede Ud. llamarme (*f.*)? —Sí, _____.

4. ¿Nos (**m.**) ayudan Uds.? —Sí, _____.

5. ¿Vas a verme mañana? —Sí, _____. (*familiar*)

6. ¿Te dejamos en tu casa? —Sí, _____.

GRAMMAR II   Reflexive Constructions and Reflexive Pronouns

A. Certain verbs in both Spanish and English are reflexive. The object of a reflexive verb is the same person or thing as the subject.

    EXS: NONREFLEXIVE: **Roberto *la* ve (a Sonia).** (*Roberto sees <u>her</u> [Sonia].*)
           REFLEXIVE: **Roberto *se* ve.** (*Roberto sees <u>himself</u>.*)

B. Memorize the reflexive construction in the chart.

lavarse (to wash oneself)			
Subject Pronoun	**Reflexive Pronoun**	**Verb**	**(English)**
yo	me	lavo	I wash myself
tú	te	lavas	you wash yourself
él	se	lava	he washes himself, it washes itself
ella	se	lava	she washes herself, it washes itself
Ud.	se	lava	you wash yourself
nosotros(as)	**nos**	lavamos	we wash ourselves
ellos/ellas	se	lavan	they wash themselves
Uds.	se	lavan	you (pl.) wash yourselves

Note that:

1. Reflexive pronouns precede the conjugated verb but follow the infinitive, just like the direct object pronouns. When the reflexive verb follows the infinitive, it is attached to it.

    EXS: **Yo *me* lavo.** (*I wash <u>myself</u>.*)
          Yo *me* voy a lavar.
          Yo voy a lavar*me*. } (*I'm going to wash <u>myself</u>.*)

2. *Se* is the reflexive pronoun for all third-person subjects, singular and plural: él/ellos, ella/ellas, Ud./Uds. The third-person reflexive pronoun *se* can mean *himself, herself, itself, oneself, yourself, yourselves,* and *themselves.*

    EXS: **Ella *se* divierte.** (*She amuses herself.*)
          Ellos *se* divierten. (*They amuse themselves.*)

3. In English the reflexive pronoun always follows the verb. It is formed with -*self* and -*selves*.

C. **Emphatic reflexive.** Reflexive pronouns are used with intransitive verbs such as **ir, salir, llegar,** and so on, to show that the action has been planned to be completed.

EXS: *Me* **voy a casa a las tres.** (*I'm going home at three.*)
Voy a casa a las tres. (*I'm going home at three.*)

This is also done with some transitive verbs to show the same kind of emphasis on completion of action.

EXS: **Ella** *se* **come la torta.** (*She is eating up the cake.*)
Ella come la torta. (*She is eating the cake.*)

D. **Impersonal se.** A sentence such as **Se habla español** (*Spanish is spoken* [or literally, *One speaks Spanish*]) is an example of an impersonal construction using *se* in Spanish where English uses an indefinite subject such as *one, you, they, people* (in general), or the passive. The sentence is called *impersonal* because the verb has no personal subject. In this case the subject *español* is inanimate.

EXS: **Se vende una casa.** (*A house is being sold.*)
Se venden dos casas. (*Two houses are being sold.*)

Note that the verb *venden* in the second sentence agrees with *casas* because the impersonal **se** does not act as a subject.

E. Not all verbs that are reflexive in Spanish are reflexive in the corresponding English. In English, a reflexive pronoun is often used only for emphasis. For example, you could say *Did you wash?* or *Did you wash yourself?* in English, but in Spanish the corresponding verb *lavarse* is always reflexive: **¿Te lavaste?**

F. Here is a list of some common reflexive verbs. Some of them have appeared in previous lessons.

abrocharse to fasten

acostarse (ue) to go to bed

afeitarse to shave (oneself)

bañarse to take a bath

despertarse (ie) to wake up

divertirse (ie) to have fun, amuse oneself

ducharse to take a shower

lavarse to wash (oneself)

levantarse to get up

llamarse to be named, called

peinarse to comb (one's hair)

ponerse to put on (one's clothes)

quitarse to take off (one's clothes)

secarse to dry (oneself)

sentarse (ie) to sit down

sentirse (ie) to feel

vestirse (i) to get dressed

PRACTIQUE LOS REFLEXIVOS

**ANSWERS
p. 192**

1. A reflexive pronoun repeats the _____ of the sentence. The reflexive pronoun for *yo* is _____, and for *tú* it is _____.

2. There is only one reflexive pronoun for all third-person subjects: _____. This is the same pronoun used to translate *one* in impersonal sentences such as *One speaks Spanish*: _____.

3. Which action is more emphatic, **Ya vas a casa** or **Ya te vas a casa**? _____.

4. *Se* is obligatory when the subject of the sentence is an inanimate noun, such as *plato* in **Los platos _____ lavan con agua caliente y jabón.**

5. *Se vende carros* is not correct because *carros* is plural; therefore the verb should be plural: _____.

6. Such personal actions as **bañarse, lavarse, sentarse,** require the _____ pronoun when the action is performed on oneself.

7. Notice the difference between *sentarse* and *sentirse;* the first one is an **-ar** verb and the second, **-ir.** How would you say *She is sitting*? **Ella _____,** and *She is feeling. . .* ? **Ella _____ ...**

EXERCISES

**ANSWERS
p. 193**

A. Fill in the blank with the present indicative of the verb in parentheses.

1. Los pasajeros _____ los cinturones en el avión. (*to fasten*)

2. Yo todos los días _____ temprano. (*to go to bed*)

3. ¿A qué hora _____ usted normalmente? (*to wake up*)

4. Lola siempre _____ mucho en las fiestas. (*to have fun*)

5. ¿Cómo _____ Ud.? —(Yo) _____ Paco. (*to be named*)

6. Después de bañarme, _____ por la mañana. (*to shave*)

7. Ella _____ un suéter (*sweater*) porque hace fresco. (*to put on*)

8. Esa señora siempre _____ muy elegante. (*to dress*)

9. Los camareros no _____ nunca en el restaurante. (*to sit down*)

10. Antes de acostarme, siempre _____ la ropa (*clothes*). (*to take off*)

11. Mi hermano y yo _____ muy bien hoy. (*to feel*)

12. Roberto no _____ muy temprano. (*to get up*)

13. Tú siempre _____ a la ventanilla. (*to sit down*)

14. Lola y yo _____ en la casa. (*to comb our hair*)

15. Si hace buen tiempo (nosotros) _____ en el mar. (*to bathe*)

ANSWERS
p. 193

B. Translate the following sentences using reflexive pronouns. Most of the sentences involve the impersonal *se.*

1. One lives well here. _____.

2. In Argentina Spanish is spoken. _____.

3. I'm *going home* now. _____.

4. He is eating up all the cake! _____.

5. The car is stopping now. _____.

6. The cars are stopping. _____.

7. House for sale. _____.

GRAMMAR III   Preterite (Past Tense) of Regular Verbs • Spelling Changes

A. Memorize the preterite of regular verbs in the chart.

	habl ar (to talk)	**com er** (to eat)	**viv ir** (to live)	(English)
yo	habl é	com í	viv í	I lived , I did live
tú	habl aste	com iste	viv iste	you lived , you did live
él/ella/ Ud.	habl ó	com ió	viv ió	he/she/you lived, he/she/you did live
nosotros(as)	habl amos	com imos	viv imos	we lived, we did live
ellos/ellas/Uds.	habl aron	com ieron	viv ieron	they/you lived, they/you did live

Note that:

1. The stems **habl-, com-, viv-,** are the same as in the present. They carry the dictionary meaning: *to talk, to eat, to live.*

2. The most important difference between the present and the preterite is the stress on the last syllable in the first and third person singular, along with new vowels. Compare *yo hablo* with *yo hablé, él come* with *él comió,* and so on.

3. The ending **-mos** for *nosotros* is the same as in the present, whereas for *tú* it is **-aste** and **-iste,** and for *ellos* it is **-aron,** and **-ieron.** Notice that **-er** and **-ir** verbs have the same endings in the preterite.

4. *Hablamos* (-ar verb) and *vivimos* (-ir verb) are the same in the present and the preterite. An adverb or the context tells us how to interpret the meaning of these forms.

    EXS: *Hablamos* con el niño *ahora.* (We <u>are talking</u> to the boy <u>now</u>.)
      Hablamos con el niño *ayer.* (We <u>talked</u> to the boy <u>yesterday</u>.)

B. Preterite means *past*. There is another tense for a past action that we will study in Lesson 9. For the time being, try to associate the Spanish preterite with the simple past in English: *lived, spoke, heard,* and so on. To translate the emphatic *did* as in *I did live in Cuba,* we use an adverb such as **sí, ciertamente: Yo sí viví en Cuba** OR **Ciertamente yo viví en Cuba.**

C. **Spelling changes.** Study the rules for spelling changes that follow.

1. *Pagar, llegar,* and any verb with a *g* before the -ar ending add a *u* after the *g* before the ending -é. This *u* is not pronounced.

   EX: **pagar → pagué** BUT **pagó**

2. *Comenzar, especializar,* and any verb with a *z* before the -ar ending change the *z* to *c* before the ending -é, just as *feliz* changes to *felices* and *felicidad*.

   EX: **comenzar → comencé** BUT **comenzó, comenzaron,** and so on.

3. *Tocar, practicar,* and any verb with a *c* before the -**ar** ending change *c* to *qu* before the ending -é. The *u* of *qu* is always silent in Spanish.

4. *Leer, caer, oír,* and any other verb with two consecutive vowels change the vowel *i* of the third person to *y* whenever it is caught between two other vowels.

   EXS: **leer → leyó → leyeron** BUT **leí, leíste, leímos**
   oír → oyó → oyeron BUT **oí, oíste, oímos**

NOTE

From *ver* we get *yo vi* (*I saw*), *él vio* (*he saw*). The *accent* is not needed because these forms have only one syllable; however, a compound verb such as **prever** (*to foresee*) will need **acento: yo preví** (*I foresaw*), **él previó** (*he foresaw*).

PRACTIQUE EL PRETÉRITO

1. The stem of a verb carries the basic _____ of the verb. The stem of *comer* is _____, and the stem of *ver* is _____.

2. The personal ending -**mos** is for _____, the endings -**aste** and -**iste** are for _____, and the endings -**é** and -**í** for _____.

3. *Hablar* has two forms with an accent (**acento**) in the preterite: _____/ _____.

4. *Vivir* has two forms with an accent: _____/ _____.

5. *Hablamos* and *vivimos* (and all the verbs ending in -**ar** and -**ir**) are the same in two tenses of the indicative: _____/ _____.

6. From *apagar* we don't say **apagé** in the preterite. It should be _____, because *g* changes to _____ in front of the vowels e and i.

7. The word *preterite* means _____. In Spanish we call it **pretérito** rather than **pasado,** the word for *past.* How would you usually translate *pagué?* _____.

8. From *creer* we don't write **creió** but _____. The reason is that the *i* between two vowels (in this case e and ó) becomes _____.

9. From *tocar* we don't write **tocé,** but _____. The reason is that the *c* changes to _____ in front of the vowels **e** and **i.**

10. From *comenzar* we don't write **comenzé,** but _____. The reason is that we change *z* to _____ in front of *e* and *i.*

11. We don't write **leiron** but _____, because the *i* is between two vowels.

12. *Ud. vio* carries no accent because this verb has _____ syllable, whereas *Ud. previó* (*you foresaw*) needs _____ because it has two syllables, and the stress is on the last syllable ending in a vowel.

EXERCISES

ANSWERS
p. 193

A. **Fill in the blanks with the correct form of the preterite. If the verb is reflexive, don't forget to write the respective reflexive pronoun: *me/te/se/nos.***

1. Mi amiga _____ a las ocho de la mañana, pero yo _____ a las siete en punto. (*llegar*)

2. Todos los estudiantes _____ la novela de García Márquez. (*leer*)

3. Este mañana (yo) no _____ por no tener tiempo. (*bañarse*)

4. ¿Dónde _____ usted esa información? (*ver*)

5. ¿A qué hora _____ (tú) ayer? (*acostarse*)

6. Yo no _____ tenis el domingo pasado. (*practicar*)

7. Ella _____ el trabajo a las nueve, pero yo _____ a las ocho. (*comenzar*)

8. Tú _____ el cigarrillo antes de entrar a la clase, y yo también lo _____. (*apagar*)

9. Mis hijos _____ de la fiesta con nosotros. (*volver*)

10. La noche pasada (yo) solamente _____ seis horas. (*dormir*)

11. Mi vaso de vino _____ y se rompió (*broke*). (*caerse*)

12. Diana _____ el piano y yo _____ la guitarra. (*tocar*)

13. Jorge _____ el vino y yo _____ la comida. (*pagar*)

14. Mi esposa y yo _____ cinco años en Cuba. (*vivir*)

15. Roberto _____ el sombrero cuando _____ a la casa.
    (*quitarse / entrar*)

16. ¿Cuándo _____ ustedes eso? (*oír*)

17. El pasado año _____ mucho en Colorado. (*nevar*)

18. Carlitos _____ toda la torta. (*comerse*)

19. El avión _____ de Chicago a las dos de la tarde. (*salir*)

20. El año pasado _____ bastante en California. (*llover*)

**ANSWERS
p. 193**

B. Practice the direct object pronouns in the preterite. Answer the questions by
replacing the noun with the corresponding pronoun.

    EX: **¿Te comiste *la paella?* —Sí, me *la* comí.** (Did you eat <u>the paella?</u> —Yes,
       I ate <u>it</u>.)

1. ¿Ya pagaste el estéreo? —Sí, ya _____.

2. ¿Quién se bebió el refresco? —Lola se _____.

3. ¿Ya invitaste a Elena? —No, no _____ todavía.

4. ¿Viste ayer a tu novia? —Sí, _____ por la tarde.

5. ¿Quién te llevó a la fiesta? —Roberto _____.

6. ¿Tocaste la guitarra en la fiesta? —Sí, _____.

**ANSWERS
p. 194**

C. **Change the present to the preterite in the following story.**

    Esta mañana (1) me despierto a las siete y cuarto, (2) me levanto de la
cama, y (3) me baño con agua bien fría. Después (4) me seco (*secarse = to
dry*) con la toalla, y (5) me visto rápidamente. (6) Me desayuno café con
pan, y (7) salgo de casa para la universidad. (8) Llego a la clase a las ocho
menos cinco, y (9) oigo las explicaciones aburridas del profesor… A las doce
(10) como una ensalada en la cafetería, y por la tarde (11) vuelvo a clase con
mis amigos. Mi clase de la tarde (12) comienza a la una en punto. El
profesor (13) explica (*explicar = to explain*) por qué el Imperio Romano
(14) se cae desastrosamente y (15) se destruye en poco tiempo.

1. _____	6. _____	11. _____
2. _____	7. _____	12. _____
3. _____	8. _____	13. _____
4. _____	9. _____	14. _____
5. _____	10. _____	15. _____

8 De compras en el supermercado
(Shopping at the Supermarket)

Spanish	English	Spanish	English
el aguacate	avocado	el mercado	market
el ajo	garlic	la merienda[6]	snack
el atún	tuna	la naranja	orange
la banana,[2]	banana	el paquete	package
el plátano		el pastel	pastry, cake
el bocadillo	sandwich	el pavo[7]	turkey
el burrito[3]	burrito	el pepino	cucumber
la caloría	calorie	la pera[8]	pear
la carne	meat	el pescado	fish
la cebolla	onion	la pierna[9]	leg
la chuleta	chop	el puerco[10]	pig, pork
el cordero	lamb	el queso	cheese
la enchilada	enchilada	la res	beef, livestock
el frijol[4]	bean	el sángüich	sandwich
la grasa	grease, fat	el solomillo	sirloin
el guisante	green pea	el taco	taco
la hamburguesa	hamburger	el té[11]	tea
el jugo, el zumo[5]	juice	la ternera	veal
la lata	can	la tortilla[12]	omelette
la leche	milk	la vaca	cow, beef
el maíz	corn	la verdura	green vegetable, greens
la manzana	apple	la zanahoria	carrot

andar	to walk	jugar (ue)	to play
asar	to roast	merendar (ie)	to snack
atender (ie)	to wait on	parar	to stop
buscar	to look for	pescar	to fish
condimentar	to season	recomendar (ie)	to recommend
cuidar	to take care	vender	to sell
haber	to have		

asado(a)	roasted	pálido(a)	pale
chileno(a)	Chilean	pasado(a) de peso	overweight
colombiano(a)	Colombian	peruano(a)	Peruvian
enfermo(a)	sick	picante	hot, spicy
estupendo(a)	fantastic	saludable	healthy
fresco(a)	fresh, cool	texano(a)	Texan
lleno(a)	full	tierno(a)	tender, soft
mexicano(a)	Mexican	tinto(a)	red wine
nervioso(a)	nervous		

acabar de (+ infinitivo)	to have just done	ir de compras	to go shopping
		no poder ver	to be unable to stand
a menudo	frequently, often	ponerse	to turn
ayer	yesterday	(+ adjetivo)	(+ adjective)
decir que sí/no	to say yes/no	ponerse a	to begin
estar a dieta[13]	to be on a diet	(+ infinitivo)	(+ infinitive)
hay que	it's necessary to	saber a	to taste like
(+ infinitivo)	(+ infinitive)	tener buena pinta	to look good

NOTAS

1. *Supermercado* is *supermarket*. In Hispanic countries, small shops are still very popular: bakery, meat shop, fruit store, fish store, and so on. After many years of competition, supermarkets are finally catching on in big cities, especially in Venezuela, Spain, Mexico, and Argentina.

2. *Banana* is one of the many words used for *banana* in Spanish. In Spain it is called **plátano**. Other common words are **banano, guineo, manzano, dominicano, Johnson**. In some Latin American countries *plátano* is the banana that is cooked in many different ways.

3. **Burrito** is one of the many Mexican dishes, although it may have started in Texas. It is made with a tortilla stuffed with meat, cheese, and beans. It is now served also for breakfast, stuffed with egg, ham, potatoes. **Enchilada** is also a Mexican dish, made with rolled corn tortillas and stuffed with ground meat, chicken, beans, and covered with chili sauce. **Taco** is made with either a soft flour tortilla or a crisp corn shell and stuffed with meat, lettuce, tomato, and cheese.

4. *Frijol* is one of many words for *bean*. In some countries it is called **fréjol, poroto,** and **alubia.**

5. *Zumo* is *juice* in Spain. In Latin America, juice is called **jugo.**

6. **Merienda** is a small meal between lunch and supper. Since supper is very late—around 9:00 or 10:00 P.M., the merienda is a midafternoon snack. *Merienda* is also the word for *picnic. Merendar* is the verb.

7. **Pavo** is called **guajolote** in Mexico and **chompipe** in Central America.

8. Hispanics eat more fruit (**fruta**) than Americans. It is the usual dessert after meals except on holidays, when cake or pastries are served after fruit. The section of canned foods, whether they be vegetables, soups, or fruits—is very small in an Hispanic supermarket. Hispanics prefer fresh foods.

9. *Pierna* translates into *leg* and applies to people, whereas *pata* is *leg* of an animal. However, if the animal is used for meat, the **patas** become **piernas.** For example, Un **cerdo tiene cuatro patas,** but **El jamón se hace con la pierna del cerdo.**

10. *Puerco* is one of the many words for *pig*. Other words are **cerdo, marrano, chancho, gocho, cochino.** In Spanish there is no difference between *pig* and *pork:* it's the same word.

11. Notice that *té* is written with **acento** to differentiate it from the pronoun **te** (*you*).

12. Tortilla is an *omelette* in Spain. It is usually pretty thick because together with eggs, they add potatoes, ham, onions, and peppers. In Mexico the **tortilla** is thin and flat, made with wheat or corn flour. It's the base for many Mexican dishes such as **taco, enchilada, burrito,** and **tostada.**

13. *Dieta* translates into *diet,* but in some Hispanic countries *dieta* suggests that it is a plan prescribed by a doctor for health reasons. For this reason *dieta* is a rather negative word, so much so that the Coca-Cola Company has had to change the name Diet Coke to Coke Light to be able to sell Diet Coke in Spain.

PRACTIQUE LAS PALABRAS NUEVAS

A. Write *el* or *la* before each noun.

1. ___ carne	6. ___ frijol	11. ___ jugo
2. ___ atún	7. ___ tortilla	12. ___ guisante
3. ___ aguacate	8. ___ té	13. ___ leche
4. ___ cebolla	9. ___ res	14. ___ hamburguesa
5. ___ maíz	10. ___ pastel	15. ___ sángüiche

ANSWERS
p. 194
B. Fill in the blanks with the following words. You may use some words twice.

a menudo	cebolla	leche	pepino	queso
bocadillo	hamburguesa	merendar	picante	solomillo
buena pinta	jugo	pavo	pierna	zanahoria

1. En el desayuno siempre tomo _____ de naranja.

2. Generalmente la carne de _____ es carne de res, pero ahora también se hace de pavo y hasta de vegetales.

3. El jamón se hace con la _____ del puerco.

4. En la fiesta de *Thanksgiving* comemos _____ en Estados Unidos.

5. Los tacos tienen carne, lechuga, tomate y _____.

6. Rita va al supermercado _____.

7. La _____ es muy buena para los niños.

8. Los latinos comen muchas cosas con _____ y ajo.

9. Voy a comer un _____ de jamón con queso.

10. Para _____ prefiero fruta o café.

11. Comemos una ensalada de tomate, cebolla, lechuga y _____.

12. La _____ es una verdura color naranja.

13. El queso se hace con _____.

14. Estas chuletas de cerdo tienen _____.

15. La carne más cara es el _____.

16. La comida mexicana generalmente es _____.

ANSWERS
p. 194
C. Complete each sentence writing the adjective corresponding to the country. (Note that adjectives of nationality are not capitalized in Spanish.)

1. Las personas de Colombia son _____.

2. Las personas de México son _____.

3. Las personas de Chile son _____.

4. Las personas de España son _____.

5. Las personas de Perú son _____.

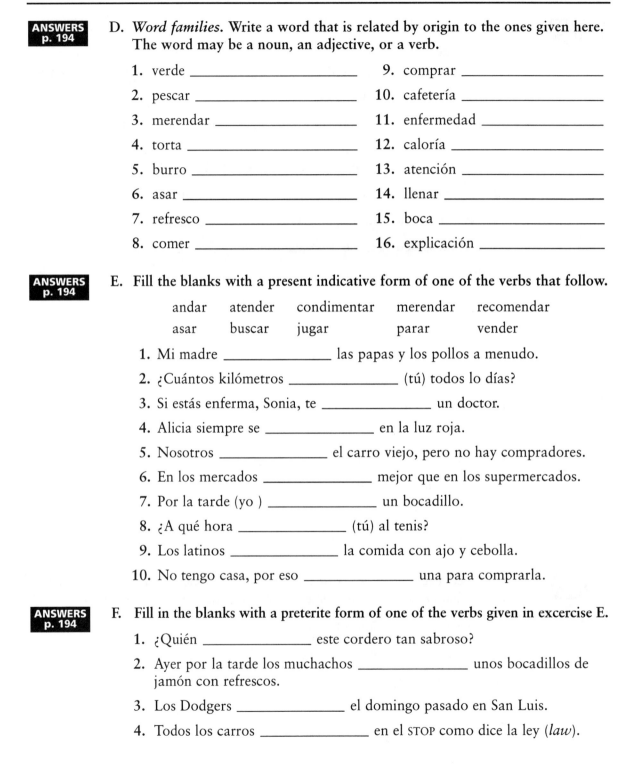

ANSWERS
p. 194

D. *Word families.* Write a word that is related by origin to the ones given here. The word may be a noun, an adjective, or a verb.

1. verde _____

2. pescar _____

3. merendar _____

4. torta _____

5. burro _____

6. asar _____

7. refresco _____

8. comer _____

9. comprar _____

10. cafetería _____

11. enfermedad _____

12. caloría _____

13. atención _____

14. llenar _____

15. boca _____

16. explicación _____

ANSWERS
p. 194

E. Fill the blanks with a present indicative form of one of the verbs that follow.

andar   atender   condimentar   merendar   recomendar
asar   buscar   jugar   parar   vender

1. Mi madre _____ las papas y los pollos a menudo.

2. ¿Cuántos kilómetros _____ (tú) todos lo días?

3. Si estás enferma, Sonia, te _____ un doctor.

4. Alicia siempre se _____ en la luz roja.

5. Nosotros _____ el carro viejo, pero no hay compradores.

6. En los mercados _____ mejor que en los supermercados.

7. Por la tarde (yo) _____ un bocadillo.

8. ¿A qué hora _____ (tú) al tenis?

9. Los latinos _____ la comida con ajo y cebolla.

10. No tengo casa, por eso _____ una para comprarla.

ANSWERS
p. 194

F. Fill in the blanks with a preterite form of one of the verbs given in excercise E.

1. ¿Quién _____ este cordero tan sabroso?

2. Ayer por la tarde los muchachos _____ unos bocadillos de jamón con refrescos.

3. Los Dodgers _____ el domingo pasado en San Luis.

4. Todos los carros _____ en el STOP como dice la ley (*law*).

5. Marcos _____ el carro viejo y compró uno nuevo.

6. La secretaria nos _____ muy bien.

7. Después de clase (yo) _____ a mi novia para invitarla a comer.

8. El doctor me _____ comer menos carne y más verduras.

DIÁLOGO   De compras en el supermercado

Rita y Mimi son buenas amigas. Están en el supermercado para hacer las compras de la semana.

MIMI: No vengo mucho al supermercado. Atienden mejor en los mercados pequeños, donde conoces a los empleados y oyes los últimos chismes de barrio.

RITA: Pues yo vengo aquí a menudo. Creo que los precios son más bajos y hay más variedad de productos.

MIMI: Tienes razón. Y no hay que andar de mercado en mercado. ¡Mira estas chuletas de cerdo a 3,50 el kilo! Un precio bien razonable.

RITA: La verdad. No tienen ninguna grasa. Voy a llevarme este paquete de cuatro kilos y medio.

MIMI: Esta carne de res tiene buena pinta, con sólo siete por ciento de grasa. Me llevo seis kilos de carne de hamburguesa y dos kilos de solomillo.

RITA: Nosotros comemos bastante cordero asado en casa. Voy a cocinar esta pierna el domingo porque somos muchos.

MIMI: Tengo que ir a la sección de verduras. Necesito zanahorias, frijoles verdes, lechuga, cebollas y ajo.

RITA: Vas a ver que aquí hay vegetales bien frescos: pepinos, guisantes, maíz, de todo, especialmente la fruta.

MIMI: Yo no puedo ver los vegetales en lata. No saben a nada.

RITA: A mí las latas también me ponen enferma, con la excepción del atún.

MIMI: Yo compro mucha fruta siempre. Mis niños la prefieren al pastel.

RITA: Sí, es más saludable y tiene menos calorías.

MIMI: Mi esposo está a dieta ahora. Se lo recomendó el médico. No toca nada dulce.

RITA: Pues mi marido también está pasado de peso. ¡Ay los hombres! ¡No se cuidan nada!

DIALOGUE   Shopping at the Supermarket

Rita and Mimi are good friends. They are in the supermarket shopping for the week.

MIMI: I don't come to the supermarket much. They wait on you better in the small stores, where you get to know the employees and can learn the latest gossip from the neighborhood.

RITA: Well, I come here often. I think the prices are lower and there is a greater variety of products.

MIMI: You're right. And you don't have to go from store to store. Look at these pork chops at 3.50 a kilo! Very reasonable price.

RITA: It's true. They don't have any fat. I'm going to take this four-and-a-half kilo package.

MIMI: This beef looks really nice with only 7 percent fat. I'll take six kilos of hamburger meat and two kilos of sirloin steak.

RITA: We eat a lot of roast lamb at home. I'm going to cook this leg on Sunday because there are going to be a lot of us.

MIMI: I have to go to the produce section. I need carrots, green beans, lettuce, onions, and garlic.

RITA: You'll see that here there are very fresh vegetables: cucumbers, green peas, corn—everything—and especially the fruit.

MIMI: I can't stand canned vegetables. They have no taste at all.

RITA: Canned food makes me sick, with the exception of tuna.

MIMI: I always buy lots of fruit. My children like it better than cake and sweets.

RITA: Of course, it's healthier and has fewer calories.

MIMI: My husband is on a diet now. The doctor recommended it to him. He doesn't touch anything sweet.

RITA: My husband is also overweight. Men! They don't know how to take care of themselves!

EXERCISES

ANSWERS p. 195

A. Complete the story using the information from the dialogue.

Rita y Mimi son dos amigas y están en el (1) _____ para hacer las (2) _____ de la semana. Mimi prefiere los (3) _____ pequeños porque la (4) _____ mejor allí, donde conoce a los (5) _____ . Rita viene al supermercado

(6) _____ porque los precios son más (7) _____, y
hay más variedad de (8) _____. Mimi cree que es buena idea no
andar de (9) _____ en mercado. Las chuletas de (10) _____
están a 3,50 el kilo, y además no tienen ninguna (11) _____.
Rita compra un (12) _____ de chuletas de cuatro kilos y medio.
La carne de res tiene buena (13) _____, y sólo tiene un 7
(14) _____ de grasa; por eso Mimi compra seis kilos de carne de
(15) _____ y dos kilos de (16) _____. En casa de
Rita comen mucho (17) _____ asado, por eso compra una
(18) _____ para asarla el domingo para todos.

Después las dos señoras hablan de las verduras del supermercado. Rita
dice que son muy (19) _____, como los (20) _____
(*cucumbers*) y las (21) _____ (*carrots*), y especialmente la fruta.
Mimi no puede ver los vegetales en (22) _____ porque no
(23) _____ a nada, y a Rita tampoco le gustan (*like*) las latas,
excepto el (24) _____. Los hijos de Mimi prefieren la fruta al
(25) _____, y Rita dice que es más (26) _____
porque tiene menos calorías. El esposo de Mimi está (27) _____
porque se lo recomendó el doctor, y por eso no toca nada de (28) _____.
El marido de Rita también está pasado (29) _____. ¡Ay los
hombres! ¡No se (30) _____ nada a la hora de comer!

**ANSWERS
p. 195**

B. Underline the word that best completes the sentence.

1. La carne de res va bien con (el pescado, el vino tinto, el jugo de tomate, los burritos).

2. De merienda prefiero (maíz picante, chuletas de cerdo, un bocadillo de pavo, zanahorias fritas).

3. Este cordero asado está (lleno, pálido, estupendo, tinto).

4. En los países tropicales hay un plato de (plátanos fritos, burritos asados, pepino fresco, cordero asado).

5. Los ingleses tienen la costumbre de beber mucho (café, té, leche, jugo).

6. En México se comen muchas tortillas de (zanahoria, pavo, cordero, maíz).

7. Prefiero poner (ajo, frijoles, queso, pastel) en mi hamburguesa.

8. En Estados Unidos son populares los sángüiches de (ternera, atún, cerdo, cordero).

9. Una vaca joven es un/una (res, chuleta, cordero, ternera).

10. Las verduras de (leche, cebolla, lata, paquete) no están frescas y no saben a nada.

11. Si estás a dieta de vegetales no debes comer (verduras, grasas, más, guisantes).

12. El azúcar tiene muchas (proteínas, calorías, grasas, peras).

13. Un vegetal tropical muy popular es (el plátano, la manzana, el guisante, el aguacate).

14. El atún es un tipo de (carne, vegeral, pescado, fruta).

C. **Match the two columns.**

1. _____ Una... española tiene papas, jamón, huevo.

2. _____ La hamburguesa se hace con... de res.

3. _____ En México y Guatemala se comen muchos...

4. _____ El... es más grande que el pollo.

5. _____ La carne de... es más tierna que la de vaca.

6. _____ El pavo de México es el... que es palabra azteca.

7. _____ Prefiero el cordero... a la plancha.

8. _____ El... es un producto derivado de la leche.

9. _____ Se comió una buena ensalada de lechuga y...

10. _____ Los tacos se hacen con tortillas de trigo (*wheat*) o de...

11. _____ La comida mexicana es más... que la americana.

12. _____ Las verduras tienen menos... que las carnes.

A. ternera

B. queso

C. picante

D. pepino

E. tortilla

F. maíz

G. guajolote

H. pavo

I. calorías

J. frijoles

K. carne

L. asado

ANSWERS p. 195

D. **Form sentences using the words in the order given. Write all the verbs in the preterite. Add words when necessary. Watch out for agreement.**

1. Rita / buscar / el / verduras / más / fresco /.

   _____

2. ellas / salir de compras / supermercado / en / carro /.

   _____

3. domingo pasado / yo / pescar / en mar /.

   _____

4. ¿cuándo / vender / tú / tu / libros / viejo /.

   _____

5. nuestro / tías / merendar / este / restaurante /.

   _____

GRAMMAR I   Preterite of Stem-Changing Verbs

A. Memorize the preterite forms of *dormir, pedir,* and *sentir.*

Subject	*dorm ir*	*ped ir*	*sent ir*	(English)
yo	dorm í	ped í	sent í	I slept, I did sleep
tú	dorm iste	ped iste	sent iste	you slept, you did sleep
él/ella/ Ud.	d*u*rm ió	p*i*d ió	s*i*nt ió	he/she/you slept, he/she/you did sleep
nosotros(as)	dorm imos	ped imos	sent imos	we slept, we did sleep
ellos/ellas/Uds.	d*u*rm ieron	p*i*d ieron	s*i*nt ieron	they/you slept, they/you did sleep

Note that:

1. The preterite of *dormir* changes *o* to *u* only in the third person, singular and plural. *Morir* shows the same change in the stem: **murió → murieron.**

2. *Pedir* and *sentir* change *e* to *i* in the third person, singular and plural. Remember that *pedir* has this change in the present: **pido, pides, pide, piden,** BUT **pedimos.** Similarly, *Sentir* changes *e* to *ie* in the present: **siento, sientes, siente, sienten,** BUT **sentimos.**

B. Look at some more stem-changing verbs and review their meaning. Notice that they are all **-ir** verbs. Remember that the vowels in parentheses remind you of the change.

divertir (ie, i) to have fun   **pedir (i)** to ask for
preferir (ie, i) to prefer   **seguir (i)** to follow
sentir (ie, i) to feel, sense   **servir (i)** to serve
repetir (i) to repeat   **vestir (i)** to dress

1. The verbs marked with (ie, i) change *e* to *ie* in the present and *e* to *i* in the preterite.

   EX: **sentir → siente** (*he/she feels*), **sintió** (*he/she felt*)

2. The verbs marked with (i) change *e* to *i* in the present and also in the preterite.

   EX: **pedir → pide** (*he/she asks for*), **pidió** (*he/she asked for*)

3. The stem-changing verbs ending in **-ar** and **-er** change the stem in the present but not in the preterite:

   EX: **volver → vuelve** (*he/she returns*), BUT **volvió** (*he/she returned*)

PRACTIQUE EL PRETÉRITO

1. The stem of *dormir* is _____, and the stem of *durmió* is _____. There has been a change in the stem from o to _____.

2. *Pedir* has the stem _____, and the stem of *pidieron* is _____. The *e* has changed to _____. How do you say *he asked for*? (Remember that you don't translate *for!*) _____.

3. *Morir* is a stem-changing verb like _____. How do you say *he died*? _____. How do you say *they died*? _____.

4. *Sentir* (*ie, i*) is also a stem-changing verb. In the present it changes *e* to _____; for example, **yo** _____. In the preterite it changes *e* to _____ in the third person singular and plural; for example, **él** _____ (*he felt*).

5. Stem-changing verbs with changes both in the present and the preterite belong to the _____ conjugation—in other words, they end in **-ir.** Verbs ending in **-ar** and **-er** change the stem in the present but not in the _____.

6. *Volver* changes o to **ue** in the present; for example, **yo** _____ and **ella** _____. However, there is no change in the preterite: **él** _____.

7. *Dormir* (*ue, u*) has a double change in the stem. In the present it changes o to _____; for example, **ella** _____ (*sleeps*). In the preterite it changes o to _____; for example, **ella** _____ and **ellas** _____.

EXERCISES

ANSWERS p. 196

A. Complete each sentence with the correct preterite form of the verb in parentheses. (Don't forget the reflexive pronoun if the verb is reflexive.)

1. Mi tío _____ mal después del viaje, pero yo _____ muy bien. (*sentirse*)

2. ¿Cuándo _____ tu abuelo en Chile? (*morir*)

3. Los Arana _____ una comida peruana el sábado pasado. (*servir*)

4. Nosotros _____ café, y ella _____ un refresco. (*pedir*)

5. Cecilia _____ cinco horas anoche, pero nosotros _____ ocho horas. (*dormir*)

6. Mi esposa _____ en una hora, pero yo _____ en diez minutos. (*vestirse*)

7. En la Guerra Civil _____ muchos inocentes. (*morir*)

8. Carlitos _____ una hamburguesa, y yo _____ dos tacos. (*preferir*)

9. ¿Cuántes veces _____ usted el ejercicio? Yo lo _____ cinco veces. (*repetir*)

10. Todos los muchachos _____ en la fiesta. (*divertirse*)

ANSWERS
p. 196

B. Change the verbs from present to preterite. Write only the verb.

1. Diana vuelve a casa de sus padres, y prefiere vivir con ellos por un tiempo.

   _____

2. Cuando me siento enfermo, me llevan a ver al médico enseguida.

   _____

3. Ellas se divierten mucho en la fiesta, y piden más champán.

   _____

4. Arturo se despierta temprano esta mañana y se viste en seguida.

   _____

5. Cuando llego al supermercado, sigo hasta la sección de la carne.

   _____

6. Este señor vive como un rico, pero muere como un pobre.

   _____

7. Por la noche me quito la ropa y me acuesto a dormir.

   _____

GRAMMAR II   Preterite of Irregular Verbs

A. Memorize the preterite forms of *ser/ir, dar, venir, decir,* and *estar.*

Subject	*ser/ir*	*d ar*	*ven ir*	*dec ir*	*est ar*
yo	fu i	d i	vin e	dij e	estuv e
tú	fu iste	d iste	vin iste	dij iste	estuv iste
él/ella/ Ud.	fu e	d io	vin o	dij o	estuv o
nosotros(as)	fu imos	d imos	vin imos	dij imos	estuv imos
ellos/ellas/Uds.	fu eron	d ieron	vin ieron	dij eron	estuv ieron

Note that:

1. *Ser* and *ir* have identical forms in the preterite. We need a context to distinguish between them.

   EXS: **El año pasado *fui* a Colombia. (*I <u>went</u> to Colombia last year.*)**
   ** *Fui* camarero en Washington. (*I <u>was</u> a waiter in Washington.*)**

2. *Dar* is irregular because it doesn't take the endings of the -ar verbs, but rather of the -er verbs. This is the only cross-conjugation in the Spanish verb system.

3. Notice that **fui, fue / di, dio** don't take an accent because they have only one syllable. The same rule applies to **va, ve / vi, vio** (*he saw*).

4. *Venir, decir,* and *estar* are irregular for two reasons:
   a) They have changes in the stem: ven-/vin-, dec-/dij-, est-/estuv-.
   b) They have special endings in the first and third person singular: *e* instead of *í* and *o* instead of *ió.*

5. *Decir* takes the ending **-eron** rather than **-ieron**. This same change occurs with the verbs for which the stem of the preterite ends in *j,* such as **traer: traje, trajeron.**

C. The following verbs are irregular in the preterite, with the same kinds of change in the endings as **venir, decir,** and **estar.** Pay attention to the changes in the stems.

andar → anduve, anduvo	poner → puse, puso
conducir → conduje, condujo	producir → produje, produjo
deshacer → deshice, deshizo	querer → quise, quiso
detener → detuve, detuvo	saber → supe, supo
haber → hube, hubo	tener → tuve, tuvo
hacer → hice, hizo	traer → traje, trajo
poder → pude, pudo	estar → estuve, estuvo

1. *Hacer* has the stem **hic-** in the preterite, and the *c* changes to *z* in *hizo.* This is a spelling change similar to that of **comenzar → comencé.**

2. Most of the verbs above have compound forms that share the same changes of the simple verbs.

   EXS: **poner → puse / componer → compuse / imponer → impuse**

3. All verbs ending in -ducir, like **producir** and **conducir,** change the *c* to *j* in the preterite; and the ending -ieron shortens to -eron.

   EX: **conducir → conduje, condujeron**

PRACTIQUE EL PRETÉRITO

ANSWERS
p. 196

1. *Dijo* is a preterite form, and it means *he/she said; digo* is a _____ indicative form, and it means _____.

2. From *saber* we say **yo sé** (*I know*) in the present. How would you say *I knew* in the preterite? _____.

3. *Hacer* has a triple stem: **hac-** in the infinitive, _____ and _____ in the preterite.

4. *Dijeron* has an irregular ending because the *j* "swallows up" the vowel
   _____. So instead of **-ieron,** the ending is _____.

5. All the verbs ending in **-ducir** change the *c* to _____ in the preterite.
   How would you say *they drove* (from **conducir**)? _____.

6. *Ponió* (from **poner**) is incorrect. It should be _____.

7. *Trajieron* is not correct. It should be _____ because of the *j*.

8. *Vino* (*he/she came*) and **vino** (*wine*) show the same spelling and sounds. How
   can you tell one from another in a conversation or writing? _____.

9. *Yo andé por el parque* sounds like good Spanish, and some native speakers
   of Spanish would say it; but the correct form should be **Yo** _____
   por el parque.

10. *Detener* is a compound of _____. How would you say in Spanish *the
    police stopped the criminal?* **La policía** _____ **al criminal.**

11. *Fue* means two things because it belongs to two verbs: _____ /
    _____. The reason is that **ser** and _____ share the same forms
    in the preterite.

12. *Dar* is irregular in the preterite because it follows the conjugation of **-er**
    verbs rather than _____ verbs. For example, we don't say **ellos daron**
    like **hablaron** but **ellos** _____.

13. *Dió* and *fué* are misspelled because of the _____. They must be
    spelled _____ and _____ because they have only one syllable.

EXERCISES

A. Fill in the blanks with the correct forms of the preterite.

1. Mi tía no _____ vender el carro viejo. (*to be able to*)

2. ¿Quién _____ los frijoles y los tacos en la mesa? (*to put*)

3. Lolita _____ ir, pero no _____. (*to want/to be able to*)

4. México y Venezuela _____ mucho petróleo. (*to produce*)

5. ¿Dónde _____ (tú) ayer todo el día? (*to be*)

6. Ellos _____ que no, pero yo _____ que sí. (*to say*)

7. ¿Quién _____ el primer presidente de Estados Unidos? (*to be*)

8. Diana _____ la torta y yo _____ la ensalada. (*to make*)

9. Rita _____ al supermercado después de desayunar. (*to go*)

10. Esteban y yo _____ a la universidad en carro. (*to come*)

11. Cuando él _____ a su esposa, no _____ qué decir. (*to see / to know*)

12. Los muchachos _____ un problema con el carro. (*to have*)

ANSWERS p. 196

B. **Change the verbs from present to preterite.**

Margarita no (1) anda al trabajo esta mañana sino que (*but*) (2) conduce su carro nuevo. Hoy no (3) está en su oficina a las ocho en punto como de costumbre, porque (4) tiene que preparar el desayuno a su hijo. Después que (5) llega, (6) deja las cosas en la mesa y (7) se pone a trabajar. Sus amigas (8) hacen café y le (9) traen una taza. Ella les (10) dice mil gracias y (11) toma su café sin crema y sin azúcar. En ese momento (12) suena el teléfono...

1. _____	5. _____	9. _____
2. _____	6. _____	10. _____
3. _____	7. _____	11. _____
4. _____	8. _____	12. _____

GRAMMAR III   Idiomatic Expressions with Verbs *hay, hay que, acabar de, ponerse a*

A. To indicate the idea of *there is / there are,* we use **hay** from the verb **haber.** In the preterite we use **hubo** for *there was / there were.*

EXS: *Hay* buenas chuletas aquí. (*There are good pork chops here.*)
El viernes *hubo* una fiesta. (*There was a party on Friday.*)

B. *Estar* is used with a *definite* noun. *Hay* and *hubo* are used with an *indefinite* noun.

EXS: *Hay un* taco en la mesa. (*There is a taco on the table.*)
Está el taco en la mesa. (*The taco is on the table.*)

C. *Hay* and *hubo* are used with a noun (**sol, calor, viento, buen tiempo**) to decribe the *weather.* They have the same meaning, just like *hace* and *hizo.*

EXS: Esta mañana *hay* (*hace*) calor. (*It's hot this morning.*)
Ayer *hubo* (*hizo*) mucho viento. (*It was very windy yesterday.*)

D. *Hay que* (+ infinitive) indicates obligation to do something, just like *tener que,* but without a specific subject, such as **yo, tú,** and so on.

EXS: *Hay que* estudiar mucho. (*It's necessary to study hard.*)
Tengo que estudiar mucho. (*I have to study hard.*)

E. *Acabar de* (+ infinitive) indicates that the action just took place: "to have just done something."

> EX: José *acaba de salir* para casa. (*José just left for home.*)

F. *Ponerse a* (+ infinitive) indicates the beginning of an action with more determination or speed than *comenzar. Ponerse a* can be used in the preterite and other tenses.

> EX: Cuando llegó *se puso a escribir* una carta. (*When he arrived, he started writing a letter.*)

G. *Ponerse* (+ adjective) carries the idea of *to turn red, pale, hysterical.* It suggests a sudden change. The adjective has to agree with the subject of the sentence in gender and number.

> EX: Cuando Elena vio al policía, *se puso* roja. (*When Helen saw the policeman, she turned red.*)

PRACTIQUE LOS MODISMOS (*Idioms*)

ANSWERS
p. 196

1. To translate *there is / there are,* we use the present of *haber:* _____.
   For the past *there was / there were,* we use the preterite: _____.

2. *Estar* is used to indicate the location of people and things, but the noun has to be _____. A noun is made definite with a definite article, a short possessive (like **mi, tu, su**), or a demonstrative (like **este, ese**)

3. *Hay* and *hubo* are third-person singular forms from the verb _____, and they indicate the location of an _____ noun.

4. *Está un libro aquí* is incorrect. If we keep the indefinite **un libro,** we must change *está* to _____.

5. *Hay que* (+ infinitive) carries the idea of _____ to do something, but in an impersonal way, since there is not a specific subject involved.

6. To describe the weather, we can use *hace* as well as _____ in the present, and *hizo* and _____ in the preterite.

7. *Hay muy viento* is incorrect, because **viento** is a noun; you have to change the adverb **muy** to the adjective _____.

8. *Acabar* means *to finish,* and *acabar de* (+ infinitive) shows that the action has _____.

9. *Ponerse a* (+ infinitive) means to _____ an action with determination or speed.

10. How do you say idiomatically **He began to eat (suddenly)?**
    _____.

EXERCISES

ANSWERS
p. 196

A. Combine each expression from column 1 with expressions from column 3. You may need a word from column 2. Write your answers in the blanks provided for each expression. (Note that each expression has three possible combinations except for number 5, which has one, and number 6, which has two.)

Hay		
Está		practicar
Hubo		una fiesta aquí
Acabamos	de	viento
Hace	que	alegre
Carlota se puso	a	el libro aquí
Me pongo		pálido
Tenemos		

1. Hay una fiesta aquí.

   Hay _____.

   Hay _____.

2. Está _____.

   Está _____.

   Está _____.

3. Hubo _____.

   Hubo _____.

   Hubo _____.

4. Acabamos _____.

   Acabamos _____.

   Acabamos _____.

5. Hace _____.

6. Carlota se puso _____.

   Carlota se puso _____.

7. Me pongo _____.

   Me pongo _____.

   Me pongo _____.

8. Tenemos _____.

    Tenemos _____.

    Tenemos _____.

ANSWERS
p. 197

B. Complete the sentences with *a, de,* or *que.* Write *X* where nothing is necessary.

1. Hay _____ comer hamburguesas esta tarde.

2. Ella quiere _____ invitarte _____ su fiesta de cumpleaños.

3. Rita se puso _____ trabajar después que llegó.

4. Jorge dejó _____ fumar la semana pasada.

5. ¿Usted acaba _____ llegar de Europa?

6. No puedo _____ ir con ella, porque tengo _____ trabajar hoy.

7. Cuando vi _____ Carlos, me puse _____ pálido.

8. Ayer traté _____ llamarte por la tarde _____ tu casa.

9. Nosotros quisimos _____ parar, pero no pudimos.

10. Pepe acabó _____ salir cuando llegó su novia.

11. Cuando estoy _____ dieta, debo _____ comer poco.

12. Mi suegra se fue _____ compras temprano.

13. No invité _____ Rosaura porque siempre me dice _____ no.

14. Esta pizza sabe mucho _____ ajo y cebolla.

15. Venimos _____ menudo _____ este supermercado.

9 En un banco de la ciudad de México
(At a Bank in Mexico City)

el banco	bank	el gasto	expense
el billete	bill, ticket	el giro (postal)	money order
el/la cajero(a)	cashier	giro internacional	international money order
la cartera	wallet, purse		
el centavo	cent	la hipoteca	mortgage
el cheque[1]	check	el impuesto	tax
la chequera	checkbook	la moneda	currency, coin
la cuenta	account	la necesidad	need
cuenta corriente	checking account	el préstamo	loan
cuenta de ahorros	savings account	el presupuesto	budget
		el salario[3]	salary
el dinero	money	el sueldo	salary
la divisa	foreign money	la tarjeta de crédito	credit card
la factura[2]	bill, invoice	la tienda	store
la ganancia	earnings	el valor[4]	value, stock
la ganga	bargain		

agradar	to please	gustar	to like
ahorrar	to save	importar[5]	to matter
alegrarse	to be happy	interesar	to interest
aumentar	to increase	meter	to put into
cargar	to load, charge	nadar	to swim
convenir (ie)	to suit	parecer[6]	to seem
descrubrir	to discover	prestar	to lend
disfrutar de	to enjoy	quejarse	to complain
encantar	to like, please	reducir	to reduce
encontrar (ue)	to find	sacar	to take out
faltar	to miss	sobrar	to be left (over)
ganar	to win, earn	valer	to be worth
gastar	to spend	**valer la pena**	to be worthwhile

actual[7]	present	necesario(a)	necessary
agradecido(a)	thankful	encantado(a)	pleased
débil	weak	serio(a)	serious
fuerte	strong	valioso(a)	valuable
lujoso(a)	luxurious		

a fines de	at the end of	¡ni modo!	no way!
a plazos	in installments	un par de	a couple of
a propósito	by the way	por ciento	percent, per cent
al contado	cash (to pay)	por fin	finally
aunque	although	sobre todo[8]	above all
de lujo, lujoso(a)	deluxe, luxurious		

NOTAS

1. *Cheque* is the word used in Latin America for check, *talón* is the word used in Spain. *Checkbook* is *talonario* in Spain, and *chequera* in Latin America.

2. *Factura* is the commercial word for *bill,* just like *invoice.* We use *cuenta* when the bill is small, such as those you get in a restaurant, drugstore. Do not confuse it with *billete,* which is used for currency bills as well as for travel tickets.

3. *Salario* was used originally for *low wages,* while *sueldo* was used for *high wages.* Nowadays the two words are interchangeable for *salary.*

4. *Valor* means *value* in general as well as *stock* in the stock market. *La bolsa de valores* translates *the stock market.*

5. *Importar* can be two different things: *to import* (from another country), and *to matter.* With the first meaning, we use *importar* like *hablar,* with different subjects:

yo, tú, and so on. With the second meaning *to matter*, it is used in the third person, like *gustar*, which is explained in the Grammar II section of this lesson.

6. *Parecer* means *to seem, to look like*; the reflexive *parecerse a* means *to take after, resemble*.

EXS: ¿*Te parece* bien el precio? (*Does the price look okay to you?*)
Yo *me parezco* a mi padre. (*I take after my father.*)

7. *Actual* means *present, now*, whereas English *actual* means **real, verdadero**. The same principle applies to **actualmente,** meaning *presently, now*, whereas *actually* is **verdaderamente.**

8. *Sobre todo* is an adverb meaning *above all*, whereas **el sobretodo** is the overcoat.

9. There is an important difference between the banking system in the United States and that in Latin America and Spain. A personal check in the United States is backed by the law, and a bad check is liable to a penalty; whereas in Latin America a check is not backed by the law, it's simply a paper whose value is based on trust between the bank and the client. Obviously the bank doesn't pay any interest on these accounts.

PRACTIQUE LAS PALABRAS NUEVAS

ANSWERS p. 197

A. Write *el, la, los,* or *las* before each noun.

1. _____ billete	5. _____ fin	9. _____ ahorros
2. _____ cheques	6. _____ valor	10. _____ divisas
3. _____ necesidad	7. _____ impuestos	11. _____ ganancia
4. _____ interés	8. _____ tiendas	12. _____ fines

ANSWERS p. 197

B. *Word families.* Write one word related to each of the following.

1. ahorros _____	10. alegre _____
2. encantado _____	11. interés _____
3. valioso _____	12. lujo _____
4. conveniente _____	13. préstamo _____
5. centavo _____	14. cheque _____
6. necesitar _____	15. cuenta (ue=o) _____
7. encargarse _____	16. ganar _____
8. gasto _____	17. pareja _____
9. peso _____	18. importancia _____

ANSWERS
p. 197

C. Fill in the blanks with one of the following words or expressions. You may need the plural forms of nouns and adjectives. Use the verbs in the present or preterite according to the context.

ahorrar	de lujo	ganar	moneda	préstamo
a plazos	descubrir	ganga	nadar	tienda
cartera	divisa	giro postal	por ciento	un par de

1. Necesito un _____ del banco para comprar un coche nuevo.

2. Muchas personas creen que el Cadillac es un carro _____.

3. El 8 _____ de doscientos es dieciséis, ¿no es cierto?

4. La _____ de México es el peso, y la de España, la peseta.

5. Es más difícil (*difficult*) _____ dinero que gastarlo.

6. El turismo trae muchas _____ a México y a España.

7. Tengo cinco billetes de un dólar en mi _____.

8. ¿Cuánto _____ usted de salario por semana?

9. Si hay sol mañana, vamos a _____ al mar.

10. ¿Puedes prestarme _____ dólares para comer algo?

11. En esta tienda todo está barato. Hay muchas _____.

12. Me gusta pagar las facturas _____ y no al contado.

13. Cristóbal Colón _____ América en 1492.

14. Mi tía me mandó (*sent*) un _____ de treinta dólares.

15. En esta _____ solamente vendemos pescado y mariscos.

ANSWERS
p. 197

D. Complete each sentence with one of the verbs below. Use the preterite tense.

alegrarse	cargar	gastar	prestar	sacar
aumentar	encontrar	meter	quejarse	valer

1. Mi novia me _____ su carro porque el mío se descompuso (*broke*).

2. Los empleados _____ del sueldo bajo que les pagan.

3. Cuando volví del trabajo, _____ el carro en el garaje.

4. Tus amigos _____ de tu buena suerte en la lotería.

5. Algunos conquistadores _____ oro (*gold*) en América y se hicieron ricos.

6. Los bancos _____ los intereses con las buenas noticias (*news*) económicas.

7. (Yo) _____ un billete de mi cartera y pagué la cuenta.

8. Mi tío vendió la casa y le _____ como 150 mil dólares.

9. Julián no ahorró nada; al contrario, lo _____ todo.

10. Los empleados _____ los paquetes en la camioneta (*pickup*).

ANSWERS p. 198

E. Write *true* or *false* (T / F).

1. _____ Abrimos una cuenta de ahorros en una tienda de mariscos.

2. _____ Una cuenta corriente da más interés que una cuenta de ahorros.

3. _____ Lo contrario de reducir el interés es aumentarlo.

4. _____ Cuando Ud. está muy feliz, Ud. está encantado.

5. _____ George Washington está en los billetes de veinte dólares.

6. _____ Lo contrario de **fuerte** es **valioso**.

7. _____ Si un americano gasta dólares en México, deja divisas en México.

8. _____ Si Ud. compra a plazos, tiene que pagar facturas todos los meses.

9. _____ En algunos estados de la Unión no se pagan impuestos federales.

10. _____ Una hipoteca es un préstamo grande para pagar a largo plazo.

11. _____ Vale la pena hacer dieta si uno está pasado de peso.

12. _____ Estados Unidos importa muchas bananas de Latinoamérica.

DIÁLOGO   En un banco de la ciudad de México

Susana es de Estados Unidos y acaba de llegar a México para estudiar un año allí y conocer el país. Entra a un banco para cambiar dinero y abrir una cuenta corriente.

CAJERO: Buenos días, señorita. ¿En qué puedo servirle?

SUSANA: Necesito cambiar quinientos dólares a pesos. ¿A cómo está el cambio?

CAJERO: Hoy está a 6,20 el dólar si está en cheques de viajero y a 6,10 si está en moneda.

SUSANA: ¡Qué suerte! Traigo todo mi dinero en cheques de viajero.

CAJERO: El banco cobra el 1 por ciento de comisión. Por favor, necesito el número de su pasaporte para poder cambiarle el dinero.

SUSANA: Aquí lo tiene. También quiero abrir una cuenta corriente. ¿Cuánto pagan de interés en una cuenta corriente?

CAJERO: Aquí solamente pagamos interés en las cuentas de ahorros. ¿Cuánto dinero va a depositar?

SUSANA: Este giro postal de quinientos dólares y quinientos más en cheques de viajero. A propósito, ¿me pueden hacer un préstamo si algún día lo necesito?

CAJERO: Sí, si tiene una tarjeta de crédito, y el préstamo no es muy grande, como una hipoteca.

SUSANA: No, no pensaba comprarme un piso aquí. Pero me gusta pagar a plazos mejor que al contado.

CAJERO: Sí, claro. ¡Ustedes los americanos viven del futuro!

SUSANA: ¡Ni modo! Yo vine a México a descubrir los valores del pasado.

CAJERO: Pues a los mexicanos nos gusta vivir y disfrutar del presente.

DIALOGUE   At a Bank in Mexico City

Susan is from the United States and has just arrived in Mexico to study there for one year and get to know the country. She goes into a bank.

TELLER: Good morning, miss. How can I help you?

SUSAN: I need to change five hundred dollars to pesos. What's the rate of exchange?

TELLER: Today the rate is 6.20 to the dollar if it's traveler's checks, and 6.10 if it's currency.

SUSAN: How lucky! All my money is in traveler's checks!

TELLER: The bank charges a commission of 1 percent. I need the number of your passport to exchange the money, please.

SUSAN: Here it is. I also want to open a checking account. How much interest do you pay on checking accounts?

TELLER: Here we only pay interest on the savings accounts. How much money are you going to deposit?

SUSAN: This money order for five hundred dollars and five hundred dollars more in traveler's checks. By the way, can I get a loan if I need it some day?

TELLER: Sure, if you have a credit card and the loan is not a big one, like for a mortgage.

SUSAN: No, I'm not thinking of buying an apartment here. However, I like to pay in installments rather than in cash.

TELLER: Of course. You Americans live in the future!

SUSAN: No way! I came to Mexico to discover the values of the past!

TELLER: Well, we Mexicans like to live and enjoy the present.

NOTES

1. The reason for asking for the passport number is to find out if you are a foreigner or a tourist living in another country. There are strict international regulations as to the amount of money you can "import" or "export."

2. Traveler's checks have a higher exchange rate than currency in most of the countries. I have asked why in Madrid, and I was told that the exchange operations between banks were easier with traveler's checks. In Mexico I was told that the consumer had to buy the traveler's checks and pay for them, and therefore the exchange had to be higher. Your guess is as good as mine!

EXERCISES

ANSWERS p. 198

A. **Complete the story with the information from the dialogue. Imagine that everything happened in the past, and use the verbs in the preterite unless the infinitive is needed.**

Susana es de Estados Unidos y llegó a México para (1) _____ un año allí y para (2) _____ el país. Ella (3) _____ a un banco para (4) _____ quinientos dólares a pesos. Un (5) _____ atendió a Susana en la operación bancaria. Ese día el (6) _____ estaba (*was*) a 6,20 pesos por los cheques de viajero y a 6,10 la (7) _____. Susana (8) _____ suerte porque solamente traía (*brought*) cheques de (9) _____ de EE UU. El banco le (10) _____ una comisión del 1 por (11) _____. El cajero le pidió el (12) _____ a Susana para escribir su número y nombre en la transacción.

Susana (13) _____ una cuenta corriente con un (14) _____ postal de quinientos dólares y otros quinientos dólares en (15) _____ de viajero. El cajero le (16) _____ a Susana que en México las cuentas (17) _____ no ganan interés, per sí las cuentas de (18) _____. También le informó que, si tiene una tarjeta de crédito, el banco le puede dar un (19) _____, pero no una hipoteca. A Susana le gusta pagar (20) _____, no al contado; por eso el cajero le dijo que los americanos viven del (21) _____, pero Susana dice que (22) _____ a México a descubrir los valores del pasado. El cajero le informó que los mexicanos prefieren vivir y (23) _____ del presente.

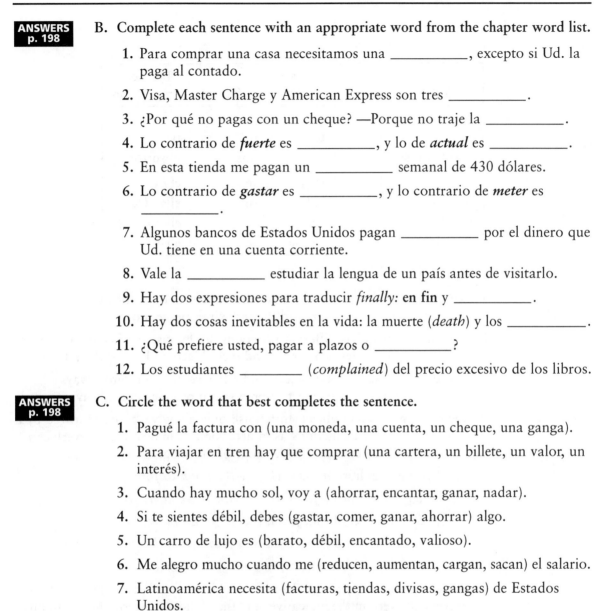

ANSWERS
p. 198 B. **Complete each sentence with an appropriate word from the chapter word list.**

1. Para comprar una casa necesitamos una _____, excepto si Ud. la paga al contado.

2. Visa, Master Charge y American Express son tres _____.

3. ¿Por qué no pagas con un cheque? —Porque no traje la _____.

4. Lo contrario de *fuerte* es _____, y lo de *actual* es _____.

5. En esta tienda me pagan un _____ semanal de 430 dólares.

6. Lo contrario de *gastar* es _____, y lo contrario de *meter* es _____.

7. Algunos bancos de Estados Unidos pagan _____ por el dinero que Ud. tiene en una cuenta corriente.

8. Vale la _____ estudiar la lengua de un país antes de visitarlo.

9. Hay dos expresiones para traducir *finally:* **en fin** y _____.

10. Hay dos cosas inevitables en la vida: la muerte (*death*) y los _____.

11. ¿Qué prefiere usted, pagar a plazos o _____?

12. Los estudiantes _____ (*complained*) del precio excesivo de los libros.

ANSWERS
p. 198 C. **Circle the word that best completes the sentence.**

1. Pagué la factura con (una moneda, una cuenta, un cheque, una ganga).

2. Para viajar en tren hay que comprar (una cartera, un billete, un valor, un interés).

3. Cuando hay mucho sol, voy a (ahorrar, encantar, ganar, nadar).

4. Si te sientes débil, debes (gastar, comer, ganar, ahorrar) algo.

5. Un carro de lujo es (barato, débil, encantado, valioso).

6. Me alegro mucho cuando me (reducen, aumentan, cargan, sacan) el salario.

7. Latinoamérica necesita (facturas, tiendas, divisas, gangas) de Estados Unidos.

8. Mis sobrinos (gustan, se alegran, se parecen, se agradan) a su madre.

GRAMMAR I   Indirect Object Pronouns

A. When you give a book to a friend, *friend* functions as the indirect object (IO) and *book* as the direct object (DO). In Spanish when a noun functions as the indirect object, it always takes the preposition *a:* **Usted dio el libro a su amiga.**

B. In this chart we see the direct object, indirect object, reflexive, and object-of-preposition pronouns.

Subject	Direct Object	Indirect Object	Reflexive	Object of Preposition
yo	me	me	me	mí
tú	te	te	te	ti
nosotros(as)	nos	nos	nos	nosotros
él/Ud.	lo	le (se)	se	él / Ud.
ella/Ud.	la	le (se)	se	ella / Ud.
ellos/Uds.	los	les (se)	se	ellos / Uds.
ellas/Uds.	las	les (se)	se	ellas / Uds.

Note that:

1. The first and second persons have the same pronouns for the direct object, the indirect object, and the reflexive: **me, te, nos.**

2. The third person has different pronouns: **lo, la, los,** and **las** for the direct object; **le (se)** and **les (se)** for the indirect object; and **se** for the reflexive.

3. The direct object, indirect object, and reflexive pronouns are always unstressed; whereas the object-of-preposition pronouns are always stressed.

C. **Meaning of the indirect object.** In English only a few verbs are followed by a noun or pronoun that functions as indirect object. In Spanish any verb can take an indirect object with a wide range of meanings.

1. BENEFIT: *Le di el libro a Juan.* (*I gave the book to John.*)

2. LOSS: *Le quité el libro a Juan.* (*I took the book away from John.*)

3. POSSESSION: *Le vi el libro a Juan.* (*I saw John's book.*)

4. GENERAL INTEREST: *Le gusta el libro a Juan.* (*John likes the book.*)

D. Direct object and indirect object pronouns in the same sentence:

1. If both the direct object and the indirect object nouns become pronouns, they precede the verb in the indicative, and they follow the verb in the infinitive.

   EXS: Ella *me* dio el libro *a mí.* → Ella *me lo* dio. (*She gave it to me.*)
   Ella va a darme el libro a mí. → Ella va a dár*melo.* (*She is going to give it to me.*)

2. The indirect object pronoun precedes the direct object, either with the indicative or the infinitive.

   EX: Ella va a dár*melo.* → Ella *me lo* va a dar. (*She will give it to me.*)

3. If both the direct object and the indirect object are third person, the indirect object pronouns *le, les* become *se* as shown in parentheses in the

chart. The indirect object pronoun precedes the direct object.

EX: **Juan dio el lápiz a su amiga.** → **Juan** *le lo* **dio.** → **Juan** *se lo* **dio.**

E. The pronouns used as object of prepositions can be added to the direct object and indirect object to add emphasis: **Ud. me vio a mí** is more emphatic than **Ud. me vio.**

Ud. vio a mí is incorrect. It needs *me* before the verb: **Ud me vio a mí.** This means that we cannot use the object-of-preposition pronouns for direct object and indirect object without the matching unstressed pronoun: **me, te, le, lo, la,** and so on.

F. When the indirect object is a noun, one often adds the corresponding pronoun *le, les* to anticipate the noun. It is not obligatory.

EX: **Le di el libro a Juan** is more frequent than **Di el libro a Juan.**

PRACTIQUE LOS PRONOMBRES

ANSWERS p. 198

1. The pronouns *me, te, nos* are the same for the reflexive, the direct object, and the _____.

2. The pronouns *lo/la, los/las,* are third person direct object pronouns; _____ are indirect object pronouns, and *se* is the only _____ pronoun for the third person.

3. The indirect object has a wide range of uses and meanings in Spanish, such as benefit, loss, possession, and general _____ or involvement.

4. Do the direct object pronouns precede or follow the indirect object pronouns? _____. The two pronouns stay together before the verb in the _____ tenses, such as present, preterite, future, and so on.

5. If the infinitive follows the indicative in the same sentence, the direct object, indirect object, and reflexive pronouns may precede the _____ or follow the _____.

6. The indirect object pronouns *le, les,* become _____ when they are in front of any of the four direct object pronouns *lo/la, los/las.* Therefore, *Le lo vendo a ella* is wrong. The correct version is _____ a ella. (*I'm selling it to her.*)

7. The sentence *Te vi ayer con tu novia* is less _____ than *Te vi ayer a ti con tu novia.* It seems obvious because *te* and *a ti* are a repetition of the same information.

8. If the indirect object is a noun instead of a pronoun, we frequently anticipate this noun with the unstressed pronouns _____, but it's not obligatory.

9. *Yo invité a ella* is not correct. We have to add _____ in front of *invité.*

EXERCISES

ANSWERS p. 198 A. Complete each sentence with a direct or indirect object pronoun.

1. Elena _____ prestó el carro a su hija.

2. ¿Por qué tú no _____ dijiste la verdad a mí?

3. Señora, se _____ cayó la cartera a usted.

4. Creo que mi hijo no _____ dijo toda la verdad a nosotros.

5. El carro se _____ paró a mí en la avenida (*avenue*).

6. A tu novio, ¿_____ gusta la comida italiana?

7. ¿Dónde está mi chequera? —_____ dejaste en casa.

8. ¿Estos libros? —_____ compré en la universidad.

9. ¿Los boletos del teatro? —_____ di a Carmen.

10. ¿Las monedas? —_____ dejé a mi hijo para su colección.

11. ¿_____ gusta nadar a ustedes?

12. A mí _____ encanta el pastel de chocolate.

ANSWERS p. 198 B. Answer the questions changing the direct and indirect object nouns to pronouns. Pay attention to the verbs in present or preterite.

EX: ¿Quién oye la radio? —Yo la oigo.

1. ¿Cuándo vas a pagarme la cuenta? —Mañana voy _____. (*Use the familiar pronoun.*)

2. ¿Cuándo va Ud. a pagarme la cuenta? —El martes voy _____. (*Use the formal pronoun.*)

3. ¿Quién le dio el cheque a Susana? —El cajero _____.

4. ¿Quién le prestó cinco dólares a mi primo? —Cecilia _____.

5. ¿Quién le trajo este flan a mi mamá? —Paco _____.

6. ¿Desea Ud. abrir la ventana? —Sí, _____.

7. ¿Por qué vas a lavarle el coche a tu papá? —Voy a _____ porque él está muy ocupado (*busy*).

8. ¿Aumentó Ud. el sueldo a las camareras? —Sí, yo _____.

9. ¿Dónde quieres poner estas maletas? —Aquí _____.

10. ¿Dónde quieres poner estas maletas? —Aquí _____. (*Answer in another way.*)

ANSWERS
p. 198 C. Form sentences using the words in the order given. Make any changes and add words when necessary, especially the indirect object pronouns. Use the preterite tense.

1. tú / comprar / bocadillos / sabroso / nosotros /.

_____

2. camareros / servir / la comida / pasajeros /.

_____

3. tu / tíos / vender / Volkswagen / mí /.

_____

4. botones / subir / maletas / turistas /.

_____

5. Enrique / prestar / carro / nadie /.

GRAMMAR II   The Indirect Object with *gustar* and with Unplanned Occurrences

A. The sentence *El libro me gusta* translates literally as *The book is pleasing to me*—in everyday English, *I like the book.* *Libro* is the subject and must always have a definite article, a short form of the possessive, or a demonstrative. If we change *libro* to *libros,* we have to change the verb to the plural: **Los libros me gustan.**

Me is an indirect object in *El libro me gusta.* The indirect object is obligatory with *gustar* and verbs like it. Here are examples:

(A mí)   **me** ⎫
(A ti)   **te** ⎬ gusta(n) la(s) casa(s). ⎧ *I like the house(s).*
(A ella) **le** ⎭   ⎨ *You like the house(s).*
                                                ⎩ *She likes the house(s).*

B. There are many verbs in Spanish with a construction like that of *gustar.* Here are some of them.

agradar to like	**interesar** to interest
apetecer to like (*food, drink*)	**molestar** to bother, annoy
convenir to be suitable, be convenient	**ocurrir** to happen, occur
doler (ue) to hurt, ache	**parecer** to seem, look like
encantar to like	**pasar** to happen, to be the matter with
faltar to miss, lack	**sobrar** to be left
importar to matter, be important	**valer la pena** to be worthwhile

C. *Convenir* means both *to agree* and *to be suitable, convenient.* When it means *to agree,* it is conjugated with a regular subject pronoun, like **yo, tú,** and so on. When it means *to be suitable* or *convenient,* it follows the same construction as that of *gustar;* and it is conjugated only in the third person singular and plural.

EXS: **Ella y yo *convinimos* en eso.** (*She and I* <u>agreed</u> *on that.*)
      Ese banco *te conviene* más. (*That bank* <u>is</u> *more* <u>convenient to you</u>.)

Other examples of verbs that work like *gustar* follow.

EXS: **A Lucía *le duelen* las manos.** (*Lucy's hands* <u>hurt</u>.)
      A ellos *les encanta* el helado. (*They like* [*love*] *ice cream.*)
      ¿Qué *te pasa?* (*What* <u>is the matter with you</u>?)

D. **Unplanned occurrences.** When we talk about an action that is or was not planned—especially something unwanted or unpleasant—we use an impersonal construction with *se,* similar to **Se habla español** and the like. We don't plan actions like forgetting, falling, dropping, or breaking. These actions seem to "just happen."

EX: **El vaso *se me cayó.* = *Se me cayó* el vaso.** (*I* <u>dropped</u> *the glass.*)

In this example *vaso* is the subject of *cayó,* and *me* is the indirect object. A literal translation is *The glass dropped itself on me.* If we change *vaso* to the plural **vasos,** *cayó* has to change to *cayeron.* The full sentence is **Se me cayeron los vasos.** More examples:

¿Se *te olvidó* el libro? (*Did you forget the book?*)
¿Se *te olvidaron* los libros? (*Did you forget the books?*)
A Sonia *se le paró* el carro. (*Sonia's car stopped.*)

PRACTIQUE LA GRAMÁTICA

ANSWERS p. 199

1. In a sentence like **Me gusta el libro,** the subject is _____, and the indirect object is _____. If we change *libro* to *libros,* we say _____ los libros.

2. *Usted* and *Ustedes* are second person in meaning (you), but _____ person grammatically . This is why their indirect objects are the pronouns _____.

3. Which is more emphatic, (a) **Me gusta eso** or (b) **A mí me gusta eso?** _____. Any repetition of information seems to be emphatic.

4. If *Me duele la mano* means *My hand hurts,* it seems obvious that the indirect object *me* has been rendered in English by the word _____.

5. When we say **Se me cayó el plato,** *se* is the same impersonal pronoun of **Se habla español.** Notice that *plato* is an _____ noun just like *español.*

6. In *Se me cayó el plato* the pronoun *me* functions as the _____ of the sentence, and it means that *I* (*me*) was involved with the *plato* (*dish*), either because I own it or because I was holding it at the time of the fall. The indirect object can be very ambiguous in Spanish!

7. *Plato* is the subject of the verb in *Se le cayó el plato al niño.* How would you write the sentence with *platos* as subject? _____ los platos al niño.

8. *Parecer* (*to seem*) needs an indirect object like *gustar.* How would you translate *That idea seems good to me?* **Esa idea** _____.

EXERCISES

ANSWERS p. 199

A. Complete the sentences with the verbs suggested. Use the present tense except when the preterite is indicated. Don't forget the indirect object pronouns.

1. A mis padres _____ los camarones a la plancha. (*to like*)

2. ¿Qué _____ a usted en el accidente? —Pues a mí no _____ nada. (*to happen,* preterite)

3. A mí _____ muy simpática la cajera. (*to seem*)

4. Hoy no puedo ir porque _____ la cabeza (*head*). (*to hurt, ache*)

5. Ustedes son muchos; por eso _____ una casa grande. (*to be suitable*)

6. ¿A ti no _____ ahorrar dinero para más tarde? (*to interest*)

7. Este carro viejo siempre _____ en la calle (a mí). (*to stop*)

8. Al camarero _____ los vasos ayer. (*to drop,* preterite)

9. Después de pagar la comida _____ un dólar a ella. (*to be left over*)

10. ¿Quieres un refresco de limón? —Gracias, no _____ en este momento. (*to like*)

11. A mi suegra _____ mucho el cigarrillo. (*to bother, annoy*)

12. A mi esposa y a mí _____ viajar por Europa. (*to like*)

ANSWERS
p. 199

B. Form sentences using the words in the order given. Add any necessary words. Use the present indicative.

1. nadie/gustar/cosas/malo/.

_____

2. tus/abuelos/encantar/comida/español/.

_____

3. alumnos/interesar/clases/bueno/.

_____

4. mí/faltar/dos/dólar/de/cartera/.

_____

5. usted/no/gustar/nadar/en/mar/.

_____

6. A ella/parar/carro en/avenida 5/.

_____

7. ti/caer/dos/billete/de/cinco /dólar/.

_____

ANSWERS
p. 199

C. Translate the following sentences.

1. My children like to listen to the radio.

_____

2. That girl looks very pretty to me.

_____

3. My hands hurt a lot today.

_____

4. What's happening to you today, my son?

_____

5. My watch fell on the floor.

_____

6. Your problems interest me.

_____

7. This class is suitable for her.

_____

GRAMMAR III   The Imperfect Indicative

A. Memorize the the imperfect indicative of the verbs in the chart.

Subject	*habl ar*	*com er*	*viv ir*	*ir*	*s er*	*v er*
yo	habl aba	com ía	viv ía	iba	era	ve ía
tú	habl abas	com ías	viv ías	ibas	eras	ve ías
él/ella/Ud.	habl aba	com ía	viv ía	iba	era	ve ía
nosotros(as)	habl ábamos	com íamos	viv íamos	íbamos	éramos	ve íamos
ellos/ellas/Uds.	habl aban	com ían	viv ían	iban	eran	ve ían

Note that:

1. The stem of *hablar, comer, vivir,* are the same as for the present: **habl-, com-, viv-.** The endings are **-aba** for the -ar verbs, and **-ía** for the -er and -ir verbs. Notice that *-s* is the ending for *tú*, *-mos* for **nosotros,** and *-n* for *ellos, ellas, Uds.*

2. All verbs are regular in the imperfect indicative except *ir, ser* and *ver.* As you can see from the chart, the imperfect, of *ir* is *iba* and of *ser* is *era,* which reminds you of the present **tú eres.** *Ver* adds an *e* to the stem **v-** to make **ve,** so the imperfect is *veía* instead of *vía.*

3. Notice the accent on the ending *-ía* in all the persons to break up the diphthong, and also the accent in the first person plural: **hablábamos, éramos, íbamos, veíamos.**

4. Stem-changing verbs do not change the stem in the imperfect. For example, **volver** → **vuelvo** BUT **volvía; pensar** → **pienso** BUT **pensaba; pedir** → **pido** BUT **pedía.**

B. **Basic use of the imperfect.** The imperfect is a past tense like the preterite, but it is used in a different way. The preterite indicates an entire action completed in the past, whereas the imperfect shows an action going on in the past, with no reference to a beginning or an end. For this reason the imperfect is usually translated by *was* + (-ing form of the verb) in English; in other words, it's an action in progress. Since a habit is an action that repeats itself, the imperfect is used to show a habit. More details will be explained further in the next lesson.

EXS: **Mi madre *hablaba* por teléfono cuando llegué.** (*My mother was talking on the phone when I arrived.*)
Los aztecas *comían* mucho maíz. (*Aztecs used to eat a lot of corn.*)

PRACTIQUE EL IMPERFECTO

ANSWERS
p. 199

1. Verbs ending in **-ar** take the ending _____ in the imperfect tense. For example, from *gustar* we say **Me _____ ese libro.**

2. Verbs ending in **-er** and **-ir** have the same ending for the imperfect: _____. For example, from *beber* we have **él _____**, and from *salir,* **ella _____**.

3. The shortest verb in Spanish is **ir** (*to go*), and it is also the most irregular verb. It is **yo fui** (*I went*) in the preterite, and now the imperfect is **yo _____**. How do you say *we were going?* _____.

4. *Ser* (*to be*) is also irregular. Remember **tú eres** in the present. The imperfect shows the same stem: **Yo _____.**

5. *Ver* (*to see, watch*) is also irregular in the imperfect. The regular form should be **yo vía,** but instead we say **yo _____.**

6. All persons with the ending **-ía** need an accent to break up the diphthong, like *día.* Verbs ending in **-ar** only carry the accent in the first person plural. For example, *hablar* has **nosotros _____; ir** has **_____.**

7. We have two tenses to refer to past time: the preterite and the _____. The preterite suggests that the action is completed, finished, whereas the imperfect suggests that the action is _____ in the past.

8. Remember that **hay** (*there is / there are*) is the present of **haber.** How would you say in the imperfect *there was / there were?* _____.

9. If we repeat an action many times, it becomes a habit, as if it were going on forever. For this reason the _____ is used to show a habit in the past. The adverbs to suggest this repetition are **siempre, muchas veces, a menudo,** and so on.

EXERCISES

ANSWERS
p. 199

A. **Fill in each blank with the correct imperfect tense form of the verb given.**

1. Mis abuelos _____ mucho dinero. (*ahorrar*)

2. Ella siempre _____ las novelas de García Márquez. (*leer*)

3. ¿Dónde _____ (tú) cuando te llamé anoche? (*estar*)

4. ¿Por qué Carlota no _____ con sus amigas? (*ir*)

5. Mi esposa y yo _____ españoles, pero ahora somos americanos. (*ser*)

6. A mi abuela le _____ mucho el ruido (*noise*). (*molestar*)

7. ¿Sabe cuánto _____ un dólar en pesos en 1970? (*valer*)

8. Esa señora me _____ muy elegante cuando la conocí. (*parecer*)

9. A Carlos siempre se le _____ los vasos de las manos. (*caer*)

10. Juan y yo _____ a menudo en la piscina (*swimming pool*). (*nadar*)

11. Mis hijos _____ antes ese programa de TV, pero ahora no. (*ver*)

12. A ella le _____ hacer ejercicios aeróbicos. (*gustar*)

13. ¿Cuántos invitados _____ en la fiesta de cumpleaños? (*haber*)

14. Por aquellos años mi familia _____ en Brasil. (*vivir*)

B. **Change the verbs from the present to the imperfect. Remember that irregular verbs in the present are not necessarily irregular in the imperfect. (Write the verbs only.)**

1. A ti te conviene este présta____ _____

2. José carga todo en la tarjeta ___ rédito. _____

3. No vale la pena comenzar otra ____ ___rra (*war*). _____

4. Ustedes encuentran muchos erro___ _____

5. Los niños duermen ocho horas to__ ___ los días. _____

6. ¿Cuánto dinero te falta para pagar ____ ___enta? _____

7. Después de pagar la cuenta me sobra__ ___nco dólares. _____

8. ¿Dónde metes tu dinero, en el banco o ____ ___u casa? _____

9. ¿Dónde ve usted esos programas tan terr____ ___? _____

10. Camila y yo vamos a nadar en el mar. _____

11. Mi suegro se queja de todo. _____

12. Siempre comienzo mi trabajo a las 8:00 en pun___ _____

13. ¿Qué piensas hacer con esos cheques de viajero? _____

14. Esta mano me duele después de trabajar. _____

15. Yo siempre tengo que hacer la comida. _____

16. Ella siempre se viste muy elegante. _____

17. Muchos niños se mueren de hambre. _____

18. Yo no conozco a tu novia. _____

19. Todos los días hace un sol estupendo. _____

20. Hay muchas personas en el banco esta mañana. _____

10 En la estación de trenes de Madrid
(At the Train Station in Madrid)

el andén	platform	el maletero	porter
el boleto	ticket	el mapa	map
la calle	street	la milla[2]	mile
el coche	car, coach	la parada	stop
el coche cama	sleeping car	la partida	departure
el coche comedor	dining car	el pelo, el cabello	hair
el electrotrén	electric train	la propina	tip, gratuity
el exprés[1]	express	la rapidez	speed, rapidity
el ferrocarril	railroad	la salud	health
el hombre de negocios	businessman	la taquilla	ticket window
		el/la taquillero(a)[3]	ticket agent, clerk
el horario	schedule	el tranvía[4]	trolley, train
la ida	one-way ticket	las vacaciones[5]	vacation
ida y vuelta	round-trip	el vagón	car, wagon
la litera	berth	la velocidad	speed
la llegada	arrival	la vía del tren	railroad track
la locomotora	engine (*train*)	la vuelta[6]	return, change

confirmar	to confirm	**hacer la maleta**	to pack the
correr	to run		suitcase
cruzar	to cross	**informar**	to inform
demorar	to delay	**mandar**	to send, order
deshacer la	to unpack the	**olvidar**[8]	to forget
maleta	suitcase	**perder (ie)**	to lose, miss
entregar	to deliver	**reservar**	to reserve
estar de	to be on vacation	**romper**	to break
vacaciones		**tomar**	to drink
firmar	to sign	**tomar una**	to have a drink
funcionar[7]	to work	**copa**	
hacer caso	to pay attention	**tomar el pelo**	to pull one's leg

descontento(a)	unhappy	**lento(a)**	slow
desocupado(a)	free, vacant	**limpio(a)**	clean
difícil	difficult	**medio(a)**[10]	half
eléctrico(a)	electric	**ocupado(a)**	busy
entero(a)	all, entire	**rápido(a)**	fast
fácil	easy	**roto(a)**	broken, torn
gratis[9]	free, free of	**sucio(a)**	dirty
	charge	**vacío(a)**	empty

a mediodía	at noon	**en medio de**	in the middle of
de primera	excellent, first-class	**millas por hora**	miles per hour
despacio	slowly	**sin falta**	without fail

NOTAS

1. With the new transportation techniques, names of trains have been changing in Spain lately. The **Exprés** is a rather slow train, because it stops at every station and it runs long distances. Called officially **TER** (**Tren Eléctrico Rápido**) or **Electrotrén**, the **Rápido** is a fast train. The **TALGO** is the fastest train, and passengers pay a surcharge for speed. The **AVE** is a new and very fast train that was inaugurated for the World Exposition in Seville in 1992, and it runs only between Madrid and Seville.

2. *Milla* is approximately 1.6 kilometers. *Metro* is a little bigger than a yard. Short for tren metropolitano, the word *metro* also means *subway*.

3. Taquillero(a) is a noun for the *agent* or *person selling tickets*. Taquillero(a) is also an adjective; and it is used for a movie or a play that sells a lot of tickets, in other words, a *hit*.

   EX: **Esa película es taquillera.** (*That movie is a hit.*)

4. Tranvía is the old *streetcar*, which has disappeared and has been replaced by buses. However, the word *tranvía* is still used to refer to a train that travels rather short

distances and stops at every station. Notice that we say **el tranvía, el coche cama**—that is, we use the masculine article, just as with **el paraguas** (*umbrella*).

5. *Vacación* is rarely used in the singular; usually it's in the plural, **vacaciones**, even if it is only one day of vacation: **Hoy tenemos vacaciones.**

6. *Vuelta* is both *return* (as in *a return ticket*) and *change* (as in *the money you get back when you pay for something*). In some countries they say **vuelto** instead of **vuelta**. **Una vuelta** also means *a walk* or *a ride*, as in the expression *dar una vuelta.*

7. *Funcionar* means *to function* in general, and it is used for people and machines. In English machines "*work*"; in Spanish, they "funcionan," because *trabajar* is used only for people.

   EXS: **Carlos trabaja en una compañía grande.** (*Charles works in a large company.*)
   El carro no funciona bien. (*The car doesn't work well.*)

8. *Olvidar* translates *to forget,* and it is frequently used as the reflexive *olvidarse,* usually followed by *de.*

   EX: **Olvidé la llave. = Me olvidé de la llave.** (*I forgot the key.*)

9. *Gratis* is an adjective and an adverb for *free of charge;* it doesn't change for gender or number. The adjective *gratuito(a),* *gratuitos(as)* is used with the same meaning. To refer to *free* and to *freedom,* we use **libre** and **libertad;** and to refer to a free or vacant room, we use *desocupado(a).*

10. *Medio(a)* means *half,* as in **Compré medio kilo** (*I bought half a kilo*). When **medio** is used with another number, it follows the unit of measure (like **kilo**), not the number: **Compré dos kilos y medio** (*I bought two and a half kilos*). *Medio* is also used as an ordinary adjective after a noun with the meaning of *average:* **el salario medio** means *the average salary.*

PRACTIQUE LAS PALABRAS NUEVAS

A. Write *el, la, los,* or *las* before each noun.

1. ___ bar	6. ___ vías	11. ___ vacaciones	16. ___ estación
2. ___ andén	7. ___ vagón	12. ___ ferrocarril	17. ___ tranvía
3. ___ calles	8. ___ rapidez	13. ___ coche cama	18. ___ salud
4. ___ exprés	9. ___ trenes	14. ___ electrotrén	19. ___ expreses
5. ___ velocidad	10. ___ mapa	15. ___ andenes	20. ___ tren

B. Complete each sentence with a word or expression from the list below. You may need the plural of some nouns.

a mediodía	despacio	horario	milla	sin falta
andén	en medio de	ida y vuelta	parada	TALGO
bar	fácil	litera	roto	taquilla
correr	hacer caso	maletero	salud	vacío

1. Este tren es lento; tiene _____ en todas las estaciones.

2. Si quieres dormir en el tren, debes comprar un billete con
_____.

3. Vamos a la _____ a comprar los boletos.

4. Hay que tomar el TALGO para Madrid en el _____
número 8.

5. Está comprobado que el tabaco no es bueno para la _____.

6. Una _____ tiene un poco más de un kilómetro y medio.

7. Aquí está el _____ con todos los trenes de Madrid a
Barcelona.

8. El tren se demora media hora en llegar. Vamos a tomar una copa en el
_____.

9. Antes de entrar en la estación, el tren va muy _____.

10. Ahí dice «No fumar», pero nadie le _____.

11. El taquillero almuerza _____ todos los días.

12. ¡Qué fatal! ¡El carro se me rompió _____ la calle!

13. Los trenes son puntuales en sus salidas. Si no quieres perder el tren,
debes estar en el andén numéro 6 a las 8:00 _____.

14. Si tengo que ir y volver, necesito comprar un boleto de _____.

15. Si Ud. quiere llegar pronto, debe comprar boletos para el _____.

16. El _____ lleva las maletas en el aeropuerto.

17. Este elevador no funciona porque está _____.

18. No hay ninguna lengua _____. Todas las lenguas son
difíciles.

19. A esa hora no hay nadie en la estación; está _____.

20. Los trenes _____ más que los autobuses en España.

C. Write the synonym for each of the following words.

ANSWERS
p. 200

1. boleto _____   5. vagón _____

2. partida _____   6. todo _____

3. vía _____   7. gratis _____

4. olvidar _____   8. ascensor _____

ANSWERS
p. 200

D. Write the opposite of these words.

1. salida _____   8. ocupado _____

2. ida _____   9. lento _____

3. enfermedad _____   10. ganar _____

4. medianoche _____   11. contento _____

5. sucio _____   12. medio _____

6. lleno _____   13. hacer _____

7. fácil _____   14. encontrar _____

ANSWERS
p. 200

E. Fill the blanks with the preterite of one of the following verbs.

correr   demorar   funcionar   informar   olvidar   romper
cruzar   entregar   hacer caso   mandar   perder   tomar el pelo

1. Mi tía Elena me _____ un giro postal de cuarenta dólares para mi cumpleaños.

2. Por supuesto; (yo) _____ la calle cuando no había tráfico.

3. Lo siento. No puedo pagar porque se me _____ la cartera en casa.

4. El elevador no _____ y tuvimos que subir por la escalera.

5. El TALGO es muy rápido; _____ hasta ciento cincuenta kilómetros por hora.

6. El vaso se me cayó al suelo y _____ me _____.

7. Los turistas no ganaron dinero en Las Vegas; al contrario, lo _____ todo.

8. Usted no me dijo la verdad. ¡Ud. me _____!

9. Roberto nos _____ que se va a casar con su novia en mayo.

10. El tranvía es lento; se _____ tres horas entre Madrid y Segovia.

11. El profesor insistió en que los alumnos llegaran (*arrive*) a tiempo, pero ellos no le _____, y llegaron bastante tarde.

12. Ayer el cartero (*mailman*) me _____ una carta (*letter*) certificada.

ANSWERS
p. 200

F. Go back to the sentences in exercise E, and change the verbs from the preterite to the imperfect. Write the verbs only.

1. _____   3. _____   5. _____

2. _____   4. _____   6. _____

7. _____ 9. _____ 11. _____

8. _____ 10. _____ 12. _____

DIÁLOGO Un americano en la estación de ferrocarril de Madrid

Un hombre de negocios de Estados Unidos habla con el taquillero de la estación principal de trenes de Madrid.

TAQUILLERO: Buenas tardes, señor. ¿En qué puedo servirle?

AMERICANO: Tengo que ir a Bilbao en viaje de negocios y necesito información sobre los trenes.

TAQUILLERO: Ud. puede tomar diferentes trenes. Tenemos el Exprés, el Electrotrén y el TALGO. ¿Cuál prefiere Ud.?

AMERICANO: ¿Cuál es el más rápido?

TAQUILLERO: El TALGO. Solamente tiene parada en las ciudades grandes.

AMERICANO: ¿Cuánto tiempo se demora en llegar?

TAQUILLERO: Cinco horas y media. La velocidad media es ciento quince kilómetros por hora, pero hay que pagar un suplemento por la rapidez.

AMERICANO: Está bien. ¿Tiene coche comedor y literas?

TAQUILLERO: No, solamente un bar pequeño con bocadillos y bebidas.

AMERICANO: Bueno, quiero un boleto de ida y vuelta a Bilbao en la sección de no fumar. Primera clase.

TAQUILLERO: El TALGO tiene vagones de fumar y no fumar, pero todos los asientos son de primera, muy amplios; no hay distinción de clases.

AMERICANO: Entonces me da el asiento en un vagón de no fumar.

TAQUILLERO: ¿Qué día piensa volver de Bilbao?

AMERICANO: El viernes que viene. ¿Cuánto es el billete?

TAQUILLERO: Siete mil quinientas pesetas incluyendo el IVA.

AMERICANO: ¿Puedo pagar con tarjeta de crédito?

TAQUILLERO: Por supuesto. Aceptamos casi todas las tarjetas, incluyendo varias de Estados Unidos.

AMERICANO: Aquí tiene mi «dinero plástico».

TAQUILLERO: Dinero es dinero... Firme la factura, por favor... Aquí tiene su billete. El TALGO sale del andén 2 a las 13:00 horas en punto. ¡Buen viaje!

AMERICANO: Muy agradecido. Adiós.

DIALOGUE   An American at the Railroad Station in Madrid

A businessman from the United States is talking to the ticket agent at the main train station in Madrid.

AGENT: Good afternoon, sir. How can I help you?

AMERICAN: I have to go to Bilbao on a business trip, and I need some information about the trains.

AGENT: You can take several trains. We have the *Exprés,* the *Electrotrén,* and the *TALGO.* Which one do you prefer?

AMERICAN: Which is the fastest?

AGENT: The TALGO. It stops only in the largest cities.

AMERICAN: How long does it take to get there?

AGENT: Five and a half hours. The average speed is seventy-five miles an hour, but you have to pay a surcharge for the speed.

AMERICAN: It's O.K. Does it have a dining car and berths?

AGENT: No, it has only a small bar with snacks and drinks.

AMERICAN: Fine. I want a round-trip ticket to Bilbao, in the nonsmoking section, first-class.

AGENT: The TALGO has smoking and nonsmoking cars, but all the seats are first-class, very wide; there is no class distinction.

AMERICAN: Then give me a seat in a nonsmoking car.

AGENT: What day do you plan to return from Bilbao?

AMERICAN: This coming Friday. How much is the ticket?

AGENT: Seven thousand five hundred pesetas, taxes included.

AMERICAN: Can I pay with a credit card?

AGENT: Of course. We accept most credit cards, including several from the United States.

AMERICAN: Here is my "plastic money."

AGENT: Money is money. . . . Sign the invoice, please. . . . Here is your ticket. The TALGO leaves from platfom 2 at 1:00 P.M. sharp. Have a nice trip!

AMERICAN: Thanks a lot. Good-bye.

NOTE

IVA stands for *Impuesto al Valor Agregado,* and it's equivalent to the American tax. The prices in the stores always have the **IVA** included. This same method is followed in Mexico. Only hotels and certain stores separate price and taxes.

EXERCISES

ANSWERS
p. 201

A. *Un hombre de negocios en la estación del tren.* Complete the story using the information from the dialogue.

El hombre de (1) _____ de Estados Unidos habla con un taquillero de la (2) _____ de ferrocarril de Madrid porque tiene que (3) _____ a Bilbao. El taquillero le explica que hay varios trenes, pero el más (4) _____ es el TALGO que corre a una (5) _____ media de ciento quince kilómetros por hora (6) _____, y hay que pagar un (7) _____ por la rapidez. El TALGO no tiene comedor ni literas; sólo un pequeño (8) _____ con bocadillos y (9) _____. También tiene (10) _____ de fumar y no fumar. El americano pide un boleto de (11) _____ en primera clase, pero el taquillero le explica que todos los asientos de ese tren son (12) _____, sin distinción de clases. El hombre de negocios quiere (13) _____ de Bilbao el viernes que (14) _____. El boleto vale siete mil (15) _____ pesetas, incluyendo el IVA, que es la manera oficial de llamar a los (16) _____. Puede pagarlo con (17) _____ de crédito o al contado. El americano lo paga con tarjeta de (18) _____ o «dinero (19) _____», como él llama a las tarjetas. Luego (20) _____ la factura del viaje como es la costumbre cuando se compra con tarjeta. El TALGO para Bilbao sale del (21) _____ número 2, y ¡muy importante!: debe ser puntual para tomar el tren porque sale a las 13:00 horas (22) _____. ¡Buen viaje!

ANSWERS
p. 201

B. Write *true* or *false* (T / F).

1. _____ Una milla es más pequeña que un kilómetro.

2. _____ El TALGO es más rápido que el Exprés en España.

3. _____ Si Ud. quiere dormir en el tren, pide un boleto de ida y vuelta.

4. _____ Para saber la hora de salida y de llegada de los trenes y aviones leemos el horario.

5. _____ Damos una propina al maletero porque nos lleva el equipaje.

6. _____ Ud. debe cruzar la calle cuando el semáforo (la luz roja) está a su favor.

7. _____ El taquillero sube y baja las maletas de los trenes al andén.

8. _____ Si la locomotora del tren está rota, el tren no puede funcionar.

9. _____ Cuando Ud. no tiene que pagar nada, quiere decir que es gratis.

10. _____ *IVA* es una manera de llamar a los impuestos en España y México.

11. _____ El TALGO tiene asientos de primera, segunda y tercera clase.

12. _____ Un boleto de ida y vuelta es más barato que un billete sencillo.

13. _____ Usted puede tomar un vagón de fumar o de no fumar en el TALGO.

14. _____ Los boletos del tren se pueden pagar en España con tarjetas de crédito.

C. Complete each sentence with an appropriate word or expression.

despacio	hacer caso	propina	tomar el pelo
difícil	medio	roto	vacaciones
gratis	ocupado	sin falta	vacío

1. Aprender bien una lengua no es fácil; al contrario, es _____.

2. Si no hay nadie en esta casa, la casa está _____.

3. ¿París la capital de Italia? Tú me _____.

4. El viento fuerte rompió la ventana; está _____.

5. Ese grupo de americanos son turistas; por eso están de _____.

6. No puedo hablar con ella ahora porque está muy _____.

7. Fuimos al mercado y compramos dos kilos y _____ de carne.

8. Te dije que fumar es malo para la salud, pero tú nunca me _____.

9. Para tomar el tren, tienes que llegar a las 13:00 horas _____.

10. Si el camarero nos da buen servicio, le damos una _____.

11. Antes de llegar al STOP con mi carro, siempre voy muy _____.

12. Ud. no paga nada para entrar al museo; es _____.

D. Write sentences using the imperfect tense only. Add any words required by the context, such as articles and prepositions. Don't forget the indirect object pronoun if needed.

1. mi / esposa / deshacer / maletas / después / viaje /.

   _____

2. su / tíos / siempre / mandar / dinero / a él /.

   _____

3. niños / hacer caso / nadie / en / fiesta /.

   _____

4. carro / viejo / siempre / romper / a mí /.

   _____

5. todo / días / parar / carro / a ella /.

_____

6. Carlos / gustar / libros / americano / de ficción /.

_____

GRAMMAR I   Preterite and Imperfect in Contrast

A. Use of the preterite

There are two tenses in the indicative to refer to an action in the past: the preterite and the imperfect. In order to understand the difference, we must think of an action as having three stages: beginning, middle, and end. We use the preterite to mark the beginning or end of an action, or to show the whole action as a completed event.

EXS: **Ayer *comimos* a la una.** (*Yesterday we <u>ate</u> at one o'clock.*) (Emphasis on the *beginning:* We started to eat at one, and we don't know how long the dinner took.)
Julia *llegó* a la una. (*Julia <u>arrived</u> at one o'clock.*) (Emphasis on the *end:* There is no action after one.)
José *vivió* en Chile. (*Joe <u>lived</u> in Chile.*) (The whole action is completed.)

B. Uses of the imperfect

1. *Basic idea.* The imperfect shows the action in the middle or in progress, without any reference to the beginning or end. The English progressive form *was* + (*-ing* form of the verb) translates the imperfect best. Consider this tense as showing an action in its middle stage.

   EXS: **Cuando llegué, él *no estaba* allí.** (*When I arrived, he <u>wasn't</u> there.*) (My arrival occurred *in the midst* of his not being there.)
   ***Trabajaba* en la escuela en ese tiempo.** (*I <u>was working</u> at the school at that time.*) (I was *in the midst of working* there at some time in the past.)

2. *Habit.* We use the imperfect to indicate a habit in the past, since a habit is an action that occurs repeatedly as if it had no beginning or end. Its English equivalent is *used to* (+ verb).

   EX: **Mi tío *fumaba* mucho.** (*My uncle <u>used to smoke</u> a lot.*)

3. *Description.* To describe persons, things, or places in the past, we use the imperfect, even when the situation no longer exists.

   EXS: **El pueblo *estaba* cerca de la vía del tren.** (*The village <u>was</u> near the railroad tracks.*)
   Los indios *vivían* en las montañas. (*The Indians <u>lived</u> in the mountains.*)

4. *Time and age.* To tell time and age with *ser* and *tener,* respectively, the imperfect must be used. The preterite cannot be used in these instances, perhaps because "time" is always in the middle of its course and cannot be stopped.

EXS: **Cuando entré *eran* las doce.** (*It <u>was</u> twelve o'clock when I came in.*)
Cuando murió *tenía* setenta años. (*He <u>was</u> seventy when he died.*)

C. **Combination of imperfect and preterite**

It is very common to use the imperfect to indicate the background for the preterite—that is, to show an ongoing action in the background (imperfect) when something else happpened in the foreground (preterite). Once again, the imperfect is better translated by the progressive form in English, and the preterite by the *-ed* past tense form.

EX: **Cuando mi esposa *cocinaba,* mi tío *llamó* por teléfono.** (*My uncle <u>called</u> on the phone when my wife <u>was cooking</u>.*)

PRACTIQUE EL IMPERFECTO Y EL PRETÉRITO

ANSWERS
p. 201

1. An action or event has three stages: beginning, _____, and _____.

2. The word *imperfect* suggests that something was going on, but is as yet incomplete, unfinished. Actually, the imperfect tense shows the _____ of an action, without reference to its beginning or _____.

3. The preterite shows the action as a whole upon completion, but this tense often points out either the _____ or the _____ of the action.

4. *Cenamos a las nueve* shows clearly that nine o'clock is only the _____ of supper, which could go to 9:15, 9:30, 10:00, and so on. On the other hand, *Llegamos a las nueve* points out the end, since there is no more _____ after nine.

5. To describe places, people, and things in the past, we use the _____, because a description doesn't seem to have limits.

EX: **Roma _____** (*was*) **una ciudad grande y _____** (*had*) **monumentos muy bellos.**

6. A habit is something unfinished and suggests repetition, as if it were in a middle stage. For this reason we use the _____ for a habit in the past.

EX: **Mi abuelo _____ mucho, pero no _____.** (*fumar / beber*)

7. Sometimes we picture a habit as a unit, a sum of many single actions. In this case we use the preterite. For example, **Mi abuelo _____ mucho dinero por años, pero no se lo pudo llevar al cementerio.** (*ahorrar*)

8. To tell time in the past, do we use the imperfect or the preterite? _____.
This is perhaps because time has no limits, it cannot be stopped.

   EX: **Cuando llegué a casa, ya _____ las tres de la mañana.**

9. To tell someone's age with **tener,** do we use the imperfect or the preterite?
_____.

   EX: **Mi suegra _____ dieciocho años cuando se casó.**

10. The progressive form, as in *I was working,* shows the ongoing nature of the
action. Is it best translated by the imperfect or the preterite? _____.

11. The ending *-ed,* as in *I walked two miles,* usually suggests the completion of
an action. Is it best translated by the imperfect or the preterite? _____.

12. Very often the imperfect indicates the background for the preterite—that is,
it shows an action that continued in the background (imperfect) when
something else happened in the foreground (preterite).

   EX: **Carmen _____ por la calle cuando _____ el accidente.** (*ir/tener*)

EXERCISES

A. **Answer the questions in the preterite and in the imperfect, using the cues in
parentheses.**

1. ¿Dónde vivía su familia cuando usted nació? (*Kansas*)

   _____

2. ¿Cuántos años tenía su abuelo cuando murió? (*ochenta*)

   _____

3. ¿Qué hora era cuando llegaron tus tíos? (*3:00*)

   _____

4. ¿Quién llamó cuando yo estaba en el jardín? (*Estela*)

   _____

5. ¿Qué le pasó a tu hermano cuando se cayó? (*nada grave*)

   _____

6. ¿A quién vio usted cuando abrió la ventana? (*su hermano*)

   _____

ANSWERS
p. 202

B. Complete each sentence, using the imperfect or the preterite of the verbs in parentheses. (Remember that the imperfect is like the background of a picture and the preterite, the foreground.)

1. A la medianoche me _____ a dormir porque _____ sueño. (*ir / tener*)

2. Mi esposa _____ en la cocina cuando el teléfono _____. (*estar / sonar*)

3. Cuando nosotros _____ en Canadá, _____ buenos amigos. (*vivir / ser*)

4. Cuando el turista _____ a la taquilla _____ un boleto sencillo. (*llegar / pedir*)

5. El médico me _____ que mi papá _____ buena salud. (*decir / tener*)

6. El tren _____ por la estación a las seis, pero no se _____. (*pasar / parar*)

7. El taquillero siempre _____ a mediodía, y después _____ un cigarrillo. (*comer / fumar*)

8. Ayer ellos no _____ el carro porque _____ roto. (*traer / estar*)

ANSWERS
p. 202

C. *Dos turistas americanas en Barcelona.* Complete the story with the preterite or imperfect of the verbs given. Read the entire paragraph first to get an understanding of the story; this will help you determine the correct tense.

Cuando Josefina y yo _____ ayer al hotel, ya _____ las
          (1. *llegar*)   (2. *ser*)
once y media de la noche. Nosotras _____ muy cansadas (*tired*) del
                                (3. *estar*)
viaje, nos _____ y nos _____ en seguida. Esta mañana nos
      (4. *duchar*)   (5. *acostar*)
_____ temprano, y _____ un desayuno delicioso. El día
(6. *despertar*)   (7. *tener*)
_____ nublado (*cloudy*), pero _____ mucho calor.
(8. *estar*)   (9. *hacer*)
Nosotras _____ un autobús para ir de compras al centro
       (10. *tomar*)
(*downtown*). Después de varias horas de compras y de andar, _____
                             (11. *estar*)
muy cansadas y con mucha hambre, y _____ en el restaurante Los
                (12. *almorzar*)
Caracoles (*The Snails*). Mientras (*while*) _____ en el restaurante,
                (13, *almorzar*)
_____ a llover y _____ que volver al hotel en taxi. El
(14. *comenzar*)   (15. *tener*)
taxista nos _____ por unas calles muy antiguas y muy estrechas,
      (16. *llevar*)
donde _____ tiendas pequeñas, templos antiguos y muchas personas
    (17. *haber*)
con paraguas. Después de llegar al hotel, _____ la siesta hasta las
                           (18. *dormir*)
seis de la tarde al estilo español.

GRAMMAR II   *Hacer* + (Time Expressions) + *que* + (Present Tense) • *Llevar* + (Time Expressions) (+ *de*)

A. EXS: 1. *Hace tres años que* vivo aquí.
      2. Vivo aquí *hace tres años.*
      3. Vivo aquí *desde hace tres años.*
      } (*I have been living here* <u>*for three years*</u>.)

We use *hace* + (a time expression) + *que* + (the present tense) (see example 1) to express an action that began in the past and is still going on in the present. We omit *que* when the main verb precedes *hace.* (See example 2.) This construction can also be used with the preposition *desde* in front of *hace.* (See example 3.)

B. EXS: 1. *Hace un mes que* fui a Chile.
      2. Fui a Chile *hace un mes.*
      } (*I went to Chile* <u>*a month ago*</u>.)

We use *hace* + (a time expression) + *que* + (the preterite tense) to express the time that elapsed between an action carried out in the past and the present time. (See example 1.) We omit *que* when *hace* + (the expression of time) follows the main verb. (See example 2.)

C. EXS: *Hacía una hora que* llovía.
      Llovía *hacía una hora.*
      Llovía *desde hacía una hora.*
      } (*It had been raining* <u>*for one hour*</u>.)

The construction *hacía* + (a time expression) + *que* + (the imperfect tense) is used to describe an action that began in the past and continued in the past. (See example 1.) We omit *que* when *hacía* + (the time expression) follows the main verb. (See example 2.) This construction can also be used with the preposition *desde* in front of *hacía.* (See example 3.)

D. EXS: Ellos *llevan treinta años de* casados. = *Hace treinta años que* ellos se casaron.
      Llevo una hora en la oficina. = *Hace una hora que* estoy en la oficina.

Llevar + (a time expression) is used without any other verb to indicate how long a person or a thing has been in a place. The preposition *de* is added if a job or a condition is added, like **de secretaria, de casado,** and so on.

PRACTIQUE LOS MODISMOS

ANSWERS
p. 202

1. *Hace* + (time expression) can be placed before or after the main verb. For example, another way to say **Hace un mes que llegué** is _____.

2. In the sentence *No te veo desde hace un año,* the word _____ can be omitted without changing the meaning.

3. *Hace una hora se fue Juan* is incorrect; the linking conjunction _____ is needed before the main verb, *se fue*.

4. The construction *hacía* + (time expression) requires the main verb to be in the _____ tense.

    EX: Hacía cinco años que José no _____. (*fumar*)

5. *Hacía dos días no trabajaba* is incorrect ; the linking conjunction _____ is missing before the main verb *no trabajaba.*

6. Another way to say **No fumaba hacía dos meses** is _____.

7. *Llevar* + (time expression) is another way to convey the idea of being in a place. Another way to say **Hace diez minutos que estoy aquí** with *llevar* is _____.

EXERCISES

A. The following questions are directed to you. Answer them using the cues given.

1. ¿Cuánto tiempo hace que Ud. vive aquí? (*cinco años*)

    _____

2. ¿Cuánto tiempo hace que Ud. viajó a Panamá? (*ocho años*)

    _____

3. ¿Cuánto tiempo hace que Ud. toca el piano? (*media hora*)

    _____

4. ¿Cuántos años hace que Ud. salió de España? (*veinticinco años*)

    _____

5. ¿Cuántos días hace que Ud. no viaja en autobús? (*una semana*)

    _____

6. ¿Cuánto tiempo hacía que no llovía en Arizona? (*cuatro meses*)

    _____

7. ¿Cuánto tiempo hacía que Ud. hablaba por teléfono? (*cinco minutos*)

    _____

8. ¿Cuánto tiempo hacía que Ud. no llamaba a sus padres? (*dos días*)

    _____

ANSWERS
p. 202

B. Rewrite the sentences, changing the position of *hace* or *hacía* in the sentence. Remember that *desde* is optional.

1. Hace como mil años que murió el Cid. = _____.

2. Hacía un año que no llovía. = _____.

3. Rita se fue hace dos años. = _____.

4. Tú fumas desde hace veinte años. = _____.

5. Hace cinco minutos que pasó el tren. = _____.

6. Llevo aquí ya diez años. = _____.

7. Saqué los billetes hace una hora. = _____.

8. Llevo cinco años de profesor. = _____.

GRAMMAR III   Ordinal Numbers • Days of the Week • Seasons • Months of the Year

A. These are the ten ordinal numbers in Spanish. They are in numerical order: *first, second,* and so on. They agree in gender and number with the noun. After ten we use ordinary, or cardinal, numbers: **once, doce, trece.**

primero(a)	tercero(a)	quinto(a)	séptimo(a)	noveno(a)
segundo(a)	cuarto(a)	sexto(a)	octavo(a)	décimo(a)

1. *Primero* and *tercero* drop the *o* when they precede a masculine noun.

    EX: Estamos en el *primer piso,* no en el tercero.

2. The ordinal numbers can precede or follow the noun without change of meaning.

    EX: Leímos *el tercer capítulo.* = Leímos *el capítulo tercero.* (*We read the third chapter.*)

3. To show the order of kings, queens, popes, we use ordinal numbers after the noun, omitting the definite article.

    EXS: la reina Isabel *Segunda* (*Queen Elizabeth the Second*)
    el rey Carlos *Tercero* (*King Charles the Third*)

4. *Séptimo* is also written **sétimo,** according to the *Diccionario de la lengua española,* of the Real Academia Española, the highest authority in the field.

B. The seven days of the week are not capitalized in Spanish. Note that the five weekdays end in the letter *s* and the two weekend days end in *o*.

lunes Monday   **jueves** Thursday   **domingo** Sunday
martes Tuesday   **viernes** Friday
miércoles Wednesday   **sábado** Saturday

We don't translate *on* in expressions such as *on Monday* and *on Tuesdays.* Instead, we replace it with the definite article *el* if the day of the week is singular, *los* if it is plural.

EXS: **Sonia llegó el martes.** (*Sonia arrived on Tuesday.*)
     No trabajo los lunes. (*I don't work on Mondays.*)

C. The four seasons of the year are:

primavera (*spring*) / **verano** (*summer*) / **otoño** (*fall*) / **invierno** (*winter*)

D. Memorize the months of the year starting with January.

    enero   marzo mayo julio   septiembre noviembre
    febrero abril   junio agosto octubre   diciembre

1. The months are capitalized in English, not in Spanish.

   EX: **Se fue el dos de enero.** (*He left on January the second.*)

2. When giving the date, we use *cardinal* numbers for days of the month. They are preceded by the article *el,* and the noun *día* is usually omitted. Notice that in English the ordinals are used instead with days of the month.

   EX: **Hoy es el (día) 5 (cinco) de marzo.** (*Today is March [the] fifth.*)

3. The only ordinal number ever used for days of the month is *primero;* and even in this case, *uno* is used as much as *primero.*

   EX: **Hoy es el primero de enero. = Hoy es el uno de enero.**

4. *Septiembre* is also written **setiembre,** just like **séptimo** and **sétimo.**

PRACTIQUE LA GRAMÁTICA

1. The ordinal numbers are adjectives with four endings; they change in gender and _____ according to the noun.

   EX: libro primero, mesa _____

2. The two numerals that drop the ending o are **primero** and _____. When is the ending dropped, before or after the masculine noun? _____.

3. The ordinal numbers can be placed before or _____ the noun they modify.

   EX: **El primer día** is the same as _____ .

4. *Carlos El Primero* is not correct for *Charles the First*. It should be _____, because we don't use the article in Spanish.

5. *Hoy es Lunes* is not written correctly because the days of the week are not _____ in Spanish. Do you capitalize the months of the year in Spanish? _____ .

6. *¿Llegaste en martes?* is not correct. It should be ¿Llegaste _____?

7. The four seasons are not capitalized in Spanish nor in English. The coldest season of the year is _____, and the hottest _____ .

8. When it's autumn in the United States, it's _____ in Argentina.

9. The first month of the year is _____, and the shortest month is _____ .

10. We celebrate the Independence of the United States in the month of _____, and Christmas falls in the month of _____ .

11. There are two ways to say the first of the month: _____ .

12. Do you translate *on* in expressions such as *on Monday?* _____ . Instead, we use the definite articles _____ or _____ .

EXERCISES

ANSWERS
p. 203

A. **Complete each sentence with an appropriate word.**

1. Después de setiembre viene el mes de _____, y después del mes de abril viene el mes de _____ .

2. Los tres meses de primavera en el hemisferio norte son marzo, _____ y _____ .

3. Si hoy es el primero de enero, mañana es _____ (de enero).

4. Si hoy es el 28 de febrero, mañana es _____ .

5. En Estados Unidos celebramos la Independencia el _____ .

6. Celebramos la Navidad (*Christmas*) el _____ .

7. Celebramos el Año Nuevo el _____ .

8. ¿Qué día de la semana celebramos la fiesta de *Thanskgiving?*
   _____.

9. ¿Cuál es la estación más fría en Norteamérica? _____.

10. ¿Cuál es la estación de más calor en Europa? _____.

11. ¿Cómo traduce usted *Charles the Fifth?* _____.

12. ¿Cuál es el primer mes del año? _____.

13. ¿Vive Ud. en el primer piso o en el segundo? _____.

14. Después del piso quinto viene el _____, y después del sétimo viene el _____.

15. La calle que sigue a la calle novena es la _____. La calle que está antes de la calle veinte es la calle _____.

B. Write sentences using the words in the order given. Make the necessary changes and add words needed. Use the present.

1. mí/gustar/primavera/y/verano/.

   _____

2. Emilio/vivir/en/8/calle/.

   _____

3. Uds./viajar/México/12/junio/.

   _____

4. Nosotros/tener/vacación/1/abril/.

   _____

5. Hoy/ser/lunes,/8/setiembre/.

   _____

C. Translate the following sentences.

1. I bought the tickets on Tuesday.

   _____

2. We like the Fourth of July.

   _____

3. Spring goes from March 21 to June 21.

   _____

4. Henry (**Enrique**) the Eighth had eight wives.

_____

5. Today is November the second.

_____

EXAM 2   LESSONS 6–10

Part I.   Practique las palabras nuevas (50 puntos)

A. Match the two columns. The article is not always needed.

1. ___ el sobrino	A. María cocinó… para tu cumpleaños.
2. ___ el sillón	B. El dinero de un… en otro, se llama divisas.
3. ___ el tejado	C. Un tiempo corto; unos minutos; unas horas
4. ___ la cama	D. No pude ir a la fiesta por…
5. ___ el jabón	E. Voy a comer una ensalada de lechuga, tomate y…
6. ___ la llave	
7. ___ el botones	F. Una vaca joven es una…
8. ___ la escalera	G. Ayer comimos… de puerco.
9. ___ el arroz	H. Botana, bocadillo, tapa, hors d'oeuvre, antojitos
10. ___ el resfriado	I. Es un producto derivado de la leche.
11. ___ el entremés	J. Mueble para sentarse.
12. ___ el rato	K. Si está roto el ascensor, subimos por…
13. ___ el país	L. El hijo de mi hermana es mi…
14. ___ la torta	M. Nos bañamos y duchamos con agua y…
15. ___ la ternera	N. Me gusta mucho… con pollo.
16. ___ el queso	O. Abrimos y cerramos la puerta con…
17. ___ el pepino	P. Mueble para dormir.
18. ___ la chuleta	Q. La parte más alta de la casa es el…
	R. El mozo que lleva las maletas a los cuartos.

ANSWERS
p. 203

B. Underline the best of the four choices.

19. Si Ud. no quiere perder el tren, debe ir enseguida (al maletero, al andén, a la propina, al horario).

20. Si Ud. desea dormir bien durante el viaje en tren, es mejor tomar (una vuelta, una vacación, un exprés, una litera).

21. Para escribir cheques Ud. necesita (una cuenta corriente, un préstamo a plazos, un giro postal, un presupuesto grande).

22. Si Ud. no tiene dinero ahora, puede pagarnos (al contado, sin falta, a plazos, al por ciento).

23. Si Ud. trabaja para una tienda, Ud. cobra (una hipoteca, un sueldo, un préstamo, un interés).

24. La carne más tierna y sabrosa es (el pescado, el cerdo, el solomillo, la res).

25. Hay muchas marcas (*trademarks*) de vino (tinto, picante, vacío, amplio).

26. En el pastel de cumpleaños de Elsa pusimos veintiuna (zanahorias, copas, velas, divisas).

27. Me gusta mi habitación porque (da al, trata de, deja de, entra al) campo de golf.

28. No me gustan las zanahorias porque son (amarillas, color café, muy rojas, color naranja).

ANSWERS p. 203

C. **Write the opposite word.**

29. lleno _____, fuerte _____

30. sucio _____, difícil _____

31. rápido _____, ancho _____

32. disponible _____, doble _____

33. abrir _____, gracioso _____

34. gastar _____, entrar _____

35. apagar _____, ganar _____

ANSWERS p. 203

D. **Complete the sentences with the correct words.**

36. Si el camarero nos da buen servicio, le dejamos una buena _____.

37. Cuando hace mucho calor, vamos al mar para bañarnos y _____.

38. Una casa vale mucho dinero. Para comprarla necesitamos _____.

39. Por la mañana me gusta tomar un vaso de _____ de naranja.

40. Los hijos de mis hijos son mis _____.

41. La semana pasada hizo frío, y las montañas tienen mucha _____ para esquiar (*to ski*).

42. Después de bañarme, me seco (*dry*) con _____.

43. El atún , las sardinas, el salmón, no son carnes sino (*but*) _____.

ANSWERS p. 203

E. Circle the letter of the best reply.

44. A mí me encantan las verduras frescas sin excepción.
    A. Sí, ya veo que no puede ver el maíz.
    B. Sí, muchas verduras saben a chocolate.
    C. Sí, creo que son más saludables que la carne.
    D. Sí, ya veo que estás a dieta hace un mes.

45. El taquillero dice que el tren exprés se demora mucho tiempo.
    A. Claro; tiene parada en todas las estaciones.
    B. Tiene razón; ese tren corre noventa millas por hora.
    C. Por supuesto; ese hombre no hace caso a nadie.
    D. ¡Cómo no! Ese tren siempre nos toma el pelo.

46. ¿Quieres comprar ese carro el lunes que viene sin falta?
    A. Sí, es un carro valioso y de lujo.
    B. A propósito; cobran un veinte por ciento de interés.
    C. No, no me conviene abrir una cuenta de ahorros.
    D. ¡Ni modo! Me faltan dos cosas: dinero y crédito.

47. Estas chuletas de cordero tienen muy buena pinta.
    A. Sí, aquí la carne de res siempre es buena.
    B. Por supuesto; el pescado en este mercado es de primera.
    C. Tienes razón; me parecen muy frescas y con poca grasa.
    D. Es verdad. Esta carne siempre tiene muchas calorías.

48. ¿Por qué se puso Ud. a merendar cuando se levantó de la siesta?
    A. Porque era ya mediodía.
    B. Porque me encanta jugar a menudo.
    C. Porque acababa de desayunar.
    D. Porque tenía un hambre terrible.

49. Te mereces un buen pastel porque cumples veinte años.
    A. Sí, no puedo creer que comencé la universidad hace dos años.
    B. No, el cumpleaños de mi hermana no es hasta el sábado.
    C. No, los mariachis ya tocaron en la fiesta de cumpleaños.
    D. Sí, pero mi cumpleaños fue hace dos años.

50. Vd. tuvo mucho éxito en la venta de su casa.
    A. Con mucho gusto. Voy a salir enseguida.
    B. Sí, tuve suerte en venderla enseguida.
    C. Aquí tiene la llave. El elevador está allí.
    D. Sí, el pagar impuestos no vale la pena.

Part II.   Practique la gramática (50 puntos)

ANSWERS
p. 204

A. Complete each sentence with the correct form of the preterite.

1. Cuando _____ me fui a dormir. (*to be sleepy*)

2. El domingo _____ y fuimos a las montañas. (*to be sunny*)

3. Cuando ella _____ se bebió una cerveza. (*to be thirsty*)

4. Me puse mucha ropa porque _____. (*to be cold*)

5. Los turistas no _____ dormir en toda la noche. (*to be able to*)

6. Lo niños _____ mucho en la fiesta. (*to have fun*)

7. No puedes quejarte; yo _____ a las tres en punto. (*to arrive*)

8. Mi padre _____ ir también, pero no pudo. (*to want, try*)

9. Nuestra prima _____ otra botella de champán. (*to ask for*)

10. Pepe se sentía un poco enfermo y _____ a casa. (*to go*)

11. Esta mañana no _____ porque no tuve tiempo. (*to shave*)

12. Yo no sé cómo ella _____ en 10 minutos. (*to get dressed*)

13. Mi hijo _____ el violín y yo _____ el piano. (*to play*)

14. ¿Por qué _____ Uds. tantos entremeses? (*to bring*)

15. La semana pasada _____ una fiesta en casa de los Arana. (*to be*)

ANSWERS
p. 204

B. Read the story that follows, and then change the verbs from present to past. You will have to decide between the preterite and the imperfect. Write the answers below.

Carlitos (16) *se levanta* temprano esta mañana porque (17) *quiere* desayunar bien antes de ir al colegio. Su madre ya (18) *está* en la cocina cuando él (19) *va* a buscar café. Primero él (20) *se baña* con agua y jabón, pero no (21) *se seca* bien el pelo hasta después del desayuno. Como (22) *tiene* mucha hambre, (23) *se come* dos huevos, jamón, tostadas y mermelada. Le (24) *dice* a su mamá que no (25) *duerme* muy bien esa noche porque (26) *sueña* en cosas muy difíciles en los exámenes del colegio… Esta mañana (27) *anda* al colegio porque (28) *tiene* la bicicleta (*bicycle*) rota. (29) *Hace* un día estupendo para caminar y no (30) *hay* una sola nube en el cielo (*sky*)…

16. _____	21. _____	26. _____
17. _____	22. _____	27. _____
18. _____	23. _____	28. _____
19. _____	24. _____	29. _____
20. _____	25. _____	30. _____

ANSWERS
p. 204

C. Select the best answer and circle the letter.

31. El supermercado de la ciudad no... lejos del hotel.
    - **A.** había
    - **C.** tenía
    - **B.** estaba
    - **D.** hacía

32. Me gusta mucho más este tren que... porque es más rápido.
    - **A.** ese uno
    - **C.** aquél
    - **B.** aquel uno
    - **D.** ése uno

33. Si José no tiene lápiz, yo le puedo prestar...
    - **A.** el mío
    - **C.** mío
    - **B.** la mía
    - **D.** mía

34. Cuando mi hija era niña, ella... hablar español bastante bien.
    - **A.** supo
    - **C.** sabía
    - **B.** conoció
    - **D.** conocía

35. Cuando Felipe II... rey (*king*) de España, preparó la Armada Invencible.
    - **A.** fue
    - **C.** estuvo
    - **B.** estaba
    - **D.** era

36. Hoy estoy cansado porque ayer... tenis por dos horas.
    - **A.** jugaba
    - **C.** jugué
    - **B.** juegué
    - **D.** juegaba

37. ... a las diez las puertas de esta tienda.
    - **A.** Las cierran
    - **C.** Se cierra
    - **B.** Se cierran
    - **D.** La cierra

38. ¿Qué pasó con el billete del avión? —... a mi madre.
    - **A.** Se lo dí
    - **D.** Se la di
    - **B.** Le la di
    - **E.** Se lo di
    - **C.** Se la dí
    - **F.** Le lo di

39. ... le dio dinero a Cristóbal Colón para el viaje a América.
    - **A.** Isabel la Primera
    - **C.** Isabel Primera
    - **B.** La Primera Isabel
    - **D.** Primera Isabel

40. Mi abuelo siempre... mucho, pero mi abuela, nada.
    - **A.** fumaba
    - **C.** fumó
    - **B.** fumía
    - **D.** fumió

41. A Margarita... ocho dólares en el supermercado.
    - **A.** le cayeron
    - **B.** le caieron
    - **C.** se le cayeron
    - **D.** se les caieron
    - **E.** se le caieron
    - **F.** se les cayeron

42. La pobre niñita... mucho frío cuando la encontramos.
    - **A.** hacía
    - **B.** había
    - **C.** estaba
    - **D.** tenía

43. Cuando volvimos de la fiesta, la ventana ya... rota.
    - **A.** fue
    - **B.** era
    - **C.** estuvo
    - **D.** estaba

44. Ayer ustedes... mi automóvil por dos horas.
    - **A.** conducieron
    - **B.** condujeron
    - **C.** conduzían
    - **D.** conducían
    - **E.** condujieron
    - **F.** conduzieron

45. Tu abuelita... ochenta y ocho años cuando murió.
    - **A.** era
    - **B.** fue
    - **C.** tenía
    - **D.** tuvo

46. Después que llegué a mi cuarto, el teléfono... dos veces (*twice*).
    - **A.** suenó
    - **B.** sueñó
    - **C.** sonaba
    - **D.** suenaba
    - **E.** sonó
    - **F.** soño

47. No tienes que pagar la cuenta. Ya... yo hace unos momentos.
    - **A.** le pagué
    - **B.** le pagé
    - **C.** la pagé
    - **D.** la pagué
    - **E.** la pagaba
    - **F.** le pagaba

48. Cuando conocimos esta ciudad,... buenas tiendas de ropa.
    - **A.** habían
    - **B.** hubo
    - **C.** había
    - **D.** hubieron

49. Los platos... a la camarera cuando iba a servir la comida.
    - **A.** se rompieron
    - **B.** se les rompió
    - **C.** se le rompió
    - **D.** se le rompieron

50. ¿Dónde... ayer cuando te llamé a las cuatro de la tarde?
    - **A.** estabas
    - **B.** eras
    - **C.** estuviste
    - **D.** fuiste

ANSWERS   LESSONS 6–10 AND EXAM 2

Lesson 6

Practique las palabras nuevas

A.

1. el	5. el	9. las	13. la
2. el	6. la	10. el	14. la
3. el/los	7. el	11. la	15. las
4. el	8. los	12. el	16. el

B.

1. servir	11. calor (calentar)	21. casar (casa)
2. bañarse	12. oír (oyente)	22. estar
3. desayunar	13. ver (visión)	23. nublado
4. fumar	14. viaje (viajero)	24. cocina (cocinar)
5. perdonar	15. pasaje (pasar)	25. señor (señorita)
6. registrar	16. rosado (rosal)	26. cenar
7. llover	17. lavaplatos	27. llegada
8. nevar (nevada)	18. invitación	28. marisco (marina)
9. reservar	19. dormitorio	29. salida
10. turismo	20. sentarse	30. vuelo (volador)

C.

1. estrecho	4. sed	7. cerrar	10. subir
2. antiguo	5. sencillo (simple)	8. mal tiempo	11. viejo
3. frío	6. lejos	9. entrar a (en)	12. permitir

D.

1. desayuno	5. doble	9. jabón	13. frío
2. peso	6. banco	10. botones (maletero)	14. sed
3. elevador (ascensor)	7. plaza	11. razonable	15. nublado
4. lluvia	8. lejos	12. habitaciones (recámara, cuarto)	16. telenovela

E.

1. G	4. I	7. A	10. C
2. E	5. K	8. B	11. D
3. J	6. H	9. F	

F. 1. llueve
   2. nieva
   3. divierto
   4. visitamos
   5. da a
   6. cobra
   7. Prefieren
   8. registran
   9. abre
   10. sube
   11. entran al (en el)
   12. cierran
   13. está
   14. incluye
   15. trata... de
   16. interesan
   17. decide
   18. permite
   19. cambio
   20. reservan
   21. divertimos
   22. prefiero
   23. es/es

Exercises

A. 1. visitar
   2. hotel
   3. dinero
   4. recámara
   5. doble
   6. época
   7. disponible
   8. piso
   9. da a
   10. cobra(n)
   11. comida
   12. caliente
   13. jabón
   14. telenovelas
   15. desayuno
   16. cierra
   17. bar
   18. firma
   19. llave
   20. abrir
   21. botones
   22. en seguida (enseguida)

B. 1. la escalera
   2. llueve
   3. servicio
   4. da
   5. razonable
   6. divisas
   7. doble
   8. el ascensor
   9. nubes
   10. sed
   11. nombre
   12. hambre
   13. divertirme
   14. un cheque
   15. el hotel

Practique las expresiones

1. a noun/mucho frío
2. hace mucho sol
3. tengo hambre
4. mucha hambre
5. no tener razón
6. I have thirst
7. de/ganas (ansias) de dormir
8. norm/es
9. change/está

Exercise

1. hace (hay)
2. hace (hay)
3. tiene
4. está
5. está
6. está
7. tengo
8. es/son
9. están
10. hace (hay)
11. está
12. tengo sueño
13. tiene razón
14. hace (hay) malo (hace [hay] mal tiempo)
15. es/está
16. tienes suerte
17. hace (hay) fresco
18. tiene hambre
19. tengo cuidado
20. tiene ganas de (tiene ansias de)

Practique los demostrativos

1. este/estos, esta/estas
2. ese/esos, esa/esas
3. number
4. aquel/aquellos, aquella/aquellas.
5. one
6. pronouns
7. ése
8. noun/no
9. e
10. eso/aquello

Exercise

1. aquel
2. Este/ése
3. eso
4. Estos
5. Este/ése
6. aquello
7. este
8. esta/ésa
9. eso que (lo que)
10. Éste
11. aquel
12. esta
13. eso
14. Esta/aquel
15. eso

Practique los posesivos

1. mi, tu, su/mis, tus, sus
2. no/emphasis
3. his, her, its, their, your
4. tus hijos
5. After
6. mío/tuyo/suyo
7. mis/tus
8. you/your
9. el
10. la casa de ella
11. noun
12. nuestro jabón

Exercise

1. mi/tuyo
2. Nuestra
3. mío/el tuyo (el suyo)
4. su
5. mía/la suya
6. sus
7. su
8. Nuestra
9. Mis/Su
10. nuestro
11. sus/de él/de ella
12. sus/las mías

Lesson 7

Practique las palabras nuevas

A. 1. el
2. el
3. la
4. el (los)
5. el (los)
6. el
7. el (los)
8. el (los)
9. el
10. el
11. el
12. la
13. el
14. el
15. el (los)

B. 1. meses
2. felices
3. viernes
4. países
5. puntuales
6. alegres
7. mariachis
8. tocadiscos
9. entremeses
10. miércoles

C. 1. G 5. A 9. E 13. H 17. C 21. S 25. R

2. I 6. P 10. B 14. V 18. O 22. W

3. F 7. K 11. D 15. L 19. J 23. Y

4. N 8. U 12. Q 16. X 20. M 24. T

D. 1. oscuro 5. bebida 8. alguien

2. encender 6. gracioso; 9. alegre (contento)

3. simpático alegre (interesante) 10. dejar de

4. puntual 7. antiguo

E. 1. comienza 6. suena 11. encarga 16. prometen

2. celebramos 7. apago 12. entiendo 17. cumplen

3. baila 8. sueñas 13. merezco 18. enciende

4. entiende 9. molestan 14. avisa 19. cumple

5. comienzan 10. tocas 15. deja 20. suena

Exercises

A. 1. cumpleaños 9. entremeses 17. deliciosa (¡Mmmm!...)

2. teléfono 10. arroz con pollo 18. tomar (beber)

3. invitar 11. ensalada 19. champán

4. viernes 12. torta 20. refresco

5. universidad 13. inspector 21. cigarrillo

6. resfriado 14. bebidas 22. bailar

7. asistir 15. divierte 23. ritmos

8. preparar 16. llega

B. 1. velas 5. domingos 9. una semana 13. cumple

2. miércoles 6. la guitarra 10. sueñan 14. apagar

3. una copa 7. enciendes 11. avisa 15. el estéreo

4. botanas 8. resfriado 12. este país

C. 1. atrasado 3. sabroso 5. aburrido

2. oscuro 4. próxima 6. oscuro

D. 1. José tiene ganas de leer el libro *Hawaii*.

    2. ¿Por qué tú no dejas de fumar hoy?

    3. La fiesta de mi cumpleaños es el sábado próximo.

    4. La torta del cumpleaños de Roberto tiene veintitrés velas.

    5. María quiere bailar (los) ritmos modernos.

    6. Ustedes llegan atrasados a la fiesta.

    7. Estos entremeses están muy sabrosos.

    8. Tus sobrinos son bastante graciosos.

Practique los pronombres

1. direct object
2. a tu tía/a
3. No/a/alguien
4. stress/verb
5. lo/la/los/las
6. lo veo/los
7. Precede/Follow
8. infinitive/indicative
9. Both are correct.
10. a/camareras

Exercises

A. 1. las traigo
   2. la oigo
   3. lo hago
   4. la conozco
   5. lo quiero
   6. lo hablo
   7. los fumo
   8. la veo
   9. quiero leerlo
  10. lo quiero ver
  11. tengo que oírla
  12. la tengo que oír

B. 1. a   2. a   3. (nothing)   4. (nothing)   5. al   6. A/A

C. 1. te llama
   2. los (las) felicita
   3. puedo llamarla (la puedo llamar)
   4. los ayudamos
   5. voy a verte (te voy a ver)
   6. me dejan en casa

Practique los reflexivos

1. subject/me/te
2. se/Se habla español
3. Ya te vas a casa
4. inanimate/se
5. se venden
6. reflexive
7. se sienta/se siente

Exercises

A. 1. se abrochan   6. me afeito   11. nos sentimos

 2. me acuesto   7. se pone   12. se levanta

 3. se despierta   8. se viste   13. te sientas

 4. se divierte   9. se sientan   14. nos peinamos

 5. se llama/me llamo   10. me quito   15. nos bañamos

B. 1. Se vive bien aquí.   5. El carro se detiene (para) ahora.

 2. En Argentina se habla español.   6. Los carros se detienen (paran).

 3. Me voy a casa ahora.   7. Se vende la casa.

 4. Se come toda la torta.

Practique el pretérito

1. meaning/com-/v-   5. present/preterite   9. toqué/qu

2. nosotros/tú/yo   6. apagué/gu   10. comencé/c

3. hablé/habló   7. past/I paid   11. leyeron

4. viví/vivió   8. creyó/y   12. one/acento

Exercises

A. 1. llegó/llegué   8. apagaste/apagué   15. se quitó/entró

 2. leyeron   9. volvieron   16. oyeron

 3. me bañé   10. dormí   17. nevó

 4. vio   11. se cayó   18. se comió

 5. te acostaste   12. tocó/toqué   19. salió

 6. practiqué   13. pagó/pagué   20. llovió

 7. comenzó/comencé   14. vivimos

B. 1. lo pagué   3. la invité   5. me llevó

 2. lo bebió   4. la vi   6. la toqué

C. 1. me desperté   6. me desayuné   11. volví

    2. me levanté   7. salí   12. comenzó

    3. me bañé   8. llegué   13. explicó

    4. me sequé   9. oí   14. se cayó

    5. me vestí   10. comí   15. se destruyó

Lesson 8

Practique las palabras nuevas

A. 1. la   4. la   7. la   10. el   13. la

    2. el   5. el   8. el   11. el   14. la

    3. el   6. el   9. la   12. el   15. el

B. 1. jugo   5. queso   9. bocadillo   13. leche

    2. hamburguesa   6. a menudo   10. merendar   14. buena pinta

    3. pierna   7. leche   11. pepino   15. solomillo

    4. pavo   8. cebolla   12. zanahoria   16. picante

C. 1. colombianas   3. chilenas   5. peruanas

    2. mexicanas   4. españolas

D. 1. verdura   5. burrito (burrada)   9. compra   13. atender

    2. pescado   6. asado   10. café   14. lleno

    3. merienda   7. fresco (refrescar)   11. enfermo   15. bocadillo

    4. tortilla   8. comedor   12. calor (caliente)   16. explicar

E. 1. asa   4. para   7. meriendo   10. busco

    2. andas   5. vendemos   8. juegas

    3. recomiendo   6. atienden   9. condimentan

F. 1. asó   3. jugaron   5. vendió   7. busqué

    2. merendaron   4. se pararon   6. atendió   8. recomendó

Exercises

A.

1. supermercado	9. mercado	17. cordero	25. pastel
2. compras	10. cerdo	18. pierna	26. saludable
3. mercados	11. grasa	19. frescas	27. a dieta
4. atienden	12. paquete	20. pepinos	28. dulce
5. empleados	13. pinta	21. zanahorias	29. de peso
6. a menudo	14. por ciento	22. lata	30. cuidan
7. bajos	15. hamburguesa	23. saben	
8. productos	16. solomillo	24. atún	

B.

1. el vino tinto	5. té	9. ternera	13. el aguacate
2. un bocadillo de pavo	6. maíz	10. lata	14. pescado
3. estupendo	7. queso	11. grasas	
4. plátanos fritos	8. atún	12. calorías	

C.

1. E	4. H	7. L	10. F
2. K	5. A	8. B	11. C
3. J	6. G	9. D	12. I

D.
1. Rita buscó las verduras más frescas.
2. Ellas salieron de compras al supermercado en carro.
3. El domingo pasado yo pesqué en el mar.
4. ¿Cuándo vendiste tú tus libros viejos?
5. Nuestras tías merendaron en este restaurante.

Practique el pretérito

1. dorm- / durm- / u
2. ped- / pid- / i / Pidió
3. dormir / Murió / Murieron
4. ie / siento / i / sintió
5. third / preterite
6. vuelvo / vuelve / volvió
7. ue / duerme / u / durmió / durmieron

Exercises

A. 1. se sintió/me sentí   5. durmió/dormimos   9. repitió/repetí

     2. murió   6. se vistió/me vestí   10. se divirtieron

     3. sirvieron   7. murieron

     4. pedimos/pidió   8. prefirió/preferí

B. 1. volvió/prefirió   4. se despertó/se vistió   6. vivió/murió

     2. sentí/llevaron   5. llegué/seguí   7. me quité/me acosté

     3. se divirtieron/pidieron

Practique el pretérito

1. present/I say   5. j/Condujeron   9. anduve   12. -ar/dieron

2. Supe   6. puso   10. tener/detuvo   13. acento/dio/fue

3. hic-/hiz-   7. trajeron   11. I was/I went/ir

4. i/-eron   8. From the context.

Exercises

A. 1. pudo   4. produjeron   7. fue   10. vinimos

     2. puso   5. estuviste   8. hizo/hice   11. vio/supo

     3. quiso/pudo   6. dijeron/dije   9. fue   12. tuvieron

B. 1. anduvo   4. tuvo   7. se puso   10. dijo

     2. condujo   5. llegó   8. hicieron   11. tomó

     3. estuvo   6. dejó   9. trajeron   12. sonó

Practique los modismos (*Idioms*)

1. hay/hubo   4. hay   7. mucho   9. start

2. definite   5. obligation   8. just taken place   10. Se puso a comer

3. haber/indefinite   6. hay/hubo

Exercises

A. 1. viento   2. el libro aquí

     que practicar   alegre

                            pálido

3. una fiesta aquí
   que practicar
   viento

4. de practicar
   una fiesta aquí
   el libro aquí

5. viento

6. a practicar
   alegre

7. a practicar
   alegre
   pálido

8. que practicar
   una fiesta aquí
   el libro aquí

B. 1. que   5. de   9. X   13. a/que
   2. X/a   6. X/que   10. de   14. a
   3. a   7. a/X   11. a/X (de) 15. a/a
   4. de   8. de/a   12. de

Lesson 9

Practique las palabras nuevas

A. 1. el   3. la   5. el   7. los   9. los   11. la
   2. los   4. el   6. el   8. las   10. las 12. los

B. 1. ahorrar   6. necesidad   11. interesar   16. ganancia
   2. encantar   7. cargo, encargado   12. lujoso   17. par
   3. valor   8. gastar   13. prestar   18. importar
   4. convenir   9. pesado, pesar   14. chequera   (importante)
   5. ciento, cien 10. alegrarse   15. contar

C. 1. préstamo   5. ahorrar   9. nadar   13. descubrió
   2. de lujo   6. divisas   10. un par de   14. giro postal
   3. por ciento 7. cartera   11. gangas   15. tienda
   4. moneda   8. gana   12. a plazos

D. 1. prestó   4. se alegraron   7. saqué   10. cargaron
   2. se quejaron 5. encontraron   8. valió
   3. metí   6. aumentan   9. gastó

E. 1. F   3. T   5. F   7. T   9. F   11. T

  2. F   4. T   6. F   8. T   10. T   12. T

Exercises

A. 1. estudiar   7. moneda   13. abrió   19. préstamo

  2. conocer   8. tuvo   14. giro   20. a plazos

  3. entró (fue)   9. viajero   15. cheques   21. futuro

  4. cambiar   10. cobró   16. dijo (informó) 22. vino

  5. cajero   11. ciento   17. corrientes   23. disfrutar

  6. dólar (cambio) 12. pasaporte 18. ahorros

B. 1. hipoteca   5. salario (sueldo)   9. por fin

  2. tarjetas de   6. ahorrar/sacar   10. impuestos
     crédito
                         7. interés   11. al contado
  3. chequera   (intereses)
                                               12. se quejaron
  4. débil/antiguo   8. pena

C. 1. un cheque   3. nadar   5. valioso   7. divisas

  2. un billete   4. comer   6. aumentan   8. se parecen

Practique los pronombres

1. indirect object   4. follow/indicative   7. emphatic

2. le/les, reflexive   5. indicative/infinitive 8. le, les

3. interest   6. se/Se lo vendo   9. la

Exercises

A. 1. le   3. le   5. me   7. La   9. Se los   11. Les

  2. me   4. nos   6. le   8. Los   10. Se las   12. me

B. 1. a pagártela   5. se lo trajo   8. se lo aumenté

  2. a pagársela   6. deseo abrirla   9. quiero ponerlas

  3. se lo dio   (la deseo abrir)   10. las quiero poner

  4. se los prestó   7. lavárselo

C. 1. Tú nos compraste bocadillos sabrosos a nosotros.

  2. Los camareros les sirvieron la comida a los pasajeros.

  3. Tus tíos me vendieron el (su) Volkswagen a mí.

  4. El botones les subió las maletas a los turistas.

5. Enrique no le prestó el carro a nadie.

Practique la gramática

1. libro / me / Me gustan   3. (b)   5. inanimate   7. Se le cayeron
2. third / le, les   4. my   6. indirect object   8. me parece buena

Exercises

A. 1. les gustan   4. me duele   7. se me para   10. me apetece
   2. le pasó / me pasó   5. les conviene   8. se le cayeron   11. le molesta
   3. me parece   6. te interesa   9. le sobró   12. nos gusta

B. 1. A nadie le gustan las cosas malas.
   2. A tus abuelos les encanta la comida española.
   3. A los alumnos les interesan las clases buenas.
   4. A mí me faltan dos dólares de la cartera.
   5. A usted no le gusta nadar en el mar.
   6. A ella se le para (paró) el carro en la avenida 5.
   7. A ti se te cayeron dos billetes de cinco dólares.

C. 1. A mis hijos (niños) les gusta oír la radio.
   2. Esa muchacha me parece muy linda (bonita) (a mí).
   3. Me duelen mucho las manos hoy.
   4. ¿Qué te pasa (a ti) hoy, mi hijo?
   5. Se me cayó el reloj al piso (suelo).
   6. Me interesan tus (sus) problemas.
   7. Le conviene esta clase (a ella).

Practique el imperfecto

1. -aba / gustaba   4. era   7. imperfect / going on
2. -ía / bebía / salía   5. veía   8. había
3. iba / Íbamos   6. hablábamos / íbamos   9. imperfect

Exercises

A. 1. ahorraban   5. éramos   9. caían   12. gustaba
   2. leía   6. molestaba   10. nadábamos   13. había
   3. estabas   7. valía   11. veían   14. vivía
   4. iba   8. parecía

B. 1. convenía   6. faltaba   11. quejaba   16. vestía

    2. cargaba   7. sobraban   12. comenzaba   17. morían

    3. valía   8. metías   13. pensabas   18. conocía

    4. encontraban   9. veía   14. dolía   19. hacía

    5. dormían   10. íbamos   15. tenía   20. había

Lesson 10

Practique las palabras nuevas

A. 1. el   4. el   7. el   10. el   13. el   16. la   19. los

    2. el   5. la   8. la   11. las   14. el   17. el   20. el

    3. las   6. las   9. los   12. el   15. los   18. la

B. 1. paradas   6. milla   11. a mediodía   16. maletero (mozo)

    2. litera   7. horario   12. en medio de   17. roto

    3. taquilla   8. bar   13. sin falta   18. fácil

    4. andén   9. despacio   14. ida y vuelta   19. vacía

    5. salud   10. hace caso   15. TALGO   20. corren

C. 1. billete   3. ferrocarril   5. coche (carro)   7. gratuito

    2. salida   4. olvidarse   6. entero (completo)   8. elevador

D. 1. llegada (entrada)   6. vacío   11. triste

    2. vuelta   7. difícil   12. entero (completo)

    3. salud   8. desocupado (libre)   13. deshacer

    4. mediodía   9. rápido   14. perder

    5. limpio   10. perder

E. 1. mandó   4. funcionó   7. perdieron   10. demoró

    2. crucé   5. corrió   8. tomó el pelo   11. hicieron caso

    3. olvidó   6. se... rompió   9. informó   12. entregó

F. 1. mandaba   4. funcionaba   7. perdían   10. demoraba

    2. cruzaba   5. corría   8. tomaba el pelo   11. hacían caso

    3. olvidaba   6. se me rompía   9. informaba   12. entregaba

Exercises

A.
1. negocios	7. suplemento	13. volver	19. plástico
2. estación	8. bar	14. viene	20. firma
3. viajar	9. bebidas	15. quinientas	21. andén
4. rápido	10. vagones (coches)	16. impuestos	22. sin falta
5. velocidad	11. ida y vuelta	17. tarjetas	
6. por hora	12. de primera	18. crédito	

B. 1. F   3. F   5. T   7. F   9. T   11. F   13. T
   2. T   4. T   6. T   8. T   10. T   12. F   14. T

C.
1. difícil	4. rota	7. medio	10. propina
2. vacía	5. vacaciones	8. haces caso	11. despacio
3. tomas el pelo	6. ocupada	9. sin falta	12. gratis

D. 1. Mi esposa deshacía las maletas después del viaje.

2. Sus tíos siempre le mandaban dinero a él.

3. Los niños no hacían caso a nadie en la fiesta.

4. El carro viejo siempre se me rompía a mí.

5. Todos los días se le paraba el carro a ella.

6. A Carlos le gustaban los libros americanos de ficción.

Practique el imperfecto y el pretérito

1. middle/end	5. imperfect/era/tenía	9. The imperfect/tenía
2. middle/end	6. imperfect/fumaba/bebía	10. The imperfect
3. beginning/end	7. ahorró	11. The preterite
4. beginning/action	8. The imperfect/eran	12. iba/tuvo

Exercises

A. 1. Mi familia vivía en Kansas cuando (yo) nací.

2. Mi abuelo tenía ochenta años cuando murió.

3. Eran las tres cuando llegaron mis tíos.

4. Estela llamó cuando estabas (Ud. estaba) en el jardín.

5. No le pasó nada grave a mi hermano cuando se cayó.

6. Vi a mi hermano cuando abrí la ventana.

B. 1. fui/tenía   3. vivíamos/éramos   5. dijo/tenía   7. comía/fumaba

   2. estaba/sonó   4. llegó/pidió   6. pasó/paró   8. trajeron/estaba

C. 1. llegamos   7. tuvimos   13. almorzábamos

   2. eran   8. estaba   14. comenzó

   3. estábamos   9. hacía   15. tuvimos

   4. duchamos   10. tomamos   16. llevó

   5. acostamos   11. estábamos   17. había

   6. despertamos   12. almorzamos   18. dormimos

Practique los modismos

1. Llegué hace un mes   4. Imperfect/fumaba   7. Llevo diez minutos aquí

2. desde   5. que

3. que   6. Hacía dos meses que no fumaba
                             (Llevaba dos meses sin fumar)

Exercises

A. 1. Hace cinco años que vivo aquí.

   2. Viajé a Panamá hace ocho años.

   3. Hace media hora que toco el piano.

   4. Salí de España hace veinticinco años.

   5. Hace una semana que no viajo en autobús.

   6. Hacía cuatro meses que no llovía en Arizona.

   7. Hacía cinco minutos que hablaba por teléfono.

   8. Hacía dos días que no llamaba a mis padres.

B. 1. El Cid murió hace como mil años

   2. No llovía (desde) hacía un año

   3. Hace dos años que se fue Rita

   4. Hace veinte años que fumas

   5. El tren pasó hace cinco minutos

   6. Hace diez años que estoy (vivo) aquí

   7. Hace una hora que saqué los billetes

   8. Hace cinco años que soy profesor

Practique la gramática

1. number/primera
2. tercero/Before
3. after/el día primero
4. Carlos Primero

5. capitalized/No
6. el martes
7. el invierno/el verano
8. primavera

9. enero/febrero
10. julio/diciembre
11. primero, uno
12. No/el/los

Exercises

A. 1. octubre/mayo
   2. abril/mayo
   3. el dos
   4. el uno (primero) de marzo
   5. el cuatro de julio
   6. veinticinco de diciembre
   7. el uno (el primero) de enero
   8. el jueves

   9. El invierno
   10. El verano
   11. Carlos Quinto
   12. Enero
   13. Vivo en el primero (segundo)
   14. sexto/octavo
   15. décima/diecinueve (19)

B. 1. A mí me gustan la primavera y el verano.
   2. Emilio vive en la calle Ocho (8).
   3. Ustedes viajan a México el doce (12) de junio.
   4. Nosotros tenemos vacaciones el uno (primero) de abril.
   5. Hoy es lunes, el ocho (8) de setiembre.

C. 1. Compré los boletos (billetes) el martes.
   2. (A nosotros) nos gusta el «Cuatro de Julio».
   3. La primavera va del 21 de marzo al 21 de junio.
   4. Enrique Octavo tuvo ocho esposas (mujeres).
   5. Hoy es el dos de noviembre.

Exam 2

Part I.   Practique las palabras nuevas (50 puntos)

1. L	4. P	7. R	10. D
2. J	5. M	8. K	11. H
3. Q	6. O	9. N	12. C

13. B
14. A
15. F
16. I
17. E
18. G
19. al andén
20. una litera
21. una cuenta corriente
22. a plazos
23. un sueldo
24. el solomillo
25. tinto

26. velas
27. da al
28. color naranja
29. vacío/débil
30. limpio/fácil
31. lento/estrecho
32. ocupado/sencillo
33. cerrar/aburrido
34. ahorrar/salir
35. encender/perder
36. propina
37. nadar
38. una hipoteca

39. jugo
40. nietos
41. nieve
42. (una) (la) toalla
43. pescados
44. C
45. A
46. D
47. C
48. D
49. A
50. B

Part II. Practique la gramática (50 puntos)

1. tuve sueño
2. hizo (hubo) sol
3. tuvo sed
4. hizo mucho frío
5. pudieron
6. se divirtieron
7. llegué
8. quiso/pudo
9. pidió
10. se sintió/(se) fue
11. me afeité
12. se vistió
13. tocó/toqué

14. trajeron
15. hubo
16. se levantó
17. quería
18. estaba
19. fue
20. se bañó
21. se secó
22. tenía
23. se comió
24. dijo
25. durmió
26. soñó

27. anduvo
28. tenía
29. Hacía
30. había
31. B
32. C
33. A
34. C
35. D
36. C
37. B
38. E
39. C

40. A
41. C
42. D
43. D
44. B
45. C
46. E
47. D
48. C
49. D
50. A

11 Las partes del cuerpo
(The Parts of the Body)

la barbilla	chin	el labio	lip
la boca	mouth	la mejilla	cheek
el brazo	arm	la muleta	crutch
el cabello[1]	hair	la muñeca	wrist; doll
la cabeza	head	el muslo	thigh
la cadera	hip	la nariz[5]	nose
la cara	face	el ojo	eye
la ceja	eyebrow	la oreja[6]	(outer) ear
la cintura	waist	el par	couple (things)
el codo	elbow	el párpado	eyelid
el cuello	neck	la patilla	sideburn
el dedo[2]	finger, toe	el pecho	breast
los deportes	sports	el pelo	hair
el diente	tooth	la pestaña	eyelash
la escalera[3]	stairs	el pie[7]	foot
la espalda	back (person)	la pierna	leg
la frente[4]	forehead	la rodilla	knee
la garganta	throat	el tobillo	ankle
el hombro	shoulder	el yeso	cast (plaster)
el hueso	bone		

besar	to kiss	ocurrir	to happen
cojear	to limp	oler[8] (hue)	to smell
doler (ue)	to hurt, ache	pasar	to happen
encontrarse	to meet, find	torcer (ue)	to twist, sprain
enyesar	to put a cast		

cojo(a)	lame, crippled	**imprevisto(a)**	unexpected
estúpido(a)	bastard	**increíble**	incredible
ligero(a)	light, quick	**serio(a)**	serious

A mal tiempo, buena cara.	Smile in the face of adversity.
echar de menos, extrañar	to miss
en serio	seriously
hacer ver las estrellas	to make one feel a terrible pain ("see the stars")
tener mala estrella	to be unlucky ("to have bad star")
tener mala pata	to be unlucky ("to have bad foot")
un par de	a couple of (*things*), a few

NOTAS

1. *Cabello* is the *hair* on a person's head. *Pelo* is both the *hair* on a person's head as well as the *hair* on any other part of the body of a person or animal.

2. *Dedo* is *finger* as well as *toe*. To tell the difference, we sometimes add *de la mano* or *del pie*.

3. *Escalera* is *stairs* as well as *ladder*. Sometimes we say *escalera de mano* for *ladder*. *Escalera rodante* is used for *escalator*.

4. **La frente** is the *forehead*. **El frente** is the *front* of a house or any other place. **El frente** is also *battlefront*. The change of gender makes a difference in meaning.

5. *Nariz* is *nose*. We use the plural **narices** to refer to *nostrils* and also in idiomatic expressions such as **dar con la puerta en las narices** (to say no emphatically).

6. *Orejas* is the standard word for *ears,* that is, *outer ears.* The word for *inner ear* is *oído.* Since Spanish has the tendency to have a different word for the same organ in animals and in persons, in some regions people use *oreja* for animals and *oído* for persons.

7. *Pie* is the *foot of a person*. *Ir a pie* means *to walk, go on foot*. We use the word *pata* for the *foot* or *leg of an animal,* but in idiomatic expressions we also use *pata* for people. *Meter la pata* is *to stick one's foot in it. Tener mala pata* is *to be unlucky.*

8. *Oler* changes *o* to *ue* and at the same time takes a silent *h:* **huelo, hueles, huele,** BUT **olemos.** *Olía* is the imperfect, and *olí* is the preterite.

9. *Estúpido* translates *bastard* rather than *stupid*. The term is very strong in Spanish and is an insult to be avoided. *Stupid* is best translated as **tonto(a), absurdo(a),** conveying the idea of *"silly."*

10. *Echar de menos* is used in Spain for *to miss* (as a nostalgic thought or as an awareness of not having something), whereas in Latin America *extrañar* is used for the same concept.

Practique las palabras nuevas

ANSWERS
p. 308

A. Write *el, la, los,* or *las* before each noun.

1. _____ diente	6. _____ narices	11. _____ cuello
2. _____ nariz	7. _____ cabello	12. _____ frente (*forehead*)
3. _____ deportes	8. _____ rodilla	13. _____ frente (*front*)
4. _____ cejas	9. _____ pares	14. _____ patillas
5. _____ pie	10. _____ ojos	15. _____ estrella

ANSWERS
p. 308

B. Complete each sentence with one of the idioms below. Make the necessary changes.

A mal tiempo, buena cara.	en serio	meter la pata
echar de menos	hacer ver las estrellas	tener mala pata
encontrarse con	ir a pie	un par de

1. El año pasado perdí a mi padre, y ahora todavía lo _____.

2. ¿Lo dices en broma (*as a joke*) o _____?

3. Mi carro está roto; por eso ayer _____ a la universidad.

4. El verano pasado perdí bastante dinero en Las Vegas. Siempre que juego dinero (*gamble*) _____.

5. No debes estar triste por eso; a mal _____.

6. Si no sabes nada de eso, no debes _____.

7. ¿Me puedes prestar _____ dólares para comprar un refresco?

8. Este dolor de cabeza es tan grande que me _____.

9. Cuando (yo) iba a pie al trabajo ayer _____ Roberto.

ANSWERS
p. 308

C. Complete each sentence with one of the words below. Make the necessary changes.

cabello	cojear	escalera	frente	imprevisto	muleta	párpado
codo	dedo	espalda	hueso	ligero	nariz	rodilla

1. Tenemos veinte _____: diez en las manos y diez en los pies.

2. Ayer tuve una visita _____ de mis tíos de Miami.

3. Parece que Lourdes tiene un problema en el pie porque _____ un poco.

4. Si no hay ascensor (elevador), bajamos y subimos por la _____.

5. Algunas mujeres se pintan las cejas y los _____.

6. El tobillo, el pie y la _____ son parte de la pierna.

7. Vemos con los ojos y olemos con la _____.

8. Delante tenemos el pecho, y detrás tenemos la _____.

9. No tengo mucha hambre; voy a comer algo _____.

10. La cabeza está cubierta de pelo o _____.

11. El _____ más grande del cuerpo es el fémur; está en el muslo.

12. Si Ud. no puede caminar bien, puede usar dos _____.

13. La parte del brazo que se dobla (*bends*) es el _____.

14. La parte de la cabeza que está entre el pelo y los ojos es la _____.

ANSWERS p. 308

D. Complete each sentence with the correct preterite form of the verb in parentheses.

1. Ayer me caí y me _____ el tobillo. (*torcer*)

2. ¿Qué le _____ a Juanito después del baile? (*ocurrir*)

3. Lolita y yo _____ en la cafetería del colegio. (*encontrarse*)

4. Mi novia tuvo un accidente en el pie y _____ bastante la semana pasada, pero ya está bien. (*cojear*)

5. Los médicos me _____ el brazo derecho. (*enyesar*)

6. Ahora no me duele el brazo, pero ayer me _____ mucho. (*doler*)

7. Los perros de la policía _____ la cocaína en el aeropuerto. (*oler*)

8. Cuando me fui de Cuba, _____ a mi país por un tiempo. (*extrañar*)

9. Los novios _____ cuando el sacerdote (*priest*) les declaró marido y mujer. (*besarse*)

ANSWERS p. 308

E. Complete each sentence with the correct name for the part of the body implied.

1. Abrimos y cerramos los ojos por medio de los _____.

2. Vemos con los ojos; besamos con los _____.

3. Mi _____ no es rojo ni rubio (*blond*) sino negro.

4. Doblamos el brazo en el codo, y doblamos la pierna en _____.

5. A los lados del cuello tenemos los dos _____.

6. Detrás del cuerpo está la espalda; delante del cuerpo está el _____.

7. La parte del cuerpo entre el brazo y la mano es la _____.

8. El fémur es el _____ más grande del cuerpo humano.

9. No es lo mismo el frente de batalla que la _____ de la cabeza.

10. A los lados de la boca tenemos las dos _____ que algunos países llaman cachetes.

11. El fémur está en la parte de la pierna que llamamos el _____.

12. El _____ une la cabeza con el resto del cuerpo.

DIÁLOGO   Un accidente imprevisto

Sonia y Mario son buenos amigos y se encuentran antes de la clase. Mario tiene el pie derecho enyesado, y camina con muletas.

SONIA: ¡Hola, Mario! ¿Qué te pasó en la pierna?

MARIO: Nada serio. Me caí por la escalera de casa y me torcí el tobillo.

SONIA: ¡Increíble! Yo pensé que esos accidentes sólo ocurrían en deportes como el fúbol y en las películas.

MARIO: Ya ves; parece que yo siempre tengo mala pata. Todo me ocurre de la manera más tonta.

SONIA: ¿Estás seguro que no fue un accidente cuando volvías de la fiesta de Carmen a mil kilómetros por hora?

MARIO: No, hablo en serio. Si no me crees, pregúntale a mi hermana.

SONIA: Bueno, ¿y te duele mucho?

MARIO: No, apenas si siento un ligero dolor.

SONIA: ¿Te dolió mucho cuando te pusieron el yeso?

MARIO: Sí, especialmente cuando el médico me ponía los huesos en su lugar. ¡Me hizo ver las estrellas!

SONIA: ¿Y cuánto tiempo llevarás el yeso y las muletas?

MARIO: Un par de semanas, si todo va bien. Voy a echar de menos el baile del cumpleaños de Margarita.

SONIA: Bueno, ¿qué le vas a hacer? ¡A mal tiempo, buena cara!

DIALOGUE   An Unexpected Accident

Sonia and Mario are good friends, and they meet before class. Mario has his right foot in a cast and walks with crutches.

SONIA: Hi! Mario. What's wrong with your leg?

MARIO: Nothing serious. I fell down the stairs at home and twisted my ankle.

SONIA: Incredible! I thought such things happened only in sports such as football and in the movies.

MARIO: As you can see, it seems I always have bad luck. Everything happens to me in the silliest way.

SONIA: Are you sure it wasn't an accident when you were coming back at full speed from Carmen's party?

MARIO: Of course not, I'm serious. If you don't believe me, ask my sister.

SONIA: Well, does it hurt a lot?

MARIO: No, I hardly feel any pain.

SONIA: Did it hurt a lot when they put on the cast?

MARIO: Plenty. Especially when the doctor was setting the bones. He made me
see stars!

SONIA: And how long will you have the cast and the crutches?

MARIO: A couple of weeks if everything goes well. I'm going to miss the dance
on Margaret's birthday.

SONIA: Well, what can you do? Smile in the face of adversity!

EXERCISES

**ANSWERS
p. 308**

A. *Un accidente imprevisto.* **Complete the story using the information from the
dialogue.**

Sonia y Mario son buenos (1) _____ y se (2) _____
antes de la clase. Mario tiene el pie derecho (3) _____ y tiene que
caminar con dos (4) _____. Él se cayó de la (5) _____ de
su casa y se (6) _____ el tobillo. Con frecuencia ocurre este tipo de
(7) _____ en los deportes como el fútbol y en las (8) _____
donde todo es posible. Mario cree que él siempre tiene (9) _____
porque le ocurren los accidentes de la manera más (10) _____.
Sonia tiene sus dudas (*doubts*) y se imagina que Mario tuvo un problema
con el carro cuando (11) _____ de la fiesta de cumpleaños de
Carmen a mil kilómetros (12) _____. Mario le asegura que habla
(13) _____. Además él le dice que puede preguntar a su
(14) _____ si no lo cree. En ese momento Mario sólo tiene un dolor
(15) _____ en el tobillo pero éste le dolió mucho cuando le pusieron
el (16) _____. El doctor le puso primero los (17) _____
en su lugar, y eso le hizo ver las (18) _____. Mario tiene que llevar
el yeso y las (19) _____ por un par de (20) _____. Él va a
echar de (21) _____el baile del cumpleaños de su amiga Margarita,
pero, ¡qué le va a hacer! ¡A mal tiempo, (22) _____!

**ANSWERS
p. 309**

B. **Answer** *true* **or** *false* **(T/F).**

1. _____ Sonia y Mario se encuentran y hablan después de la clase.

2. _____ Mario tiene enyesado el pie izquierdo porque se cayó en su casa.

3. _____ Él se cayó por la escalera de su casa y se torció el tobillo.

4. _____ Sonia siempre tiene mala pata porque le ocurren los accidentes más tontos.

5. _____ Sonia sabe que Mario estuvo en la fiesta de Carmen y que le gusta correr bastante con el carro.

6. _____ El accidente del tobillo ocurrió cuando Mario volvía de una fiesta a mil kilómetros por hora.

7. _____ Mario apenas si siente un ligero dolor en el tobillo en este momento.

8. _____ Ayer él vio las estrellas cuando el médico le puso los huesos en su lugar.

9. _____ Mario tiene que llevar el yeso y las muletas por una semana solamente.

10. _____ Él va a echar de menos un baile de cumpleaños de una amiga.

11. _____ Sonia cree que es mejor estar alegre en una dificultad que ponerse triste.

12. _____ Después de leer el diálogo y la historia concluimos que Sonia y Mario son novios.

ANSWERS p. 309

C. Underline the best answer.

1. Si Ud. tiene un problema para caminar, puede usar (cinturas, muletas, rodillas, patillas).

2. Sentimos los olores con (los ojos, los oídos, la nariz, la boca).

3. Sonia y Mario forman un(a) buen(a) (pareja, muñeca, par, deporte).

4. El fútbol y el béisbol son dos clases de (huesos, deportes, muslos, caderas).

5. El fémur es una clase de (tobillo, muslo, hueso, hombro).

6. La (garganta, espalda, cara, pestaña) es muy importante para hablar.

7. Para doblar el brazo usamos (la rodilla, el cuello, el hombro, el codo).

8. Un accidente que Ud. no espera es (ligero, increíble, imprevisto, serio).

9. Unas personas se besan en los labios; otras se besan en (las mejillas, las patillas, las cejas, las rodillas).

10. Nos ponemos el reloj en (el brazo, el pecho, la muñeca, las pestañas).

ANSWERS p. 309

D. Form sentences in the preterite. Use the words given in the order of appearance, and make all necessary adjustments.

1. Mario / caerse / por / escalera / su casa / .

2. él / torcerse / tobillo / derecho / en / accidente /.

_____

3. Sonia / no / creer / Mario / primero /.

_____

4. Mario / sentir / bastante / dolor / en / operación /.

_____

5. médico / poner / huesos / en / su / lugar /.

_____

6. doctor / hacer ver / estrellas / Mario / de / el dolor /.

_____

7. Mario / cojear / par de / semana /.

_____

GRAMMAR I Comparisons of Inequality

A. Comparisons with nouns, adjectives, and adverbs

Spanish Structure	English Equivalent
más menos + { (noun) (adjective) + **que** (adverb)	more less, fewer + { (noun) (adjective) + than (verb)

EXS: Ella tiene _más_ libros _que_ yo. (_She has <u>more</u> books <u>than</u> I do._)
José es _más_ tonto _que_ yo. (_José is sill<u>ier</u> <u>than</u> I am._)
Escribes _menos_ rápido _que_ yo. (_You write <u>less</u> quickly <u>than</u> I do._)

Note that in English short adjectives and adverbs take the comparative ending _-er_ rather than the adverb _more: happier, faster, funnier._

B. Comparisons with numbers and amounts

Spanish Structure	English Equivalent
más menos + **de** + (number, amount)	more less, fewer + than + (number, amount)

EXS: Compré _más de_ cinco libros. (_I bought <u>more than</u> five books._)
Compré _más de_ lo que quería. (_I bought <u>more than</u> I wanted._)

C. **Emphatic way to indicate an exact amount**

no + (verb) + **más que** + (amount) → only + (verb) + (amount)

EXS: 1. No tengo *más que* cinco pesos. (*I have <u>only</u> five pesos.*)
2. Tengo *exactamente* cinco pesos. (*I have <u>exactly</u> five pesos.*)

Example 1 is more emphatic and more idiomatic than example 2.

D. **Comparisons with verbs**

Spanish Structure	English Equivalent
(Subject) + (verb) + más que / menos que + (subject)	(Subject) + (verb) + more than / less than + (subject)

EXS: Ella trabaja *más que* yo. (*She works <u>more than</u> I do.*)
Ella pagó *menos que* yo. (*She paid <u>less than</u> I did.*)

PRACTIQUE LOS COMPARATIVOS

ANSWERS p. 309

1. The expressions *más que* and *menos que* are used to compare nouns, verbs, adjectives, and _____.

   EX: Ellos corrieron _____ yo. (*more than*)

2. To compare numbers and general amounts, the expression _____ is used instead of *más que,* and _____ is used instead of *menos que.*

3. How do you complete the sentence **Ud. bebió** _____ **cuatro cervezas?** (*more than*)

4. How do you complete the sentence **En mi familia tenemos** _____ **un carro?** (*more than*)

5. Sometimes it's necessary to compare a general amount rather than an exact number. For example, the idea of *more than you think* is translated into Spanish as _____ **lo que Ud. piensa.**

6. The English ending *-er* added to an adjective or adverb is translated into Spanish by the full word _____. For example, *She is taller than I am* becomes in Spanish **Ella es** _____ **yo.**

7. In Spanish *un, una,* are indefinite articles as well as numbers for *one.* Therefore, it's a mistake to say **Tienes más que un carro.** It should be **Tienes** _____ **un carro.**

8. If I say **No tengo más que dos pesos,** how many pesos do I have exactly? _____.

9. If I say **No tengo más de dos pesos,** I probably have fewer than _____, somewhere between one and two.

10. *Compraron exactamente tres libros* is equivalent but less emphatic than *No compraron _____ tres libros.*

EXERCISES

ANSWERS p. 309

A. Complete the sentences with the comparative forms.

1. Paco se fue a casa _____ temprano _____ yo. (*earlier than*)

2. ¿Tiene Ud. _____ veinte dólares en la cartera? (*more than*)

3. No puedo comprarlo porque tengo _____ un dólar. (*less than*)

4. Mi hija estudia _____ mi hijo. (*more than*)

5. Tenía ocho dólares y pagué cinco dólares por la comida. Ahora no tengo _____ tres dólares. (*only*)

6. Mi esposa es _____ alta _____ yo. (*taller*)

7. Antonio trabaja _____ lo que Ud. se imagina. (*more than*)

8. Uds. compraron _____ libros _____ Juan. (*less than*)

9. En realidad siempre comemos _____ lo que necesitamos. (*more than*)

10. Si Ud. tiene exactamente un televisor, Ud. no tiene _____ un televisor. (*only*)

ANSWERS p. 309

B. Combine the sentences according to the example.

EX: **Ana compró tres libros. Yo compré dos libros.**
    Ana compró más libros que yo.

1. Pablo se rompió dos huesos en el accidente. María se rompió un hueso.

   _____

2. Mario tuvo un accidente. Sonia no tuvo ningún accidente.

   _____

3. Marcos tiene seis pies de alto. Lola tiene cinco pies y medio. (*Use the Spanish equivalent of "taller."*)

   _____

4. José estudia mucho, pero su hermano estudia poco.

   _____

5. Estudio cuatro horas todos los días. Ud. piensa que yo estudio sólo dos horas.

    _____

6. Miriam tiene exactamente dos hermanos. No tiene ni más ni menos. (*only*)

    _____

7. Carlos gana poco dinero. Ud. se imagina que Carlos gana mucho.

    _____

GRAMMAR II   Comparisons of Equality • Superlatives

A. **Comparisons with adjectives and adverbs**

Spanish Structure	English Equivalent
tan + (adjective) / (adverb) **+ como**	as + (adjective) / (adverb) + as

EXS: María es *tan* alta *como* yo. (*Mary is* <u>as</u> *tall* <u>as</u> *I am.*)
    Ella corre *tan* rápido *como* yo. (*She runs* <u>as</u> *fast* <u>as</u> *I do.*)

B. **Comparisons with verbs**

(Verb) + **tanto** + **como** → (Verb) + as much as

EXS: Mario no fuma *tanto como* tú. (*Mario doesn't smoke* <u>as much as</u> *you do.*)
    Ella estudia *tanto como* yo. (*She studies* <u>as much as</u> *I do.*)

C. **Comparisons with nouns**

Spanish Structure	English Equivalent
tanto / tanta / **tantos / tantas** **+ (noun) + como**	as much / as many + (noun) + as

Note that *tanto, tanta, tantos,* and *tantas* agree with the noun in gender and number.

EXS: No tengo *tanto* dinero *como* tú. (*I don't have* <u>as much</u> *money* <u>as</u> *you.*)
    No trabajo *tantas* horas *como* tú. (*I don't work* <u>as many</u> *hours* <u>as</u> *you.*)

D. **Superlatives**

Study the following examples carefully.

EXS: Mario es *el más* alto *de* la clase. (*Mario is* <u>the tallest in</u> *the class.*)
    Sonia es *la más* alta *de* la clase. (*Sonia is* <u>the tallest in</u> *the class.*)

Note that the articles (**el, la**) and the adjectives (**alto, alta**) have to agree with the nouns in gender and number. However, the most common mistake is to translate *in* by Spanish *en* instead of *de*.

EX: **Marcos corre** *lo más* **rápido posible.** (*Mark runs* <u>as</u> *fast* <u>as</u> *possible.*)

In this case, the neuter article *lo* has no translation in English, just as the second *as* of the English equivalent has no translation in Spanish.

EX: **Marcos está gordísimo. = Marcos está** *muy* **gordo.** (*Mark is* <u>very</u> *fat.*)

The ending *-ísimo* is equivalent to the adverb *muy* in Spanish and *very* in English. It is more colloquial Spanish to use *muy* instead of *-ísimo*.

E. **Irregular comparatives and superlatives**

A few adjectives in Spanish—such as **bueno, malo, grande,** and **pequeño**—have the ending *-or* for the comparative (parallel to English *-er*). They can also form the comparative by using their regular forms in combination with other words: **más + (adjetivo) + que.** For example, **mejor que = más bueno que.**

These adjectives also have an irregular superlative besides **muy + (adjective).**

Adjective	Comparative	Superlative	(English)
bueno	mejor	óptimo	good, better, best
malo	peor	pésimo	bad, worse, worst
grande	mayor	máximo	big, bigger, biggest
pequeño	menor	mínimo	small, smaller, smallest

Mayor translates *older/oldest* when talking about people, and *menor* translates *younger/youngest*. In some countries *mayor* is used for *very old* (like a very old person), and as a noun *los mayores* means *ancestors*.

EX: **Mi hermana es** *menor que* **yo.** (*My sister is* <u>younger than</u> *I am.*)

PRACTIQUE LA GRAMÁTICA

ANSWERS
p. 310

1. The comparatives *tan, tanto, tanta, tantos,* and *tantas* are completed with the word _____, which translates *as* in English.

   EX: **Trabajé tanto** _____ **tú.**

2. *Tanto, tanta,* show the same gender and _____ as the noun they modify.

   EX: **Tengo** _____ **dedos como ella.** (*I have as many fingers as she does.*)

3. *Tan* is the short form of *tanto,* and it is used only in front of adjectives and _____.

   EX: **Tu pelo es** _____ **negro como el mío.**

4. What English word is not translated in the expression *as much as?*
   _____.

   EX: *I work as much as you do.* = **Trabajo** _____ **tú.**

5. How do you translate *older* if we are talking about people? _____.
   The same word is used for *oldest* with the articles *el, la, los, las.*

   EX: **Mi abuela es** _____ **de la familia.** (*oldest*)

6. How do you say *younger* in Spanish? _____. This word will
   change to the plural, for example, **Tengo dos hermanos** _____
   que yo. (*younger*)

7. We can use the word _____ instead of **más bueno,** and the word
   _____ instead of **más malo.**

   EX: **Tu casa es** _____ **la mía.** (*better than*)

8. Another way to say the superlative **muy lindo** in one word is _____.

   EX: **Mario está** _____. (*very lame*)

9. How do you complete the sentence *Anita es la más inteligente* _____
   la clase? This means that the English equivalent *in* is not *en* in Spanish but
   _____.

10. How do you translate **Lo más pronto posible?** _____. This
    means that the neuter article *lo* is not translated, and the English word
    _____ has no equivalent in Spanish.

11. If you are **optimista,** you look for the **óptimo** (*the best*) — in Spanish, **Usted**
    busca lo _____ **en la vida.** But if you are **pesimista,** you look
    only at **lo** _____. (*the worst*).

12. The maximum speed on United States highways used to be fifty-five miles per
    hour. It is now sixty-five miles per hour. You would tell a Spanish tourist that
    La velocidad _____ **es sesenta y cinco millas por hora.**

EXERCISES

**ANSWERS
p. 310**

A. Complete each sentence with the suggested items.

1. Mi hermano es _____ yo, pero es _____ alto _____
   yo. (*younger/as . . . as*)

2. Tus patillas no son _____ largas _____ las mías. (*as . . . as*)

3. Elena no trabaja _____ horas _____ Ud. (*as many . . . as*)

4. Después de clase tengo que irme _____. (*as soon as*
   possible)

5. José está demasiado gordo; está _____. (*very fat*)

6. ¿Quién es _____, tu padre o tu madre? (*older*)

7. Emilio, no corres _____ los atletas. (*as much as*)

8. Los dedos del pie no son _____ largos _____ los de la mano. (*as . . . as*)

9. Antonio no tiene _____ hambre _____ yo. (*as . . . as*)

10. Creo que hablo el inglés _____ el español. (*worse than*)

11. Colorado es el estado _____ montañoso _____ Estados Unidos. (*the most . . . in*)

12. Otra palabra para decir **muy grande** es _____.

13. Marta y Sofía son _____ Elena. (*older*)

14. Otra palabra para decir **más malo** es _____.

15. Un _____ siempre busca lo mejor en la vida.

16. Un _____ siempre ve lo negativo, lo peor de las cosas.

B. **Change the comparisons from** *tan... como* **to** *más... que.*

1. Lola tiene el pelo tan rubio como su hermana.

   _____

2. Guillermo tiene tanta suerte como su amiga.

   _____

3. En Alaska hace tanto frío como en Siberia.

   _____

4. Esta comida es tan ligera como esa otra.

   _____

C. **Translate into Spanish.**

1. Meat is as expensive as fish. _____

2. You are younger than I (am). _____

3. My car is as old as yours (is). _____

4. I did it as soon as possible. _____

5. She works as much as you (do). _____

6. She is the best of them all. _____

7. My son is very tall. _____

8. This is the tallest building (edificio) in the United States. _____

GRAMMAR III   Future Indicative of Regular Verbs

A. Memorize the future indicative forms of the verbs in the chart.

Subject	*hablar*	*comer*	*vivir*	*ser*	*estar*
yo	hablar é	comer é	vivir é	ser é	estar é
tú	hablar ás	comer ás	vivir ás	ser ás	estar ás
él/ella/Ud.	hablar á	comer á	vivir á	ser á	estar á
nosotros(as)	hablar emos	comer emos	vivir emos	ser emos	estar emos
ellos/ellas/Uds.	hablar án	comer án	vivir án	ser án	estar án

Note that:

1. The infinitive is the future stem for each verb: **hablar, comer, vivir, ser, estar.**

2. The endings are the same for all five verbs: **é, ás, á, emos, án.**

3. Except for **-emos**, all the endings have an accent: **comeré** BUT **comeremos.**

B. Use of the future indicative and other ways of expressing future time

1. We use the future indicative to indicate an action that is supposed to occur at some time after the present moment.

   EX: **La carta *llegará* mañana.** (*The letter <u>will arrive</u> tomorrow.*)

2. A future action may also be expressed by the use of the present indicative.

   EX: **La carta *llega* mañana.** (*The letter <u>will arrive</u> tomorow.*)

3. Finally, we may express a future action by using the present indicative of *ir* followed by *a* and the infinitive of the main verb.

   EX: **La carta *va a llegar* mañana.** (*The letter <u>will arrive</u> tomorrow.*)

4. Frequency of usage of the three different ways of expressing future time varies from country to country. For example, the future indicative is much more used in Spain than in Latin America, where use of *ir a* plus the main verb prevails.

C. Future of probability

The future indicative is also used to indicate wonderment or probability at the present time. Its English equivalent often has expressions like *I wonder, probably, can, must be.*

   EXS: **Sonia no vino a clase hoy. *Estará* enferma.** (*Sonia didn't come to class today. <u>Probably she is</u> sick.*)
   ¿Qué hora *será*? (*<u>I wonder</u> what time it is [what time it <u>can be</u>].*)
   No tengo reloj. *Serán* las tres de la tarde. (*I don't have a watch. It <u>must be</u> three o'clock in the afternoon.*)

PRACTIQUE EL FUTURO

ANSWERS p. 310

1. The stem of the future is the whole _____. For example, the stem of *comerán* is _____; the stem of *seremos* is _____.

2. The endings are the same for all the verbs, but each person has a different ending. For example, -*é* means _____, -*ás* means _____, -*emos* means _____.

3. All the endings have an accent mark except the ending _____.

4. English usually needs the auxiliary *will* or the contracted *'ll* to form the future tense. How do you say *we'll buy* in Spanish? _____.

5. The word *future* is interpreted as an action that will take place after the _____ moment.

6. The future tense is not the only way to express a future action. In Spanish we can use the _____ tense as well as the future tense forms. For example, *Ella llegará mañana* is the same as *Ella _____ mañana.*

7. Another way to indicate a future action is using the present of the auxiliary _____ followed by *a* and by the infinitve of the main verb. For example, *Ella nos va a hablar mañana* carries the same idea as *Ella nos _____ mañana.*

8. To indicate that an action is probable at the present time, we could use one of the several adverbs such as *posible, probable, tal vez* (*maybe*), *quizás* (*perhaps*). However, in Spanish we can use the future tense to indicate the same idea of probability. For example, *Tal vez Mario está enfermo* could be rendered as *Mario _____ enfermo.*

EXERCISES

ANSWERS p. 311

A. Complete each sentence with the correct future tense form.

1. El año próximo (nosotros) _____ en Buenos Aires. (*vivir*)

2. Si no llueve mañana, Carolina y yo _____ a la playa. (*ir*)

3. Después de la clase Pepe _____ con su novia. (*encontrarse*)

4. Mario _____ con muletas por dos semanas. (*caminar*)

5. Los médicos te _____ el tobillo. (*enyesar*)

6. Si no tienes más problemas, no te _____ nada serio. (*pasar*)

7. El codo derecho te _____ mañana menos que hoy. (*doler*)

8. El presidente _____ en Denver el domingo que viene. (*estar*)

9. ¿Crees que tu esposo te _____ cuando llegue del trabajo? (*besar*)

10. Si no tiene cuidado, _____ el tobillo otra vez. (*torcerse*)

11. Nadie sabe exactamente lo que _____ mañana. (*ocurrir*)

12. Estas rosas _____ muy bien cuando se abran más tarde. (*oler*)

13. Los recién casados _____ muy felices. (*ser*)

14. Si no hay sillas libres, (yo) _____ en el piso. (*sentarse*)

B. Change each verb from present to future. Remember that an irregular verb in the present is not necessarily irregular in the future. Look for the infinitive; then add the endings. Don't forget the accent marks!

1. hablas _____

2. vuelvo _____

3. piensan _____

4. estamos _____

5. somos _____

6. pide _____

7. sigo _____

8. duele _____

9. hueles _____

10. eres _____

11. vivimos _____

12. das _____

13. vemos _____

14. vas _____

15. es _____

16. conozco _____

17. empieza _____

18. diviertes _____

19. entramos _____

20. oyes _____

C. Change each verb from preterite to future. Remember that an irregular verb in the preterite is not necessarily irregular in the future.

1. volvió _____

2. fueron (*went*) _____

3. fueron (*were*) _____

4. hablaron _____

5. torcí _____

6. cojeé _____

7. oyó _____

8. cayeron _____

9. pidió _____

10. sirvieron _____

11. lavaste _____

12. diste _____

13. oyeron _____

14. murió _____

15. durmieron _____

16. siguió _____

17. estuvo _____

18. enyesó _____

19. me caí _____

20. creyó _____

ANSWERS
p. 311

ANSWERS
p. 311

12 La buena salud
(Good Health)

la alergia	allergy	el músculo	muscle
el antibiótico	antibiotic	la náusea	nausea
la camisa	shirt	la pastilla	tablet
la camiseta	undershirt	el peligro	danger
la consulta de doctor	doctor's office	la píldora	pill
		la póliza	policy
el corazón	heart	el pulmón	lung
el cura / la cura[1]	priest / cure	la radiografía	X-ray
el domicilio	address; home	la receta[5]	prescription; recipe
la enfermedad	sickness	el remedio	remedy
el / la enfermero(a)	nurse	el resfriado[6]	cold
el estómago	stomach	la salud	health
el estrés[2]	mental stress	el seguro	insurance
la farmacia	pharmacy	el síntoma	symptom
la fatiga	fatigue	la tarjeta	card
la fiebre	fever	la temperatura	temperature
la gripe[3]	flu	la tensión	pressure
la indigestión	indigestion	la tos	cough
la inyección	shot	la úlcera	ulcer
el mareo[4]	dizziness	la vacuna	vaccine
la medicina	medicine	la vitamina	vitamin

agradecer	to thank	enfermarse	to get sick
aliviar	to relieve	marearse	to get dizzy
arreglar	to arrange	molestar[8]	to bother, annoy
calmar[7]	to calm	quitar[9]	to take away, remove
calmarse	to calm down	quitarse	to move away, stay away
curar	to cure, heal	recetar	to prescribe
descansar	to rest	toser	to cough

alegre	happy		**pálido(a)**	pale
enfermo(a)	sick, ill		**preferible**	preferable
médico(a)	medical		**saludable**	healthy

a lo mejor	perhaps	**perder el tiempo**	to waste time
¡cómo no!	of course	**¡Sólo me falta eso!**	That's all I need!
guardar cama	to stay in bed	**tener mareos**	to be dizzy
llenar una receta	to fill a prescription	**tener tos**	to have a cough
no tener remedio	to have no solution	**tomar asiento**	to take a seat

NOTAS

1. *Cura* means *cure* as a feminine noun: **la cura.** However, *el cura* means *the priest,* as the person who "cures souls." *Una curita* is an adhesive bandage.

2. *Estrés* was accepted by the Real Academia in their dictionary in 1984 as the equivalent of *mental stress.* Hispanics have added the verb *estresar* and the adjective *estresante.*

3. *Gripe* is feminine in all dialects, but in some countries they use *la gripa.* The official word for this illness is *influenza,* an Italian term.

4. *Mareo* is *dizziness.* It comes from *mar* (*sea*), but it applies to any kind of dizziness. The plural *mareos* is more common than the singular. The verb for *to get dizzy* is *marearse* as well as the expressions *tener mareos* and *dar mareos.*

5. *Receta* is not only *medical prescription,* but also (*cooking*) *recipe.*

6. **Resfriado** is one of the many words for the common cold. Other words used in different countries are **resfrío, trancazo, catarro, constipado.**

7. *Calmar* means *to calm,* and the reflexive *calmarse* is *to calm down. Calma* is *calm* as well as *slowness. Tener calma* is *to be slow* as well as *to quiet down.*

8. *Molestar* is not *to molest* as the spelling suggests, but *to bother, annoy. To molest* is rendered as *abusar sexualmente.*

9. *Quitar* is not *to quit* as the spelling suggests; it means *to take away, remove, steal.* The reflexive *quitarse* is *to move away, stay away, disappear.* Notice that *quitarse, molestar, aliviar, calmar,* are conjugated like *gustar,* with an indirect object.

   EX: **A mí se me quitó la tos con las píldoras.** (*My cough disappeared with the pills.*)

10. If you travel to Hispanic countries, you will find that generally the medicine is stronger than in the USA, for instance, aspirin. Be sure to read the labels; you will find that the doses in milligrams are higher. One aspirin at a time is enough. Some medicines that require a prescription in the USA are sold over the counter in Mexico and other countries.

PRACTIQUE LAS PALABRAS NUEVAS

ANSWERS
p. 311

A. Write *el, la, los,* or *las* before each noun.

1. _____ tensión	6. _____ camisas	11. _____ cura (*cure*)
2. _____ síntoma	7. _____ gripe	12. _____ cura (*priest*)
3. _____ salud	8. _____ tos	13. _____ pulmón
4. _____ mareos	9. _____ seguros	14. _____ náuseas
5. _____ fiebre	10. _____ inyección	15. _____ enfermedad

ANSWERS
p. 311

B. Complete each sentence with one of the idioms below. Make necessary adjustments.

a lo mejor	no tener remedio	tener calma
¡Cómo no!	perder el tiempo	tener mareos
guardar cama	ponerse pálido	tener tos
llenar una receta	¡Sólo me falta eso!	tomar asiento

1. El médico me dijo que debo _____ para descansar para curar la anemia.

2. No debes fumar tanto porque _____ mucha _____.

3. Sólo faltan diez minutos para salir el avión; no podemos _____.

4. Ese problema no se puede resolver; _____.

5. Si tengo bastante dinero, _____ voy a Las Vegas a gastarlo.

6. El médico está ocupado y Ud. tiene que esperar; favor de _____.

7. ¿Quieres venir conmigo (*with me*) al concierto? —_____. Me encanta esa música.

8. Elena espera un bebé; por eso _____ a menudo.

9. Hoy tenemos mucho estrés; es mejor _____ que desesperarse.

10. Primero perdí mi dinero en el juego. Ahora me dicen que tengo que pagar como dos mil dólares al *IRS*. _____.

11. José se _____ cuando la policía lo detuvo en la calle.

12. El farmacéutico _____ que me escribió el médico.

ANSWERS
p. 311

C. Complete each sentence with one of the words below. Make necessary adjustments.

domicilio	fatiga	pulmón	receta	tensión	vacuna
farmacia	póliza	radiografía	salud	úlcera	vitamina

1. Es necesario hacerte una _____ para ver si el hueso está roto.

2. La _____ contra la polio salva muchas vidas.

3. Las naranjas y limones tienen mucha _____ C.

4. ¿Cuál es más importante, la _____ o el dinero?

5. Vamos a la _____ a comprar medicinas.

6. ¿Sabes de memoria el número de tu _____ de seguro de carro?

7. Mi _____ oficial para votar está en Los Ángeles.

8. Si sientes mucha _____, debes descansar unos minutos.

9. Respiramos el aire por la boca y la nariz, pero los órganos encargados de procesar ese aire son los _____.

10. La enfermera tomó la _____ del enfermo.

11. El médico me escribió una _____ para llevarla a la farmacia.

12. Si te duele tanto el estómago, es posible que tengas una _____.

ANSWERS
p. 311

D. Complete each sentence with the correct form of the future.

1. Si me ayudas, te lo _____. (*agradecer*)

2. Si fumas tanto, te _____ de cáncer. (*enfermar*)

3. Ella _____ las maletas más tarde. (*arreglar*)

4. Mario, este tobillo no te _____ más. (*molestar*)

5. Esta gripe se _____ muy pronto con estas píldoras. (*curar*)

6. El doctor te _____ unas pastillas contra la tos. (*recetar*)

7. Mi esposa y yo _____ en Acapulco. (*descansar*)

8. Ese dolor se te _____ con estas píldoras. (*quitar*)

9. Los niños _____ antes de dormir. (*calmarse*)

10. Los Arana _____ mucho, como todos los veranos. (*viajar*)

ANSWERS
p. 312

E. Write a synonym for each word or expression.

1. resfriado _____   5. gripe _____

2. dirección _____   6. contento _____

3. pastilla _____   7. posiblemente _____

4. por supuesto _____   8. dar gracias _____

ANSWERS
p. 312

F. Write a related word for each item.

1. alérgico _____   5. digerir _____

2. fatigoso _____   6. curativo _____

3. estomacal _____   7. pulmonar _____

4. farmacéutico _____   8. vaca _____

9. toser _____

10. saludable _____

11. peligroso _____

12. sintomático _____

13. remediar _____

14. receta _____

15. muslo _____

16. inyectar _____

17. alivio _____

18. preferir _____

19. palidecer _____

20. alegrarse _____

21. calmante _____

22. mar _____

23. asegurar _____

24. guardia _____

DIÁLOGO   En la consulta del médico

Guillermo Cabrera López no se siente nada bien y va a la consulta de su doctor.

ENFERMERA: ¿Me da usted su nombre, por favor?

GUILLERMO: ¡Cómo no! Guillermo Cabrera López.

ENFERMERA: ¿Domicilio y número de teléfono?

GUILLERMO: Avenida de los Mártires, 28. Mi teléfono es 6-30-48-46.

ENFERMERA: ¿Tiene usted seguro médico?

GUILLERMO: Sí; aquí tiene mi tarjeta con la póliza.

* * *

DOCTOR: ¿Qué le trae por aquí, señor Cabrera?

GUILLERMO: Un dólor de estómago terrible. No quería molestarlo, pero ya llevo dos días con náuseas, mareos, y este dolor terrible que no se me quita. Además la tos que tanto me molesta.

DOCTOR: Veo que tiene bastante fiebre y la presión alta.

GUILLERMO: ¿Cree usted que será una úlcera?

DOCTOR: A lo mejor es el resultado de una indigestión. Quítese la camisa y la camiseta para ver cómo andan el corazón y los pulmones.

GUILLERMO: ¡Sólo falta que tenga complicaciones en los pulmones!

DOCTOR: Me imagino que ya dejó de fumar definitivamente.

GUILLERMO: No, pero sólo fumo unos diez cigarrillos por día.

DOCTOR: ¡Ay! ¡La nicotina!… Esa es la razón de la tos… Veo que los pulmones y el corazón están bien. Le voy a poner una inyección para calmar el dolor.

GUILLERMO: ¿Debo guardar cama?

DOCTOR: Sí, por varios días. Me parece ser un simple caso de gripe. Le daré una receta y ya verá que con estas píldoras todo se curará.

GUILLERMO: Se lo agradezco mucho, doctor.

DOCTOR: Bueno, a la cama y a descansar. ¡Y cuidado con los cigarrillos! Adiós.

DIALOGUE   At the Doctor's Office

Guillermo Cabrera López is not feeling well and visits his doctor.

NURSE: Your name, please?

GUILLERMO: Of course. Guillermo Cabrera López.

NURSE: Your address and telephone number?

GUILLERMO: 28 Avenida de los Mártires. My phone is 630-4846.

NURSE: Do you have medical insurance?

GUILLERMO: Yes; here's the card with the policy number.

*   *   *

DOCTOR: What brings you here, Mr. Cabrera?

GUILLERMO: A terrible stomachache. I didn't want to bother you, but I've been nauseated and dizzy for two days, and this terrible pain that doesn't go away. Besides, this coughing that bothers me so.

DOCTOR: I see you have a rather high fever and high blood pressure.

GUILLERMO: Do you think it could be an ulcer?

DOCTOR: Perhaps it's the result of indigestion. Take off your shirt and undershirt so I can see how your heart and your lungs are doing.

GUILLERMO: All I need is complications in the lungs!

DOCTOR: I assume you definitively quit smoking.

GUILLERMO: Not quite. I only smoke about ten cigarettes a day.

DOCTOR: Ah! The nicotine! . . . That's the reason for your coughing. . . . I see your lungs and heart are okay. I'm going to give you a shot to stop the pain.

GUILLERMO: Should I stay in bed?

DOCTOR: Yes, for a few days. It seems to be a simple case of flu. I'll give you a prescription, and you'll see that everything will be cured with these pills.

GUILLERMO: I thank you very much, doctor.

DOCTOR: Well, go to bed and rest. And be careful with those cigarettes! Good-bye.

EXERCISES

ANSWERS p. 312

A. *Don Guillermo en la consulta del médico.* **Complete the story using the information from the dialogue.**

La enfermera le pide el nombre, el (1) _____ y el número de

(2) _____ a Don Guillermo; éste vive en la Avenida de los

(3) _____ y presenta a la enfermera la tarjeta con la (4) _____

del seguro médico. Don Guillermo dice que no quería (5) _____ al doctor, pero tiene un dolor terrible de (6) _____; ya lleva dos días con náuseas y (7) _____, y por eso llega a la conclusión de que tal vez tenga una (8) _____ en el estómago. Además la (9) _____ le molesta mucho. El doctor ve que Don Guillermo tiene bastante (10) _____ y la tensión arterial (11) _____, y le pide quitarse la (12) _____ y la camiseta para examinarle el corazón y los (13) _____. El doctor le pregunta si dejó de (14) _____, y él se excusa diciendo (*saying*) que ya sólo fuma unos diez (15) _____ por día. ¡Es tan difícil dejar la adicción a la (16) _____! Parece que los pulmones y el (17) _____ están bien y el doctor cree que se trata de un simple caso de (18) _____. Por eso le pondrá una (19) _____ para calmar el dolor de estómago. También le ordena (20) _____ cama por unos días y le da una receta de unas (21) _____ que curarán todo. Don Guillermo se lo (22) _____ mucho, y el doctor le recuerda que tenga (23) _____ con los cigarrillos. ¡La nicotina no es ninguna vitamina!

ANSWERS p. 312

B. Answer *true* or *false* (T/F).

1. _____ La enfermera necesita saber el nombre, el domicilio y el número de teléfono de Guillermo.

2. _____ Guillermo le da el nombre y el domicilio, pero no tiene teléfono.

3. _____ El domicilio de Guillermo está en la Avenida del Cinco de Mayo.

4. _____ Guillermo le da la tarjeta con la póliza del seguro médico a la enfermera.

5. _____ El doctor del diálogo se llama Don Guillermo Cabrera López.

6. _____ La nicotina causa una de las adicciones más difíciles de dejar.

7. _____ Guillermo tiene mucho dolor de estómago, y siente mareos y náuseas.

8. _____ La temperatura y la tensión de Guillermo son normales.

9. _____ El doctor piensa que Guillermo tiene una indigestión o un simple caso de gripe.

10. _____ El diálogo sugiere que Guillermo tiene miedo (*is scared*) de tener úlcera y complicaciones en los pulmones.

11. _____ Guillermo no quiere inyecciones ni píldoras contra el dolor.

12. _____ Fumar diez cigarrillos por día no es ningún peligro para la salud.

13. _____ El doctor le receta unas píldoras y le manda guardar cama por unos días.

14. _____ Guillermo está muy agradecido con la enfermera y le dice adiós.

15. _____ El doctor le recuerda que debe tener cuidado con el tabaco.

ANSWERS p. 312

C. **Complete each sentence with an appropriate word.**

1. Lo contrario de *salud* es _____.

2. Una enfermedad incurable como el SIDA (*AIDS*) es una enfermedad que no tiene _____.

3. Lo contrario de *paciente* (*enfermo*) es _____.

4. Algunas personas se ponen una _____ debajo de la camisa.

5. En una _____ se pueden ver los huesos y los órganos internos de una persona.

6. Lo contrario de *saludable* es _____.

7. La enfermera toma la _____ para ver si uno tiene fiebre.

8. Lo contrario de *curarse* es _____.

9. Fumar es un _____ porque el tabaco puede causar cáncer, enfisema.

10. El doctor busca las causas de una _____ para curarla.

ANSWERS p. 312

D. **Write sentences using the following words in the order given. Make the necessary changes and add articles, prepositions, and so on.**

1. Guillermo / tener / mareo / porque / tener / tensión / alto / .

   _____

2. Lola / estar / pálido / porque / tener / fiebre / .

   _____

3. mí / molestar / dolor / estómago / .

   _____

4. a Ud. / doler / músculos / porque / tener / gripe / .

   _____

5. ¿ti / quitarse / dolor / cabeza / con aspirina? /

   _____

6. a José / no / aliviarse / tos / con / pastillas / .

   _____

GRAMMAR I   Conditional Tense of Regular Verbs

A. Memorize the conditional forms of the verbs in the chart.

Subject	*hablar*	*comer*	*vivir*	*ser*	*ir*
yo	hablar ía	comer ía	vivir ía	ser ía	ir ía
tú	hablar ías	comer ías	vivir ías	ser ías	ir ías
él/ella/Ud.	hablar ía	comer ía	vivir ía	ser ía	ir ía
nosotros(as)	hablar íamos	comer íamos	vivir íamos	ser íamos	ir íamos
ellos/ellas/Uds.	hablar ían	comer ían	vivir ían	ser ían	ir ían

Note that:

1. The stem of the conditional, just like the stem of the future tense, is the full infinitive.

   EXS: hablar → hablaría, comer → comería, vivir → viviría, ser → sería, ir → iría

2. The endings are the same for all the verbs: ía, ías, ía, íamos, ían. Remember that these endings are the same as those of the imperfect tense of -er and -ir verbs. The conditional has one more syllable than the imperfect: comía → comería.

3. Just like the imperfect tense forms (**comía, comías,** and so on), all of the forms of the conditional take an accent mark to break the dipthong: -ía.

B. Uses of the conditional tense

1. The conditional (*would* + [verb]) is used to indicate an action that is supposed to occur some time after a moment in the past, just as the future refers to an action that occurs after the time of speaking. The two tenses are parallel.

   EXS: **Te prometo que *volveré.*** (*I promise you that I will be back.*)
   Te prometí que *volvería.* (*I promised you that I would be back.*)

2. We also use the imperfect tense of *ir a* + (verb) to indicate the same idea of the conditional.

   EX: **Te prometí que *iba a volver.* = Te prometí que *volvería.***

3. We frequently use the conditional in English to show a habit in the past. This conditional must be translated by the imperfect in Spanish, as we have studied before. The conditional never shows a habit in Spanish.

   EX: **Cuando estaba en México, yo siempre *hablaba* español.**
   (*When I was in Mexico, I would speak Spanish all the time.*)

C. Conditional of probability

The conditional is also used to indicate an action that was *probable* at a past moment, just as the future tense refers to probability at the present time.

EX: **Jaime no estuvo en clase.** *Iría* **a la playa.** (*James wasn't in class. He probably went to the beach.*)

PRACTIQUE EL CONDICIONAL

ANSWERS p. 313

1. The stem used in the conditional tense is the full _____. For example, the conditional of the *yo* form of *estar* is _____.

2. The _____ of the conditional are the same for all the verbs: **ía, ías,** and so on.

3. The conditional has the same endings as the _____ tense of verbs ending in -er, -ir. For example, **comía** →_____.

4. The difference between the imperfect and the conditional forms or -er and -ir verbs is one syllable. The conditional is always longer: **vívía** → _____.

5. We use the conditional to show that an action is supposed to happen after a moment in the _____, just as the future shows an action that takes place after the _____ of speaking.

6. The conditional tense can be replaced by the _____ of *ir a* + (verb). For example, **Me dijo que llegaría tarde. = Me dijo que** _____ **tarde.**

7. The conditional is used in English to show a habit in the past, just like *used to* + (verb). In Spanish the conditional is never used to show a habit. Instead, we use the _____.

8. To indicate probability at the moment of speaking, we use the _____, whereas to show probability in the past, we use the _____.

9. A more idiomatic way of saying **Ella estuvo tal vez en casa** is **Ella** _____ **en casa.**

EXERCISES

ANSWERS p. 313

A. **Imagine that you are a patient and that the doctor tells you what to do and what not to do. Fill in the blanks using the conditional tense of the verbs in parentheses.**

El doctor me dijo ayer que...

1. me _____ pronto de la tos. (*curar*)

2. me _____ del dolor de garganta. (*aliviar*)

3. _____ guardar cama por una semana. (*deber*)

4. él no _____ el tiempo con aspirinas. (*perder*)

5. él no _____ por una semana. (*fumar*)

6. me _____ con una inyección. (*calmar*)

7. no me _____ otra vez. (*enfermar*)

8. _____ mejor con un calmante. (*descansar*)

9. no _____ comer carne ni pollo. (*deber*)

10. la tos no me _____ más. (*molestar*)

11. el dolor de estómago se me _____. (*quitar*)

12. él me _____ unos antibióticos. (*recetar*)

13. las cosas se _____ pronto. (*arreglar*)

14. él me _____ los pulmones. (*examinar*)

15. él me _____ a examinar en una semana. (*volver*)

ANSWERS p. 313

B. Change each verb from the present indicative to the conditional. Remember that an irregular verb in the present is not necessarily irregular in the conditional. (You may want to go back to the infinitive.)

1. soy _____

2. pido _____

3. estás _____

4. vuelven _____

5. piensan _____

6. eres _____

7. conozco _____

8. vamos _____

9. pago _____

10. duerme _____

11. escribo _____

12. mueren _____

13. sigue _____

14. oyes _____

ANSWERS p. 313

C. Now change each verb from the preterite to the conditional. (You may want to go back to the infinitive to get the right stem for the conditional.)

1. entré _____

2. oyó _____

3. fue (*went*) _____

4. fue (*was*) _____

5. pidieron _____

6. murió _____

7. cayó _____

8. durmieron _____

9. seguiste _____

10. compraron _____

11. estuve _____

12. anduvo _____

GRAMMAR II   Future and Conditional of Irregular Verbs

A. Memorize the future and conditional forms of the irregular verbs in the chart.

Subject	saber		venir	
	Future	Conditional	Future	Conditional
yo	sabr é	sabr ía	vendr é	vendr ía
tú	sabr ás	sabr ías	vendr ás	vendr ías
él/ella/Ud.	sabr á	sabr ía	vendr á	vendr ía
nosotros(as)	sabr emos	sabr íamos	vendr emos	vendr íamos
ellos/ellas/Uds.	sabr án	sabr ían	vendr án	vendr ían

Note that:

1. All the verbs that are irregular in the future show the same irregularities in the conditional, with the same kinds of changes. For example, *sabré* and *sabría* are irregular because they drop the *e: saberé → sabré* and *sabería → sabría.*

2. *Vendré* and *vendría* are the irregular forms of *venir*. In this case the *i* is replaced by a *d:* instead of *veniré* the future is *vendré,* and instead of *veniría* the conditional is *vendría.*

B. Memorize the future and conditional forms of the twelve irregular verbs below.

Infinitive	Future	Conditional	Infinitive	Future	Conditional
caber	cabré	cabría	querer	querré	querría
haber	habré	habría	saber	sabré	sabría
hacer	haré	haría	salir	saldré	saldría
decir	diré	diría	tener	tendré	tendría
poder	podré	podría	valer	valdré	valdría
poner	pondré	pondría	venir	vendré	vendría

C. Compound verbs

The twelve verbs mentioned above have compound forms that show the same irregularities. Here is a partial list that you will encounter at different stages of your learning process. Notice that many of them are cognates of English.

deshacer to undo, melt
rehacer to redo, do again
satisfacer to satisfy

abstener to abstain
contener to contain

detener to detain
mantener to maintain
obtener to obtain
sostener to sustain

convenir to be convenient
prevenir to prevent
provenir to originate in

componer to compose, fix
exponer to expose
imponer to impose
oponer to oppose
proponer to propose
suponer to suppose

1. The compounds of *decir* are regular in the future and in the conditional.

   bendecir → bendeciré → bendeciría (*I will/would bless*)
   maldecir → maldeciré → maldeciría (*I will/would curse*)

2. *Caber* means to *fit in, to have room for.*

   EX: **En mi carro *caben* cuatro personas.** (*Four people <u>fit in</u> my car.*)

PRACTIQUE EL FUTURO Y CONDICIONAL

ANSWERS
p. 313

1. The future form of *saber* is not *saberé* but _____. This means that the vowel _____ was dropped.

2. The conditional of *venir* is not *veniría* but _____. This means that the letter *i* was replaced by the letter _____.

3. Every verb that is irregular in the future is also irregular in the _____. For example, from *hacer* we have *haré* and _____.

4. From *querer* we have *quería* in the imperfect. In this case the conditional is not a syllable longer as in *querería,* because the vowel *e* is dropped, and the correct form is _____.

5. *Caber* means *to fit in.* How do you say *We won't fit in your VW?* **No _____ en tu VW.**

6. *Satisfacer* is a compound of *hacer* (old Spanish *facer*). If the future of *hacer* is *haré,* the future of *satisfacer* is _____.

7. If the future of *tener* is *tendré,* the future of *contener* (*to contain*) is _____, and the conditional _____.

8. If the future of *poner* is *pondré,* the future of *suponer* (*to suppose*) is _____, and the conditional _____.

9. If the conditional of *hacer* is *haría,* the conditional of *rehacer* (*to redo*) is _____, and the future _____.

10. If the conditional of *poner* is *pondría,* the conditional of *oponer* (*to oppose*) is _____, and the future _____.

EXERCISES

A. Complete each sentence with the correct form of the future.

   1. Anita y yo _____ para México el lunes próximo. (*salir*)

2. Pasado mañana _____ una fiesta de cumpleaños en mi casa. (*haber*)

3. El calor del sol _____ la nieve. (*deshacer*)

4. El presidente _____ unas reglas nuevas. (*proponer*)

5. Algunos senadores se _____ de votar. (*abstener*)

6. Esa composición tiene errores; Ud. la _____ para mañana. (*rehacer*)

7. ¿Cuánto _____ un Cadillac en diez años? (*valer*)

8. Puedes invitar a Estela; estoy seguro que no _____ venir. (*querer*)

9. Hoy hace fresco, pero mañana _____ calor. (*hacer*)

10. Estoy seguro que el testigo (*witness*) _____ la verdad. (*decir*)

ANSWERS p. 314

B. *Listen to your doctor's advice!* Complete each sentence with the conditional tense of the suggested verb.

El doctor me dijo que...

1. _____ que guardar cama por una semana. (*tener*)

2. él _____ escribirme una receta. (*poder*)

3. _____ bien de la operación de apendicitis. (*salir*)

4. _____ mejores resultados sin fumar. (*obtener*)

5. _____ más saludable si no bebía alcohol. (*ser*)

6. _____ tomar unas píldoras. (*deber*)

7. él me _____ la verdad sobre mi enfermedad. (*decir*)

8. él _____ verme otra vez en una semana. (*querer*)

9. él me _____ unos exámenes de la sangre (*blood*). (*hacer*)

10. _____ que operar el cáncer inmediatamente. (*haber*)

11. él se _____ en contacto conmigo (*with me*). (*mantener*)

12. _____ la pena guardar cama. (*valer*)

13. la aspirina _____ el dolor de cabeza. (*prevenir*)

14. la vacuna _____ buen resultado. (*tener*)

15. los antibióticos _____ la infección. (*detener*)

ANSWERS
p. 314

C. You have now studied the five tenses of the indicative: present, preterite, imperfect, future, and conditional. This exercise is a summary of these tenses. You have the present and the imperfect. Write the preterite and the future.

Present	Imperfect	Preterite	Future
1. vamos	íbamos		
2. somos	éramos		
3. estoy	estaba		
4. dan	daban		
5. pido	pedía		
6. veo	veía		
7. hace	hacía		
8. digo	decía		
9. oigo	oía		
10. cree	creía		
11. salgo	salía		
12. tiene	tenía		
13. vuelve	volvía		
14. sé	sabía		
15. pongo	ponía		
16. oyen	oían		
17. es	era		
18. huye	huía		
19. puedo	podía		
20. quiere	quería		
21. hay	había		
22. anda	andaba		
23. muere	moría		
24. sigue	seguía		
25. ofrezco	ofrecía		
26. pago	pagaba		

GRAMMAR III   Familiar Commands (*tú*)

A. Regular commands
   Commands are also called imperatives. They are used to give orders or make requests. The forms for the affirmative commands are different from those for negative commands.

   1. **Affirmative commands.** The form is identical to the third person singular of the present indicative: **hablar** → **habla; comer** → **come.**

      EX: *Trae* el libro de ejercicios. (*Bring the exercise book.*)

   2. **Negative commands.** Verbs ending in -ar take the ending -es, and verbs ending in -er and -ir take the ending -as. A negative is required in front of the verb.

      EXS: *No hables* tanto. (*Don't talk so much.*)
      No comas esa ensalada. (*Don't eat that salad.*)

B. Irregular commands

   1. All stem-changing verbs have the same changes in the command forms as in their present indicatives.

      EXS: dormir → duerme → no duermas / pedir → pide → no pidas /
      pensar → piensa → no pienses / volver → vuelve → no vuelvas

   2. Most verbs that are irregular in the first person of the present tense show the same irregularity in the negative command.

      EXS: conducir → conduzco → no conduzcas / decir → digo → no digas /
      huir → huyo → no huyas / oír → oigo → no oigas /
      salir → salgo → no salgas / tener → tengo → no tengas

   3. Here are ten verbs that are irregular either because they drop the ending -e in the affirmative command or because they take unexpected forms.

decir → di → no digas	salir → sal → no salgas
hacer → haz → no hagas	ser → sé → no seas
poner → pon → no pongas	tener → ten → no tengas
saber → sabe → no sepas	venir → ven → no vengas

C. Object pronouns with command forms
   Unstressed object pronouns (including reflexive pronouns) follow the affirmative command, and they are attached to it. They precede the verb if the command is negative.

   EXS: **Lláma*me*. No *me* llames.** (*Call me. / Don't call me.*)
   Díme*lo*. No *me lo* digas. (*Tell it to me. / Don't tell it to me.*)
   Siénte*se*. No *se* siente. (*Sit down. / Don't sit down.*)

PRACTIQUE EL IMPERATIVO

ANSWERS
p. 314

1. We use the command forms (sometimes called imperatives) to give a direct order. There are two kinds of commands: formal commands, addressed to Ud., and familiar _____, addressed to _____. We will cover the formal commands in the next lesson.

2. The affirmative command forms are the same as the third person singular forms of the present _____. For example, **hablar** → _____.

3. For negative commands, verbs ending in -**ar** take the ending _____; verbs ending in -**er** and -**ir** take the ending _____. For example, **hablar** → **no** _____ / **comer** → **no** _____. A negative sentence always requires a negative word in front of the verb.

4. Stem-changing verbs show the same changes in the command forms as in the present _____. For example, **dormir** → **duermo** → **no** _____.

5. Most verbs that are irregular in the present indicative show the same irregularities in the _____ command forms. Example, **salir** → **salgo** → **no** _____.

6. A few verbs are irregular in the affirmative command because they show no ending; they drop the *e*. Examples, **venir** → _____; **tener** → _____; **salir** → _____.

7. The word *di* is two different things in Spanish: a) the preterite of *dar,* and it means _____; b) the familiar command form of *decir,* and it means _____. Notice that *di* does not take an accent mark!

8. *Sé* is also two different things: a) the present of *saber,* and it means _____, b) the familiar command form of *ser,* and it means _____. In both cases it needs an accent.

9. Unstressed pronouns, such as **me, se, lo, la,** follow the _____ commands, but precede the _____ commands.

10. To translate *call me* in Spanish, we follow the same order as in English: _____. However, in *Don't call me* the order is different: **No** _____.

11. Compound verbs follow the same rules as simple verbs. If the familiar command form of *poner* is *pon,* the familiar command form of *suponer* is _____. (It needs an accent because it has two syllables.)

12. If the familiar command form of *tener* is *ten,* the familiar command of *mantener* is _____. If the familiar command form of *venir* is *ven,* the familiar command of *prevenir* is _____.

EXERCISES

A. Change the statements to affirmative familiar commands. Write the verb only.

EX: Carlos *me llama* esta noche. = Carlos, llámame…

1. Lola *me habla* en español. = Lola, _____
2. Luis *me escribe* a menudo. = Luis, _____
3. José *me dice* la verdad. = José, _____
4. Marcos *me hace* un favor. = Marcos, _____
5. Ana *viene* conmigo a la fiesta. = Ana, _____
6. Esteban *me oye* bien. = Esteban, _____
7. Luisa *sale* temprano hoy. = Luisa, _____
8. Felipe *se lava* las manos. = Felipe, _____
9. Anita *se bebe* toda la leche. = Anita, _____

B. Now change these statements to negative familiar commands.

1. Luisa no llega tarde. = Luisa, no _____.
2. Guillermo no dice nada. = Guillermo, no _____.
3. Sonia no me llama hoy. = Sonia, no me _____.
4. Julia no hace caso. = Julia, no _____.
5. Lolita no se lava las manos. = Lolita, no _____.
6. Mario no se duerme tarde. = Mario, no _____.
7. Anita no me lo compra. = Anita, no _____.
8. Carlos no deshace la maleta. = Carlos, no _____.
9. Lucía no lo propone. = Lucía, no _____.
10. Marcos no se sienta. = Marcos, no _____.
11. Mi hijo no miente (*lies*). = Hijo, no _____. (*don't lie*)
12. Evelio no se acuesta tarde. = Evelio, no _____.

C. Answer the questions, first affirmatively and then negatively. Replace the direct and indirect object nouns with pronouns.

EX: ¿Preparo la comida? —Sí, *prepárala.* —No, *no la prepares.*

1. ¿Contesto el teléfono?

—Sí, _____. —No, _____.

2. ¿Escribo la receta?

—Sí, _____. —No, _____.

3. ¿Traigo a mi amiga Luisa?

—Sí, _____. —No, _____.

4. ¿Me lavo las manos?

—Sí, _____. —No, _____.

5. ¿Le pido el carro a papá?

—Sí, _____. —No, _____.

6. ¿Le digo la verdad a tu amiga?

—Sí, _____. —No, _____.

7. ¿Tomo las pastillas ahora?

—Sí, _____. —No, _____.

ANSWERS p. 315 D. Change these familiar commands from affirmative to negative.

EX: **Llámame mañana.**
    —No me llames mañana.

1. Siéntate aquí. —_____.

2. Dame la cuenta ahora. —_____.

3. Háblame siempre en español. —_____.

4. Dímelo todo. —_____.

5. Arréglatelo. —_____.

6. Bébetela. —_____.

Now change these familiar commands from negative to affirmative.

EX: **No te laves las manos.**
    —Lávate las manos.

7. No te lo tomes todo. —_____.

8. No la llames temprano. —_____.

9. No te vistas ahora. —_____.

10. No lo toques, por favor. —_____.

11. No lo empieces mañana. —_____.

12. No te lo lleves. —_____.

13 Dos amigos en la farmacia
(Two Friends at the Pharmacy)

el acero	steel	el jarabe	syrup
el alimento	food	el líquido	liquid
la balanza	scale	la marca	trademark
la barbería	barbershop	el narcótico	narcotic
el calmante	sedative	la panadería	bakery
la caloría	calorie	la pastelería	pastry shop
la carnicería	butcher's shop	la peluquería[3]	hairdresser's
la crema dental	toothpaste	la pescadería	fish store
la dieta[1]	diet	la sangre	blood
el/la dietista	dietitian	el/la sastre(a)	tailor
la droga	drug	la sastrería	tailor shop
la droguería[2]	drugstore	el talco	powder, talc
el ejercicio	exercise	el tubo	pipe, tube
la florería	flower shop	la variedad	variety
la frutería	fruit store	la verdulería	greengrocer's
la gota	drop, gout	la verdura	vegetable
la hoja de afeitar	razor blade	la vuelta[4]	change, ride
la irritación	irritation	el yogur	yogurt
el jabón	soap	la zapatería	shoe store

abusar[5]	to abuse	contestar	to answer
acostumbrarse	to get/become accustomed to	convertir(ie, i)	to convert
		durar	to last
adelgazar	to lose weight	gotear	to drip
alimentar	to feed	padecer (c)	to suffer
balancear	to balance	preocuparse	to worry
conseguir[6] (i)	to get, obtain	tardar	to be long, last
contener	to contain	tragar	to swallow

balanceado(a)	balanced	gordito(a)	chubby
complicado(a)	complicated	gordo(a)	fat
delgado(a)[7]	thin, slim	grueso(a)	fat
drogadicto(a)	drug addicted	inoxidable	stainless
estricto(a)	strict, severe	obeso(a)	obese
flaco(a)	thin, skinny	reciente	recent

bajar de peso	to lose weight	farmacia de guardia	24-hour pharmacy
cortar el pelo	to cut the hair		
estar a dieta	to be on a diet	perder peso	to lose weight

NOTAS

1. *Dieta* still has the connotation of *medical diet* in Hispanic countries; it's a rather negative concept, like something prescribed by the doctor. The Coca-Cola company does not export Diet Coke to Hispanic countries but Coke Light, with this English label. Mexico is the only country that imports American products just as they are in the USA; some American companies add typically Mexican commodities to their product lines for sale in that country, such as **jalapeño** soup by Campbell Soup Company.

2. *Droguería* is also called *farmacia*. In Hispanic countries the *farmacia* is not as large as the American drugstore. Obviously it has a pharmacist to prepare all kinds of medicines; and it sells only a few products such as toothpaste, razor blades, some cosmetic and perfume items, baby food, diapers, bathroom paper.

3. *Peluquería* or *salón de belleza* is *hairdresser's* (for women). *Barbería* is *barbershop*, but in some countries the word *peluquería* is used instead for *barbershop*.

4. *Vuelta* means *change* (money), and also *ride, return* (trip), *bend* (in road). Some dialects use **vuelto, cambio, calderilla, feria,** for *change* (money). *Viaje de ida y vuelta* means *round-trip*.

5. *Abusar* is not *to abuse* but *to misuse, use too much, go too far, take advange of;* whereas *to abuse* means to *use immorally* and translates **maltratar, injuriar, insultar.**

   EXS: **Algunos padres *maltratan* a sus hijos.** (*Some parents <u>abuse</u> their children.*)
   No *abuses* del tabaco. (*Don't <u>smoke too much</u>.*)

6. *Conseguir* is a compound of *seguir,* and it changes *e* to *i* as the *i* within parentheses indicates: **consigo, consigues,** and so on. *Convertir* changes *e* to *ie* in the present and the *e* to *i* in the preterite: **convierto, conviertes,** BUT **convirtió.**

7. *Delgado* means *thin; flaco* is used to indicate *very thin, skinny*. However, different dialects will interchange these words. A universal expression is *estar como un palillo* for *to be very thin* (literally, to be like a toothpick).

8. In Hispanic countries *obesity* (**obesidad**) is not a serious problem like in the United States. There are fewer *obese people,* **obesos,** in spite of the fact that the average person in Spain and Latin America takes about three hundred calories more than an American person on a daily basis. One reason is that Hispanics exercise a lot as a habit and as a necessity. Furthermore, American foods in general are very rich in calories. You will find quite a few **gorditos** (*chubby people*) in Latin America, but only a few **obesos** (*obese people*).

PRACTIQUE LAS PALABRAS NUEVAS

**ANSWERS
p. 315**

A. Write *el, la, los,* or *las* before each noun.

1. _____ sastre
2. _____ vuelta
3. _____ variedades
4. _____ jabón

5. _____ jarabe
6. _____ yogures
7. _____ calmante
8. _____ irritaciones

9. _____ dietista
10. _____ narcóticos
11. _____ sangre
12. _____ yogur

**ANSWERS
p. 315**

B. The ending *-ería* is used in Spanish to indicate the place where a product is made, sold, or fixed. Write the name of that place for each item below.

EX: zapato → zapatería.

1. pescado _____
2. verduras _____
3. frutas _____
4. flores _____
5. libros _____
6. tortillas _____
7. drogas _____

8. zapatos _____
9. pan _____
10. carne _____
11. relojes _____
12. tacos _____
13. pasteles _____
14. ropa, trajes _____

**ANSWERS
p. 315**

C. Complete each sentence with one of the words or expressions below. Make the necessary adjustments.

acostumbrarse   farmacia de guardia (turno)   perder peso
crema dental   hoja de afeitar   preocuparse
drogadicto   peluquería   seguir una dieta

1. Estas _____ son de acero inoxidable.

2. Ana _____ mucho porque su esposo fuma demasiado.

3. Las señoras van a _____ a cortarse y arreglarse el pelo.

4–5. Jaime, estás muy gordo, o como dicen los científicos, obeso. Debes _____ con el propósito de _____.

6. La nicotina es como una droga; los fumadores habituales son verdaderos _____.

7. En Cuba hace mucho calor, pero después de cuatro años (yo) _____ al clima cálido.

8. ¿Cómo te vas a lavar los dientes sin _____?

9. Ya son las dos de la mañana; la única manera de comprar esa medicina es ir a la _____.

ANSWERS
p. 315

D. **Review the future by completing each sentence with the verb suggested.**

1. El vuelo de Madrid a Nueva York _____ siete horas. (*durar*)

2. Roberto _____ mucho si no deja de fumar. (*padecer*)

3. ¿Cuánto tiempo _____ en llegar la secretaria? (*tardar*)

4. Aquí en el banco (ellos) te _____ los dólares en pesos. (*convertir*)

5. Pronto (yo) _____ los boletos del viaje. (*conseguir*)

6. (Nosotros) _____ si seguimos una buena dieta. (*adelgazar*)

7. Si llegamos tarde, mamá _____ mucho. (*preocuparse*)

8. Usted _____ estas píldoras sin masticarlas (*chewing them*). (*tragar*)

9. Los padres _____ a su familia con su trabajo. (*mantener*)

10. Si llamas tarde, nadie _____ el teléfono. (*contestar*)

ANSWERS
p. 315

E. **Complete each sentence with a word from the list below. Make the necessary adjustments.**

acero   caloría   florería   jabón   marca   talco   verdura
balanza   droga   gota   jarabe   sangre   tubo   yogur

1. En esta dieta sólo podemos comer mil doscientas _____ por día.

2. La cocaína es una _____ peligrosa.

3. Voy a pasar por la _____ para comprar una docena de rosas para mi novia

4. Tú dices que sólo pesas ciento cincuenta libras, pero la _____ dice ciento cincuenta y cinco.

5. Ford, Toyota, Chevrolet, son tres _____ de automóviles.

6. Estas hojas de afeitar son de _____ inoxidable.

7. Creo que tu tensión de _____ está un poco alta.

8. Para bañarte necesitas _____, champú y una toalla.

9. Los dietistas dicen que las _____ son mejores que las carnes.

10. Si te molestan los pies, debes ponerte un poco de _____.

11. El _____ tiene pocas calorías; es bueno para la salud.

12. Voy a comprar un _____ de crema dental.

13. Los niños prefieren el _____ a las pastillas porque es dulce.

14. Es necesario poner tres _____ de este líquido en los ojos porque los tienes irritados.

DIÁLOGO   En la farmacia

Don Guillermo Cabrera López y Don Tomás Ruiz Pérez son viejos (longtime)
*amigos. Don Guillermo es el mismo paciente de la lección anterior y Don
Tomás es el farmacéutico.*

TOMÁS: ¡Hola, Guillermo! ¡Hacía tanto tiempo que no te veía! ¿Cómo
            estás?

GUILLERMO: No muy bien, Tomás. Tengo un dolor terrible de estómago, con
            mareos, náuseas,...

TOMÁS: Pero, ¿cómo vas a estar bien si sigues fumando (*smoking*) como
            una chimenea?

GUILLERMO: ¡No exageres! Sólo fumo unos diez cigarrillos por día.

TOMÁS: No te engañes, Guillermo. El tabaco es fatal.

GUILLERMO: Sí, pero más fatal es dejarlo para un fumador de treinta años.

TOMÁS: ¿Y ya viste al doctor?

GUILLERMO: Sí, de allí vengo.

TOMÁS: ¿Y qué te dijo?

GUILLERMO: Que no parece nada serio, un simple caso de gripe, pero me
            ordenó guardar cama por varios días.

TOMÁS: ¿Y no te recetó nada para el dolor?

GUILLERMO: Sí, aquí está la receta. Llénamela lo más pronto posible.

TOMÁS: A ver. No es complicada. Es un calmante. Te la puedo preparar
            en pastillas o en jarabe.

GUILLERMO: Prepárala en jarabe. Siempre me molesta tragar pastillas. Ese
            calmante, ¿contiene algún narcótico?

TOMÁS: No te preocupes. Este jarabe no te convertirá en drogadicto como
            la nicotina.

GUILLERMO: Mientras preparas la receta voy a buscar unas cosas que necesito.
            Un tubo de crema dental, talco para los pies y unas hojas de afeitar.

TOMÁS: Esas hojas son de acero inoxidable. Te deben durar mucho tiempo.

GUILLERMO: Sí, no puedo acostumbrarme a las maquinitas modernas de
            afeitar. A propósito, recientemente me molestan los ojos cuando
            leo mucho. ¿Tienes algo para eso?

TOMÁS: ¡Cómo no! Te recomiendo estas gotas; deben aliviarte la
            irritación. Ponte tres gotas en cada ojo antes de acostarte.

GUILLERMO: Gracias, Tomás. ¿Cuánto te debo?

TOMÁS: Son ciento setenta y dos pesos en total. ¡Alíviate pronto y no
            abuses del tabaco!

DIALOGUE   At the Pharmacy

Don Guillermo Cabrera López and Don Tomás Ruiz Pérez are longtime friends.
Don Guillermo is the same patient we met in the previous lesson. Don Tomás is
the pharmacist. We will call them Tom and Bill.

TOM: Hi, Bill! I haven't seen you in a long time! How are you?

BILL: Not so well, Tom. I have a terrible stomachache, with dizziness, nausea, . . .

TOM: But how can you feel well if you keep smoking like a chimney?

BILL: Don't exaggerate! I only smoke about ten cigarettes a day.

TOM: Don't deceive yourself, Bill. Tobacco is fatal.

BILL: Sure, but more fatal is to stop smoking after thirty years!

TOM: And have you seen the doctor?

BILL: Yes, that's where I'm coming from.

TOM: What did he say?

BILL: That it doesn't seem serious, a simple case of the flu, but he told me to stay in bed for a few days.

TOM: And didn't he prescribe anything for the pain?

BILL: Yes, here is the prescription. Fill it for me as soon as possible.

TOM: Let me see. It's not complicated. It's a sedative. I can make it for you in pills or in syrup.

BILL: Prepare it in syrup. It always bothers me to swallow pills. Does the sedative contain a narcotic?

TOM: Don't worry. This syrup won't turn you into a drug addict like the nicotine.

BILL: While you fill the prescription, I'm going to look for a few things I need. Toothpaste, foot powder, and razor blades.

TOM: Those blades are made of stainless steel. They should last you a long time.

BILL: I just cannot get used to the modern shavers. By the way, my eyes have been bothering me recently when I read a lot. Do you have anything for that?

TOM: Of course! I recommend these drops. They should relieve the irritation. Put three drops in each eye before you go to bed.

BILL: Thanks, Tom. How much do I owe you?

TOM: It's a hundred seventy-two pesos altogether. I hope you'll feel better soon! And don't smoke too much!

NOTE

Hispanics have two family names (*apellidos*) in all their documents: father's family name followed by mother's family name. Women keep their two family names after they get married—in other words, every person has the two family names from birth to death. In a few countries banks allow a married woman to use her husband's first family name after her own first family name in bank accounts.

EXERCISES

ANSWERS
p. 316

A. *Dos amigos en la farmacia.* **Complete the story using the information from the dialogue.**

Guillermo y Tomás son (1) _____ amigos, pero hace mucho tiempo que ellos no se (2) _____. Guillermo tiene un (3) _____ terrible de estómago, con náuseas y (4) _____. Tomás lo acusa de seguir fumando como una (5) _____, pero él le dice que no (6) _____, porque sólo fuma (7) _____ diez cigarrillos al día. Tomás le asegura que el tabaco es (8) _____ para la salud, pero Guillermo le dice que es más fatal (9) _____ de fumar después de treinta años.

Guillermo acaba de ver al (10) _____ que cree que su enfermedad no es seria; probablemente un simple caso de (11) _____, pero debe guardar (12) _____ por unos días. Guillermo le da la (13) _____ para que la llene lo más pronto (14) _____. El farmacéutico puede prepararla en pastillas o en (15) _____, y Guillermo prefiere éste porque le molesta (16) _____ las píldoras. Mientras Tomás prepara la receta, Guillermo busca algunas cosas que necesita: un tubo de (17) _____ dental, talco para los (18) _____ y unas hojas de (19) _____ porque no puede acostumbrarse a las (20) _____ modernas. Las hojas de afeitar son de (21) _____ inoxidable y (22) _____ mucho tiempo. A Guillermo le molestan los ojos cuando (23) _____ mucho, y Tomás le recomienda unas gotas que le curarán la (24) _____. Debe ponerse tres gotas de ese líquido en cada ojo antes de (25) _____. Guillermo le paga al farmacéutico los ciento setenta y dos pesos que le (26) _____ por las cosas que compró. Tomás le recuerda a su amigo que no (27) _____ del tabaco y espera que se alivie (28) _____.

ANSWERS
p. 316

B. **Circle the best answer.**

1. Si Ud. desea cortarse el pelo va a la (droguería, farmacia, barbería, florería).

2. Si Ud. quiere perder peso debe (seguir una dieta, ver al farmacéutico, tomar narcóticos, fumar cigarrillos).

3. Si Ud. quiere lavarse los dientes necesita (jabón, jarabe, crema dental, una buena marca).

4. Si Ud. quiere dulces va a la (frutería, pastelería, panadería, verdulería).

5. Si Ud. quiere hacerse un traje va a la (sastrería, pescadería, zapatería, florería).

6. Si Ud. quiere saber su peso necesita una (marca, droga, gota, balanza).

7. Si Ud. necesita bañarse debe tener (yogur, jabón, acero, alimento).

8. Si Ud. tiene la tensión alta debe (comer más carne, tragar píldoras, tomar alcohol, comer sin sal).

9. Si Ud. tiene los ojos irritados es bueno (comer menos calorías, ponerse gotas, leer y escribir más, tomar un calmante).

10. Si Ud. tiene problemas en los pulmones, no (coma tanto, abuse del tabaco, cuide sus calorías, tome tantas píldoras).

C. Complete each sentence with one of the words below. Make the necessary changes.

abusar	complicado	en total	líquido	reciente
alimento	drogadicto	gordo	marca	sastre
balanceado	durar	inoxidable	peluquería	tragar

1. Una cosa que no es sencilla es _____.

2. Es un accidente _____; acaba de pasar hace poco tiempo.

3. Si Ud. paga por todo, Ud. paga _____.

4. Lo contrario de *delgado* es _____.

5. Las hojas de afeitar son de acero _____.

6. La persona que sabe hacer trajes y ropa es un _____.

7. Me _____ la pastilla con un vaso de agua.

8. _____ en español es *usar demasiado*. No tiene que ver con la moral.

9. El jarabe no es sólido sino _____.

10. Una persona que siempre toma cocaína es un _____.

11. Los dietistas recomiendan una dieta _____ para tener buena salud.

12. Las señoras van a la _____ a arreglarse el cabello.

13. La tortilla es el _____ básico de los mexicanos

14. Mis vacaciones de verano _____ casi dos meses.

15. ¿Qué _____ de cigarrillos fuma usted?

ANSWERS
p. 316

D. Form sentences with the following words in the order given. Add the missing words, and make necessary changes. Use all the verbs in the familiar command form.

1. preparar / este / receta / a mí /.

   _____

2. no / preocuparse (tú) / de / ese / problemas /.

   _____

3. ponerse (tú) / dos / gota / antes / acostarse /.

   _____

4. (yo) / acostumbrarse / a / este / píldoras /.

   _____

5. conseguir / un / balanza / para / pesarse /.

   _____

6. Guillermo, / no / abusar / de / tabaco /.

   _____

GRAMMAR I   Conjunctions *y, e, o, u, sino, pero* • Formation and Uses of Adverbs Ending in *-mente*

I. Conjunctions *y, e, o, u, sino, pero*

   A. There are two words in Spanish for the word *and:* y and e. We use *e* when the word that follows begins with the sound [*i*], which corresponds to the letters *i* and *hi.* (Remember that *h* is always silent.)

   EXS: **Daniel *e* Isabel / padre *e* hijo**

   There are a few words that begin with *hie;* in this case *hie* sounds like [*ye*] instead of [*ie*], and the conjunction *y* is used.

   EX: **agua *y* hielo** (*water and ice*)

   B. There are two words in Spanish for the word *or:* o and u. We use *u* when the word that follows begins with the sound [*o*], which corresponds to the letters *o* and *ho.* If the word begins with the diphthong *hue* as in **hueso,** we use *o.*

   EXS: **siete *u* ocho, minutos *u* horas,** BUT **músculos *o* huesos**

C. There are three ways to translate the word *but:* **pero, sino,** and **sino que.** In order to use *sino,* two conditions are required:

1. The first part of the sentence must be negative:

   EX: **Ese muchacho *no* es Pedro *sino* Pablo.** (*That boy is <u>not</u> Pedro <u>but</u> Pablo.*)

2. The two parts of the sentence must be parallel—that is, the contrast must be between two nouns, two adjectives, and so on. At the same time those two parts must be on the same level of meaning: two colors, two religions, two affiliations. Otherwise *pero* must be used.

   EXS: **No es gorda *sino* delgada.** (*She's not fat <u>but</u> thin.*): Fatness and thinness are on the same level.
   No es gordo *pero* es alto. (*He's not fat <u>but</u> tall.*): Fatness and height are on different levels.

   Sino que is used when each of the two parts of the sentence contains a subject and a verb.

   EXS: **Pepe no fuma *sino que* bebe.** (*Joe doesn't smoke, <u>but</u> he drinks.*)
   BUT **Pepe no quiere fumar *sino* beber.** (*Joe doesn't want to smoke <u>but</u> to drink.*)

II. **Formation and uses of adverbs ending in -*mente***

A. Every descriptive adjective becomes an adverb with the ending **-mente** added to the feminine form of the adjective: **bueno** → **buena** → **buenamente / claro** → **clara** → **claramente.**

B. If the adjective has a written accent, this accent is preserved in the adverb.

   fácil → **fácilmente / rápido** → **rápida** → **rápidamente.**

   Actually these adverbs are the only Spanish compound words with two stresses: one on the adjectival part, the other on the first *e* of -*mente.*

C. If there are two or more adverbs in a sequence, only the last adverb takes the ending **-mente,** but all of them must be feminine.

   EX: **Pepe habló clara, concisa y amablemente.** (*Joe spoke clearly, concisely, and amiably.*)

PRACTIQUE LA GRAMÁTICA

1. The usual Spanish translation of *and* is **y,** but if the following word begins with the sound [*i*], we don't use **y** but _____; for example, **padre** _____ **hijo.** There are two possible spellings for the sound [*i*]: _____ and _____.

2. *Hielo* (*ice*) begins with the [*ye*] rather than the [*ie*] sound. Therefore we say **agua** _____ **hielo.** The same rule applies to *acero* _____ *hierro* (*steel and iron*).

3. We usually translate *or* by *o*, but if the following word begins with the sound [*o*], we use _____ rather than *o;* for example, **setenta** _____ **ochenta.** The two spellings for the sound [*o*] are _____ and _____.

4. *Pero* and *sino* mean the same thing: *but*. Most of the time we use *pero*. In order to use *sino,* the first part of the sentence must be _____. If the sentence is affirmative, _____ must be used.

5. Another condition for using *sino* is that the two parts in contrast must be parallel, such as two colors, two nationalities, two professions, and so on.

   EX: **Ella no es mexicana** _____ **chilena.**

6. *Sino que* is used when each of the two parts of the sentence contains a _____ and a verb; for example, **Ella no es de México** _____ **es de Chile.**

7. The sentence *María no quiere bailar* _____ *charlar* (*chat*) requires *sino* instead of *sino que* because *bailar* and *charlar* are two infinitives; they are not full sentences.

8. To form an adverb from an adjective, we add *-mente* to the _____ form of the adjective, the reason being that *la mente* (*mind*) is feminine. If the adjective has only one form for both masculine and feminine, we use that form.

   EX: **triste** →_____

9. If the adjective has a written accent, we _____ that accent.

   EX: **fácil** →_____

10. If we have two or more adverbs in a sequence, only the _____ one takes the ending *-mente,* but all the others must be in the feminine gender.

    EX: **Habla** _____ **y** _____. (*clearly and easily*)

EXERCISES

ANSWERS p. 316

A. Translate the words in parentheses.

1. Marta _____ Isabel son bonitas _____ inteligentes. (*and*)

2. El agua tiene dos elementos: oxígeno _____ hidrógeno. (*and*)

3. ¿Cuántos años tiene tu abuela, setenta _____ ochenta? (*or*)

4. Dos metales importantes son oro _____ hierro. (*and*)

5. Andrés Segovia no tocaba el violín _____ la guitarra. (*but*)

6. No me importa si son minutos _____ horas. (*or*)

7. Aquí no está la entrada del aeropuesto _____ la salida. (*but*)

8. No tomamos la calle Dos _____ fuimos por la Avenida Martí. (*but*)

9. María Elena es gordita _____ bonita. (*but*)

10. Carlos vio el STOP _____ no se paró. (*but*)

11. Irma _____ Sonia son buenas amigas. (*and*)

12. Sírveme tortilla española _____ huevos. (*or*)

B. **Form adverbs from the following adjectives.**

1. tonto _____

2. reciente _____

3. claro _____

4. feliz _____

5. amable _____

6. suave _____

7. fácil _____

8. difícil _____

9. triste _____

10. alegre _____

11. bueno _____

12. total _____

C. **Answer the questions using the cues given. Change adjectives to adverbs.**

EX: ¿A qué hora sale el tren? (*tres de la tarde/puntual*)
Sale a las tres de la tarde puntualmente.

1. ¿Qué hace Ud. cuando su mamá tiene sed? (*llevar/refresco/rápido*)

_____

2. ¿Qué hace Ud. cuando está muy cansada? (*sentarse/cómodo/en/sillón*)

_____

3. ¿Cómo podemos llevar todos estos libros? (*poder/llevar/fácil/en/carro*)

_____

4. ¿Qué hace Ud. para el cumpleaños de su amiga? (*gustar/celebrar/alegre*)

_____

5. ¿Qué hace Ud. cuando sus amigos la visitan? (*servir/bocadillos/bebida/probable*)

_____

GRAMMAR II   Formal Commands (*usted/ustedes*)

A. Commands with regular verbs

Verbs ending in -ar take the ending -e for *usted* and -en for *ustedes*. Verbs ending in -er and -ir take the ending -a for *usted* and -an for *ustedes*.

habl ar	*com er*	*escrib ir*	*segu ir*
habl e Ud.	com a Ud.	escrib a Ud.	sig a Ud.
habl en Uds.	com an Uds.	escrib an Uds.	sig an Uds.

Note that:

1. The pronouns **Ud.** and **Uds.** are not required, but using them is sometimes considered both more polite and more formal.

2. Formal affirmative and negative commands have the same forms.

   EX: hablar → hable Ud. → no hable Ud.

B. Commands with irregular verbs

1. Stem-changing verbs show the same changes in the command forms as in the present indicative.

   EXS: pensar → piense Ud. / volver → vuelva Ud. / pedir → pida Ud.

2. Verbs with irregularities in the first person singular of the present indicative show the same irregularities in the formal command. Study the following verbs.

   hacer → hago → haga Ud.   decir → digo → diga Ud.
   ofrecer → ofrezco → ofrezca Ud.   huir → huyo → huya Ud.
   poner → pongo → ponga Ud.   oír → oigo → oiga Ud.
   tener → tengo → tenga Ud.   salir → salgo → salga Ud.
                                     venir → vengo → venga Ud.

3. Also study the following verbs.

   ir → voy → vaya Ud. / saber→ sé→ sepa Ud. / ser → soy → sea Ud.

C. Spelling changes

1. Verbs with a *z* in the stem change the *z* to *c* before *e,* just as *feliz* changes to *felices.*

   EXS: empezar → empiece Ud. / comenzar → comience Ud.

2. Verbs with a *g* at the end of the stem add *u* before *e.*

   EXS: pagar → pague Ud. / llegar → llegue Ud.

3. Verbs with the letters *gu* before the -ir infinitive ending drop the *u* before *a*.

EXS: seguir → siga Ud. / conseguir → consiga Ud.

4. Verbs with a *c* before the -ar infinitive ending change the *c* to *qu* before *e*.

EXS: practicar → practique Ud. / sacar → saque Ud.

D. **Unstressed object and reflexive pronouns**

Unstressed object and reflexive pronouns—such as **me, te, se, lo, la**—follow the affirmative, and precede the negative, commands.

EXS: decir → dígame → no me diga / lavarse → lávese → no se lave

NOTE

Parents usually use the familiar (*tú*) commands when addressing their children. However, when they are angry at their children, they may switch to the formal commands in order to keep a distance between them and the child. For this reason the *tú* pronoun has been called the pronoun of intimacy.

PRACTIQUE EL IMPERATIVO FORMAL

ANSWERS
p. 317

1. Verbs endings in -ar change the *a* to _____ for the command with **usted.** The ending for the plural command *ustedes* is _____.

EX: hablar →_____ Ud.

2. Verbs ending in -er, -ir, take the ending _____ for **usted** and _____ for **ustedes.**

EX: comer →_____ Ud. →_____ Uds.

3. The expression *Mande Ud.* is used in Mexico to ask a speaker to repeat what he or she said. Actually *Mande Ud.* is the command form of the verb _____.

4. The stem-changing verbs show the same changes in the formal commands as in the present _____.

EX: pensar →_____ Ud.

5. *Dormir* changes *o* to *ue* in **duermo, duermes,** and so on. The command form for **usted** shows the same change: _____ Ud. PLURAL: _____ Uds.

6. The present indicative of *decir* is *digo*. This same stem **dig-** appears in the command forms _____ Ud. and _____ Uds.

7. The formal command for *empezar* is not **empieze Ud.**, but _____ Ud. There is a spelling rule in Spanish that never allows a *z* in front of a(n) _____.

8. The formal command of *pagar* is not **page usted,** but _____ **usted.** In order to preserve the hard sound of the *g* in front of *e,* we have to add a silent _____.

9. The formal command of *seguir* is not **sigua usted,** but _____ **usted.** The *u* from *seguir* is silent and is not needed in front of *o,* as in **sigo** or _____.

10. The unstressed object pronouns (like **me, te, lo, se**) follow the _____ command forms, but they precede the _____ command forms.

11. If you want your supervisor to call you, you don't say **Me llame Ud.,** but _____ **Ud.** If you want to say **Don't call me,** you would say **No** _____.

12. *Lavarse* is a reflexive verb, and it requires the reflexive pronoun. The affirmative command is _____ **Ud.** (Did you remember the accent?) The plural is _____ **Uds.** (Also with an accent!)

EXERCISES

ANSWERS p. 317

A. Write the affirmative formal command for each verb. Use the *Ud.* form.

1. abusar _____
2. alimentar _____
3. balancear _____
4. conseguir _____
5. contestar _____
6. convertir _____
7. cortar _____
8. durar _____
9. padecer _____
10. tragar _____
11. preocuparse _____
12. acostumbrarse _____

ANSWERS p. 317

B. Answer the questions, first affirmatively and then negatively. Replace nouns with pronouns.

EX: ¿Compro esta camisa ? —Sí, cómprela. —No, no la compre.

1. ¿Escribo la carta? —Sí, _____. —No, _____.
2. ¿Pido más café? —Sí, _____. —No, _____.
3. ¿Lleno esta receta? —Sí, _____. —No, _____.
4. ¿Me siento en el sofá? —Sí, _____. —No, _____.
5. ¿Pago la cuenta? —Sí, _____. —No, _____.
6. ¿Trago las píldoras? —Sí, _____. —No, _____.
7. ¿Empiezo la cena? —Sí, _____. —No, _____.
8. ¿Consigo los libros? —Sí, _____. —No, _____.

9. ¿Me lavo las manos? —Sí, _____. —No, _____.

10. ¿Me voy a casa? —Sí, _____. —No, _____.

ANSWERS
p. 317

C. Imagine that you are a doctor and are giving advice to a group of people. Tell them what to do and what not to do using the *Uds.* formal command.

1. No abusar de las aspirinas. _____.
2. Tragarse las pastillas. _____.
3. Empezar la dieta mañana. _____.
4. Guardar cama unos días. _____.
5. No tomar ni café ni soda. _____.
6. No fumar absolutamente nada. _____.
7. Lavarse bien los dientes. _____.
8. No preocuparse demasiado. _____.
9. Acostumbrarse a comer poco. _____.
10. Acostarse temprano. _____.
11. Dormir siete horas por lo menos. _____.
12. Balancear bien las comidas. _____.

GRAMMAR III   Present Subjunctive of Regular and of Stem-Changing Verbs • Uses of the Present Subjunctive

I. Present subjunctive of regular and of stem-changing verbs

A. Memorize the present subjunctive of the verbs in the chart.

Subject	*habl ar*	*com er*	*volv er*	*pens ar*	*ped ir*
yo	habl e	com a	vuelv a	piens e	pid a
tú	habl es	com as	vuelv as	piens es	pid as
él/ella/Ud.	habl e	com a	vuelv a	piens e	pid a
nosotros(as)	habl emos	com amos	volv amos	pens emos	pid amos
ellos/ellas/Uds.	habl en	com an	vuelv an	piens en	pid an

Note that:

1. Verbs ending in -ar take the endings -e, -es, -emos, -en, in the present subjunctive; whereas verbs ending in -er, -ir, take the endings -a, -as, -amos, -an. The formal commands show the same switch of vowels: a → e, e → a.

2. Stem-changing verbs show the same changes in the present subjunctive as in the present indicative: o → ue (volver) / e → ie (pensar).

3. Verbs like **pedir, vestir,** and **seguir,** change *e* to *i* in all the persons.

4. *Morir* and *dormir* change o to **ue** in all the persons except in the first plural, where o changes to *u:* **duerma, duermas, duerman,** BUT **durmamos.**

5. Verbs like *sentir, divertir, convertir, preferir, sugerir, mentir,* show a double change: *e* changes to *ie* in all the persons except in the first plural, where *e* changes to *i:* **sienta, sientas, sientan,** BUT **sintamos.**

B. The spelling rules for verbs in the present subjunctive are the same as those for verbs in the formal command.

1. *z → c* in front of *e:* **comenzar → comience**
2. *c → z* in front of *a:* **convencer → convenza**
3. *g → gu* in front of *e:* **llegar → llegue**
4. *gu → g* in front of *a:* **seguir → siga**
5. *c → qu* in front of *e:* **tocar → toque**
6. *g → j* in front of *a:* **recoger → recoja** (*pick up*)

II. Uses of the present subjunctive

The present subjunctive is used rather frequently in compound sentences in Spanish. In the next lesson we will cover some of the most common uses. For the time being we will use it after verbs of command, desire, request, suggestion, and the like, as you can see in exercises B and C that follow.

PRACTIQUE EL SUBJUNTIVO

**ANSWERS
p. 317**

1. Verbs ending in -ar change the *a* to _____ in the present subjunctive, and verbs ending in -er, -ir, change *e* or *i* to _____.

   EX: **hablar** → _____.

2. You have noticed that the command forms for *usted* and *ustedes* are the same as the forms of the present _____ in all the verbs.

3. The negative commands for *tú,* such as **hablar** → **no hables,** are also the same forms as the present _____.

   EX: **comer** → no _____ (*tú*).

4. *Volver* changes the stem **volv-** to _____ in the present indicative as well as in the present subjunctive: **volver** → **vuelvo** → _____. However, there is no change in the first person plural: **volvamos.**

5. *Sentarse* changes *e* to *ie* in all the persons of the present indicative and subjuctive: **te sientas** → **te** _____. The first person plural is regular: **nos** _____.

6. *Pedir* changes the vowel *e* into _____ in all the persons of the present subjunctive: **tú** _____, **nosotros** _____.

7. *Dormir* and *morir* show a double change in the present subjunctive: *o* changes to *ue* in all the persons except in the first _____: **yo duerma** → **nosotros** _____.

8. *Sentir, divertir,* too, show a double change: *e* changes to *ie* in all the persons except in the first person plural, where *e* becomes *i*: **yo sienta** → **nosotros** _____.

9. Many verbs have spelling changes because they follow general rules of spelling in Spanish. These same rules apply to the preterite, where we have the ending -é. For example, *z* changes to _____ in front of *e*: **comenzar** → **yo** _____.

10. *Tragar* has a *g* at the end of the stem. This *g* changes to _____ in front of *e*. For example, in the preterite: _____ (*I swallowed*). The same thing happens in the present subjunctive: **yo** _____.

11. *Seguir* has a silent *u*. This *u* disappears in front of *o* (**sigo**) and in front of _____ in the present subjunctive: **yo** _____.

12. The last *c* of *practicar* and other verbs ending in -car change *c* to *qu* in front of the vowel _____. You have seen the command form of this verb at the beginning of this section: _____ (Ud.) **el subjuntivo.**

13. Have you noticed that the only difference between the first person of the preterite and the present subjunctive in -ar verbs is a written accent? **hablé** → **hable.** Show this contrast with *llegar:* _____ → _____.

EXERCISES

ANSWERS p. 318

A. **Write the first person singular of the present subjunctive.**

1. abusar _____
2. adelgazar _____
3. balancear _____
4. convertir _____
5. alimentar _____
6. divertir _____
7. vestirse _____
8. tocar _____
9. apagar _____
10. sentarse _____
11. sentirse _____
12. torcer (ue) _____
13. servir (i) _____
14. conseguir _____

15. poner _____   17. jugar (ue) _____

16. aliviarse _____   18. comenzar _____

ANSWERS p. 318

B. You work in your doctor's office. You are repeating what the doctor wants his patients to do and not do. Use the verbs suggested in the present subjunctive.

El doctor quiere que...

1. yo no _____ una dieta muy estricta. (*seguir*)
2. usted _____ estas píldoras tres veces al día. (*tomar*)
3. ella _____ temprano. (*acostarse*)
4. nosotros _____ mejor de salud. (*sentirse*)
5. ustedes _____ a verlo en tres días. (*volver*)
6. tú _____ veinte kilos de peso. (*perder*)
7. mi padre _____ a trabajar menos horas. (*empezar*)
8. Marta y yo _____ más verduras. (*comer*)
9. ustedes _____ la cuenta pronto. (*pagar*)
10. tú no _____ tanto. (*fumar*)
11. yo _____ del dolor de estómago. (*aliviarse*)
12. ella _____ una receta nueva. (*pedir*)

ANSWERS p. 318

C. *¿Qué quiere el profesor de sus estudiantes?* You are just coming from your Spanish class. Tell what the profesor wants the students to do or not do.

El profesor quiere que sus estudiantes...

1. no _____ tarde a clase. (*llegar*)
2. _____ bien sus ejercicios. (*escribir*)
3. _____ los acentos cuando son necesarios. (*marcar*)
4–5. no _____ ni _____ en la clase. (*fumar/comer*)
6. no _____ en clase con los amigos. (*hablar*)
7. no _____ chicle (*chewing gum*). (*masticar:* to chew)
8. _____ bien en los asientos. (*sentarse*)
9. _____ los deportes para hacer ejercicio. (*practicar*)
10. _____ bien en casa para no dormir en clase. (*dormir*)
11. no _____ en la clase. (*dormir*)
12. _____ los fines de semana. (*divertirse*)

14 El automóvil de alquiler
(The Rental Car)

el aceite	oil	la licencia	license
el acelerador	accelerator	el limpiaparabrisas	windshield wiper
el acumulador	battery	la llanta	tire
el alquiler	rent, rental	el maletero	trunk (*of a car*)
el arranque	starter	el mapa	map
la batería	battery	la matrícula	license plate
el baúl[2]	trunk	la milla	mile
la bocina	horn	el motor	engine
el cacharro	jalopy	el neumático[5]	tire
la cajuela	trunk	el parabrisas	windshield
la calefacción	heating	el parachoques	bumper
el capó	hood	el pedal	pedal
el carné[3]	license	la placa	license plate
el cinturón	belt	la rueda	wheel
el desastre	disaster	la seguridad	safety
el embrague	clutch	el tablero de mandos	dashboard
el faro	headlight	la tarifa	tariff, fee
el freno	brake	la transmisión	standard
el galón	gallon	manual, de cambios	transmission
la ganga	bargain	la velocidad	speed
el kilómetro[4]	kilometer	el volante[6]	steering wheel

alquilar	to rent	funcionar	to work
apagar	to turn off	guiar	to guide
aparcar	to park	inflar	to inflate
arrancar[7]	to start, root out	llenar	to fill
cobrar	to charge	manejar	to drive
conducir[8]	to drive	parquear	to park
desinflar	to deflate	pincharse	to get a flat tire
estacionar	to park	pitar	to blow a horn
frenar	to brake	tocar	to touch

asegurado(a)	insured	gastado(a)	worn out
automático(a)	automatic	lujoso(a)	luxurious
cómodo(a)	comfortable	manual[9]	standard shift
destruido(a)	destroyed	mecánico(a)	mechanical
diario(a)	daily	roto(a)	broken, torn
disponible	available	torcido(a)	twisted, bent

a... millas por hora	at . . . miles per hour	en fin, por fin	in short
a todo riesgo	at all risk	olerle mal a uno	to smell fishy
de segunda mano	secondhand	por ser usted	just for you
		tocar la bocina	to blow the horn

NOTAS

1. *Automóvil* is used for *car* in all of the Spanish-speaking world, but different words are preferred in different countries: *carro* is common in Latin America, and *coche* in Spain. Most of the words for new models such as *station wagon, van, jeep,* are not translated; they prefer to use the English words. This is also the case with new technology words such as *fax, laser, beeper,* which in Spanish may end up looking like *fax, láser, bíper. Yipi* has been used for many years for *jeep.* An old car is called **cacharro**; the word for *jalopy* in Mexico is **carcacha.**

2. *Baúl* is *car trunk* and also *large suitcase.* In Mexico they use **cajuela** for the *car trunk,* and in Spain they use **maletero,** which happens to be the same word for *suitcase carrier* or *porter.*

3. *Carné,* the old **carnet,** is used not only for *driver's license* but also for any identification document. The Real Academia has dropped the final *t* in many words: **bufé, bidé, cabaré, chalé.**

4. *Kilómetro* is used in all Hispanic countries. It's .62 mile; in other words, a mile is 1.6 kilometers.

5. The word *neumático, tire,* reminds us of the times when the tire had an inner tube to inflate. *Cámara* used to be used in some dialects for **neumático.** The modern word is **llanta,** which used to be used for the outer part of the tire. In some countries *tire* is called **goma,** literally, *rubber.*

6. *Volante* (from *volar*) is *steering wheel* of a car, a boat, a tractor, and so on. Lately *timón* is used with the same meaning, although it used to be used for boats only. *Volante* is also a *flier,* a "piece of paper that can *fly*," *volar* in Spanish.

7. *Arrancar* is *to start* (an engine), but the ordinary meaning is *to pull out by the roots* (plants or things).

8. *Conducir* is *to conduct* in all the countries, but in Spain it is used for *to drive vehicles,* which in Latin America is always *manejar. Manejar* also means *to handle.*

9. *Manual* (*un*) as a noun is a *booklet, notebook.* As an adjective it means *by hand,* and it is used for the *standard shift,* along with *mecánico* and *de cambios.*

PRACTIQUE LAS PALABRAS NUEVAS

A. Write *el* or *la* before each noun.

1. _____ motor	7. _____ baúl	13. _____ arranque
2. _____ velocidad	8. _____ capó	14. _____ embrague
3. _____ galón	9. _____ carné	15. _____ acelerador
4. _____ aceite	10. _____ placa	16. _____ cinturón
5. _____ batería	11. _____ mapa	17. _____ pedal
6. _____ alquiler	12. _____ volante	18. _____ timón

B. Write a synonym for each of these words.

1. batería _____
2. coche _____
3. aparcar _____
4. carné _____
5. baúl _____
6. conducir _____
7. matrícula _____
8. neumático _____
9. manual _____
10. en fin _____

C. Complete each sentence with a word or expression from the list below.

a todo riesgo	diario	maletero	por ser usted
cacharro	ganga	mapa	tablero de mandos
carné	gastado	olerle mal a uno	tocar la bocina
cinturón	llanta	pedal	torcido
de segunda mano	lujoso	por fin	volante

1. Ponemos el equipaje en el _____ del carro.

2. No, este coche no es nuevo; es _____.

3. Ud. necesita llantas nuevas porque las que tiene ya están muy _____.

4. Para manejar el carro ponemos las manos en el _____.

5. Tenemos precios baratos en los carros; hay verdaderas _____.

6. Para acelerar ponemos el pie en el _____ del acelerador.

7. ¡Por supuesto! Este carro está asegurado _____.

8. Nuestras tarifas de alquiler son bajas: quince dólares _____.

9. Mi carro no tiene reloj en el _____, pero sí tiene radio.

10. Después del accidente, todo el parachoques quedó _____.

11. Es necesario tener las _____ bien infladas para ahorrar gasolina.

12. Este coche es muy viejo, y está roto; me parece un _____.

13. Por favor, no _____ en esta zona de hospital para no molestar a los enfermos.

14. Este carro es nuevo y _____; tiene toda clase de comodidades.

15. Por favor, abróchense los _____ de seguridad.

16. Si no conoce esta región, debe comprar un _____ para no perderse.

17. Después de manejar todo el día, _____ llegamos a Chicago.

18. La tarifa normal es diez dólares diarios, pero _____, se la bajo a ocho dólares.

19. Es ilegal en Estados Unidos manejar un carro sin _____.

20. Me parece una ganga increíble. ¡Esto empieza a _____ a mí!

ANSWERS p. 319

D. **Write a related noun for each verb.**

1. alquilar _____
2. estacionar _____
3. parquear _____
4. conducir _____
5. frenar _____
6. arrancar _____
7. funcionar _____
8. oler _____

DIÁLOGO   ¡Qué desastre!

Un turista de Estados Unidos está en un país hispano y va a una agencia de carros de alquiler para alquilar un coche. Habla con el agente.

AGENTE: ¿En qué puedo servirle, señor?

TURISTA: Querría alquilar un carro pequeño, pero cómodo.

AGENTE: ¿Por cuánto tiempo lo desea?

TURISTA: Por tres semanas.

AGENTE: Sólo tengo uno disponible. Es de segunda mano, pero está en perfectas condiciones.

TURISTA: ¿Automático o de cambios?

AGENTE: De cambios. Así ahorra gasolina.

TURISTA: Mmmm... ¡de segunda mano! ¿Cómo están los frenos?

AGENTE: Acabo de ponerlos nuevos. También la batería es nueva, y el arranque y el embrague... En fin, está como nuevo.

TURISTA: ¿Está asegurado contra todo riesgo?

AGENTE: No, señor, Usted lo alquila y maneja a su propio riesgo.

TURISTA: ¿Cuál es la tarifa diaria?

AGENTE: Normalmente cobro treinta dólares diarios, pero por ser usted se lo dejo en veinticinco. Una ganga ¿no?

TURISTA: Esta clase de ganga me huele mal. ¿Podría ver el carro antes de alquilarlo?

AGENTE: Por supuesto. Venga usted conmigo. Está aquí mismo.

* * *

TURISTA: ¿De segunda mano? Yo diría de «última mano.» Las llantas están muy gastadas, un faro roto, el parachoques torcido, los asientos destruidos, el tablero de mandos...

AGENTE: Pero el motor todavía funciona, señor,

TURISTA: ¡No me diga más! ¡Este cacharro es un verdadero desastre!

DIALOGUE   What a Disaster!

An American tourist is in a Hispanic country, and goes to a car rental agency to rent a car. He is speaking with the agent.

AGENT: How can I help you, sir?

TOURIST: I would like to rent a small but comfortable car.

AGENT: How long do you want it for?

TOURIST: Three weeks.

AGENT: I have just one available. It's secondhand, but it's in perfect condition.

TOURIST: Is it automatic or standard shift?

AGENT: Standard. That way you save gas.

TOURIST: Mmmmm. . . . Secondhand! How are the brakes?

AGENT: I just put in new ones. The battery, too, is new, as well as the starter and the clutch. . . . In short, it's like new.

TOURIST: It is insured against all kinds of risk?

AGENT: No, sir. You rent it and drive at your own risk.

TOURIST: How much is it per day?

AGENT: Normally I charge thirty dollars a day, but I'll give you a special price: twenty-five dollars. It's a bargain, isn't it?

TOURIST: This kind of bargain smells fishy to me. Could I see the car before I rent it?

AGENT: Of course. Come with me, sir. It's right here.

* * *

TOURIST: Secondhand car? I'd say 'last hand'! The tires look all worn out, one of the headlights is broken, the bumper is all bent, the seats are in rags, the dashboard. . . .

AGENT: But, sir, the engine still works.

TOURIST: Don't say another word! This jalopy is a total disaster!

NOTE

This dialogue shows a gloomy picture of the car business in Latin America. We have exaggerated the tendency to keep cars as long as possible because of the high price of new cars and because mechanical labor is still cheap. Lately things have improved a lot in some countries; they are still behind in others. If you plan to rent a car while you travel in a Hispanic country, it's cheaper to do it from the United States. The main rental companies, such as Hertz, Avis, and Alamo, have affiliates in Latin America.

EXERCISES

ANSWERS p. 319

A. *¿Realidad o fantasía?* **Complete the story using the information from the dialogue.**

Un turista americano fue a una (1) _____ de carros de alquiler para alquilar un carro pequeño pero (2) _____. Quería alquilarlo por tres (3) _____. El agente sólo tenía un carro (4) _____, y no es nuevo sino (5) _____, pero estaba en perfectas (6) _____. El turista le preguntó si el carro era automático o (7) _____, y como es de transmisión manual él podrá (8) _____ gasolina. El agente le dijo que acababa de ponerle (9) _____ nuevos, y también batería, pero no estaba (10) _____ contra todo riesgo. El turista podía alquilarlo y (11) _____ a su propio riesgo. La tarifa normal era de treinta dólares (12) _____, pero por ser él, le podía hacer una buena rebaja de cinco dólares, una verdadera (13) _____. Esta clase de gangas le (14) _____ mal al turista y éste quiso ver el carro antes de (15) _____. El agente lo llevó a ver el carro disponible. El turista reaccionó inmediatamente cuando lo vio y (16) _____ que no le parecía de «segunda (17) _____», sino de «última». Las llantas estaban muy (18) _____, uno de los faros estaba (19) _____, el parachoques todo (20) _____, los asientos destruidos,... El agente le interrumpió diciendo (*by saying*) que el motor todavía (21) _____, pero el turista se fue porque aquel cacharro era ¡un verdadero (22) _____!

En conclusión, tenemos aquí un caso exagerado de lo peor que le puede pasar a un turista en Latinoamérica. Por supuesto que no todas las agencias de alquiler son tan malas como la que aquí se pinta, ni tienen tantos problemas en un solo carro. Muchas agencias americanas, como Hertz, Avis, tienen afiliadas en bastantes países latinoamericanos.

ANSWERS p. 319

B. **Answer *true* or *false* (T/F). Think of the correct answer for each false statement.**

1. _____ El turista americano quería alquilar un carro lujoso, cómodo y grande.

2. _____ El turista desea alquilar el carro por tres días para él y su familia.

3. _____ El agente dice que sólo tiene un carro disponible, pero que está en buenas condiciones.

4. _____ El agente cree que un carro de cambios ahorra gasolina.

5. _____ La tarifa normal de alquiler de ese carro es veinticinco dólares diarios.

6. _____ Todos los coches de la agencia están asegurados contra todo riesgo.

7. _____ El carro tiene los frenos nuevos, pero la batería es muy vieja.

8. _____ El americano piensa que el coche no es de segunda mano sino de «última mano».

9. _____ Las llantas están muy gastadas, pero los faros están bien.

10. _____ El parachoques está torcido y los asientos muy destruidos.

11. _____ El agente asegura que el motor todavía funciona bien.

12. _____ El turista piensa que el carro es un cacharro, un verdadero desastre.

C. *Review the subjunctive.* Imagine that you are lending your car to a friend who doesn't know much about cars. Tell him the conditions under which he can have it. Use the present subjunctive. Make any necessary changes.

Oye, Carlitos, te doy mi carro por esta tarde; pero quiero que...

1. (tú) _____ siempre con mucho cuidado. (*manejar*)

2. _____ bien antes de llegar a un STOP. (*frenar*)

3. _____ el carro en lugares legales. (*estacionar*)

4. no te _____ en la carretera (*road*). (*pinchar*)

5. el motor te _____ sin problemas. (*funcionar*)

6. _____ la bocina sólo cuando es necesario. (*tocar*)

7. siempre _____ tu licencia de manejar. (*llevar*)

8. nunca te _____ en la zona roja. (*parquear*)

9. nunca _____ frente a un hospital. (*pitar*)

10. la batería te _____ sin dificultad. (*arrancar*)

11. nunca _____ a velocidad excesiva. (*conducir*)

12. _____ los faros cuando es de noche. (*encender*)

13. _____ los faros cuando no son necesarios. (*apagar*)

14. _____ el tanque de gasolina. (*llenar*)

GRAMMAR I   Verbs Irregular in the Present Subjunctive

A. Memorize the present subjunctive of the verbs in the chart.

Subject	*sal ir*	*conoc er*	*ten er*	*hu ir*
yo	salg a	conozc a	teng a	huy a
tú	salg as	conozc as	teng as	huy as
él/ella/Ud.	salg a	conozc a	teng a	huy a
nosotros(as)	salg amos	conozc amos	teng amos	huy amos
ellos/ellas/Uds.	salg an	conozc an	teng an	huy an

Note that:

1. *Salir* and *tener* are irregular because they add *g* to the stems, just as they do for the first person singular of the present indicative.

2. *Conocer* is irregular because it adds *c* to the stem after changing the last letter of the stem from *c* to *z*. Most of the verbs ending in *-cer, -cir,* have this same change: **ofrecer, nacer, conducir, seducir, reducir.**

3. *Huir* is irregular because it adds *y* to the stem. All the verbs ending in *-uir* have this same change: **construir, destruir, concluir, incluir, excluir.**

B. Memorize this list of the present subjunctive of irregular verbs. The present subjunctive stems stay the same for all the persons, singular and plural.

caer	**caiga**	hacer	**haga**	saber	**sepa**	valer	**valga**
dar	**dé**	huir	**huya**	salir	**salga**	venir	**venga**
decir	**diga**	ir	**vaya**	ser	**sea**	ver	**vea**
estar	**esté**	oír	**oiga**	traer	**traiga**		
haber	**haya**	poner	**ponga**	tener	**tenga**		

1. Notice that **esté, estés, estén,** need an accent. From *dar* we have **dé** with an accent, which helps to differentiate it from the preposition *de*. The forms **des, demos, den,** don't need an accent.

2. The same irregular forms that are used in the present subjunctive are also used in the formal commands: **traer → traiga Ud.** These same forms are used in the negative commands for the familiar *tú:* **traer → no traigas.**

3. Compound verbs show the same irregularities as the simple verbs from which they are derived: **mantener → mantenga / deshacer → deshaga / suponer → suponga.**

PRACTIQUE EL SUBJUNTIVO

ANSWERS
p. 319

1. *Preferir* is a stem-changing verb like *sentir.* The present subjunctive of *preferir* is yo _____ and **nosotros** _____.

2. *Conocer* and other verbs ending in *-cer, -cir,* are irregular because they add the letter _____ to the stem after changing the last letter of the stem from *c* to _____.

3. *Producir* is like *conocer.* The present subjunctive is yo _____; nosotros _____.

4. *Huir, concluir, destruir,* have the same irregularity: they add _____ to the stem. The subjunctive of *concluir* is yo _____.

5. You have heard the expression and song *Vaya con Dios.* Actually this is the command form (expressing a wish in this case) of the verb _____. How do you translate the expression literally? _____.

6. Only two verbs have written accents in the present subjunctive: **estar** and **dar.** From *estar* we have three forms with an accent: _____ /

_____ / _____. And from *dar* we have only one
form—that is, **yo, él / ella / Ud.** _____.

7. *Saber* is very irregular because it has **yo sé** in the present indicative, **yo supe**
in the preterite, yo _____ in the future, and now yo
_____ in the present subjunctive.

8. *Hacer* is another very irregular verb with many stems: **yo hago** in the
present indicative, **yo hice** in the preterite, yo _____ in the
future, and now **yo** _____ in the subjunctive.

9. *Decir* is another verb that is irregular in many tenses: **yo digo** in the present
indicative, **yo dije** in the preterite, yo _____ in the future, and
yo _____ in the present subjunctive.

10. From *hacer* we have **yo haga** in the subjunctive. *Satisfacer* is a compound
of *hacer* (the old *facer*). The present subjunctive is yo _____.

11. From *tener* we have **tenga** in the subjunctive; from *mantener,* we have
_____.

12. From *poner* we have **ponga** in the subjunctive; from *suponer,* we have
_____.

13. Remember that some Hispanics answer the phone by saying **Diga** or
Dígame. Actually this is the formal command form of the verb
_____.

EXERCISES

**ANSWERS
p. 319**

A. Imagine that you are a mechanic and that you have just fixed your friend
Luisa's car. Make your recommendations about the car and express your
good wishes to Luisa using the *tú* form of the present subjunctive.

Oye, Luisa, tu carro está en buenas condiciones; espero que (*I hope that*)...

1. no _____ con el aceite bajo en el motor. (*manejar*)

2. _____ gasolina sin plomo (*unleaded*) en el tanque. (*poner*)

3. _____ oír bien la radio ahora. (*poder*)

4. _____ siempre calmada cuando manejes. (*estar*)

5. no _____ cosas tontas con el carro. (*hacer*)

6. no te _____ con la mano en el volante. (*dormir*)

7. siempre _____ el cinturón de seguridad. (*abrocharse*)

8. siempre _____ los peligros de la carretera. (*prevenir*)

9. siempre _____ la velocidad marcada. (*mantener*)

10. siempre _____ una llanta de repuesto (*spare*). (*traer*)

11. tus amigos _____ usar bien tu carro. (*saber*)

12. tus padres _____ la cuenta del arreglo. (*pagar*)

13. nunca _____ a una velocidad excesiva. (*ir*)

14. nunca _____ de viaje sin el tanque lleno de gasolina. (*salir*)

15. nunca _____ del lugar de un accidente. (*huir*)

16. nunca te _____ nada malo con el carro. (*pasar*)

17. nunca más me _____ de problemas de tu carro. (*hablar*)

B. You are given infinitives. Fill in the rest of the chart by writing the first person of the present indicative, the third person of the preterite, and the first person plural of the present subjunctive for each verb. Follow the examples.

Infinitive	*Present Indicative*	*Preterite*	*Present Subjunctive*
vestirse	me visto	se vistió	nos vistamos
sentir	siento	sintió	sintamos
1. dormir	_____	_____	_____
2. servir	_____	_____	_____
3. mentir (*to lie*)	_____	_____	_____
4. morir	_____	_____	_____
5. preferir	_____	_____	_____
6. divertir	_____	_____	_____
7. seguir	_____	_____	_____
8. tener	_____	_____	_____
9. hacer	_____	_____	_____
10. leer	_____	_____	_____
11. irse	_____	_____	_____
12. oír	_____	_____	_____
13. caer	_____	_____	_____
14. ser	_____	_____	_____

GRAMMAR II Indicative and Subjunctive in Contrast: Information vs. Influence

A. In Spanish, a sentence is often composed of two clauses joined by the conjunction *que* (*that*). In this case, the subordinate clause follows *que* and is dependent upon the first clause, which is the main clause.

EX: **Nosotros sabemos** (= *main clause*) **que Roberto es mexicano** (= *subordinate clause*). (*We know that Robert is Mexican.*)

B. Verbs of information take the indicative.

1. If the main clause contains a verb of information, such as **decir, leer, saber, conocer, informar,** the verb in the subordinate clause must be in the indicative.

EXS: **Ella sabe que Ud.** *habla* **español.** (*She knows [that] you speak Spanish.*)
Ud. dice que *necesito* **una dieta.** (*You say [that] I need a diet.*)

2. Here is a partial list of verbs and expressions of information.

conocer to know	**es cierto que** it's true that	**informar** to inform
contar to tell	**es claro que** it's clear that	**leer** to read
decir to say	**escribir** to write	**reconocer** to recognize
declarar to declare	**es verdad que** it's true that	**saber** to know

C. Verbs of influence take the subjunctive.

1. If the main clause contains a verb of influence—that is, a verb that indicates something that is not a fact—the verb in the subordinate clause must be in the subjunctive. By verbs of *influence,* we mean verbs of advice, command, request, suggestion, preference, desire, hope, permission, prohibition, and so on.

EX: **Ella quiere que yo** *hable* **español.** (*She wants me to speak Spanish.*)

It is important to note that here the subject of the main clause tries to impose her will on the subject of the subordinate clause. Therefore, they must be different persons. If the subject is the same in both clauses, then we use the infinitive.

EXS: **Ella quiere** *volver.* (*She wants to come back.*)
Ella quiere que *tú vuelvas.* (*She wants you to come back.*)

2. Here is a partial list of verbs of influence.

aconsejar to advise	**impedir** to prevent	**preferir** to prefer
decir to tell	**insistir** to insist	**prohibir** to forbid
dejar to allow, let	**mandar** to order	**querer** to want
desear to wish	**oponerse** to oppose	**recomendar** to recommend
escribir to write	**ordenar** to order	**sugerir** to suggest
esperar to hope	**pedir** to ask for	**suplicar** to beg
gritar to scream	**permitir** to allow	

D. Expressions of influence take the subjunctive, just like verbs of influence.

1. When we say to a person "It's necessary that you do it," we are trying to influence that person; in other words, instead of saying directly "I want you to do it," we are using the impersonal expression to convey the same idea. Therefore, the subjunctive is required in the subordinate clause.

   EX: **Es importante que lo** *hagas.* (*It's important that <u>you do</u> it.*)

2. Here is a partial list of impersonal expressions of influence.

es aconsejable it's advisable	**es malo** it's bad
es bueno it's good	**es mejor** it's better
es conveniente it's convenient	**es necesario** it's necessary
es deseable it's desirable	**es peor** it's worse
es imperativo it's imperative	**es preciso** it's necessary
es importante it's important	**está prohibido** it's forbidden
es inútil it's useless	**es útil** it's useful

E. Some verbs are both verbs of information and verbs of influence. You may have noticed that a few verbs appear both under letter *B* as verbs of information and under letter *C* as verbs of influence. These verbs are *decir, escribir, insistir, gritar.* Actually these verbs have a double meaning; for example, *decir* means both to state with words (*information*) and to request something (*influence*). The difference is illustrated by the use of either the indicative or the subjunctive.

   EX: *INFORMATION:* **Papá dice que** *eres* **bueno.** (*Dad says that you are good.*)
   INFLUENCE: **Papá dice que** *seas* **bueno.** (*Dad requests [asks] that you be good.*)

PRACTIQUE EL SUBJUNTIVO

ANSWERS p. 320

1. A clause that depends on another clause is called a _____ clause. The independent clause is called the _____ clause.

2. In English the linking conjunction between the main and the subordinate clauses is *that,* which is omitted very frequently. In Spanish the conjunction is _____ and is never omitted.

3. If the main clause contains a verb of information, the verb in the subordinate clause must be in the _____. For example, **Usted no sabe que su hijo** _____ **cigarrillos.** (*fumar*)

4. If the main clause contains a verb of influence, the subordinate clause must have its verb in the _____. For example, **Usted no quiere que su hijo** _____. (*fumar*)

5. By influence we mean verbs that denote imposition of will, from a strong command to a soft suggestion. Usually these verbs are listed as command, request, desire, wish, prohibition, advice, opposition, and the like.

   EX: **El profesor sugiere que (nosotros)** _____ **el español con los hispanos.** (*practicar*)

6. If the main clause and the subordinate clause have the same subject, there actually is no subordinate clause. We use the _____ in the second part of the sentence.

   EX: **El profesor quiere** _____ **vacaciones.** (*tomar*)

7. Verbs like *saber, declarar, leer,* denote information. Therefore, the verb in the subordinate clause must be in the _____.

8. If you read a notice at work that says *It is important that all of you . . . ,* you will probably interpret it as an order, even if your name is not mentioned there. Complete this sentence: **Es necesario que ustedes** _____ **a tiempo.** (*llegar*)

9. Notice that impersonal expressions like **es bueno** and **es mejor** contain an adjective. If this adjective in the main clause contains a message of information—like **cierto, claro, verdad**—the subordinate clause must be completed in the _____.

   EX: **Es cierto que ella** _____ **francés.** (*hablar*)

10. How do you translate **El director dice que Ud. trabaja mucho?** *The director* _____ *a lot.*

11. How do you translate **El director dice que Ud. trabaje mucho?** *The director* _____ *a lot.*

EXERCISES

ANSWERS p. 320

A. **Complete each sentence with a present indicative or a present subjunctive form of the verb in parentheses.**

1. La abuelita quiere que el nieto _____ temprano. (*dormirse*)

2. No es necesario que el carro _____ nuevo. (*ser*)

3. Es verdad que ustedes _____ bien el carro. (*manejar*)

4. Espero que todos ustedes _____ a tiempo. (*llegar*)

5. Es cierto que el agente sólo _____ un carro disponible. (*tener*)

6. El turista desea que Ud. le _____ un carro pequeño. (*alquilar*)

7. Todos reconocemos que Juan _____ muy bien. (*nadar*)

8. Mi amiga me escribe que su mamá _____ enferma. (*estar*)

9. Tus padres no permiten que tú _____ tarde a casa. (*volver*)

10. El médico insiste en que el paciente _____ las pastillas. (*tomar*)

11. Es mucho mejor que yo _____ con mi amiga. (*ir*)

12. Es importante que tú _____ en vacaciones. (*divertirse*)

13. Acabo de leer aquí que _____ una guerra en África. (*haber*)

14. El presidente declara que los camioneros (*truckers*) _____ razón. (*tener*)

15. Prefiero que Ud. me _____ antes de mediodía. (*llamar*)

16. Es cierto que Cecilia _____ en un banco grande. (*trabajar*)

17. No es bueno que los niños _____ sin usted. (*salir*)

18. El mecánico dice que Ud. no _____ el aceite a tiempo. (*cambiar*)

19. El policía no permite que (nosotros) _____ aquí. (*aparcar*)

20. Mi eposa prefiere que (yo) _____ en casa. (*desayunar*)

21. Los senadores se oponen a que _____ los impuestos. (*subir*)

22. ¿Me sugiere Ud. que _____ en tren desde Chicago? (*venir*)

23. Mi hijo siempre me pide que le _____ pasteles. (*traer*)

24. El director nos informa que mañana _____ vacaciones. (*haber*)

25. Es claro que Elena _____ bien en español. (*escribir*)

ANSWERS p. 320

B. **What do teachers and students expect of one another? Complete each sentence using the present subjunctive.**

Quiero que mis estudiantes...

1. _____ (*decir*) la verdad.

2. _____ (*llegar*) a tiempo.

3. _____ (*hablar*) español en clase.

4. _____ (*hacer*) sus trabajos.

5. _____ (*escribir*) los ejercicios.

6. _____ (*no fumar*) en clase.

7. _____ (*saber*) respetarme.

8. _____ (*divertirse*) en vacaciones.

Los estudiantes esperan que su maestro...

9. _____ (*hablar*) siempre español.

10. _____ (*darles*) buenas notas (*grades*).

11. _____ (*ser*) muy alegre.

12. _____ (*tener*) paciencia con ellos.

13. _____ (*preparar*) bien las clases.

14. _____ (*terminar*) la clase a tiempo.

15. _____ (*mantener*) la disciplina.

16. _____ (*empezar*) la clase a tiempo.

ANSWERS p. 320 C. Complete the sentences with one of the ideas given below. Decide to use the indicative or subjunctive according to the rules.

acostarse muy tarde   llegar más temprano   visitarme en agosto
cambiar el día del examen   tomar una cerveza fría   volver a la consulta

1. José vio al médico hace una semana porque tenía mucho dolor en el pecho. Todavía no se le quita el dolor. Es necesario que él _____.

2. Mis padres trabajan todos los meses del año excepto tres semanas en agosto. Ayer recibí su carta y me dicen que _____.

3. «Mi hija, ya son las doce de la noche; ya sabes que mañana tienes que trabajar a las siete y media. Es mejor que no _____».

4. Ya sabemos mucha gramática y muchos verbos, pero necesitamos más tiempo para aprender tantas palabras nuevas. Por eso hoy le vamos a pedir a la maestra que _____ para más tarde.

5. Hace un calor terrible y llevamos dos horas de trabajo; vamos a descansar un rato, y sugiero que (nosotros) _____.

6. Todas las mañanas hay mucho tráfico en la sección donde vivo. Siempre salgo de casa con bastante tiempo, y por eso nunca llego tarde. Esta mañana me dice el director que yo _____ que los otros empleados.

GRAMMAR III   A Review of the Written Accent

A. The written accent (´) is used in Spanish to facilitate reading. It is written on the stressed vowel of a word according to spelling rules that have changed somehow along the years. You should be able to hear the stress in order to apply the rules. Quite a few Hispanics cannot hear it. For example, if you hear the stress on *la* of *lápiz,* you should be able to apply rule number 2 from letter *B* below and write the accent.

B. There are three important rules for the use of the written accent.

1. Words with the stress on the last syllable need an accent mark if the last letter is a vowel or the consonant *n* or *s*. If the word has only one syllable, the rule doesn't apply.

   EXS: comió, menú, menús, estén, café, dieciséis
   BUT dio, di, fue, vio, seis, mes

2. Words with the stress on the next-to-the-last syllable need an accent mark if the last letter is any consonant except *n* or *s*.

   EXS: árbol, fácil, lápiz, álbum, Pérez (BUT Peres), eslálom, sángüich, estándar

3. Words with the stress two syllables before the last always need an accent. The last letter doesn't matter.

   EXS: águila, águilas, número, dígame, lávese, área, estéreo, gramática

C. Following are two special cases for the use of the written accent.

1. Whenever the weak vowel *i* or *u* precedes or follows any of the so-called strong vowels—a, e, or o—the two vowels form one syllable, with the stress on the strong vowel. This combination is called a diphthong. For example, *oiga* has two syllables: *oi-ga*, with the stress on the *o*.

   When the stress is on the weak vowels, *i* or *u*, the diphthong is broken. This is shown with a written accent: *oído* has three syllables: o-í-do, Ma-rí-a, and so on.

   EXS: oír, día, mío, baúl, dúo, maíz (BUT maizal), país, países (BUT paisano), reúnes (BUT reunir), prohíbo (BUT prohibir), oí, oíste (BUT oigo)

2. When a word has two or more meanings, one meaning is arbitrarily singled out by the use of an accent mark. Altogether there are ten such words.

   aún (*yet*) vs. aun (*even*)   sé (*I know, be*) vs. se (*himself, herself, etc.*)
   dé (*give*) vs. de (*of, 's*)   sí (*yes, oneself*) vs. si (*if*)
   él (*he*) vs. el (*the*)   sólo (*only*) vs. solo (*alone*)
   más (*more*) vs. mas (*but*)   té (*tea*) vs. te (*you*)
   mí (*me*) vs. mi (*my, mine*)   tú (*you*) vs. tu (*your*)

D. Question words take an accent mark in questions and in exclamatory expressions, such as ¡Qué desastre! Question words are cuánto, dónde, cómo, qué, por qué, cuál, quién, para qué. Question words take an accent mark even when they are used in indirect questions. A question is indirect because it depends on verbs of asking, knowing, finding out, and the like.

   EX: Quiero saber *cómo* te llamas. (*I want to know <u>what</u> your name is.*)

E. The demonstrative words **este, ese, aquel,** and so on, take an accent mark when they are used without a noun—that is, when they are pronouns.

EX: **Prefiero esta camisa a *aquélla*.** (*I prefer this shirt to* <u>*that one*</u>.)

NOTE

If you don't hear the stress, your memory and common sense are the only things you have to go by. Why do you write **hablar** with an *h?* Because you have a good memory. Follow the same instincts and hope that some day the Real Academia will eliminate all the accents!

PRACTIQUE LOS ACENTOS

ANSWERS p. 321

1. The accent is written over the _____ vowel of a word.

2. If a word ends in a vowel, we write the accent if the stress is on the _____ syllable, but the word must have _____ or more syllables: **comeré, oí, champú.**

3. If a word ends in *n, s,* we write the accent if the _____ is on the last syllable. Again, we need at least _____ syllables, because this rule doesn't apply to one-syllable words: **dos → veintidós, mes → entremés, dios → adiós.**

4. *Fue, dio, vio, vi, di, fui,* used to have an accent. However, in 1959 the Real Academia decided that the accent on a one-syllable word was useless unless the word had two meanings, like *tú* meaning _____ and *tu* meaning _____ .

5. *Lápiz* needs an accent because the _____ is on the next-to-the-last syllable, and the last letter is a consonant other than _____ , in this case a *z*. The plural **lápices** needs the accent because of a different rule: the stress is on _____ syllables before the last.

6. Foreign words follow the same rules for the accent. For example, *sandwich* gave us *sángüich,* which needs an accent for the same reason that *lápiz, azúcar, Cristóbal, eslálom,* do: the last letter is a consonant, and the stress is on the _____ syllable.

7. Some Spanish speakers say **sángüiche,** and this word needs the accent because the stress is _____ syllables before the last, just as in **lápices** and **pirámide.**

8. *Diga* doesn't need the accent, but *dígame* does, because the stress is on *di-,* which is _____ syllables before the last. In a few cases, there are

three syllables before the last, and obviously they need the accent: **dígamelo** (*tell it to me*).

9. *Sí* needs an accent mark when it means: (1) _____, (2) _____. However, *si* does not need an accent (nor stress) when it means _____.

10. *Mi* means _____, whereas *mí* means _____.

    EX: A _____ me gusta _____ casa. (*I like my home.*)

11. *Yo sé donde vive usted* is not correct because an accent is missing on

    _____.

12. We put an accent mark on a question word that appears in a question or in an exclamatory expression. For example, ¡_____ carro tan desastroso! (*What a terrible car!*)

13. *Día, María, mío, dúo, país, baúl*—they all need an accent mark for the same reason: the stress is on the weak vowels, *i, ú,* and the _____ is broken.

14. Do you put an accent mark on *oir?* _____, because the stress is on -**ir,** as in all the verbs with this same ending. *Oiga* doesn't need the accent because it has two syllables (**oi-ga**) and the stress is on the vowel _____.

EXERCISE

ANSWERS p. 321

Write the accent when needed.

1. El baul de mi automovil es bastante grande y ayer lo llene de libros.

2. El doctor me receto unas pildoras y me puso una inyeccion de antibioticos.

3. Solamente quiero saber cuando te vas y a donde llevaras a tu familia.

4. Yo compraria ese hotel, pero tu no quieres ayudarme con tu dinero.

5. En este album de fotografias esta toda mi familia con mis papas.

6. Jose prefirio compar este coche en lugar de aquel.

7. Digame por que no llego a tiempo al dia veintitres de abril.

8. Cristobal Colon descrubrio America el doce de octubre de 1492.

9. Todos los indios de America comian maiz y hacian pan con el.

10. Tu carro es automatico, pero esta en pesimas condiciones.

11. No entiendo eso del acento en la ultima silaba; ¿puede explicarmelo?

12. ¡Como no! Para mi, eso esta mas claro que el agua del rio.

13. Te dire que si, porque asi me volveras a invitar a tu cumpleaños.

14. Este te esta mas caliente que ese cafe, pero a mi no me gusta el te.

15 En un camión mexicano
(On a Mexican Bus)

el autobús[1]	bus	la llanta de respuesto	spare tire
la autopista	highway	la loma	hill
el autoservicio	self-service	la manguera	hose
la avería	breakdown	la onda[3]	wave
la bienvenida	welcome	el paisaje	landscape
la bomba	pump, bomb	la parada	stop
el camino	road, way	el petróleo	oil
el camión	truck, bus	la pirámide	pyramid
el campo	field	el pozo	well
la carretera	road	el puente	bridge
el cerro	hill	el radiador	radiator
el choque	crash	el ranchero	rancher
el cruce	intersection	el rancho	ranch
la cuadra	block	el stop,[4] el alto	stop
el cumplido	compliment	el surtidor	pump
la emergencia	emergency	el tanque	tank
el engrase	lubrication	el terreno	terrain
el freno de emergencia	emergency brake	el turismo	tourism
la intersección	intersection	el velocímetro	speedometer
la lana[2]	wool		

acompañar	to accompany	doblar	to turn, bend
asustar	to scare	engrasar	to lubricate
cargar	to load, charge	limpiar	to clean
chocar[5]	to crash, collide;	ocupar[6]	to occupy
	to shock	ocuparse	to take care
consultar	to consult	parar(se)[7]	to stop
convencer	to convince	prohibir	to forbid
cruzar	to cross	resbalar	to slip
cultivar	to cultivate	revisar	to check
dañar	to damage	subir	to go up, climb

atento(a)	polite	güero(a)[8]	blond
breve	short, brief	listo(a)	ready, smart
chistoso(a)	funny	ondulado(a)	wavy, hilly
derecho(a)	right, straight	petrolero(a)	oil-producing
despierto(a)	awake, alert	prudente(a)	prudent
espontáneo(a)	spontaneous	quebrado(a)	abrupt
estrecho(a)	narrow	recto(a)	straight
fascinante	fascinating	resbaladizo(a)	slippery
gentil	elegant	romántico(a)	romantic

con anticipación	ahead of time	¡qué buena onda!	how nice!
dar la bienvenida	to welcome	¡qué casualidad!	what a
estar en onda	to be up to date		coincidence!
prestar atención	to pay attention	traérselas[9]	to get worse

NOTAS

1. *Autobús* is the word for *bus* in all Spanish-speaking countries. More common words exist, however, and they vary from country to country: **camión** in Mexico, **guagua** in the Caribbean, **colectivo** in Argentina and Chile, **autocar** and **coche de línea** in Spain, and so on.

2. *Lana* means *wool,* but in colloquial speech in Mexico it is frequently used to mean *money,* similar to American "dough." *Pasta* is the word for *money* in Spain, and *plata* is the word for *money* in all of the Spanish-speaking world.

3. *Onda* means *wave* and **un microondas** is *a microwave.* The expression *estar en onda* is used for *to be up to date, hip. ¡Qué buena onda!* translates the idea of *How nice!*

4. STOP is the international sign for *STOP,* but some countries use their own signs: ALTO is used in Mexico, PARE in Colombia and Ecuador.

5. *Chocar* means two different things: *to crash* or *collide* and also *to shock.* The noun is *choque* for *collision* or *crash,* and *choque cultural* is *culture shock.* The verb *chocar* is used also for *to shake hands,* the whole expression being *chocar la mano.* As it is shown at the end of the dialogue, Hispanics shake hands when they get a surprise or some good news. The expression is *¡Chócala!,* literally, *Shake it!*

6. *Ocupar* means *to occupy,* but the reflexive *ocuparse de* means *to take care of.*

   EX: Sonia *se ocupa de* su papá. (*Sonia takes care of her father.*)

7. *Parar* and *pararse* mean the same: *to stop.* However, in Latin America *pararse* is also *to stand up.* We have to decide the meaning by the context.

8. *Güero* and *güera* are used in Mexico for *blond.* The other countries use the word *rubio* and *rubia.* It is interesting to note that Mexicans use *güero* for anybody who has a fair complexion, but the hair color doesn't have to be what we usually call blond.

9. *Traérselas, to get worse,* is an idiomatic expression, with the reflexive *se* and the direct object *las,* that doesn't replace anything in this case, just like the Mexican *le* in *ándale, híjole,* and so on.

   EX: Este chico *se las trae.* (*This boy is getting worse and worse.*)

PRACTIQUE LAS PALABRAS NUEVAS

A. Write *el* or *la* before each noun.

1. ___ autobús	5. ___ choque	9. ___ pirámide	13. ___ stop
2. ___ camión	6. ___ engrase	10. ___ puente	14. ___ tanque
3. ___ intersección	7. ___ estación	11. ___ radiador	15. ___ cruce
4. ___ avería	8. ___ paisaje	12. ___ surtidor	16. ___ autopista

B. Complete each sentence with one of the following expressions. Make the necessary changes.

con anticipación	llanta de repuesto	prestar atención
dar la bienvenida	microondas (el)	¡Qué casualidad!
estar en onda	ocuparse de	traérselas

1. Amelia, llevas un vestido y unos zapatos de última moda. Se ve que te gusta _____.

2. La _____ está en el maletero del carro.

3. Las enfermeras _____ de los enfermos del hospital.

4. Es muy fácil calentar (*to heat*) la comida: ponla tres o cuatro minutos en el _____ y ya está.

5. Si vas a hacer un viaje largo, es mejor que lo prepares _____.

6. Mañana llegan unos amigos de Canadá y voy a tener una fiesta para

   _____.

7. ¿Su apellido es Rosicler? pues el mío también: ¡_____! ¿Usted cree que seamos familia?

8. Ese dolor de pecho puede ser serio; creo que debes _____ y ver al médico.

9. No creas que este trabajo es fácil; en realidad _____.

ANSWERS p. 322

C. Write an adjective related to each of the following verbs.

1. atender _____   5. fascinar _____

2. abreviar _____   6. resbalar _____

3. despertar _____   7. estrechar _____

4. quebrar _____   8. ondular _____

ANSWERS p. 322

D. Write a synonym for each of the following words.

1. autobús _____   6. bomba _____

2. cruce _____   7. STOP _____

3. cerro _____   8. campo _____

4. depósito _____   9. cuidar de _____

5. accidente _____   10. autopista _____

ANSWERS p. 322

E. Complete each sentence with an appropriate word.

1. Para poner gasolina en el tanque usamos una _____ de autoservicio.

2. En Texas y en California hay muchos _____ de petróleo.

3. Los mexicanos llaman _____ a las mujeres rubias.

4. El viento hace muchas _____ con las aguas del mar.

5. San Francisco tiene un _____ famoso que se llama Golden Gate.

6. Ayer se me paró el carro en la autopista; tuve una _____ en el motor.

7. Colorado es un estado muy bonito; tiene montañas y _____ muy lindos.

8. Los faraones de Egipto y los indios de México construyeron _____ muy altas.

9. Ponemos agua en el _____ del carro para enfriar el motor.

10. Leemos la velocidad del carro en el _____ que está en el tablero de mandos.

11. Los autobuses son lentos porque tienen muchas _____ para que la gente suba y baje del autobús.

12. La tienda está en la _____ de la Calle 20 y la Avenida Lincoln.

ANSWERS
p. 322

F. *A few tips from your travel agent!* Complete each sentence with the present subjunctive of the verb in parentheses.

Antes de empezar el viaje, es importante que...

1. un mecánico te _____ el motor. (*engrasar*)

2. (tú) _____ bien todas las ventanillas. (*limpiar*)

3. un mecánico te _____ el aceite. (*revisar*)

4. (tú) _____ el tanque de gasolina. (*llenar*)

5. (tú) _____ bien las llantas en una estación de gasolina. (*inflar*)

6. (tú) _____ agua y refrescos para toda la familia. (*preparar*)

7. tus padres _____ de tu casa y tu perro. (*ocuparse de*)

8. (tú) _____ un mapa de la región que vas a visitar. (*comprar*)

ANSWERS
p. 322

G. Complete each sentence with a word from the list below.

atento   chistoso   esquina   lana   petrolero   ruina
cerro   cuadra   estrecho   listo   quebrado   surtidor

1. Anita no vive lejos de aquí; hay solamente tres _____.

2. Don Tomás es un caballero muy _____ con las damas.

3. En España hay muchas _____ romanas, como templos, puentes, acueductos, anfiteatros.

4. Vamos a pasar por un terreno muy _____, con cerros y montañas.

5. La carretera se hace más pequeña porque llegamos a un puente _____.

6. Marta siempre está _____ para cualquier emergencia.

7. La consulta del doctor está en la _____ de la calle Martí y Miramar.

8. Don Paco es millonario; tiene toda la _____ del mundo.

9. Una montaña pequeña es una loma o _____.

10. En la televisión hay artistas _____ que nos hacen reír (*laugh*).

11. Para poner gasolina en el tanque tiene que manejar cerca del _____.

12. Muchos de los países árabes son muy _____. Venden petróleo a todo el mundo.

DIÁLOGO   ¡Qué casualidad!

Una turista americana decide viajar en autobús desde la ciudad de México hasta Acapulco. En el autobús se sienta al lado de un joven mexicano.

AMERICANA: Buenos días, ¿puedo pasar hacia la ventanilla?

MEXICANO: Claro. ¿Hasta dónde va usted, señorita?

AMERICANA: Hasta Acapulco. Es un viaje largo, ¿no?

MEXICANO: Sí, bastante. Pero, ¿qué hace una güera como usted viajando en este camión? ¿Dónde está su Cadillac?

AMERICANA: No se crea Ud. que todos los americanos tengamos un Cadillac. En realidad, muchos jóvenes manejan un Volkswagen hecho en México. Pero me gusta viajar con la gente del pueblo para conocerla mejor.

MEXICANO: Ándale, pues. Ya verá que este "viajecito" se las trae.

AMERICANA: Eso no me asusta. Estoy lista para cualquier emergencia.

* * *

AMERICANA: ¡Qué lindos campos de maíz!

MEXICANO: Sí, gracias a eso seguiremos comiendo tortillas, tacos, enchiladas.

AMERICANA: ¡Qué poco romántico es usted! Es mejor que admire la naturaleza. ¡Mire allá lejos las ruinas de un templo y una pirámide altísima!

MEXICANO: Sí, sí, muy lindo; pero hablando de otras cosas, ¿de qué parte de Estado Unidos viene usted?

AMERICANA: De una pequeña ciudad de California. Se llama Calabasas.

MEXICANO: ¡Qué casualidad! Tengo un primo allí que trabaja de camarero en un restaurante.

AMERICANA: ¿No me diga usted que ese restaurante es «El Torito», mi lugar favorito?

MEXICANO: Efectivamente. Hace ya más de un año que trabaja allí y está bien cargado de lana. Se llama Carlos.

AMERICANA: Pero si lo conozco yo. ¡Otra casualidad! ¡Es un chico bien simpático!

MEXICANO: ¡Chócala!

DIALOGUE   What a Coincidence!

An American tourist decides to go from Mexico City to Acapulco by bus. On the bus she sits next to a young Mexican man.

AMERICAN: Good morning. May I sit next to the window?

MEXICAN: Of course. How far are you going, miss?

AMERICAN: To Acapulco. It's a long trip, isn't it?

MEXICAN: Yes, pretty long. But, what's a blonde like you doing traveling in this bus? Where's your Cadillac?

AMERICAN: Don't think all Americans own a Cadillac. Actually many young people drive a Volkswagen made in Mexico. But I like to travel with people to get to know them better.

MEXICAN: Well, then. You'll see that this "little trip" will get worse and worse.

AMERICAN: That doesn't scare me. I'm ready for any emergency.

* * *

AMERICAN: What pretty corn fields!

MEXICAN: Sure; thanks to that we'll keep on eating tortillas, tacos, enchiladas.

AMERICAN: You're not very romantic! It's better to admire nature. Look over there, the ruins of a temple and a very tall pyramid!

MEXICAN: Yes, yes, very pretty. But let's talk about something else. What part of the United States do you come from?

AMERICAN: From a small city in California. It's called Calabasas.

MEXICAN: What a coincidence! I have a cousin there who works as a waiter in a restaurant.

AMERICAN: Don't tell me the restaurant is "El Torito," my favorite place?

MEXICAN: Exactly. He has been working there over a year, and he's loaded with dough. His name is Carlos.

AMERICAN: Another coincidence! But I know him! He is a very nice guy!

MEXICAN: Shake it! (= *Shake hands!*)

EXERCISES

A. *Una coincidencia increíble.* **Complete the story in the past using the information from the dialogue. Use the imperfect tense or preterite as needed.**

La turista americana decidió (1) _____ en autobús desde la ciudad de México (2) _____ Acapulco. En el autobús se encontró con un (3) _____ mexicano, y quería (4) _____ junto a la ventanilla, y (5) _____ permiso para pasar. El mexicano se sorprendió de ver a una (6) _____ como ella viajando en autobús porque él (7) _____ que todos los americanos tienen un Cadillac. La turista le dijo que muchos jóvenes en Estados Unidos (8) _____ un carro pequeño hecho en México, pero a ella le (9) _____ viajar con la gente para conocerla mejor. El mexicano le (10) _____ que el viaje a Acapulco es muy largo y que se (11) _____, pero ella estaba (12) _____ para cualquier emergencia.

Después de viajar un tiempo por la carretera, la americana observó los campos de (13) _____, las ruinas de un templo, y una (14) _____ muy alta. El mexicano cambió la conversación y le preguntó de dónde (15) _____, y ella le (16) _____ que de una ciudad pequeña llamada Calabasas. El joven mexicano se sorprendió mucho al oír este nombre porque él (17) _____ un primo que vivía allí y que trabajaba de (18) _____ en un restaurante llamado «El Torito». La turista le aseguró que ése era su restaurante (19) _____, y que además, ella conocía a su simpático primo Carlos. ¡Qué (20) _____! Con esta sorpresa y buena noticia, el mexicano extendió la mano y le dijo muy contento a la americana: (21) «¡_____!»

ANSWERS p. 322 **B.** **Answer *true* or *false* (T/F). Think of the correct answer for each false statement.**

1. _____ La turista americana es romántica, simpática y morena.

2. _____ La turista dice que va a viajar de México a Acapulco y de allí a Mazatlán.

3. _____ La americana prefiere sentarse junto a la ventanilla.

4. _____ El mexicano se sorprende de ver a una joven americana viajando en autobús.

5. _____ Los mexicanos en general piensan que los americanos manejan carros lujosos.

6. _____ La turista dice que viaja en autobús para ver los campos de maíz.

7. _____ Al mexicano le interesa el maíz desde el punto de vista práctico: la comida.

8. _____ A la turista le parecen románticos el campo, las ruinas, las pirámides.

9. _____ La americana dice que vive en una ciudad pequeña de Arizona, llamada Calabasas.

10. _____ El mexicano tiene un hermano que trabaja de camarero en Estados Unidos.

11. _____ El restaurante «El Torito» es el favorito de la americana en Calabasas.

12. _____ La turista conoce al primo del mexicano y lo considera muy simpático.

13. _____ Este diálogo sugiere que muchos turistas americanos viajan en autobús en México.

14. _____ Este diálogo sugiere que los mexicanos piensan que en Estados Unidos se gana mucho dinero, incluyendo los camareros.

15. _____ Este diálogo sugiere que es bueno que los turistas conozcan a la gente del país que visitan.

ANSWERS p. 322

C. A friend is riding in your car with you. He has one annoying remark after the other. Complete his remarks using the present subjunctive of the verbs in parentheses.

1. Pepe, es mejor que (nosotros) _____ el aceite. (*revisar*)

2. Te sugiero que te _____ en aquella estación de gasolina. (*parar*)

3. Es necesario que (tú) _____ con cuidado el ferrocarril. (*cruzar*)

4. Es importante que (tú) _____ a la derecha en esa esquina. (*doblar*)

5. Será mejor que el carro no _____ con esta lluvia. (*resbalar*)

6. Te pido que no _____ esta loma rápidamente. (*subir*)

7. Espero que (nosotros) no _____ con nadie. (*chocar*)

8. Estamos perdidos. Es mejor que (tú) _____ el mapa. (*consultar*)

9. Espero que (nosotros) no _____ ninguna avería. (*tener*)

10. Para en esta estación. Es mejor que (yo) _____ al baño aquí. (*ir*)

11. Espero que el motor no se _____ con el calor. (*dañar*)

12. Será mejor que (nosotros) _____ un rato aquí. (*descansar*)

ANSWERS p. 322

D. You are going overseas for the first time. Listen to your travel agent give you advice. Complete her statements using the *Ud.* formal command.

1. _____ los boletos a tiempo. (*comprar*)

2. No _____ las cosas para el último momento. (*dejar*)

3. _____ algunos libros sobre el país que va a visisitar. (*leer*)

4. _____ los mapas de la región que visita. (*consultar*)

5. No _____ demasiado equipaje. Es molesto. (*llevar*)

6. No _____ el pasaporte en casa. (*olvidar*)

7. No _____ un asiento en la sección de fumar. (*pedir*)

8. _____ las maletas con anticipación. (*hacer*)

9. No _____ los cheques de viajero. (*perder*)

10. _____ cuidado con la comida y el agua de otros países. (*tener*)

GRAMMAR I   Indicative and Subjunctive in Contrast: Perception vs. Emotion

A. If the main clause contains a verb or an expression of perception—such as **oír, ver, observar, es obvio**—the verb in the subordinate clause must be in the indicative. The verbs or expressions of perception are not many. They are as follows:

notar to notice	**es claro** it's clear
observar to observe	**es evidente** it's evident
oír to hear	**es obvio** it's obvious
sentir to feel	**está claro** it's clear
ver to see	

EXS: **Usted ve que** *yo hablo* **francés.** (*You see I speak French.*)
Es obvio que *ella estudia* **aquí.** (*It's obvious that she studies here.*)

B. If the main clause contains a verb of emotion, the verb in the subordinate clause must be in the subjunctive. Verbs of emotion are those that denote sadness, happiness, like, dislike, surprise, hate, love, fear, pity, anger, gratitude, and so on.

EXS: **Me gusta que** *vayas* **a Madrid.** (*I like that you're going to Madrid.*)
Es triste que él *esté* **enfermo.** (*It's sad that he is sick.*)

If the two clauses have the same subject, the second clause takes the infinitive, although the subjunctive is still possible.

EXS: **Siento mucho no** *ir*... (*I'm sorry I am not going. . . .*)
Siento mucho que no *vaya*...(*I'm sorry I am not going. . . .*)

Here is a partial list of verbs and expressions of emotion:

agradar to please, like	**es extraño** it's strange
agradecer to thank	**es maravilloso** it's marvelous
alegrarse to be glad	**es sorprendente** it's surprising
asustar to scare	**es triste** it's sad
disgustar to upset	**es (una) lástima** it's a pity
enojarse to get angry	**es una pena** it's a pity
gustar to like	**tener miedo** to be afraid
molestar to bother	
sentir to be sorry	
sorprender to surprise	
temer to be afraid	

C. Note that:

1. Sentir means both *to be sorry* and *to feel, sense*. When it means *to be sorry,* it takes the subjunctive, because being sorry is an emotion. When it means *to feel, sense,* it takes the indicative, because feeling or sensing is a perception.

    EXS: Siento mucho que *estés* enfermo. (*I'm sorry that you're are sick.*)
    Siento por el pulso que *estás* enfermo. (*I feel [sense] by your pulse that you're sick.*)

2. *Ojalá* (*que*) means *I hope that,* implying an emotion or a wish. It is not a verb; it's a frozen expression borrowed from Arabic. It always takes the subjunctive, and it may or may not be followed by **que**.

    EXS: Ojalá *llegues* a tiempo. (*I hope [that] you will be on time.*)
    Ojalá *que tenga* suerte. (*I hope [that] I will be lucky.*)

PRACTIQUE LA GRAMÁTICA

ANSWERS
p. 323

1. If the main clause contains a verb of perception, the subordinate clause must be in the _____.

   EX: Es evidente que ella _____ español. (*saber*)

2. If the main clause contains a verb of emotion, the subordinate clause must be in the _____.

   EX: Me alegra que (tú) _____. (*estudiar*)

3. In the previous lesson we saw that a verb of information requires the indicative. *Perception* is information through our senses. Also remember that a verb of *influence* requires the _____. Somehow an emotion is an *influence* on somebody, and as such, requires the verb in the

   _____.

4. Gratitude is an emotion. How would you finish the sentence **José te agradece que (tú)** _____ **a verlo.** (*venir*)

5. *Molestar* is not *to molest* but *to bother,* an emotion of dislike. Complete the sentence **Me molesta que Ud.** _____. (*fumar*)

6. *Asustar* is an emotion of surprise combined with fear. How do you complete the sentence **Me asusta que ellos** _____ **a noventa millas por hora?** (*manejar*)

7. *Evidente* is related to *ver, video;* it refers to something everybody can see and understand.

   EX: Es evidente que él _____ dinero. (*tener*)

8. *Ojalá* is one of the many words that Spanish got from the Arabic language. Originally it meant *may Allah grant that*. However, nowadays it means *I hope that*. Complete the sentence.

   Ojalá (que) no _____ **mañana.** (*llover*)

9. In the expresion *Es una lástima que* (*It's a pity that*), **una** may be omitted. This is an emotion of sadness and compassion, and it requires the verb in _____.

10. *Sentir* means both *to be sorry* and *to feel, sense, hear*. When it means *to be sorry*, it takes the _____; when it means *to feel, sense, hear*, it takes the _____.

EXERCISES

ANSWERS
p. 323

A. Complete each sentence with a present indicative or a present subjunctive form of the verb in parentheses.

1. Me sorprende que tu amigo no _____ vino ni cerveza. (*beber*)

2. Es una lástima que ustedes _____ tarde. (*llegar*)

3. Es obvio que ustedes no _____ un español perfecto. (*hablar*)

4. El director me asegura que ese alumno _____ mucho. (*estudiar*)

5. Me pone furioso que los estudiantes no _____ la lección. (*saber*)

6. ¿Te gusta que yo _____ en tu libro? (*escribir*)

7. Todos vemos que Cristina _____ lista para su trabajo. (*estar*)

8–9. Es evidente que Ud. no _____ ni _____. (*fumar/beber*)

10. Ojalá que el coche no _____ ninguna avería. (*tener*)

11. Es claro que esta americana _____ conocer a la gente. (*querer*)

12. Sentimos mucho que Ud. no _____ venir a la fiesta. (*poder*)

13. Me sorprende bastante que (tú) no _____ más café. (*pedir*)

14. Ella tiene miedo que el carro se le _____ en la autopista. (*parar*)

15. Es maravilloso que Ud. _____ tan rápidamente. (*vestirse*)

ANSWERS
p. 323

B. Write sentences with the following words in the order given. Make any necessary adjustments.

1. me sorprende/ella/no ir/vacaciones/.

2. nos alegramos mucho/ustedes/tener/bueno/trabajo/.

_____

3. ojalá/nosotros/ganar/mucho/dólares/en Las Vegas/.

_____

4. es una lástima/tú/no poder/acompañar/a mí/.

_____

5. nos molesta/vecinos (neighbors)/poner/radio/muy alto/.

_____

6. agradecemos/usted/cambiar/aceite/de/mi carro/.

_____

GRAMMAR II Indicative and Subjunctive in Constrast: Certainty vs. Doubt

A. **Indicative with verbs of certainty**

1. If the main clause contains a verb of certainty or belief, the verb in the subordinate clause is in the indicative.

   EXS: **Ud. cree que su amiga _está_ enferma.** (_You believe your friend is sick._)
   Supongo que ella _está_ enferma. (_I suppose she is sick._)

2. Here is a partial list of verbs and expressions of certainty, belief, and sureness.

creer to believe	**estar convencido** to be convinced
imaginarse to imagine	**es verdad** it's true
parecer to seem	**no dudar** to not doubt
pensar to think	**no hay duda** there is no doubt
suponer to suppose	**tener por cierto** to be certain
es que the fact is	**tener por seguro** to be sure

B. **Subjunctive with verbs of doubt, disbelief**

1. If the main clause contains a verb of doubt, disbelief, denial, the verb in the subordinate clause is in the subjunctive.

   EXS: **Ud. no cree que ella _esté_ enferma.** (_You don't believe she is sick._)
   Es posible que _llueva_ mañana. (_It's possible that it will rain tomorrow._)

2. Here is a partial list of verbs of disbelief, doubt, and denial.

dudar to doubt	**no es que** it isn't that
es dudoso it's doubtful	**no estar convencido** to not be convinced
es imposible it's impossible	**no es verdad** it's not true
es posible it's possible	**no imaginarse** to not imagine
es probable it's probable	**no parecer** to not seem
hay duda de there is doubt	**no pensar** to not think
no creer to not believe	**no suponer** to not suppose

3. There is no clear-cut way of being able to tell when the verbs and expressions above are expressing doubt and when they are expressing certainty. Therefore, the rules given do not apply one hundred percent of the time, but lend themselves to interpretation. You may have noticed that many of the verbs and verbal expressions in *B, 2* above are the negative counterpart of the verbs and verbal expressions in *A, 2:* creer → no creer / pensar → no pensar / es verdad → no es verdad.

C. **Indicative and subjunctive with adverbs of doubt**

The adverbs of doubt are **quizá(s), tal vez, acaso, puede ser,** and they all mean the same: *perhaps, maybe.* They are used with the indicative or subjunctive, depending on the degree of doubt the speaker feels.

EXS: **Quizás** *llueve* **mañana.** (*Perhaps it will rain tomorrow.*): The speaker is almost sure.
Tal vez *llueva* **mañana.** (*Perhaps it will rain tomorrow.*): The speaker has doubts.

PRACTIQUE LA GRAMÁTICA

ANSWERS
p. 323

1. Verbs and expressions of doubt require the verb in the subordinate clause to be in the _____.

   EX: **Es posible que mi tío me** _____. (*visitar*)

2. Verbs of certainty and belief in the main clause require the subordinate clause to be in the _____.

   EX: **Pienso que (tú)** _____ **razón.** (*tener*)

3. *Suponer* indicates more certainty than doubt. For this reason it requires the subordinate verb to be in the _____.

   EX: **Supongo que ella** _____ **bien.** (*estar*)

4. One way to emphasize a statement in English is to add *The fact is that* in front of it. To translate this idea Spanish uses the simple expression _____, which requires the indicative.

   EX: Es que Pepe _____ inglés y español. (*saber*)

5. To deny a fact with emphasis, in Spanish we use *No es que* + (statement), and the opposite usually follows with *sino que.*

   EX: No es que Pepe _____ mexicano, sino que vivió en Mexico. (*ser*)

6. Adverbs of doubt such as **quizás, tal vez,** take the _____ if the speaker is almost sure; they take the _____ if he or she is not that sure.

EXERCISES

A. Complete each sentence with a present indicative or a present subjunctive form of the verb in parentheses.

   1. Pienso que mis padres _____ en casa ahora. (*estar*)

   2. Marta no está convencida de que tú la _____. (*querer*)

   3. Es posible que los abuelos _____ a vernos para Navidad. (*venir*)

   4. Me parece muy bien que ustedes _____ una dieta. (*seguir*)

   5. El doctor piensa que mi enfermedad no _____ grave. (*ser*)

   6. No hay duda de que ellos _____ aprender el español. (*desear*)

   7. ¿Por qué dudas de que ella no te _____ el dinero? (*dar*)

   8. Suponemos que este carro _____ en buenas condiciones. (*estar*)

   9–10. No es que yo _____ infalible, pero es que tú siempre _____ tener razón. (*ser/querer*)

   11. Dudamos que Anita nos _____ el día de tu cumpleaños. (*acompañar*)

   12. Es verdad que este carro _____ poca gasolina. (*gastar*)

B. Add the expressions in parentheses to form sentences with two clauses.

   EX: Paga mucho dinero por arreglar el carro. (*dudo*)
   Dudo que pague mucho dinero por arreglar el carro.

   1. El muchacho cruza la calle sin problema. (*suponemos*)

2. Roberto se ocupa de comprar los boletos. (*me parece*)

   _____

3. Ella me asusta mucho por la noche. (*es posible*)

   _____

4. Seguimos derecho hasta la catedral. (*es probable*)

   _____

5. El carro resbala mucho cuando llueve. (*es que*)

   _____

6. El paisaje de las pirámides es fascinante. (*creemos*)

   _____

7. La americana llega a Acapulco en tres días. (*es imposible*)

   _____

GRAMMAR III   Indicative and Subjunctive in Contrast: Adjectival and Adverbial Clauses

A. Indicative-subjunctive contrast in adjectival clauses: known vs. unknown

1. Compare this pair of sentences:

   a) **Tengo una casa que *es* grande.** (*I have a house that is big.*)

   b) **Busco una casa que *sea* grande.** (*I'm looking for a house that is big.*)

   In *a)* we have a house that is known, and the verb *es* is in the indicative. In *b)* the house is unknown, and the verb *sea* is in the subjunctive. These clauses are called adjectival because they describe *house.*

2. Now compare this pair of sentences:

   a) **Aquí hay un señor que *habla* chino.** (*There is a man here who speaks Chinese.*)

   b) **Aquí no hay un señor que *hable* chino.** (*There is no man here who speaks Chinese.*)

   In *a)* the speaker states the existence of a man who is known, and therefore the verb has to be in the indicative (**habla**). In *b)* the speaker denies the existence of a man, in other words, the man is unknown. Therefore, the verb has to be in the subjunctive (**hable**).

More examples follow.

EXS: **Quiero una secretaria que hable español.** (unknown)
Conozco a una secretaria que habla español. (known)
¿Hay una secretaria que hable español? (unknown)

B. **Indicative-subjunctive contrast in adverbial clauses**

1. **Indicative to show reality.** An adverbial clause explains some circumstance of the main clause: time, location, and so on. If the main clause shows an action that has already occurred, the verb in the subordinate clause is in the indicative because it's a real fact or a definite situation.

EXS: **Te vi cuando *saliste* de clase.** (*I saw you when you left the class.*)
Te saludo cuando *llego* a casa. (*I greet you when I arrive home.*)

Notice that any action in the past is a fact. The present too can be a fact when it's a habit; as such it has happened many times before.

2. **Subjunctive to show unreality.** A future action is only a possibility; it is not yet a fact. When the main clause is in the future tense, the verb in the subordinate clause has to be in the subjunctive. Remember that the present indicative is often used to show a future action, as you can see in the second example below.

EXS: **Te veré cuando *llegues*.** (*I'll see you when you arrive.*)
Te pago cuando me *paguen*. (*I'll pay you when they pay me.*)

3. **Adverbial conjunctions.** Here is a list of adverbial conjunctions that may take the indicative or the subjunctive.

aunque although	**en seguida que** as soon as
como as	**hasta que** until
cuando when	**luego que** after
después (de) que after	**mientras (que)** while
donde where	**siempre que** whenever
en cuanto as soon as	**tan pronto como** as soon as

NOTES

1. *Mientras* can be used with *que* and without it. The modern tendency is to omit it.

EX: **Mamá cocina mientras nosotros *vemos* la TV.** (indicative = habit = reality)

2. *Antes que* always takes the subjunctive, even to show reality in the past, or when there is a real habit.

EX: **Siempre te llamo antes que *salgas*.** (*I always call you before you leave.*)

3. We use *antes que* and *antes de que* with the same meaning. The modern tendency is to omit *de*. Exactly the same happens with *después que* and *después de que*.

C. **Indicative-subjunctive contrast.** Review the uses of the indicative vs. those of the subjunctive.

Indicative	Subjunctive
1. INFORMATION:	INFLUENCE:
Ya sé que *estás* bien.	Espero que *estés* bien.
2. PERCEPTION:	EMOTION:
Ya veo que *estás* bien.	Me alegra que *estés* bien.
3. CERTAINTY:	DOUBT:
Creo que *estás* bien.	No creo que *estés* bien.
4. KNOWN ELEMENT:	UNKNOWN ELEMENT:
Tengo una casa que *tiene* dos pisos.	Busco una casa que *tenga* dos pisos.
5. REAL FACT:	FUTURE FACT:
Te invité cuando te *saludé.*	Te veré cuando *llegues.*

PRACTIQUE LA GRAMÁTICA

ANSWERS
p. 324

1. An adjective describes a noun. A subordinate clause that starts with *que* and describes a noun in the main clause is called an _____ clause.

2. The adjectival clause may describe a known noun; in this case the verb is in _____. If the noun described is unknown, the verb in the adjectival clause must be in the _____.

3. To state the existence of a noun presupposes some knowledge of that noun. Complete this sentence: **Aquí hay una pirámide que** _____ **ochocientos años.** (*tener*)

4. A speaker can mention a noun that is hypothetical or nonexistent, and therefore, unknown. Complete this sentence: **No hay un mexicano que no** _____ **chile.** (*comer*)

5. You ask for information about a noun when you don't know about that noun. Complete the sentence: **¿Hay alguna persona que** _____ **francés?** (*estudiar*)

6. You know about the things you have: your house, your car, and so on. Complete the sentence: **Tenemos un perro que** _____ **mucho.** (*comer*)

7. An adverb gives information about an action; it tells when, where, how. If we use a clause instead of an adverb to describe the verb of the main clause, this will be an _____ clause.

8. If the main clause shows an action that has already occurred, this action is a reality. The verb in the subordinate clause must be in the _____.

   EX: **Comimos después que mi padre** _____. (*llegar*)

9. A habit is something we repeat many times, and it is therefore a reality. Consequently, the subordinate clause must be in the _____.

   EX: **Usted siempre fuma un cigarrillo después que** _____. (*comer*)

10. A future action is only a possibility; it's not a reality. When the main clause is in the future tense, the subordinate clause must be in _____.

    EX: **Comeremos después que mi padre** _____. (*llegar*)

11. Complete this sentence: **Vamos a viajar cuando (nosotros)** _____ **dinero.** (*tener*)

12. In the adverb-conjunction *después de que* the preposition _____ is omitted in modern Spanish, and so is the conjunction _____ in *mientras que.*

13. *Antes que* always requires the _____, even in the past when the action has been a reality.

14. Verbs of influence and emotion require the _____, whereas verbs of information and perception require the _____.

EXERCISES

ANSWERS
p. 324

A. Complete each sentence with a present indicative or a present subjunctive form of the verb in parentheses.

1. Conozco un parque que _____ muchos árboles. (*tener*)

2. Compré una casa que me _____ mucho. (*gustar*)

3. Necesitamos un equipo (*team*) que _____ ganar y perder. (*saber*)

4. Teresa tiene un gato que _____ muy lindo. (*ser*)

5. Hablé con mi esposa después que _____ el trabajo. (*acabar*)

6. Hablaré con el director antes que se _____ a casa. (*ir*)

7. Es cierto que yo sólo _____ inglés y español. (*saber*)

8. No hay muchos españoles que _____ chino. (*hablar*)

9. María tiene un amigo que _____ en Nueva York. (*vivir*)

10. En Estados Unidos hay unos treinta millones de habitantes que _____ español. (*hablar*)

11. Tengo miedo que ellos _____ demasiado dinero. (*gastar*)

12. Quiero comprar una casa que no _____ muy cara. (*ser*)

13. Me molesta que la gente _____ en lugares públicos. (*fumar*)

14. Haré ese trabajo aunque no me _____. (*gustar*)

15. Hice el trabajo como usted me _____ (*decir*)

16. Trabajaré toda la tarde hasta que me _____. (*cansar*)

ANSWERS p. 324 **B.** Replace the verbs or verbal expressions in the main clause with those in parentheses. Make the necessary changes.

EX: **Tienen una raqueta buena.** (*buscar*)
Buscan una raqueta que sea buena.

1. Tenemos un profesor que nunca llega tarde. (*querer*)

   _____

2. Hay alguien aquí que estudia italiano. (*no hay nadie*)

   _____

3. Conocemos a una secretaria que escribe bien. (*necesitar*)

   _____

4. Hay muchos turistas que viajan en autobús. (*no hay ningún*)

   _____

5. Los estudiantes sacan buenas notas en esta clase. (*ojalá*)

   _____

ANSWERS p. 324 **C.** Translate the sentences into Spanish.

1. We don't know anyone who is going.

   _____

2. She needs an apartment that has two bedrooms.

   _____

3. There is no one here who plays the guitar.

   _____

4. Is there anyone here who has a watch?

   _____

5. I am looking for a secretary who wants to work.

   _____

ANSWERS
p. 324 D. Use the conjunctions in parentheses to combine the two sentences. Make the necessary changes.

> EX: Teresa se enfermará. Ella comerá enchiladas. (*después que*)
> Teresa se enfermará después que coma enchiladas.

1. No te olvides de llamarme. Llegarás a la oficina. (*antes que*)

   _____

2. Paco siempre llama al doctor. Tiene mareos. (*cuando*)

   _____

3. Los turistas volverán al hotel. Visitarán las ruinas. (*después que*)

   _____

4. Me ocuparé de todo. Los niños se dormirán. (*tan pronto como*)

   _____

5. Yo busco la llanta de repuesto. Ud. revisa la batería. (*mientras*)

   _____

ANSWERS
p. 324 E. Complete these sentences with the indicative or subjunctive forms of the verbs in parentheses.

1. Espero que Ud. _____ algo en el Rastro de Madrid. (*comprar*)
2. No entiendo por qué él _____ a Chacago mañana. (*irse*)
3. Puedo ver a tu amiga después que (yo) _____ de clase. (*salir*)
4. Te contaré muchas cosas cuando (nosotras) _____ a casa. (*llegar*)
5. No hay nadie aquí que no _____ español. (*hablar*)
6. Conozco a una muchacha en la oficina que _____ de Caracas. (*ser*)
7. Anita me informa que Ud. _____ a España el verano próximo. (*ir*)
8. Teresa me sugiere que (nosotros) _____ en la esquina. (*cruzar*)
9. El mecánico trabaja hasta que se _____. (*cansarse: get tired*)
10. Me sorprende que Mirta no _____ nada. (*decir*)
11. Es una pena que miles de niños _____ de hambre. (*morir*)
12. Supongo que ustedes _____ responsables en su trabajo. (*ser*)

EXAM 3   LESSONS 11–15

Part I.   Practique las palabras nuevas (50 puntos)

ANSWERS
p. 325

A. Match the two columns. The article is not always needed.

1. ___ pestañas
2. ___ tobillo
3. ___ codo.
4. ___ muletas
5. ___ rodilla.
6. ___ garganta
7. ___ muslo
8. ___ tos
9. ___ mareos
10. ___ fiebre
11. ___ pastillas
12. ___ pulmones
13. ___ gotas
14. ___ sastre
15. ___ sangre
16. ___ acero
17. ___ marca
18. ___ balanza

A. Cuando me duele el estómago, me dan muchos...

B. El doctor me recetó... para el dolor de estómago.

C. Creo que tiene la tensión de... un poco alta.

D. Voy a ir al... porque necesito un vestido nuevo.

E. Con tanto fumar, debes tener los... negros del humo.

F. Algunas señoras y señoritas se pintan las...

G. Me duelen los ojos. Voy a ponerme unas...

H. Cuando se tuerce el..., no se puede caminar bien.

I. Doblamos la pierna en la parte que se llama la...

J. Necesitas una... si quieres saber tu peso.

K. Tienes dificultad para hablar por la infección de la...

L. Doblamos el brazo en la articulación del...

M. El hueso más grande del hombre está en el...

N. Si te enyesan la pierna, tienes que caminar con...

O. No me gustan las hojas de aluminio; prefiero las de...

P. Para saber si tienes..., debes ponerte el termómetro.

Q. Con tanta... no deberías fumar.

R. No me gusta esa... de cerveza; pide otra.

ANSWERS
p. 325

B. Underline the best of four choices.

19. Debemos comprar llantas nuevas porque éstas están (desinfladas, torcidas, gastadas, disponibles).

20. Mi carro tiene el acumulador viejo; por eso no (funciona, arranca, toca, pincha) bien.

21. Si no tienes buenos (frenos, cinturones, neumáticos, faros) no puedes parar con seguridad.

22. Vamos a la droguería para (llenar una receta, bajar de peso, ponernos una inyección, estar en onda).

23. Para poder mandarle la cuenta necesito (una radiografía, el domicilio, el cacharro, la matrícula).

24. Si tiene un hueso roto, probablemente lo tendremos que (cortar, oler, enyesar, tragar).

25. Debemos estar listos para una emergencia (increíble, gruesa, imprevista, resbaladiza).

26. No puedo llenar el tanque porque la manguera está (doblada, dañada, cargada, ondulada).

27. En un cruce peligroso es mejor (bajar la velocidad, engrasar el motor, subir la loma, aparcar el carro).

28. Cuando se pincha un neumático es bueno tener (un choque con anticipación, una llanta de repuesto, una buena bocina, un puente estrecho).

29. Para que el médico pueda examinarme es conveniente (tragarme las pastillas, quitarme la camiseta, guardar cama, seguir una dieta).

30. Vamos a la florería cuando queremos (comprar unas rosas, cortarnos el cabello, conseguir un jarabe, contener la fiebre).

ANSWERS
p. 325

C. Write a synonym for each of the following words.

31. autobús _____ manejar _____

32. farmacia _____ baúl (*del carro*) _____

33. carné _____ matrícula _____

34. aparcar _____ manual _____

35. choque _____ detenerse _____

36. autopista _____ cerro _____

37. píldora _____ cruce _____

38. paciente _____ resfriado _____

39. delgado _____ grueso _____

ANSWERS
p. 325

D. Circle the letter of the best reply.

40. El lunes pasado tuve una avería imprevista en la carretera.
    A. Sí, claro; por eso echas de menos a tus amigos.
    B. Sú, claro; eso te pasa por comprar carros de segunda mano.
    C. Sí, claro; tú siempre tienes buena suerte para todo.
    D. Sí, claro; ya veo que tienes un pie enyesado y muletas.

41. Esta mañana me corté terriblemente en la mejilla cuando me afeitaba.

   A. Bueno, me imagino que eso te hizo ver las estrellas.

   B. Eso te pasa por afeitarte con una máquina eléctrica.

   C. Entonces debes ir a llenar una receta en seguida.

   D. Ya veo que tienes todavía un poco de sangre en la mano.

42. Doctor, tengo una tos terrible desde hace una semana y no se me quita.

   A. Lo mejor será que dejes el cigarrillo inmediatamente.

   B. Eso me huele mal. Será mejor que tengas mareos y úlceras.

   C. Eso no tiene remedio. Es preferible que pierdas peso.

   D. Probablemente es una indigestión con complicaciones.

43. Me parece que las tarifas de alquiler son demasiado altas, señor.

   A. Es que aquí solamente alquilamos coches de segunda mano.

   B. Ya veo que usted siempre tiene mala estrella.

   C. Es que todos nuestros carros están asegurados a todo riesgo.

   D. Una razón es que todos nuestros carros son todos de cambios.

44. Doctor, me dañé bastante la espalda cuando choqué contra el autobús.

   A. Eso te pasa porque probablemente no te pones el cinturón de seguridad.

   B. Sí, ya veo que tienes el tobillo torcido y habrá que enyesarlo.

   C. Eso te pasa porque acabas de poner los frenos nuevos al carro.

   D. Pero ese dolor se te quitará cuando tu seguro pague los daños.

45. ¿Cree usted que todo mi equipaje cabrá en el baúl de su carro?

   A. ¡Cómo no! Usted sabe que mi automóvil es de cambios.

   B. Por supuesto. Yo también llevo tres maletas grandes.

   C. Claro que sí. Mi esposa también lleva dos baúles.

   D. Creo que no. Ud. sabe que mi carro es bastante pequeño.

46. Anita, ayer me encontré con un señor muy gentil y me pagó el almuerzo.

   A. Bueno, pues ya sabes que «A mal tiempo, buena cara».

   B. Yo también me encontré con uno muy atento que se las traía.

   C. Me imagino que te casarás con él mañana mismo.

   D. Te felicito. Tú siempre tienes buena estrella.

47. Oiga, señor, aquí se prohíbe estacionar el automóvil.

   A. En ese caso me aparcaré aquí mismo.

   B. Está bien. No me importa pagar la propina.

   C. En ese caso tendré que buscar otro lugar.

   D. No importa. Éste es el carro de mi papá.

48. El turismo representa una buena entrada de dinero en nuestro país, ¿no?

    A. Sí, por eso los turistas americanos viajan en autobús.

    B. Sí, los turistas admiran mucho nuestros paisajes.

    C. Claro, los turistas dejan mucha lana en hoteles y restaurantes.

    D. ¡Cómo no! Los turistas americanos se las traen.

49. ¿Estás prestando atención a la velocidad máxima de sesenta y cinco millas?

    A. Sí, pero mi póliza de seguro pagará todo.

    B. Sí, pero mis frenos y llantas son nuevos.

    C. Aquí en Texas no hay velocidad máxima.

    D. Sí, pero yo voy solamente a cincuenta.

50. Doctor, ¿qué me recomienda para este dolor terrible de cabeza?

    A. Que vayas a la pastelería de guardia.

    B. Que te pongas esta inyección de calmante.

    C. Que te pongas unas gotas de jarabe en los ojos.

    D. Que te preocupes más de pagar las cuentas.

Part II. Practique la gramática (50 puntos)

ANSWERS p. 325

A. **Change the verb to the future in each sentence. Write the verb only.**

1. _____ Ud. tiene que poner gasolina en el tanque.

2. _____ ¿Por qué no vuelves mañana a verme?

3. _____ No sé qué hacer con este equipaje.

4. _____ Ellos no quieren venir en el autobús.

5. _____ El padre mantiene a toda su familia.

6. _____ Jaimito les dice la verdad a sus papás.

7. _____ El pueblo no se opone al presidente electo.

ANSWERS p. 325

B. **Change the verbs to the familiar command (*tú*). Make the command positive or negative according to the statement. Write the command only.**

8. _____ Teresa viene con nosotros a la fiesta.

9. _____ Eduardo no sale con el carro.

10. _____ Esteban no va en avión sino en tren.

11. _____ Mamá tiene paciencia con nosotros.

12. _____ Juanita pone la mesa con cuidado.

13. _____ Mario no es cruel con los perros.

ANSWERS
p. 325

C. Change the verbs to formal commands (Ud./Uds.). Substitute object pronouns such as *me, te, lo, la,* wherever possible.

14. _____ Ud. sabe esta lección para mañana.

15. _____ Ustedes no vienen tarde a la fiesta.

16. _____ Ud. me da un regalo para el cumpleaños.

17. _____ Uds. me lo hacen bien.

18. _____ Ud. no me lo dice.

19. _____ Usted nos lo trae.

20. _____ Usted pide el café con crema.

ANSWERS
p. 326

D. Complete each sentence with the present indicative or the present subjunctive of the verb in parentheses.

21. Es muy necesario que él _____ a tiempo. (*llegar*)

22. Es muy evidente que tú _____ muy atento. (*ser*)

23. Nadie duda que ustedes _____ buena salud. (*tener*)

24. ¿Te gusta que nosotros te _____ bromas (*tricks*)? (*hacer*)

25. Siento mucho que tu papá no _____ vernos. (*poder*)

26. ¿Es cierto que Teresa _____ para Colombia? (*irse*)

27. Yo no pienso que tú _____ tan enfermo. (*estar*)

28. Es mejor que usted _____ en una semana. (*volver*)

29. Mis padres quieren una casa que _____ un jardín grande. (*tener*)

30. Siempre me siento bien después que _____ ocho horas. (*dormir*)

31. Ellos prefieren que (yo) _____ el carro. (*conducir*)

32. Mi tía me escribe que ella _____ a verme pronto. (*venir*)

33. El doctor te informa que el caso no _____ serio. (*ser*)

34. El director quiere verte antes que _____ . (*salir*)

35. ¿Hay alguien aquí que _____ hablar árabe? (*saber*)

ANSWERS
p. 326

E. Circle the letter of the best answer.

36. En realidad tu amigo no es gordo... es bajito.

    A. sino   **C.** excepto

    B. pero   **D.** sino que

37. Aquí hay muchas minas de plata... hierro.

    A. y   **C.** o
    B. e   **D.** i

38. Prefiero que ustedes... en mi viaje de vacaciones.

    A. me acompañan   **C.** me acompañen
    B. me acompañarán   **D.** me acompañarían

39. Conozco a una familia que... diez hijos.

    A. tenga   **C.** tiene
    B. tendría   **D.** ten

40. Es una lástima que no... más en Arizona y California.

    A. llueve   **C.** lloverá
    B. llovería   **D.** llueva

41. Yo siempre tenía... dinero... tú; pero ahora no tengo nada.

    A. más que   **C.** más como
    B. tanto que   **D.** tan como

42. Jorge siempre toma una cerveza fría antes que su familia...

    A. coma   **C.** comer
    B. come   **D.** comería

43. Sentimos mucho que no... venir al teatro con nosotros.

    A. puedes   **C.** poderás
    B. podrás   **D.** puedas

44. Ella me prometió que... aquí a las ocho, y ya son las nueve.

    A. estuviera   **C.** estara
    B. estaría   **D.** esté

45. Tengo cuatro dólares. Aquí tienes uno para tu Coca-Cola. Ya no me quedan... tres para almorzar.

    A. menos de   **C.** más que
    B. pero   **D.** más de

46. Lolita quiere que... la novela este fin de semana.

    A. le lees   **C.** le leas
    B. la lees   **D.** la leas

47. Es conveniente que el niño... ocho horas al menos.

    A. dormirá   **C.** duerme
    B. duerma   **D.** dormiría

48. José me contó que ustedes... un verano estupendo en España.

    A. tengan   **C.** tuvieron

    B. tendrían   **D.** teniendo

49. A Carolina le agrada que (tú)... en español.

    A. le hablas   **C.** la hables

    B. la hablas   **D.** le hables

50. Me parece que la gente latina... más baja que la de Estados Unidos.

    A. será   **C.** sea

    B. sería   **D.** es

ANSWERS   LESSONS 11–15 AND EXAM 3

Lesson 11

Practique las palabras nuevas

A. 1. el   4. las   7. el   10. los   13. el
2. la   5. el   8. la   11. el   14. las
3. los   6. las   9. los   12. la   15. la

B. 1. echo de menos   4. tengo mala pata   7. un par de
2. en serio   5. tiempo, buena cara   8. hace ver las estrellas
3. fui a pie   6. meter la pata   9. me encontré con

C. 1. dedos   5. párpados   9. ligero   13. codo
2. imprevista   6. rodilla   10. cabello   14. frente
3. cojea   7. nariz   11. hueso
4. escalera   8. espalda   12. muletas

D. 1. torcí   4. cojeó   7. olieron
2. ocurrió   5. enyesaron   8. extrañé
3. nos encontramos   6. dolió   9. se besaron

E. 1. párpados   4. la rodilla   7. muñeca   10. mejillas
2. labios   5. hombros   8. hueso   11. muslo
3. cabello (pelo)   6. pecho   9. frente   12. cuello

Exercises

A. 1. amigos   7. accidente   13. en serio   19. muletas
2. encuentran   8. películas   14. hermana   20. semanas
3. enyesado   9. mala pata   15. ligero   21. menos
4. muletas   10. tonta   16. yeso   22. buena cara
5. escalera   11. volvía   17. huesos
6. torció   12. por hora   18. estrellas

B. 1. F   3. T   5. T   7. T   9. F   11. T
   2. F   4. F   6. F   8. T   10. T   12. F

C. 1. muletas   4. deportes   7. el codo   10. la muñeca
   2. la nariz   5. hueso   8. imprevisto
   3. pareja   6. garganta   9. las mejillas

D. 1. Mario se cayó por la escalera de su casa.
   2. Él se torció el tobillo derecho en el accidente.
   3. Sonia no creyó a Mario primero.
   4. Mario sintió bastante dolor en la operación.
   5. El médico (le) puso los huesos en su lugar.
   6. El doctor le hizo ver las estrellas a Mario del dolor.
   7. Mario cojeó un par de semanas.

Practique los comparativos

1. adverbs/más que   4. más de   7. más de   10. más que
2. más de/menos de   5. Más de   8. Dos (*Two*)
3. más de   6. más/más alta que   9. two

Exercises

A. 1. más... que   4. más que   7. más de   10. más que
   2. más de   5. más que   8. menos... que
   3. menos de   6. más... que   9. más de

B. 1. Pablo se rompió más huesos que María.
   2. Mario tuvo más accidentes que Sonia.
   3. Marcos es más alto que Lola.
   4. José estudia más que su hermano.
   5. Estudio más de lo que Ud. piensa.
   6. Miriam no tiene más que dos hermanos.
   7. Carlos gana menos dinero de lo que Ud. se imagina.

Practique la gramática

1. como / como
2. number / tantos
3. adverbs / tan
4. The second *as* / tanto como
5. Mayor / la mayor
6. Menor / menores
7. mejor / peor / mejor que
8. lindísimo / cojísimo
9. de / de
10. As soon as possible / as
11. mejor (óptimo) / peor (pésimo)
12. máxima

Exercises

A. 1. menor que / tan... como
   2. tan... como
   3. tantas... como
   4. lo más pronto posible
   5. gordísimo (muy gordo)
   6. mayor
   7. tanto como
   8. tan... como
   9. tanta... como
   10. peor que
   11. más / de
   12. grandísimo
   13. mayores que
   14. peor
   15. optimista
   16. pesimista

B. 1. Lola tiene el pelo más rubio que su hermana.
   2. Guillermo tiene más suerte que su amiga.
   3. En Alaska hace más frío que en Siberia.
   4. Esta comida es más ligera que esa otra.

C. 1. La carne es tan cara como el pescado.
   2. Eres más joven (menor) que yo.
   3. Mi carro es tan viejo como el tuyo.
   4. Lo hice lo más pronto posible.
   5. Ella trabaja tanto como Ud. (tú).
   6. Ella es la mejor de todos.
   7. Mi hijo es muy alto (altísimo).
   8. Éste es el edificio más alto de Estados Unidos.

Practique el futuro

1. infinitive / comer / ser
2. yo / tú / nosotros
3. -emos
4. compraremos
5. present
6. present / llega
7. ir / hablará (habla)
8. estará

Exercises

A.
1. viviremos	5. enyesarán	9. besará	13. serán
2. iremos	6. pasará	10. se torcerá	14. me sentaré
3. se encontrará	7. dolerá	11. ocurrirá	
4. caminará	8. estará	12. olerán	

B.
1. hablarás	6. pedirá	11. viviremos	16. conoceré
2. volveré	7. seguiré	12. darás	17. empezará
3. pensarán	8. dolerá	13. veremos	18. divertirás
4. estaremos	9. olerás	14. irás	19. entraremos
5. seremos	10. serás	15. será	20. oirás

C.
1. volverá	6. cojearé	11. lavarás	16. seguirá
2. irán	7. oirá	12. darás	17. estará
3. serán	8. caerán	13. oirán	18. enyesará
4. hablarán	9. pedirá	14. morirá	19. me caeré
5. torceré	10. servirán	15. dormirán	20. creerá

Lesson 12

Practique las palabras nuevas

A.
1. la	4. los	7. la	10. la	13. el
2. el	5. la	8. la	11. la	14. las
3. la	6. las	9. los	12. el	15. la

B.
1. guardar cama	5. a lo mejor	9. tener calma
2. tienes... tos	6. tomar asiento	10. ¡Sólo me falta eso!
3. perder el tiempo	7. ¡Cómo no!	11. puso pálido
4. no tiene remedio	8. tiene mareos	12. llenó una receta

C.
1. radiografía	4. salud	7. domicilio	10. tensión
2. vacuna	5. farmacia	8. fatiga	11. receta
3. vitaminas	6. póliza	9. pulmones	12. úlcera

D.
1. agradeceré	4. molestará	7. descansaremos	9. se calmarán
2. enfermarás	5. curará	8. quitará	10. viajarán
3. arreglará	6. recetará		

E. 1. catarro (gripe)   3. píldora   5. gripa (trancazo)   7. a lo mejor
    2. domicilio   4. ¡Cómo no!   6. feliz (alegre)   8. agradecer

F. 1. alergia   7. pulmón   13. remedio   19. pálido
    2. fatiga   8. vacuna   14. recetar   20. alegre
    3. estómago   9. tos   15. músculo   21. calma/calmar
    4. farmacia   10. salud   16. inyección   22. mareo/marina
    5. indigestión   11. peligro   17. aliviar   23. seguro/asegurado
    6. curar/cura   12. síntoma   18. preferible   24. guardar

Exercises

A. 1. domicilio   7. mareos   13. pulmones   19. inyección
    2. teléfono   8. úlcera   14. fumar   20. guardar
    3. Mártires   9. tos   15. cigarrillos 21. píldoras (pastillas)
    4. póliza   10. fiebre   16. nicotina   22. agradece
    5. molestar   11. alta   17. corazón   23. cuidado
    6. estómago   12. camisa   18. gripe

B. 1. T   3. F   5. F   7. T   9. T   11. F   13. T   15. T
    2. F   4. T   6. T   8. F   10. T   12. F   14. F

C. 1. enfermedad   4. camiseta   7. temperatura   9. peligro
    2. cura   5. radiografía 8. morirse   10. enfermedad
    3. saludable   6. enfermo

D. 1. Guillermo tiene mareos porque tiene (la) tensión alta.
    2. Lola está pálida porque tiene fiebre.
    3. A mí me molesta el dolor de estómago.
    4. A usted le duelen los músculos porque tiene gripe.
    5. ¿A ti se te quita el dolor de cabeza con aspirina?
    6. A José no se le alivia la tos con pastillas.

Practique el condicional

1. infinitive/estaría	4. viviría	7. imperfect
2. endings	5. past/time	8. future/conditional
3. imperfect/comería	6. imperfect/iba a llegar	9. estaría

Exercises

A.
1. curaría	5. fumaría	9. debería	13. arreglarían
2. aliviaría	6. calmaría	10. molestaría	14. examinaría
3. debería	7. enfermaría	11. quitaría	15. volvería
4. perdería	8. descansaría	12. recetaría	

B.
1. sería	5. pensarían	9. pagaría	13. seguiría
2. pediría	6. serías	10. dormiría	14. oirías
3. estarías	7. conocería	11. escribiría	
4. volverían	8. iríamos	12. morirían	

C.
1. entraría	4. sería	7. caería	10. comprarían
2. oiría	5. pedirían	8. dormirían	11. estaría
3. iría	6. moriría	9. seguirías	12. andaría

Practique el futuro y condicional

1. sabré/e	6. satisfaré
2. vendría/d	7. contendré/contendría
3. conditional/haría	8. supondré/supondría
4. querría	9. reharía/reharé
5. cabremos	10. opondría/opondré

Exercises

A.
1. saldremos	4. propondrá	7. valdrá	9. hará
2. habrá	5. abstendrán	8. querrá	10. dirá
3. deshará	6. rehará		

B. 1. tendría   5. sería   9. haría   13. prevendría

    2. podría   6. debería   10. habría   14. tendría

    3. saldría   7. diría   11. mantendría   15. detendrían

    4. obtendría   8. querría   12. valdría

C. 1. fuimos/iremos   10. creyó/creerá   19. pude/podré

    2. fuimos/seremos   11. salí/saldré   20. quiso/querrá

    3. estuve/estaré   12. tuvo/tendrá   21. hubo/habrá

    4. dieron/darán   13. volvió/volverá   22. anduvo/andará

    5. pedí/pediré   14. supe/sabré   23. murió/morirá

    6. vi/veré   15. puse/pondré   24. siguió/seguirá

    7. hizo/haré   16. oyeron/oirán   25. ofrecí/ofreceré

    8. dije/diré   17. fue/será   26. pagué/pagaré

    9. oí/oiré   18. huyó/huirá

Practique el imperativo

1. commands/tú   5. negative/salgas   9. affirmative/negative

2. indicative/habla   6. ven/ten/sal   10. llámame/me llames

3. -es/-as/hables/comas   7. I gave/tell (say)   11. supón

4. indicative/duerme   8. I know/be   12. mantén/prevén

Exercises

A. 1. háblame   4. házme   7. sal

    2. escríbeme   5. ven   8. lávate

    3. dime   6. óyeme   9. bébete

B. 1. llegues tarde   5. te laves las manos   9. lo propongas

    2. digas nada   6. te duermas tarde   10. te sientes

    3. llames hoy   7. me lo compres   11. mientas

    4. hagas caso   8. deshagas la maleta   12. te acuestes tarde

C. 1. contéstalo/no lo contestes   3. tráela/no la traigas

    2. escríbela/no la escribas   4. lávatelas/no te las laves

5. pídeselo/no se lo pidas   7. tómalas/no las tomes

6. dísela/no se la digas

D. 1. No te sientes aquí.   7. Tómatelo todo.

2. No me des la cuenta ahora.   8. Llámala temprano.

3. No me hables en español.   9. Vístete ahora.

4. No me lo digas todo.   10. Tócalo, por favor.

5. No te lo arregles.   11. Empiézalo mañana.

6. No te la bebas.   12. Llévatelo.

Lesson 13

Practique las palabras nuevas

A. 1. el   3. las   5. el   7. el   9. el (la)   11. la

2. la   4. el   6. los   8. las   10. los   12. el

B. 1. pescadería   5. librería   9. panadería   12. taquería

2. verdulería   6. tortillería   10. carnicería   13. pastelería

3. frutería   7. droguería   11. relojería   14. sastrería

4. florería   8. zapatería

C. 1. hojas de afeitar   4. seguir una dieta   7. me acostumbré

2. se preocupa   5. perder de peso   8. crema dental

3. la peluquería   6. drogadictos   9. farmacia de guardia

D. 1. durará   4. convertirán   7. se preocupará   9. mantendrán

2. padecerá   5. conseguiré   8. tragará   10. contestará

3. tardará   6. adelgazaremos

E. 1. calorías   5. marcas   9. verduras   12. tubo

2. droga   6. acero   10. talco   13. jarabe

3. florería   7. sangre   11. yogur   14. gotas

4. balanza   8. jabón

Exercises

A.
1. viejos
2. ven
3. dolor
4. mareos
5. chimenea
6. exagere
7. unos
8. fatal
9. dejar
10. médico
11. gripe
12. cama
13. receta
14. posible
15. jarabe
16. tragar
17. crema
18. pies
19. afeitar
20. máquinas
21. acero
22. duran
23. lee
24. irritación
25. acostarse
26. cobra (carga)
27. abuse
28. pronto

B.
1. barbería
2. seguir una dieta
3. crema dental
4. pastelería
5. sastrería
6. balanza
7. jabón
8. comer sin sal
9. ponerse gotas
10. abuse del tabaco

C.
1. complicada
2. reciente
3. en total
4. gordo (obeso)
5. inoxidable
6. sastre
7. trago
8. Abusar
9. líquido
10. drogadicto
11. balanceada
12. peluquería
13. alimento
14. duran
15. marca

D.
1. Prepárame esta receta a mí.
2. No te preocupes por esos problemas.
3. Ponte dos gotas antes de acostarte.
4. Me acostumbro a estas píldoras.
5. Consigue una balanza para pesarte.
6. Guillermo, no abuses del tabaco.

Practique la gramática

1. e/e/i, hi
2. y/y
3. u/u/o/ho
4. negative/pero
5. sino
6. subject/sino que
7. sino
8. feminine/ tristemente
9. keep/fácilmente
10. last/clara/ fácilmente

Exercises

A.
1. e/e
2. e
3. u
4. y
5. sino
6. u
7. sino
8. sino que
9. pero
10. pero
11. y
12. o

B.
1. tontamente
2. recientemente
3. claramente
4. felizmente
5. amablemente
6. suavemente
7. fácilmente
8. difícilmente
9. tristemente
10. alegremente
11. buenamente
12. totalmente

C. 1. Le llevo un refresco rápidamente.

2. Me siento cómodamente en un sillón.

3. Podemos llevarlos fácilmente en el carro.

4. Me gusta celebrarlo alegremente.

5. Les sirvo bocadillos y bebidas probablemente.

Practique el imperativo formal

1. e/en/hable
2. a/an/coma/coman
3. mandar
4. indicative/piense
5. duerma/duerman
6. diga/digan
7. empiece/e
8. pague/u
9. siga/o
10. affirmative/negative
11. llámeme/me llame
12. lávese/lávense

Exercises

A. 1. abuse
2. alimente
3. balancee
4. consiga
5. conteste
6. convierta
7. corte
8. dure
9. padezca
10. trague
11. preocúpese
12. acostúmbrese

B. 1. escríbala/no la escriba
2. pídalo/no lo pida
3. llénela/no la llene
4. siéntese/no se siente
5. páguela/no la pague
6. tráguelas/no las trague
7. empiécela/no la empiece
8. consígalos/no los consiga
9. láveselas/no se las lave
10. váyase/no se vaya

C. 1. No abusen de las aspirinas.

2. Tráguense las pastillas.

3. Empiecen la dieta mañana.

4. Guarden cama unos días.

5. No tomen café ni soda.

6. No fumen absolutamente nada.

7. Lávense bien los dientes.

8. No se preocupen demasiado.

9. Acostúmbrense a comer poco.

10. Acuéstense temprano.

11. Duerman siete horas por lo menos.

12. Balanceen bien las comidas.

Practique el subjuntivo

1. e/a/hable
2. subjunctive
3. subjunctive/comas
4. vuelv-/vuelva
5. sientes/sentemos
6. i/pidas/pidamos
7. plural/durmamos
8. sintamos
9. c/comience
10. gu/tragué/trague
11. a/siga
12. e/practique
13. llegué/llegue

Exercises

A. 1. abuse
   2. adelgace
   3. balancee
   4. convierta
   5. alimente
   6. divierta
   7. vístase
   8. toque
   9. apague
  10. siéntese
  11. siéntase
  12. tuerza
  13. sirva
  14. consiga
  15. ponga
  16. alíviese
  17. juegue
  18. comience

B. 1. siga
   2. tome
   3. se acueste
   4. nos sintamos
   5. vulevan
   6. pierdas
   7. empiece
   8. comamos
   9. paguen
  10. fumes
  11. me alivie
  12. pida

C. 1. lleguen
   2. escriban
   3. marquen
   4. fumen
   5. coman
   6. hablen
   7. mastiquen
   8. se sienten
   9. practiquen
  10. duerman
  11. duerman
  12. se diviertan

Lesson 14

Practique las palabras nuevas

A. 1. el
   2. la
   3. el
   4. el
   5. la
   6. el
   7. el
   8. el
   9. el
  10. la
  11. el
  12. el
  13. el
  14. el
  15. el
  16. el
  17. el
  18. el

B. 1. acumulador
   2. carro
   3. estacionar
   4. la licencia
   5. maletero (cajuela)
   6. manejar
   7. placa
   8. llanta (goma)
   9. de cambios (mecánico)
  10. por fin

C. 1. baúl (maletero)
   2. de segunda mano
   3. gastadas
   4. volante
   5. gangas
   6. pedal
   7. a todo riesgo
   8. diarios
   9. tablero de mandos
  10. torcido
  11. llantas
  12. cacharro
  13. toque la bocina
  14. lujoso
  15. cinturones
  16. mapa
  17. por fin
  18. por ser usted
  19. carné
  20. olerme mal

D. 1. alquiler   3. parque   5. freno   7. función

    2. estación   4. conductor   6. arranque   8. olor

Exercises

A. 1. agencia   7. manual   13. ganga   19. roto

    2. cómodo   8. ahorrar   14. olió   20. torcido

    3. semanas   9. frenos   15. alquilarlo   21. funcionaba

    4. disponible   10. asegurado   16. dijo   22. desastre

    5. de segunda mano   11. manejarlo   17. mano

    6. condiciones   12. diarios   18. gastadas

B. 1. F   3. T   5. F   7. F   9. F   11. T

    2. F   4. T   6. F   8. T   10. T   12. T

C. 1. manejes   5. funcione   9. pites   12. enciendas

    2. frenes   6. toques   10. arranque   13. apagues

    3. estaciones   7. lleves   11. conduzcas   14. llenes

    4. pinches   8. parquees

Practique el subjuntivo

1. prefiera / prefiramos   6. esté / estés / estén / dé   11. mantenga

2. c / z   7. sabré / sepa   12. suponga

3. produzca / produzcamos   8. haré / haga   13. decir

4. y / concluya   9. diré / diga

5. ir / Go with God   10. satisfaga

Exercises

A. 1. manejes   6. duermas   11. sepan   16. pase

    2. pongas   7. te abroches   12. paguen   17. hables

    3. puedas   8. prevengas   13. vayas

    4. estés   9. mantengas   14. salgas

    5. hagas   10. traigas   15. huyas

B. 1. duermo/durmió/durmamos   8. tengo/tuvo/tengamos

2. sirvo/sirvió/sirvamos   9. hago/hizo/hagamos

3. miento/mintió/mintamos   10. leo/leyó/leamos

4. muero/murió/muramos   11. me voy/se fue/nos vayamos

5. prefiero/prefirió/prefiramos   12. oigo/oyó/oigamos

6. divierto/divirtió/divirtamos   13. caigo/cayó/caigamos

7. sigo/siguió/sigamos   14. soy/fue/seamos

Practique el subjuntivo

1. subordinate/main   5. practiquemos   9. indicative/habla

2. que   6. infinitive/tomar   10. says that you work

3. indicative/fuma   7. indicative   11. tells you to work

4. subjunctive/fume   8. lleguen

Exercises

A. 1. se duerma   8. está   15. llame   22. venga

2. sea   9. vuelvas   16. trabaja   23. traiga

3. manejan   10. toma/tome   17. salgan   24. hay/habrá

4. lleguen   11. vaya   18. cambia   25. escribe

5. tiene   12. te diviertas 19. aparquemos

6. alquile   13. hay   20. desayune

7. nada   14. tienen   21. suban

B. 1. digan   5. escriban   9. hable   13. prepare

2. lleguen   6. no fumen   10. les dé   14. termine

3. hablen   7. sepan   11. sea   15. mantenga

4. hagan   8. se diviertan 12. tenga   16. empiece

C. 1. vuelva a la consulta   4. cambie el día del examen

2. me visitan (visitarán) en agosto   5. tomemos una cerveza fría

3. te acuestes muy tarde   6. llego más temprano

Practique los acentos

1. stressed
2. last/two
3. stress/two
4. you/your

5. stress/n, s/two
6. next-to-the-last
7. two
8. two

9. yes/oneself/if
10. my/me/mí/mi
11. dónde

12. ¡Qué
13. diphthong
14. Yes/o

Exercise

1. El baúl de mi automóvil es bastante grande y ayer lo llené de libros.
2. El doctor me recetó unas píldoras y me puso una inyección de antibióticos.
3. Solamente quiero saber cuándo te vas y a dónde llevarás a tu familia.
4. Yo compraría ese hotel, pero tú no quieres ayudarme con tu dinero.
5. En este álbum de fotografías está toda mi familia con mis papás.
6. José prefirió comprar este coche en lugar de aquél.
7. Dígame por qué no llegó a tiempo el día veintitrés de abril.
8. Cristóbal Colón descrubrió América el doce de octubre de 1492.
9. Todos los indios de América comían maíz y hacían pan con él.
10. Tu carro es automático, pero está en pésimas condiciones.
11. No entiendo eso del acento en la última sílaba; ¿puede explicármelo?
12. ¡Cómo no! Para mí eso está más claro que el agua del río.
13. Te diré que sí, porque así me volverás a invitar a tu cumpleaños.
14. Este té está más caliente que ese café, pero a mí no me gusta el té.

Lesson 15

Practique las palabras nuevas

A.
1. el
2. el
3. la

4. la
5. el
6. el

7. la
8. el
9. la

10. el
11. el
12. el

13. el
14. el

15. el
16. la

B.
1. estar en onda
2. llanta de repuesto
3. se ocupan de

4. microondas
5. con anticipación
6. darles la bienvenida

7. qué casualidad
8. prestarle atención
9. se las trae

C. 1. atento   3. despierto   5. fascinante   7. estrecho
   2. breve   4. quebrado   6. resbaladizo   8. ondulado

D. 1. camión/guagua   3. colina/loma   6. surtidor   8. terreno
      colectivo   4. tanque   7. alto/pare/ 9. ocuparse de
   2. intersección   5. avería   parada   10. carretera/autovía

E. 1. manguera   4. ondas (olas)   7. paisajes   10. velocímetro
   2. pozos   5. puente   8. pirámides   11. paradas
   3. güeras   6. avería   9. radiador   12. esquina

F. 1. engrases   3. revise   5. infles   7. se ocupen de
   2. limpies   4. llenes   6. prepares   8. compres

G. 1. cuadras   4. quebrado   7. esquina   10. chistosos
   2. atento   5. estrecho   8. lana (plata) 11. surtidor
   3. ruinas   6. lista   9. cerro   12. petroleros

Exercises

A. 1. viajar   7. creía (pensaba)   13. maíz   19. favorito
   2. hasta   8. manejaban   14. pirámide   20. casualidad
   3. joven   9. gustaba   15. venía   21. chócala
   4. sentarse   10. dijo (aseguró)   16. dijo (contestó)
   5. pidió   11. las trae   17. tenía
   6. güera   12. lista   18. camarero

B. 1. F   4. T   7. T   10. F   13. F
   2. F   5. T   8. T   11. T   14. T
   3. T   6. F   9. F   12. T   15. T

C. 1. revisemos   4. dobles   7. choquemos   10. vaya
   2. pares   5. resbale   8. consultes   11. dañe
   3. cruces   6. subas   9. tengamos   12. descansemos

D. 1. Compre   4. Consulte   7. pida   9. pierda
   2. deje   5. lleve   8. Haga   10. Tenga
   3. Lea   6. olvide

Practique la gramática

1. indicative / sabe
2. subjunctive / estudies
3. subjunctive / subjunctive
4. vengas
5. fume
6. manejen
7. tiene
8. llueva
9. subjunctive
10. subjunctive / indicative

Exercises

A.
1. beba
2. lleguen
3. hablan
4. estudia
5. sepan
6. escriba
7. está
8. fuma
9. bebe
10. tenga
11. quiere
12. pueda
13. pidas
14. pare
15. se vista

B.
1. Me sorprende que ella no vaya de vacaciones.
2. Nos alegramos mucho que ustedes tengan (un) buen trabajo.
3. Ojalá que nosotros ganemos muchos dólares en Las Vegas.
4. Es una lástima que (tú) no puedas acompañarme a mí.
5. Nos molesta que los vecinos pongan la radio muy alta (el radio muy alto).
6. Le agradecemos a usted que cambie el aceite de mi carro.

Practique la gramática

1. subjunctive / visites
2. indicative / tienes
3. indicative / está
4. es que / sabe
5. sea
6. indicative / subjunctive

Exercises

A.
1. están
2. quieras
3. vengan
4. sigan
5. es
6. desean
7. dé
8. está
9. sea
10. quieres
11. acompañe
12. gasta

B.
1. Suponemos que el muchacho cruza la calle sin problema.
2. Me parece que Roberto se ocupa de comprar los boletos.
3. Es posible que ella me asuste mucho por la noche.
4. Es probable que sigamos derecho hasta la catedral.
5. Es que el carro resbala mucho cuando llueve.
6. Creemos que el paisaje de las pirámides es fascinante.
7. Es imposible que la americana llegue a Acapulco en tres días.

Practique la gramática

1. adjectival	6. come	11. tengamos
2. indicative/subjunctive	7. adverbial	12. de/que
3. tiene	8. indicative/llegó	13. subjunctive
4. coma	9. indicative/come	14. subjunctive/indicative
5. estudie	10. subjunctive/llegue	

Exercises

A.
1. tiene	5. acabé	9. vive	13. fume
2. gusta (gustó)	6. vaya	10. hablan	14. guste (gusta)
3. sepa	7. sé	11. gasten	15. dijo
4. es	8. hablen	12. sea	16. canse

B.
1. Queremos un profesor que nunca llegue tarde.
2. No hay nadie aquí que estudie italiano.
3. Necesitamos una secretaria que escriba bien.
4. No hay ningún turista que viaje en autobús.
5. Ojalá que los estudiantes saquen buenas notas.

C.
1. No conocemos a nadie que vaya.
2. (Ella) necesita un apartamento que tenga dos recámaras (dormitorios).
3. No hay nadie aquí que toque la guitarra.
4. ¿Hay alguien aquí que tenga (un) reloj?
5. Busco a una secretaria que quiera (desee) trabajar.

D.
1. No te olvides de llamarme antes que llegues a la oficina.
2. Paco siempre llama al doctor cuando tiene mareos.
3. Los turistas volverán al hotel después que visiten las ruinas.
4. Me ocuparé de todo tan pronto como los niños se duerman.
5. (Yo) busco la llanta de repuesto mientras Ud. revisa la batería.

E.
1. compre	4. lleguemos	7. va (irá)	10. diga
2. se va	5. hable	8. crucemos	11. mueran
3. salga	6. es	9. cansa	12. son

Exam 3

Part I.   Practique las palabras nuevas (50 puntos)

A. 1. F   4. N   7. M   10. P   13. G   16. O

    2. H   5. I   8. Q   11. B   14. D   17. R

    3. L   6. K   9. A   12. E   15. C   18. J

B. 19. gastadas   25. imprevista

    20. arranca   26. dañada

    21. frenos   27. bajar la velocidad

    22. llenar una receta   28. una llanta de repuesto

    23. el domicilio   29. quitarse la camiseta

    24. enyesar   30. comprar unas rosas

C. 31. autocar (camión, guagua)/conducir (guiar)

    32. droguería/maletero (cajuela)

    33. licencia/placa

    34. estacionar (parquear)/mecánico (de cambios)

    35. accidente/pararse

    36. carretera (autovía)/loma (colina)

    37. pastilla/intersección

    38. enfermo/resfrío (catarro)

    39. flaco/gordo

D. 40. B   42. A   44. A   46. D   48. C   50. B

    41. A   43. C   45. D   47. C   49. D

Part II.   Practique la gramática (50 puntos)

A. 1. tendrá   3. sabré   5. mantendrá   7. opondrá

    2. volverás   4. querrán   6. dirá

B. 8. ven   10. no vayas   12. pon

    9. no salgas   11. ten   13. no seas

C. 14. sépala   16. démelo   18. no me lo diga   20. pídalo

    15. no vengan   17. háganmelo   19. tráiganoslo

D. 21. llegue   25. pueda   29. tenga   33. es

    22. eres   26. se va   30. duermo   34. salgas

    23. tienen   27. estás   31. conduzca   35. sepa

    24. hagamos   28. vuelva   32. viene (vendrá)

E. 36. B   40. D   44. B   48. C

    37. A   41. A   45. C   49. D

    38. C   42. A   46. C   50. D

    39. C   43. D   47. B

___ **Appendixes**

APPENDIX 1   Regular Verbs

Infinitive

habl ar (*to speak*)   com er (*to eat*)   viv ir (*to live*)

Present Participle

habl ando (*speaking*)   com iendo (*eating*)   viv iendo (*living*)

Past Participle

habl ado (*spoken*)   com ido (*eaten*)   viv ido (*lived*)

Indicative: Simple Tenses

PRESENT

(*I speak, am speaking, do speak, will speak*)	(*I eat, am eating, do eat, will eat*)	(*I live, am living, do live, will live*)
habl o	com o	viv o
habl as	com es	viv es
habl a	com e	viv e
habl amos	com emos	viv imos
habl an	com en	viv en

IMPERFECT

(*I was speaking, used to speak, spoke*)	(*I was eating, used to eat, ate*)	(*I was living, used to live, lived*)
habl aba	com ía	viv ía
habl abas	com ías	viv ías
habl aba	com ía	viv ía
habl ábamos	com íamos	viv íamos
habl aban	com ían	viv ían

PRETERITE

(*I spoke, did speak*)	(*I ate, did eat*)	(*I lived, did live*)
habl é	com í	viv í
habl aste	com iste	viv iste
habl ó	com ió	viv ió
habl amos	com imos	viv imos
habl aron	com ieron	viv ieron

FUTURE

(*I shall/will speak*)	(*I shall/will eat*)	(*I shall/will live*)
hablar é	comer é	vivir é
hablar ás	comer ás	vivir ás
hablar á	comer á	vivir á
hablar emos	comer emos	vivir emos
hablar án	comer án	vivir án

CONDITIONAL

(*I would speak*)	(*I would eat*)	(*I would live*)
hablar ía	comer ía	vivir ía
hablar ías	comer ías	vivir ías
hablar ía	comer ía	vivir ía
hablar íamos	comer íamos	vivir íamos
hablar ían	comer ían	vivir ían

Subjunctive: Simple Tenses

PRESENT

(*that I [may] speak*)	(*that I [may] eat*)	(*that I [may] live*)
habl e	com a	viv a
habl es	com as	viv as
habl e	com a	viv a
habl emos	com amos	viv amos
habl en	com an	viv an

IMPERFECT

(*that I [might] speak*)		(*that I [might] eat*)		(*that I [might] live*)	
habl ara	habl ase	com iera	com iese	viv iera	viv iese
habl aras	habl ases	com ieras	com ieses	viv ieras	viv ieses
habl ara	habl ase	com iera	com iese	viv iera	viv iese
habl áramos	habl ásemos	com iéramos	com iésemos	viv iéramos	viv iésemos
habl aran	habl asen	com ieran	com iesen	viv ieran	viv iesen

COMMANDS

(*speak*)	(*eat*)	(*live*)
habl a (**tú**)	com e (**tú**)	viv e (**tú**)
habl e (**Ud.**)	com a (**Ud.**)	viv a (**Ud.**)
habl en (**Uds.**)	com an (**Uds.**)	viv an (**Uds.**)

Indicative: Compound Tenses

PRESENT PERFECT

(*I have spoken*)		(*I have eaten*)		(*I have lived*)	
h e		h e		h e	
h as		h as		h as	
h a	hablado	h a	comido	h a	vivido
h emos		h emos		h emos	
h an		h an		h an	

PAST PERFECT

(*I had spoken*)		(*I had eaten*)		(*I had lived*)	
hab ía		hab ía		hab ía	
hab ías		hab ías		hab ías	
hab ía	hablado	hab ía	comido	hab ía	vivido
hab íamos		hab íamos		hab íamos	
hab ían		hab ían		hab ían	

FUTURE PERFECT

(*I will have spoken*)		(*I will have eaten*)		(*I will have lived*)	
habr é		habr é		habr é	
habr ás		habr ás		habr ás	
habr á	hablado	habr á	comido	habr á	vivido
habr emos		habr emos		habr emos	
habr án		habr án		habr án	

CONDITIONAL PERFECT

(*I would have spoken*)		(*I would have eaten*)		(*I would have lived*)	
habr ía		habr ía		habr ía	
habr ías		habr ías		habr ías	
habr ía	hablado	habr ía	comido	habr ía	vivido
habr íamos		habr íamos		habr íamos	
habr ían		habr ían		habr ían	

Subjunctive: Compound Tenses

PRESENT PERFECT

(*that I [may] have spoken*)		(*that I [may] have eaten*)		(*that I [may] have lived*)	
hay a		hay a		hay a	
hay as		hay as		hay as	
hay a	} hablado	hay a	} comido	hay a	} vivido
hay amos		hay amos		hay amos	
hay an		hay an		hay an	

PAST PERFECT

(*that I had [might have] spoken*)		(*that I had [might have] eaten*)		(*that I had [might have] lived*)	
hub iera		hub iera		hub iera	
hub ieras		hub ieras		hub ieras	
hub iera	} hablado	hub iera	} comido	hub iera	} vivido
hub iéramos		hub iéramos		hub iéramos	
hub ieran		hub ieran		hub ieran	

OR		OR		OR	
hub iese		hub iese		hub iese	
hub ieses		hub ieses		hub ieses	
hub iese	} hablado	hub iese	} comido	hub iese	} vivido
hub iésemos		hub iésemos		hub iésemos	
hub iesen		hub iesen		hub iesen	

APPENDIX 2   Irregular Verbs

(Only the tenses in which the verbs are irregular are included here.)

Andar *to walk, go*
PRETERITE: anduve, anduviste, anduvo, anduvimos, anduvieron
IMPERFECT SUBJUNCTIVE: anduviera (anduviese), anduvieras, anduviera, anduviéramos, anduvieran

Caber *to fit*
PRESENT INDICATIVE: quepo, cabes, cabe, cabemos, caben
PRETERITE: cupe, cupiste, cupo, cupimos, cupieron
FUTURE: cabré, cabrás, cabrá, cabremos, cabrán
CONDITIONAL: cabría, cabrías, cabría, cabríamos, cabrían
PRESENT SUBJUNCTIVE: quepa, quepas, quepa, quepamos, quepan
IMPERFECT SUBJUNCTIVE: cupiera (cupiese), cupieras, cupiera, cupiéramos, cupieran

Caer *to fall, drop*

PRESENT INDICATIVE: caigo, caes, cae, caemos, caen

PRESENT SUBJUNCTIVE: caiga, caigas, caiga, caigamos, caigan

Conducir *to drive, conduct*

PRESENT INDICATIVE: conduzco, conduces, conduce, conducimos, conducen

PRETERITE: conduje, condujiste, condujo, condujimos, condujeron

PRESENT SUBJUNCTIVE: conduzca, conduzcas, conduzca, conduzcamos, conduzcan

IMPERFECT SUBJUNCTIVE: condujera (condujese), condujeras, condujera, condujéramos, condujeran

Conocer *to know, be acquainted with*

PRESENT INDICATIVE: conozco, conoces, conoce, conocemos, conocen

PRESENT SUBJUNCTIVE: conozca, conozcas, conozca, conozcamos, conozcan

Construir *to build, construct*

PRESENT INDICATIVE: construyo, construyes, construye, construimos, construyen

PRESENT SUBJUNCTIVE: construya, construyas, construya, construyamos, construyan

Dar *to give*

PRESENT INDICATIVE: doy, das, da, damos, dan

PRETERITE: di, diste, dio, dimos, dieron

IMPERFECT SUBJUNCTIVE: diera (diese), dieras, diera, diéramos, dieran

Decir *to say, tell*

PRESENT INDICATIVE: digo, dices, dice, decimos, dicen

PRETERITE: dije, dijiste, dijo, dijimos, dijeron

FUTURE: diré, dirás, dirá, diremos, dirán

CONDITIONAL: diría, dirías, diría, diríamos, dirían

PRESENT SUBJUNCTIVE: diga, digas, diga, digamos, digan

IMPERFECT SUBJUNCTIVE: dijera (dijese), dijeras, dijera, dijéramos, dijeran

COMMANDS: di (tú), diga (Ud.), digan (Uds.)

PRESENT PARTICIPLE: diciendo

PAST PARTICIPLE: dicho

Estar *to be*

PRESENT INDICATIVE: estoy, estás, está, estamos, están

PRETERITE: estuve, estuviste, estuvo, estuvimos, estuvieron

PRESENT SUBJUNCTIVE: esté, estés, esté, estemos, estén

IMPERFECT SUBJUNCTIVE: estuviera (estuviese), estuvieras, estuviera, estuviéramos, estuvieran

Haber *to have* (*auxiliary*)
PRESENT INDICATIVE: he, has, ha, hemos, han
PRETERITE: hube, hubiste, hubo, hubimos, hubieron
FUTURE: habré, habrás, habrá, habremos, habrán
CONDITIONAL: habría, habrías, habría, habríamos, habrían
PRESENT SUBJUNCTIVE: haya, hayas, haya, hayamos, hayan
IMPERFECT SUBJUNCTIVE: hubiera (hubiese), hubieras, hubiera, hubiéramos,
   hubieran

Hacer *to do, make*
PRESENT INDICATIVE: hago, haces, hace, hacemos, hacen
PRETERITE: hice, hiciste, hizo, hicimos, hicieron
FUTURE: haré, harás, hará, haremos, harán
CONDITIONAL: haría, harías, haría, haríamos, harían
PRESENT SUBJUNCTIVE: haga, hagas, haga, hagamos, hagan
IMPERFECT SUBJUNCTIVE: hiciera (hiciese), hicieras, hiciera, hiciéramos, hicieran
COMMANDS: haz (tú), haga (Ud.), hagan (Uds.)
PAST PARTICIPLE: hecho

Ir *to go*
PRESENT INDICATIVE: voy, vas, va, vamos, van
IMPERFECT INDICATIVE: iba, ibas, iba, íbamos, iban
PRETERITE: fui, fuiste, fue, fuimos, fueron
PRESENT SUBJUNCTIVE: vaya, vayas, vaya, vayamos, vayan
IMPERFECT SUBJUNCTIVE: fuera (fuese), fueras, fuera, fuéramos, fueran
COMMANDS: ve (tú), vaya (Ud.), vayan (Uds.)
PRESENT PARTICIPLE: yendo

Oír *to hear, listen*
PRESENT INDICATIVE: oigo, oyes, oye, oímos, oyen
PRESENT SUBJUNCTIVE: oiga, oigas, oiga, oigamos, oigan

Poder *to be able to, can*
PRESENT INDICATIVE: puedo, puedes, puede, podemos, pueden
PRETERITE: pude, pudiste, pudo, pudimos, pudieron
FUTURE: podré, podrás, podrá, podremos, podrán
CONDITIONAL: podría, podrías, podría, podríamos, podrían
PRESENT SUBJUNCTIVE: pueda, puedas, pueda, podamos, puedan
IMPERFECT SUBJUNCTIVE: pudiera (pudiese), pudieras, pudiera, pudiéramos,
   pudieran
PRESENT PARTICIPLE: pudiendo

Poner *to put, place, set*
PRESENT INDICATIVE: pongo, pones, pone, ponemos, ponen
PRETERITE: puse, pusiste, puso, pusimos, pusieron
FUTURE: pondré, pondrás, pondrá, pondremos, pondrán
CONDITIONAL: pondría, pondrías, pondría, pondríamos, pondrían
PRESENT SUBJUNCTIVE: ponga, pongas, ponga, pongamos, pongan
IMPERFECT SUBJUNCTIVE: pusiera (pusiese), pusieras, pusiera, pusiéramos, pusieran
COMMANDS: pon (tú), ponga (Ud.), pongan (Uds.)
PAST PARTICIPLE: puesto

Querer *to wish, want; love*
PRESENT INDICATIVE: quiero, quieres, quiere, queremos, quieren
PRETERITE: quise, quisiste, quiso, quisimos, quisieron
FUTURE: querré, querrás, querrá, querremos, querrán
CONDITIONAL: querría, querrías, querría, querríamos, querrían
PRESENT SUBJUNCTIVE: quiera, quieras, quiera, queramos, quieran
IMPERFECT SUBJUNCTIVE: quisiera (quisiese), quisieras, quisiera, quisiéramos, quisieran

Saber *to know*
PRESENT INDICATIVE: sé, sabes, sabe, sabemos, saben
PRETERITE: supe, supiste, supo, supimos, supieron
FUTURE: sabré, sabrás, sabrá, sabremos, sabrán
CONDITIONAL: sabría, sabrías, sabría, sabríamos, sabrían
PRESENT SUBJUNCTIVE: sepa, sepas, sepa, sepamos, sepan
IMPERFECT SUBJUNCTIVE: supiera (supiese), supieras, supiera, supiéramos, supieran

Salir *to go out, leave*
PRESENT INDICATIVE: salgo, sales, sale, salimos, salen
FUTURE: saldré, saldrás, saldrá, saldremos, saldrán
CONDITIONAL: saldría, saldrías, saldría, saldríamos, saldrían
PRESENT SUBJUNCTIVE: salga, salgas, salga, salgamos, salgan
COMMANDS: sal (tú), salga (Ud.), salgan (Uds.)

Ser *to be*
PRESENT INDICATIVE: soy, eres, es, somos, son
IMPERFECT INDICATIVE: era, eras, era, éramos, eran
PRETERITE: fui, fuiste, fue, fuimos, fueron
PRESENT SUBJUNCTIVE: sea, seas, sea, seamos, sean
IMPERFECT SUBJUNCTIVE: fuera (fuese), fueras, fuera, fuéramos, fueran

Tener *to have*

PRESENT INDICATIVE: tengo, tienes, tiene, tenemos, tienen

PRETERITE: tuve, tuviste, tuvo, tuvimos, tuvieron

FUTURE: tendré, tendrás, tendrá, tendremos, tendrán

CONDITIONAL: tendría, tendrías, tendría, tendríamos, tendrían

PRESENT SUBJUNCTIVE: tenga, tengas, tenga, tengamos, tengan

IMPERFECT SUBJUNCTIVE: tuviera (tuviese), tuvieras, tuviera, tuviéramos, tuvieran

COMMANDS: ten (tú), tenga (Ud.), tengan (Uds.)

Traer *to bring*

PRESENT INDICATIVE: traigo, traes, trae, traemos, traen

PRETERITE: traje, trajiste, trajo, trajimos, trajeron

PRESENT SUBJUNCTIVE: traiga, traigas, traiga, traigamos, traigan

IMPERFECT SUBJUNCTIVE: trajera (trajese), trajeras, trajera, trajéramos, trajeran

Valer *to be worth, cost*

PRESENT INDICATIVE: valgo, vales, vale, valemos, valen

FUTURE: valdré, valdrás, valdrá, valdremos, valdrán

CONDITIONAL: valdría, valdrías, valdría, valdríamos, valdrían

PRESENT SUBJUNCTIVE: valga, valgas, valga, valgamos, valgan

Venir *to come, go*

PRESENT INDICATIVE: vengo, vienes, viene, venimos, vienen

PRETERITE: vine, viniste, vino, vinimos, vinieron

FUTURE: vendré, vendrás, vendrá, vendremos, vendrán

CONDITIONAL: vendría, vendrías, vendría, vendríamos, vendrían

PRESENT SUBJUNCTIVE: venga, vengas, venga, vengamos, vengan

IMPERFECT SUBJUNCTIVE: viniera (viniese), vinieras, viniera, viniéramos, vinieran

COMMANDS: ven (tú), venga (Ud.), vengan (Uds.)

Ver *to see, watch*

PRESENT INDICATIVE: veo, ves, ve, vemos, ven

IMPERFECT INDICATIVE: veía, veías, veía, veíamos, veían

PRESENT SUBJUNCTIVE: vea, veas, vea, veamos, vean

PAST PARTICIPLE: visto

APPENDIX 3   Stem-Changing Verbs • Verbs with Spelling Changes

STEM-CHANGING VERBS

1. Single change: e → ie / o → ue

Pensar *to think, plan*

PRESENT INDICATIVE: pienso, piensas, piensa, pensamos, piensan

PRESENT SUBJUNCTIVE: piense, pienses, piense, pensemos, piensen

Volver *to return*

PRESENT INDICATIVE: vuelvo, vuelves, vuelve, volvemos, vuelven

PRESENT SUBJUNCTIVE: vuelva, vuelvas, vuelva, volvamos, vuelvan

Some common verbs of this type are:

acordarse (ue) *to remember*	jugar (ue) *to play*
acostarse (ue) *to go to bed*	llover (ue) *to rain*
cerrar (ie) *to close*	mostrar (ue) *to show*
comenzar (ie) *to start, begin*	negar (ie) *to deny*
contar (ue) *to count, tell*	nevar (ie) *to snow*
costar (ue) *to cost*	perder (ie) *to miss, lose*
despertarse (ie) *to wake up*	querer (ie) *to wish, love*
doler (ue) *to hurt*	recordar (ue) *to remember, remind*
empezar (ie) *to start, begin*	sentar (ie) *to sit down*
encontrar (ue) *to find*	tener (ie) *to have*
entender (ie) *to understand*	volar (ue) *to fly*

2. Double change: e → ie, i, / o → ue, u

Preferir *to prefer*

PRESENT INDICATIVE: prefiero, prefieres, prefiere, preferimos, prefieren

PRETERITE: preferí, preferiste, prefirió, preferimos, prefirieron

PRESENT SUBJUNCTIVE: prefiera, prefieras, prefiera, prefiramos, prefieran

IMPERFECT SUBJUNCTIVE: prefiriera (prefiriese), prefirieras, prefiriera, prefiriéramos, prefirieran

PRESENT PARTICIPLE: prefiriendo

Dormir *to sleep*

PRESENT INDICATIVE: duermo, duermes, duerme, dormimos, duermen

PRETERITE: dormí, dormiste, durmió, dormimos, durmieron

PRESENT SUBJUNCTIVE: duerma, duermas, duerma, durmamos, duerman

IMPERFECT SUBJUNCTIVE: durmiera (durmiese), durmieras, durmiera, durmiéramos, durmieran

PRESENT PARTICIPLE: durmiendo

Other verbs with double changes in the stems are:

convertir (ie, i) *to convert*	morir (ue, u) *to die*
divertirse (ie, i) *to enjoy oneself*	sentir (ie, i) *to feel, sense*
mentir (ie, i) *to lie*	

3. Change from e → i
Pedir *to ask for*

PRESENT INDICATIVE: pido, pides, pide, pedimos, piden

PRETERITE: pedí, pediste, pidió, pedimos, pidieron

PRESENT SUBJUNCTIVE: pida, pidas, pida, pidamos, pidan

IMPERFECT SUBJUNCTIVE: pidiera (pidiese), pidieras, pidiera, pidiéramos, pidieran

PRESENT PARTICIPLE: pidiendo

Other verbs with this type of change:

competir (i) *to compete*	seguir (i) *to follow*
conseguir (i) *to obtain*	servir (i) *to serve*
corregir (i) *to correct*	vestirse (i) *to get dressed*
repetir (i) *to repeat*	

VERBS WITH SPELLING CHANGES

1. Verbs ending in *-zar* change *z* to *c* before *e*.
Empezar *to begin*

PRETERITE: empecé, empezaste, empezó, empezamos, empezaron

PRESENT SUBJUNCTIVE: empiece, empieces, empiece, empecemos, empiecen

Other verbs with this type of spelling changes are:

cazar *to hunt*	especializar *to specialize*
comenzar *to start, begin*	organizar *to organize*

2. Verbs ending in *-cer* change *c* to *z* before *o* and *a*.
Vencer *to defeat, conquer*

PRESENT INDICATIVE: venzo, vences, vence, vencemos, vencen

PRESENT SUBJUNCTIVE: venza, venzas, venza, venzamos, venzan

Convencer, to convince, has the same changes as *vencer.*

3. Verbs ending in *-car* change *c* to *qu* before *e*.
Buscar *to look for*

PRETERITE: busqué, buscaste, buscó, buscamos, buscaron

PRESENT SUBJUNCTIVE: busque, busques, busque, busquemos, busquen

Other verbs that end in -*car* and change *c* to *qu* before *e* are:

explicar *to explain* **sacar** *to take out*
practicar *to practice* **tocar** *to touch, play*

4. Verbs ending in *-gar* change *g* to *gu* before *e*.
Llegar *to arrive*
PRETERITE: llegué, llegaste, llegó, llegamos, llegaron
PRESENT SUBJUNCTIVE: llegue, llegues, llegue, lleguemos, lleguen

5. Verbs ending in *-guir* change *gu* to *g* before *o* and *a*.
Seguir *to follow*
PRESENT INDICATIVE: sigo, sigues, sigue, seguimos, siguen
PRESENT SUBJUNCTIVE: siga, sigas, siga, sigamos, sigan
Conseguir, to obtain, and **distinguir,** *to distinguish,* follow the same changes.

6. Verbs ending in *-ger, -gir,* change *g* to *j* before *o* and *a*.
Coger *to take, seize*
PRESENT INDICATIVE: cojo, coges, coge, cogemos, cogen
PRESENT SUBJUNCTIVE: coja, cojas, coja, cojamos, cojan

Other verbs ending in -*ger, gir,* with the same changes:
corregir *to correct* **escoger** *to choose*
dirigir *to direct, go to* **recoger** *to pick up*
elegir *to elect*

7. Verbs ending in -*aer,* -*eer,* -*uir,* change *i* to *y* when *i* is unstressed and is between two vowels.
Leer *to read*
PRETERITE: leí, leíste, leyó, leímos, leyeron
IMPERFECT SUBJUNCTIVE: leyera (leyese), leyeras, leyera, leyéramos, leyeran
PRESENT PARTICIPLE: leyendo

Other verbs changing *i* to *y:*
caer *to fall* **excluir** *to exclude*
construir *to build* **huir** *to flee*
creer *to believe* **incluir** *to include*
destruir *to destroy* **traer** *to bring*

Spanish-English Vocabulary

A

abrir to open
abrochar to fasten
abuelo(a) (el/la) grandfather, grandmother
aburrido(a) boring, bored
abusar to abuse
acabar de (+ infinitivo) to have just done
acción (la) action
aceite (el) oil
acelerador (el) accelerator
aceptar to accept
acero (el) steel
acompañar to accompany
acostumbrar to get used to
actual present
acumulador (el) battery
adelgazar to lose weight
además besides
Adiós. Good-bye.
aduana (la) customs
aerolínea (la) airline
aeropuerto (el) airport
a fines de by the end of
agradar to please
agradecer to thank
agradecido(a) thankful
agua (f.) (el) water
aguacate (el) avocado
águila (f.) (el) eagle
ahora now
ahorrar to save
ajo (el) garlic
a la plancha on the grill, grilled
al contado cash (to pay)
alegrarse to be happy
alegre happy, glad, cheerful
alergia (la) allergy

algo something
alimentar to feed
alimento (el) food
aliviar to relieve
allí there, over there
almuerzo (el) lunch
¡aló!, dígame hello!
a lo mejor perhaps
alquilar to rent
alquiler (el) rent, lease
alto(a) high, tall
amable kind, nice
amarillo(a) yellow
amigo(a) (el/la) friend
ancho(a) wide
andar to walk
andén (el) platform
animado(a) lively
antes (de) beforehand, before
antibiótico (el) antibiotic
anticipación: con ~ ahead of time
antiguo(a) ancient, former
antipático(a) unpleasant
apagar to turn off
aparcar to park
aparecer to appear
aperitivo (el) aperitif
apreciar to appreciate
aprender to learn
aquí here, over here
árbol (el) tree
arrancar to start, root
arranque (el) starter
arreglar to arrange
arroz (el) rice
asado(a) roasted
asar to roast
ascensor (el) elevator
asegurado(a) insured

asiento (el) seat
así que so
asustar to scare
atender (ie) to wait on
atento(a) polite
atrasado(a) late
atún (el) tuna
aumentar to increase
aunque although
autobús (el) bus
automático(a) automatic
autopista (la) highway
autoservicio (el) self-service
a veces sometimes
avería (la) breakdown
avión (el) airplane
avisar to warn, inform
ayer yesterday
ayudar to help
azafata (la) stewardess
azúcar (el/la) sugar

B

bailar to dance
bajar (de) to get off, go down
    bajar de peso to lose weight
bajo(a) low, short
balanceado(a) balanced
balancear to balance
balanza (la) scale
banana (la), plátano (el) banana
banco (el) bank
bañarse to bathe
baño (el) bathroom
barato(a) cheap
barbería (la) barbershop
barbilla (la) chin
bastante enough
batería (la) battery
baúl (el) trunk

beber to drink
bebida (la) drink, beverage
bebido(a) drunk
besar to kiss
bienvenida (la) welcome
billete (el) bill, ticket
bisté (el), bistec (el) beefsteak
blanco(a) white
blando(a) tender, soft
boca (la) mouth
bocadillo (el) sandwich
bocina (la) horn
boleto (el) ticket
bomba (la) pump, bomb
bonito(a) pretty
botana (*México*) (la) snack
   (*Mexico*)
botella (la) bottle
botón (el) button
botones (el) bellboy
brazo (el) arm
breve short, brief
bueno(a) good, healthy
burrito (el) burrito
buscar to look for

C

cabello (el) hair
cabeza (la) head
cacharro (el) jalopy
cadera (la) hip
caer to fall
caja (la) cash register
cajero(a) (el/la) cashier
cajuela (la) trunk
calefacción (la) heating
caliente hot
calle (la) street
calmante (el) sedative
calmar(se) to calm (down)
calor (el) heat
caloría (la) calorie
cama (la) bed
camarero(a) (el/la) waiter,
   waitress
camarón (el) shrimp
cambiar to change

camino (el) road, way
camión (el) truck, bus
camisa (la) shirt
camiseta (la) undershirt
campo (el) field
capó (el) hood
cara (la) face
cargar to load, charge
carne (la) meat
carné (el) license
carnicería (la) butcher's shop
caro(a) expensive
carretera (la) road
carro (el), coche (el) car
carta (la) menu
  a la carta à la carte
cartera (la) wallet, purse
casa (la) house
casado(a) married
casi almost
casualidad: por ~ by chance;
   ¡Qué casualidad! What a
   coincidence!
cebolla (la) onion
ceja (la) eyebrow
celebrar to celebrate
cena (la) supper
cenar to have supper
centavo (el) cent
cerca near
cerrar (ie) to close
cerro (el) hill
cerveza (la) beer
champán (el) champagne
cheque (el) check
chequera (la) checkbook
chileno(a) Chilean
chimenea (la) fireplace
chistoso(a) funny
chocar to crash, collide;
   to shock
chocolate (el) chocolate
choque (el) crash
chuleta (la) chop
ciento: por ~ percent
cigarrillo (el) cigarette
cintura (la) waist

cinturón (el) belt, seat belt
ciudad (la) city, town
claro(a) clear
clase (la) class
cobrar to charge, get paid
coche (el) car, coach
  coche cama (el) sleeping car
  coche comedor (el) dining car
cocina (la) kitchen
cocinar to cook
cocinero(a) (el/la) cook
codo (el) elbow
cojear to limp
cojo(a) lame, crippled
colombiano(a) Colombian
color (el) color
comedor (el) dining room
comenzar (ie) to start
comer to eat
comida (la) food, meal
cómodo(a) comfortable
compañero(a) (el/la)
   schoolmate, fellow student
completar to complete
complicado(a) complicated
comprar to buy
comprender to understand
concluir to conclude
condimentar to season
conducir to drive
confirmar to confirm
confusión (la) confusion
conocer to know, meet
conseguir (i) to get, obtain
construir to build
consulta de doctor (la) doctor's
   office
consultar to consult
contener to contain
contestar to answer
convencer to convince
convenir (ie) to suit
convertir(ie, i) to convert
copa (la) glass
corazón (el) heart
cordero (el) lamb
correr to run

cortar el pelo to cut the hair
corto(a) short
creer to believe
crema (la) cream
   crema dental (la) toothpaste
cruce (el) intersection
cruzar to cross
cuadra (la) block
cuarto (el) room
cuello (el) neck
cuenta (la) bill, account
   cuenta corriente (la)
   checking account; **cuenta de
   ahorros (la)** savings account
cuidar to take care of
cultivar to cultivate
cumpleaños (el) birthday
cumplido (el) compliment
cumplir to fulfill
cura (el) priest
   cura (la) cure
curar to cure, heal

D

dañar to damage
dar to give
   dar a + (a place) to face + (a
   place); **dar la bienvenida** to
   welcome
deber must, should
débil weak
decidir to decide
decir to say, tell
   decir que sí/no to say yes/no
dedo (el) finger, toe
dejar to leave
   dejar de to stop
delgado(a) thin, slim
delicioso(a) delicious
de lujo, lujoso(a) deluxe,
   luxurious
demorar to delay
deportes (los) sports
de primera excellent, first-class
derecho(a) right, straight
desastre (el) disaster

desayuno (el) breakfast
descansar to rest
descontento(a) unhappy
descrubrir to discover
desde from
desear to want, wish
deshacer to undo, melt
   deshacer la maleta to unpack
   the suitcase
desinflar to deflate
desocupado(a) free, vacant
despacio slowly
despierto(a) awake, alert
después (de) after, afterwards
destruido(a) destroyed
destruir to destroy
detener to stop, detain (*people*)
día (el) day
   a mediodía at noon; **Buenos
   días** Good morning; **por día**
   per day
diario(a) daily
diente (el) tooth
dieta (la) diet
dietista (el/la) dietitian
difícil difficult
dinero (el) money
disfrutar de to enjoy
disponible available
divertirse (ie, i) to have fun
divisa (la) foreign money
doblar to turn, bend
doble double
doler (ue, u) to hurt, ache
domicilio (el) address, home
domingo (el) Sunday
dormir (ue, u) to sleep
dormitorio (el) bedroom
dos two
droga (la) drug
drogadicto(a) (el/la) drug
   addict
droguería (la) drugstore
ducha (la) shower
dulce sweet
durar to last

E

echar de menos, **extrañar** to miss
ejercicio (el) exercise
eléctrico(a) electric
electrotrén (el) electric train
embrague (el) clutch
emergencia (la) emergency
empleado(a) (el/la) employee
encantado(a) pleased
encantar to charm, like, please
encargarse de to take charge of
encender (ie) to light
enchilada (la) enchilada
encontrar (ue) to find
encontrarse to meet, find
enfermarse to get sick
enfermedad (la) sickness
enfermero(a) (el/la) nurse
enfermo(a) sick, ill
engrasar to lubricate
engrase (el) lubrication
ensalada (la) salad
enseguida, en seguida right away
entender (ie) to understand
entero(a) all, entire
entonces then
entrar a (en) to enter
entregar to deliver
entremés (el) appetizer
enyesar to put a cast
época (la) season, epoch
equipaje (el) luggage
escalera (la) staircase, stairs
escribir to write
eso: por ~ because of that
espalda (la) back (*person*)
especializar to specialize
espontáneo(a) spontaneous
esposo(a) (el/la) spouse
estación (la) station; season
estacionamiento (el) parking
estacionar, parquear to park
esta noche tonight
estar to be
   ¿A cómo está ? What's the

price of?; **estar a dieta** to be on a diet; **estar de vacaciones** to be on vacation; **estar en onda** to be up to date; **estar nublado** to be cloudy

este (*m.*) this

estómago (el) stomach

estrecho(a) narrow

estrés (el) mental stress

estricto(a) strict, severe

estudiar to study

estupendo(a) fantastic, terrific

estúpido(a) bastard

excelente excellent

exprés (el) express

F

fácil easy

factura (la) bill, invoice

facturar to check in

falta: sin ~ without fail

faltar to miss
   ¡Sólo me falta eso! That's all I need!

familia (la) family

fantástico(a) fantastic

farmacia (la) pharmacy
   farmacia de guardia 24-hour pharmacy

faro (el) headlight

fascinante fascinating

fatiga (la) fatigue

fecha (la) date

felicidad (la) happiness
   felicidades congratulations

felicitar to congratulate

feliz happy

feo(a) ugly

ferrocarril (el) railroad

fiebre (la) fever

fiesta (la) party

filete (el), **bisté** (el) steak, fillet

fin: en ~, por ~ in short, finally

firmar to sign

flaco(a) thin, skinny

flan (el) custard

flor (la) flower

florería (la) flower shop

frenar to brake

freno (el) brake
   freno de emergencia (el) emergency brake

frente (la) forehead

fresco(a) fresh, cool

frijol (el) bean

frío(a) cold

fruta (la) fruit

frutería (la) fruit store

fuerte strong

fumar to smoke

funcionar to work

futuro(a) future

G

galón (el) gallon

ganancia (la) earnings

ganar to win, earn

ganga (la) bargain

garaje (el) garage

garganta (la) throat

gastado(a) worn-out

gastar to spend

gasto (el) expense

gato (el) cat

gentil elegant

giro internacional (el) international money order

giro (postal) (el) money order

gordito(a) chubby

gordo(a) fat

gota (la) drop, gout

gotear to drip

gracioso(a) funny

grande large, big

grasa (la) grease, fat

gratis free, free of charge

gripe (la) flu

grueso(a) fat

guapo(a) handsome

guardar cama to stay in bed

guiar to guide

guisante (el) green pea

guitarra (la) guitar

güero(a) blond

gustar to like

gusto: con mucho ~ it's a pleasure

H

haber to have

habitación (la) room

hablar to speak

hacer to do, make, to be (*weather*)
   hacer buen tiempo, hacer buen to be good weather; **hacer calor** to be hot; **hacer caso** to pay attention; **hacer fresco** to be cool; **hacer frío** to be cold; **hacer la boca agua** to make one's mouth water; **hacer la maleta** to pack the suitcase; **hacer mal tiempo, hacer mal** to be bad weather; **hacer sol** to be sunny; **hacer ver las estrellas** to make one feel a terrible pain; **hacer viento** to be windy; **¿Qué tiempo hace?** What's the weather?

hágame el favor please, do me a favor

hambre (*f.*) (el) hunger

hamburguesa (la) hamburger

hasta until, to

hay que (+ verb) it's necessary to (+ verb)

heladería (la) ice cream store

helado (el) ice cream

hermano(a) (el/la) brother, sister

hijo(a) (el/la) son, daughter

hipoteca (la) mortgage

hoja de afeitar (la) razor blade

¡Hola! Hi!

hombre (el) man
   hombre de negocios (el) businessman

hombro (el) shoulder

hora (la) hour
horario (el) schedule
hotel (el) hotel
hoy today
hueso (el) bone
huir to flee

I

ida (la) one-way ticket
   ida y vuelta (la) round-trip
idea (la) idea
importar to matter
imprevisto(a) unexpected
impuesto (el) tax
incluir (y) to include
increíble incredible
indigestión (la) indigestion
inflar to inflate
informar to inform
inglés (el) English
inoxidable stainless
inspeccionar to inspect
interesar to interest
intersección (la) intersection
invitación (la) invitation
invitar to invite
inyección (la) shot, injection
ir to go
   ir de compras to go shopping
irritación (la) irritation

J

jabón (el) soap
jamón (el) ham
jarabe (el) syrup
jardín (el) garden
joven young
jueves (el) Thursday
jugar (ue) to play
jugo (el), zumo (el) juice
junto: ~ a close to, near

K

kilómetro (el) kilometer

L

labio (el) lip
lana (la) wool

langosta (la) lobster
lápiz (el) pencil
largo(a) long
lata (la) can
lavaplatos (el) dishwasher
lavar to wash
lección (la) lesson
leche (la) milk
lechuga (la) lettuce
leer to read
legumbres (las) vegetables
lejos far away
lento(a) slow
libro (el) book
licencia (la) license
ligero(a) light, quick
limonada (la) lemonade
limpiaparabrisas (el) windshield
   wiper
limpiar to clean
limpio(a) clean
lindo(a) pretty
líquido (el) liquid
listo(a) ready, smart
litera (la) berth
llanta (la) tire
   llanta de respuesto (la) spare
   tire
llave (la) key
llegada (la) arrival
llegar to arrive
llenar to fill
   llenar una receta to fill a
   prescription
lleno(a) full
llover (ue) to rain
lluvia (la) rain
locomotora (la) engine (*train*)
loma (la) hill
luego: Hasta ~. So long.
lujoso(a) luxurious
lunes (el) Monday
luz (la) light
   luz roja (la) red light, traffic
   light

M

madre (la) mother

maíz (el) corn
maleta (la) suitcase
maletero (el) porter, trunk (*of a
   car*)
maletín (el) briefcase
malo(a) bad, sick
mamá (la) mom
mandar to send, order
manejar to drive
manguera (la) hose
mano (la) hand
   de segunda mano secondhand
mantequilla (la) butter
manual standard shift
manzana (la) apple
mañana (la) morning
   Hasta mañana. See you
   tomorrow.
mapa (el) map
mar (el) sea
marca (la) trademark
marearse to get dizzy
mareo (el) dizziness
margarina (la) margarine
mariachi (el) mariachi
marisco (el) seafood
martes (el) Tuesday
más: ~ o menos more or less
matrícula (la) license plate
mecánico(a) mechanic
medicina (la) medicine
médico(a) medical
medio(a) half
   en medio de in the middle of
mejilla (la) cheek
mejor better, best
menú (el) menu
menudo: a ~ frequently, often
mercado (el) market
merecer (c) to deserve
merendar (ie) to snack
merienda (la) snack
mes (el) month
mesa (la) table
mesero(a) (el/la) waiter,
   waitress
meter to put into

mexicano(a) Mexican
mi, mis my
miércoles (el) Wednesday
milla (la) mile
mirar to look at
moderno(a) modern
modo: ¡Ni ~! No way!
molestar to bother, annoy
moneda (la) currency, coin
morir (ue) to die
mostrar (ue) to show
motor (el) engine
mozo(a) (el/la) waiter, waitress;
    bellboy, chambermaid
mucho(a) much, a lot
mueble (el) furniture
mujer (la) woman
    mujer policía (la) policewoman
muleta (la) crutch
mundo (el) world
muñeca (la) wrist, doll
músculo (el) muscle
música (la) music
muslo (el) thigh

N

nacer to be born
nadar to swim
naranja (la) orange
narcótico (el) narcotic
nariz (la) nose
náusea (la) nausea
necesario(a) necessary
necesidad (la) need
necesitar to need
negro(a) black
nervioso(a) nervous
neumático (el) tire
nevar (ie) to snow
nieto(a) (el/la) grandson,
    granddaughter
nieve (la) snow
nieve (la) (*México*) ice cream
nievería (la) (*México*) ice cream
    store
niño(a) (el/la) boy, son
noche (la) night
    Buenas noches. Good evening.

nombre (el) name
no: ¡Como ~! Of course!
novio(a) (el/la) fiancé, fiancée
nube (la) cloud
nublado(a) cloudy
nuevo(a) new

O

o or
obeso(a) obese
ocupado(a) busy
ocupar to occupy
ocuparse to look after
ocurrir to happen
ofrecer to offer
oír to hear
ojo (el) eye
oler (hue) to smell
    olerle mal a uno to smell
    fishy
olvidar to forget
onda (la) wave
    ¡Qué buena onda! How nice!
ondulado(a) wavy, hilly
ordenar to order
oreja (la) (outer) ear
oscuro(a) dark

P

pachanga (la) (*México*) party
padecer (c) to suffer
padre (el) father
padres (los) parents
paella (la) paella
pagar to pay
país (el) country
paisaje (el) landscape
palabra (la) word
pálido(a) pale
pan (el) bread
panadería (la) bakery
papá (el) father, dad
papas fritas (las) French fries
papel (el) paper
paquete (el) package
par (el) couple (*things*)
    un par de a couple of
    (*things*), a few

para to, in order to; for
parabrisas (el) windshield
parachoques (el) bumper
parada (la) stop
paraguas (el) umbrella
parar to stop
pararse to stop
parecer to seem
pared (la) wall
pareja (la) pair
pariente (el) relative
párpado (el) eyelid
parquear to park
partida (la) departure
pasado(a) de peso overweight
pasaje (el) ticket
pasajero(a) (el/la) passenger
pasaporte (el) passport
pasar to happen, pass
pastel (el) pastry, cake
pastelería (la) pastry shop
pastilla (la) tablet
patata (la) potato
patilla (la) sideburn
pavo (el) turkey
pecho (el) breast
pedal (el) pedal
pedir (i) to ask for
peligro (el) danger
pelo (el), cabello (el) hair
peluquería (la) hairdresser's
pensar (ie) to think
pensión (la) boardinghouse
pepino (el) cucumber
pequeño(a) small
perder (ie) to lose, miss
    perder el tiempo to waste
    time; perder peso to lose
    weight
perdonar to pardon
permitir to allow
pero but
peruano(a) Peruvian
pescadería (la) fish store
pescado (el) fish
pescar to fish
peso (el) peso
pestaña (la) eyelash

petróleo (el) oil
petrolero(a) oil-producing
piano (el) piano
picante hot, spicy
pie (el) foot
pierna (la) leg
píldora (la) pill
piloto (el) pilot
pincharse to get a flat tire
pirámide (la) pyramid
piso (el) floor, story
pitar to blow the horn
placa (la) license plate
plato (el) dish, plate
plaza (la) square
plazo: a ~s in installments
pluma (la) pen
pobre poor
poco(a) little
poder (ue) to be able to
   no poder ver to be unable to
   stand
policía (el) policeman
policía (la) police department
póliza (la) policy
pollo (el) chicken
poner to put
   ponerse (+ adjective) to turn
   (+ adjective); ponerse a (+
   verb) to begin (+ verb)
por: a... millas por hora at . . .
   miles per hour; por ser usted
   just for you
porcentaje (el) percentage
porque because
postre (el) dessert
pozo (el) well
precio (el) price
preferible preferable
preferir (ie, i) to prefer
preocuparse to worry
preparar to prepare
presentar to present
préstamo (el) loan
prestar to lend
   prestar atención to pay
   attention
presupuesto (el) budget

primero(a) first
primo(a) (el/la) cousin
problema (el) problem
producir to produce
prohibir to forbid
prometer to promise
propina (la) tip, gratuity
propósito: a ~ by the way
próximo(a) next, coming
prudente prudent
puente (el) bridge
puerco (el) pig, pork
puerta (la) door, gate
pulmón (el) lung
punto: en~ sharp (*exact time*)
puntual punctual

Q

que that
quebrado(a) broken
quejarse to complain
querer (ie) to wish, want
queso (el) cheese
quitar to take away, remove
quitarse to move away, stay
   away

R

ración (la) order, serving
radiador (el) radiator
radiografía (la) X ray
ranchero (el) rancher
rancho (el) ranch
rapidez (la) speed
rápido(a) fast, quick
rato (el) a while
razonable reasonable
recado (el) message, errand
recepción (la) front desk
recepcionista (la) receptionist
receta (la) prescription; recipe
recetar to prescribe
reciente recent
recomendar (ie) to recommend
reconocer to recognize
recordar (ue) to remember
recto(a) straight
reducir to reduce

refresco (el) refreshment, cold
   drink (*nonalcoholic*)
registrarse to register
reloj (el) clock, watch
remedio (el) remedy
res (la) beef, livestock
resbaladizo(a) slippery
resbalar to slip
reservación (la) reservation
reservar to reserve
resfriado (el) cold
residencia (la) residence
revisar to check
rico(a) rich
riesgo: a todo ~ at all risk
ritmo (el) rhythm
rodilla (la) knee
rojo(a) red
romántico(a) romantic
romper to break
rosado(a) pink, rosé
roto(a) broken, torn
rueda (la) wheel

S

sábado (el) Saturday
saber to know
   saber a to taste like
sabor (el) taste, flavor
sabroso(a) tasty, delicious
sacar to take out
salario (el) salary
salida (la) departure, exit
salir to leave, go out
   salir de + (lugar) to leave (a
   place)
salsa (la) sauce
salud (la) health
saludable healthy
sangre (la) blood
sangría (la) wine cooler
sánguich (el) sandwich
sastre(a) (el/la) tailor
sastrería (la) tailor's shop
seco(a) dry
seguir (i) to follow
seguridad (la) safety
seguro (el) insurance

semana (la) week

sencillo(a) single (*room*), one-way (*ticket*); simple

sentarse (ie) to sit down

señor Sir

señora Madam

señorita Miss

ser to be

serio(a) serious

　　en serio seriously

servicio: el ~ a los cuartos room service

servir (i) to serve, help

silla (la) chair

sillón (el) armchair

simpático(a) nice, pleasant

síntoma (el) sympton

sobrar to be left

sobre about, above

　　sobre todo above all

sobrino(a) (el/la) nephew, niece

sol (el) sun

solamente only

solomillo (el) sirloin

soltero(a) single

sonar (ue) to ring, sound

soñar (ue) to dream

sopa (la) soup

stop (el), **alto** (el) stop (sign)

su, sus his/her (*s. & pl.*)

subir to go up, climb

sucio(a) dirty

suegro(a) (el/la) father-in-law, mother-in-law

sueldo (el) salary

sueño (el) dream, sleep

supuesto: por ~ of course

sur (el) south

surtidor (el) pump

T

tablero de mandos (el) dashboard

taco (el) taco

talco (el) powder, talc

también also

tanque (el) tank

taquilla (la) ticket window

taquillero(a) (el/la) ticket agent, clerk

tardar to be long, last

tarde (la) afternoon

　　Buenas tardes. Good afternoon.

tarde late

tarifa (la) tariff, fee

tarjeta (la) card; credit card

　　tarjeta de crédito (la) credit card

taxista (el/la) taxi driver

té (el) tea

tejado (el) roof

teléfono (el) telephone

telenovela (la) soap opera

tema (el) theme

temperatura (la) temperature

temprano early

tener to have

　　no tener remedio to have no solution; **tener ansias de, tener ganas de** to feel like, want to; **tener... años** to be . . . years old; **tener buena pinta** to look good; **tener calor** to feel hot; **tener éxito** to be successful; **tener frío** to feel cold; **tener hambre** to be hungry; **tener mala estrella** to be unlucky; **tener mala pata** to be unlucky; **tener mareos** to be dizzy; **tener que + (infinitivo)** to have to + (infinitive); **tener razón** to be right; **tener sed** to be thirsty; **tener sueño** to be sleepy; **tener suerte** to be lucky; **tener tos** to have a cough

tensión (la) pressure

tercero(a) third

ternera (la) veal

terreno (el) terrain

terrible terrible

texano(a) Texan

tiempo (el) time

　　A mal tiempo, buena cara. Smile in the face of adversity.

tienda (la) store

tierno(a) tender, soft

tinto(a) red (*wine*)

tío(a) (el/la) uncle, aunt

típico(a) typical

toalla (la) towel

tobillo (el) ankle

tocadiscos (el) record player

tocar to play, touch

　　tocar la bocina to blow the horn

todavía still, yet

todo(a) all

tomado(a) drunk

tomar to take, drink

　　tomar asiento to take a seat; **tomar el pelo** to pull one's leg; **tomar una copa** to have a drink

tomate (el) tomato

torcer (ue) to twist, sprain

torcido(a) twisted, bent

torta (la) cake

tortilla (la) omelette

tos (la) cough

toser to cough

trabajar to work

traducir to translate

traer to bring

　　traérselas to get worse

tragar to swallow

transmisión manual, de cambios (la) standard transmission

tranvía (el) trolley, train

tratar de to try to

tren (el) train

triste sad

tu, tus your

tubo (el) pipe, tube

turismo (el) tourism

U

usar to use

úlcera (la) ulcer

V

vaca (la) cow, beef

vacaciones (las) vacation

vacío(a) empty

vacuna (la) vaccine
vagón (el) car, wagon
valer to be worth
    valer la pena to be worthwhile
valioso(a) valuable
valor (el) value, stock
variedad (la) variety
varios(as) several, various
vaso (el) (drinking) glass
vegetales (los) vegetables
vela (la) candle
velocidad (la) speed
velocímetro (el) speedometer
vender to sell
venir to come
ventana (la) window
ventanilla (la) small window

ver to see, look at
verdad (la) truth
verde green
verdulería (la) greengrocer's
verdura (la) green vegetable
verduras (las) greens, (green) vegetables
vermut (el), vermú (el) vermouth
vez (la) time (*in a series*)
vía (la) railroad track
viajar to travel
viaje (el) travel, trip
viajero(a) (el / la) traveler
viejo(a) old
viernes (el) Friday
vino (el) wine

visitar to visit
vista (la) sight, view
vitamina (la) vitamin
vivir to live
volante (el) steering wheel
volar (ue) to fly
volver (ue) to come back
vuelo (el) flight
vuelta (la) change, ride, return

Y

yeso (el) cast (*plaster*)
yogur (el) yogurt

Z

zanahoria (la) carrot
zapatería (la) shoe store

English-Spanish Vocabulary

A

able: to be ~ to poder (ue)
about sobre
above all sobre todo
abrupt quebrado(a)
abuse (to) abusar
accelerator acelerador (el)
accept (to) aceptar
accompany (to) acompañar
account cuenta (la)
action acción (la)
address, home domicilio (el)
after, afterwards después (de)
afternoon tarde (la)
   Good ~. Buenas tardes.
airline aerolínea (la)
airplane avión (el)
airport aeropuerto (el)
all, entire todo(a)
allergy alergia (la)
allow (to) permitir
almost casi
also también
although aunque
ancient, former antiguo(a)
ankle tobillo (el)
annoy (to) molestar
answer (to) contestar
antibiotic antibiótico (el)
aperitif aperitivo (el)
appear (to) aparecer
appetizer entremés (el)
apple manzana (la)
appreciate (to) apreciar
arm brazo (el)
armchair sillón (el)
arrange (to) arreglar
arrival llegada (la)
arrive (to) llegar
ask for (to) pedir

aunt tía (la)
automatic automático(a)
available disponible
avocado aguacate (el)
awake, alert despierto(a)

B

back (*person*) espalda (la)
bad, sick malo(a)
bakery panadería (la)
balance (to) balancear
balanced balanceado(a)
banana banana (la), plátano (el)
bank banco (el)
barbershop barbería (la)
bargain ganga (la)
bastard estúpido(a)
bathe (to) bañarse
bathroom baño (el)
battery acumulador (el), batería
   (la)
be (to) estar, ser
bean frijol (el)
because porque
   because of that por eso
bed cama (la)
bedroom dormitorio (el)
beef, livestock res (la)
beefsteak bisté (el), bistec (el)
beer cerveza (la)
beforehand, before antes (de)
begin (+ verb) (to) ponerse a (+
   verb)
believe (to) creer
bellboy botones (el), mozo (el)
belt cinturón (el)
berth litera (la)
besides además
better, best mejor
bill, invoice factura (la), cuenta
   (la); bill, ticket billete (el)

birthday cumpleaños (el)
black negro(a)
block cuadra (la)
blond güero(a)
blood sangre (la)
blow the horn (to) tocar la
   bocina, pitar
boardinghouse pensión (la)
bone hueso (el)
book libro (el)
boring, bored aburrido(a)
born: to be ~ nacer
bother (to) molestar
bottle botella (la)
boy, son niño (el)
brake freno (el)
   emergency brake freno de
   emergencia (el); brake (to)
   frenar
bread pan (el)
break (to) romper
breakdown avería (la)
breakfast desayuno (el)
breast pecho (el)
bridge puente (el)
briefcase maletín (el)
bring (to) traer
broken, torn roto(a)
brother hermano (el)
budget presupuesto (el)
build (to) construir
bumper parachoques (el)
burrito burrito (el)
bus autobús (el)
businessman hombre de
   negocios (el)
busy ocupado(a)
but pero
butcher's shop carnicería (la)
butter mantequilla (la)
button botón (el)

buy (to) comprar

C

cake torta (la)
calm (to) calmar
calm down (to) calmarse
calorie caloría (la)
can lata (la)
candle vela (la)
car, coach carro (el), coche (el)
   car, wagon vagón (el)
card tarjeta (la)
carrot zanahoria (la)
carte: à la ~ a la carta
cash (to pay) al contado
cashier cajero(a) (el/la)
cash register caja (la)
cast (plaster) yeso (el)
cat gato (el)
celebrate (to) celebrar
cent centavo (el)
chair silla (la)
champagne champán (el)
chance: by ~ por casualidad
change, ride vuelta (la)
   change (to) cambiar
charge, get paid (to) cobrar
charm, like (to) encantar
cheap barato(a)
check cheque (el)
   check (to) revisar
checkbook chequera (la)
check in (to) facturar
checking account cuenta
   corriente (la)
cheek mejilla (la)
cheerful alegre
cheese queso (el)
chicken pollo (el)
Chilean chileno(a)
chin barbilla (la)
chocolate chocolate (el)
chop chuleta (la)
chubby gordito(a)
cigarette cigarrillo (el)
city, town ciudad (la)
class clase (la)
clean limpio(a)
   clean (to) limpiar

clear claro(a)
clock, watch reloj (el)
close (to) cerrar (ie)
close to, near junto a
cloud nube (la)
cloudy nublado(a)
   be cloudy (to) estar nublado
clutch embrague (el)
coincidence: What a coincidence!
   ¡Qué casualidad!
cold frío(a)
   be cold (to) (weather) hacer frío
cold resfriado (el)
collide (to) chocar
Colombian colombiano(a)
color color (el)
come (to) venir
   come back (to) volver (ue)
   come in (to) entrar a (en)
comfortable cómodo(a)
complain (to) quejarse
complete (to) completar
complicated complicado(a)
compliment cumplido (el)
conclude (to) concluir
confirm (to) confirmar
confusion confusión (la)
congratulate (to) felicitar
congratulation: ~s felicidades
consult (to) consultar
contain (to) contener
convert (to) convertir(ie, i)
convince (to) convencer
cook cocinero(a) (el/la)
   cook (to) cocinar
cool: to be ~ hacer fresco
corn maíz (el)
cough tos (la)
   cough (to) toser
country país (el)
couple (things) par (el)
   a couple of (things), a few
   un par de
course: of ~ ¡Cómo no!, por
   supuesto
cousin primo(a) (el/la)
cow, beef vaca (la)
crash choque (el)
   crash (to) chocar

cream crema (la)
credit card tarjeta de crédito (la)
cross (to) cruzar
crutch muleta (la)
cucumber pepino (el)
cultivate (to) cultivar
cure cura (la)
   cure, heal (to) curar
currency, coin moneda (la)
custard flan (el)
customs aduana (la)
cut the hair (to) cortar el pelo

D

daily diario(a)
damage (to) dañar
dance (to) bailar
danger peligro (el)
dark oscuro(a)
dashboard tablero de mandos (el)
date fecha (la)
daughter hija (la)
day día (el)
decide (to) decidir
deflate (to) desinflar
delay (to) demorar
delicious delicioso(a)
deliver (to) entregar
deluxe, luxurious de lujo,
   lujoso(a)
departure partida (la)
   departure, exit salida (la)
deserve (to) merecer (c)
dessert postre (el)
destroy (to) destruir
destroyed destruido(a)
die (to) morir (ue)
diet dieta (la)
   be on a diet (to) estar a
   dieta
dietitian dietista (el/la)
difficult difícil
dining car coche comedor (el)
dining room comedor (el)
dirty sucio(a)
disaster desastre (el)
discover (to) descubrir
dish, plate plato (el)
dishwasher lavaplatos (el)

dizziness mareo (el)

dizzy: to be ~ tener mareos; to get ~ marearse

do, make (to) hacer

doctor's office consulta de doctor (la)

door, gate puerta (la)

double doble

dream, sleep sueño (el)
    dream (to) soñar (ue)

drink bebida (la)
    drink (to) beber, tomar

drip (to) gotear

drive (to) conducir, manejar

drop, gout gota (la)

drug droga (la)

drug addict drogadicto(a)

drugstore droguería (la)

drunk bebido(a), tomado(a)

dry seco(a)

E

eagle águila (f.) (el)

ear (outer) oreja (la)

early temprano

earnings ganancia (la)

easy fácil

eat (to) comer

elbow codo (el)

electric eléctrico(a)
    electric train electrotrén (el)

elegant gentil

elevator ascensor (el)

emergency emergencia (la)

employee empleado(a) (el/la)

empty vacío(a)

enchilada enchilada (la)

end: by the ~ of a fines de

engine motor (el); (train) locomotora (la)

English inglés (el)

enjoy (to) disfrutar de

enough bastante

evening: Good ~. Buenas noches.

excellent, first-class excelente, de primera

exercise ejercicio (el)

expense gasto (el)

expensive caro(a)

express exprés (el)

eye ojo (el)

eyebrow ceja (la)

eyelash pestaña (la)

eyelid párpado (el)

F

face cara (la)

face + (a place) (to) dar a + (a place)

fail: without ~ sin falta

fall (to) caer

family familia (la)

fantastic estupendo(a), fantástico(a)

far away lejos

fascinating fascinante

fast, quick rápido(a)

fasten (to) abrochar

fat gordo(a), grueso(a)

father padre (el)
    father, dad papá (el)

father-in-law suegro (el)

fatigue fatiga (la)

favor: Please, do me a ~. Hágame el favor.

feed (to) alimentar

feel like, want to (to) tener ansias de, tener ganas de

fever fiebre (la)

fiancé novio (el)

fiancée novia (la)

field campo (el)

fill (to) llenar
    fill a prescription (to) llenar una receta

finally por fin

find (to) encontrar (ue)

finger, toe dedo (el)

fireplace chimenea (la)

first primero(a)

fish pescado (el)
    fish (to) pescar; fish store pescadería (la)

flee (to) huir

flight vuelo (el)

floor, story piso (el)

flower flor (la)
    flower shop florería (la)

flu gripe (la)

fly (to) volar (ue)

follow (to) seguir (i)

food alimento (el)
    food, meal comida (la)

foot pie (el)

for: just ~ you por ser usted

forbid (to) prohibir

forehead frente (la)

foreign money divisa (la)

forget (to) olvidar

free, free of charge gratis
    free, vacant desocupado(a)

French fries papas fritas (las)

frequently, often a menudo

fresh, cool fresco(a)

Friday viernes (el)

friend amigo(a) (el/la)

from desde

front desk recepción (la)

fruit fruta (la)

fruit store frutería (la)

fulfill (to) cumplir

full lleno(a)

funny chistoso(a), gracioso(a)

furniture mueble (el)

future futuro(a)

G

gallon galón (el)

garage garaje (el)

garden jardín (el)

garlic ajo (el)

get, obtain (to) conseguir (i)
    get a flat tire (to) pincharse;
    get off, go down (to) bajar (de);
    get used to (to) acostumbrarse;
    get worse (to) traérselas

give (to) dar

glass copa (la)

go (to) ir

go up, climb (to) subir

good, healthy bueno(a)

Good-bye. Adiós.

granddaughter nieta (la)

grandfather abuelo (el)

grandmother abuela (la)

grandson nieto (el)

grease, fat grasa (la)

green verde

greengrocer's verdulería (la)
green pea guisante (el)
greens, green vegetable(s)
   verdura(s) (la[s])
grill: on the ~, grilled a la
   plancha
guide (to) guiar
guitar guitarra (la)

H

hair pelo (el), cabello (el)
hairdresser's peluquería (la)
half medio(a)
ham jamón (el)
hamburger hamburguesa (la)
hand mano (la)
handsome guapo(a)
happen (to) ocurrir, pasar
happiness felicidad (la)
happy alegre, feliz
be happy (to) alegrarse
have (to) tener, haber
   have a cough (to) tener tos;
   have a drink (to) tomar,
   tomar una copa; have fun (to)
   divertirse (ie); have just done
   (to) acabar de (+ verb); have
   no solution (to) no tener
   remedio; have supper (to)
   cenar; have to + (infinitive)
   (to) tener que + (infinitivo)
head cabeza (la)
headlight faro (el)
health salud (la)
healthy saludable
hear (to) oír
heart corazón (el)
heat calor (el)
heating calefacción (la)
hello! ¡aló!, dígame
help (to) ayudar
here aquí
Hi! ¡Hola!
high, tall alto(a)
highway autopista (la)
hill cerro (el), loma (la)
hip cadera (la)
his/her (s. & pl.) su, sus
hood capó (el)

horn bocina (la)
hose manguera (la)
hot caliente, (spicy) picante
   be hot (to) hacer calor
   (weather)
hotel hotel (el)
hour hora (la)
house casa (la)
hunger hambre (f.) (el)
hungry: to be ~ tener hambre
hurt, ache (to) doler (ue)

I

ice cream helado (el)
   ice cream (Mexico) nieve (la);
   ice cream store heladería
   (la); ice cream store (Mexico)
   nievería (la)
idea idea (la)
ill, sick enfermo(a)
include (to) incluir (y)
increase (to) aumentar
incredible increíble
indigestion indigestión (la)
inflate (to) inflar
inform (to) informar
inspect (to) inspeccionar
installment: in ~s a plazos
insurance seguro (el)
insured asegurado(a)
interest (to) interesar
international money order giro
   internacional (el)
intersection intersección (la),
   cruce (el)
invitation invitación (la)
invite (to) invitar
irritation irritación (la)
it's necessary to (+ verb) hay que
   (+ verb)

J

jalopy cacharro (el)
juice jugo (el), zumo (el)

K

key llave (la)
kilometer kilómetro (el)
kind, nice amable

kiss (to) besar
kitchen cocina (la)
knee rodilla (la)
know (to) saber
   know, meet (to) conocer

L

lamb cordero (el)
lame, crippled cojo(a)
landscape paisaje (el)
large, big grande
last (to) durar
late atrasado(a); tarde
learn (to) aprender
leave (to) salir, dejar
   leave (a place) (to) salir de +
   (lugar)
left: be ~ over (to) sobrar
leg pierna (la)
lemonade limonada (la)
lend (to) prestar
lesson lección (la)
lettuce lechuga (la)
license carné (el), licencia (la)
   license plate matrícula (la),
   placa (la)
light luz (la)
   red light, traffic light luz roja
   (la); light (to) encender (ie)
light, quick ligero(a)
like, please (to) encantar, gustar
limp (to) cojear
lip labio (el)
liquid líquido (el)
little poco(a)
live (to) vivir
lively animado(a)
load, charge (to) cargar
loan préstamo (el)
lobster langosta (la)
long largo(a)
   be long, last (to) tardar; So
   long. Hasta luego.
look at (to) mirar
look for (to) buscar
look good (to) tener buena pinta
lose, miss (to) perder (ie)
   lose weight (to) adelgazar,
   bajar de peso, perder peso

low, short bajo(a)
lubricate (to) engrasar
lubrication engrase (el)
lucky: to be~ tener suerte
luggage equipaje (el)
lunch almuerzo (el)
lung pulmón (el)
luxurious lujoso(a)

M

Madam señora
make one feel a terrible pain
 (to) hacer ver las estrellas
make one's mouth water (to)
 hacer la boca agua
man hombre (el)
map mapa (el)
margarine margarina (la)
mariachi mariachi (el)
market mercado (el)
married casado(a)
matter (to) importar
meat carne (la)
mechanic mecánico(a)
medical médico(a)
medicine medicina (la)
meet, find (to) encontrarse
mental stress estrés (el)
menu menú (el), carta (la)
message, errand recado (el)
Mexican mexicano(a)
middle: in the ~ of en medio de
mile milla (la)
milk leche (la)
miss (to) echar de menos,
 extrañar, faltar
Miss señorita
modern moderno(a)
mom mamá (la)
Monday lunes (el)
money dinero (el)
 money order giro (postal) (el)
month mes (el)
more: ~ or less más o menos
morning mañana (la)
 Good ~. Buenos días.
mortgage hipoteca (la)
mother madre (la)
mother-in-law suegra (la)

mouth boca (la)
move away (to) quitarse
much, a lot mucho(a)
muscle músculo (el)
music música (la)
must, should deber
my mi, mis

N

name nombre (el)
narcotic narcótico (el)
narrow estrecho(a)
nausea náusea (la)
near cerca
necessary necesario(a)
neck cuello (el)
need necesidad (la)
need (to) necesitar
 That's all I need! ¡Sólo me
 falta eso!
nephew sobrino (el)
nervous nervioso(a)
new nuevo(a)
next, coming próximo(a)
nice, pleasant (*people*)
 simpático(a)
 How nice! ¡Qué buena onda!
niece sobrina (la)
night noche (la)
noon: at ~ a mediodía
nose nariz (la)
now ahora
nurse enfermero(a) (el/la)

O

obese obeso(a)
offer (to) ofrecer
oil aceite (el), petróleo (el)
oil-producing petrolero(a)
old viejo(a)
omelette tortilla (la)
onion cebolla (la)
only solamente
open (to) abrir
or o
orange naranja (la)
order, serving ración (la)
 order (to) ordenar
overweight pasado(a) de peso

P

package paquete (el)
pack the suitcase (to) hacer la
 maleta
paella paella (la)
pair pareja (la)
pale pálido(a)
paper papel (el)
pardon (to) perdonar
parents padres (los)
park (to) estacionar, parquear,
 aparcar
parking estacionamiento (el)
party fiesta (la)
 party (*Mexico*) pachanga
 (la)
pass (to) pasar
passenger pasajero(a) (el/la)
passport pasaporte (el)
pastry, cake pastel (el)
 pastry shop pastelería (la)
pay (to) pagar
 pay attention (to) hacer caso,
 prestar atención
pedal pedal (el)
pen pluma (la)
pencil lápiz (el)
percent por ciento
percentage porcentaje (el)
per: at . . . miles ~ hour a...
 millas por hora; ~ day por día
perhaps a lo mejor
Peruvian peruano(a)
peso peso (el)
pharmacy farmacia (la)
 24-hour pharmacy farmacia
 de guardia (la)
piano piano (el)
pig, pork puerco (el)
pill píldora (la)
pilot piloto (el)
pink, rosé rosado(a)
pipe, tube tubo (el)
platform andén (el)
play (to) jugar (ue)
 play, touch (to) tocar
please (to) agradar
pleased encantado(a)

pleasure: It's a pleasure. Con mucho gusto.
police department policía (la)
policeman policía (el)
policewoman mujer policía (la)
policy póliza (la)
polite atento(a)
poor pobre
porter maletero (el)
potato patata (la)
powder, talc talco (el)
prefer (to) preferir (ie)
preferable preferible
prepare (to) preparar
prescribe (to) recetar
prescription receta (la)
present actual
present (to) presentar
pressure tensión (la)
pretty bonito(a), lindo(a)
price precio (el)
  What's the ~ of? ¿A cómo está?
priest cura (el)
problem problema (el)
produce (to) producir
promise (to) prometer
prudent prudente
pull one's leg (to) tomar el pelo
pump surtidor (el)
  pump, bomb bomba (la)
punctual puntual
put (to) poner
  put in a cast (to) enyesar;
  put into (to) meter
pyramid pirámide (la)

R

radiator radiador (el)
railroad ferrocarril (el)
  railroad track vía (la)
rain lluvia (la)
  rain (to) llover (ue)
ranch rancho (el)
rancher ranchero (el)
razor blade hoja de afeitar (la)
read (to) leer
ready, smart listo(a)

reasonable razonable
recent reciente
receptionist recepcionista (la)
recognize (to) reconocer
recommend (to) recomendar (ie)
record player tocadiscos (el)
red rojo(a)
reduce (to) reducir
refreshment, cold drink (*nonalcoholic*) refresco (el)
register (to) registrarse
relative pariente (el)
relieve (to) aliviar
remedy remedio (el)
remember (to) recordar (ue)
remove (to) quitar
rent, lease alquiler (el)
  rent (to) alquilar
reservation reservación (la)
reserve (to) reservar
residence residencia (la)
rest (to) descansar
return, change vuelta (la)
rhythm ritmo (el)
rice arroz (el)
rich rico(a)
right, straight derecho(a)
  be right (to) tener razón
right away enseguida, en seguida
ring, sound (to) sonar (ue)
risk: at all ~ a todo riesgo
road carretera (la)
  road, way camino (el)
roast (to) asar
roasted asado(a)
romantic romántico(a)
roof tejado (el)
room cuarto (el), habitación (la)
  room service servicio a los cuartos (el)
run (to) correr

S

sad triste
safety seguridad (la)
salad ensalada (la)
salary salario (el), sueldo (el)

sandwich bocadillo (el), sánguich (el)
Saturday sábado (el)
sauce salsa (la)
save (to) ahorrar
savings account cuenta de ahorros (la)
say, tell (to) decir
  say yes/no (to) decir que sí/no
scale balanza (la)
scare (to) asustar
schedule horario (el)
schoolmate, fellow student compañero(a) (el/la)
sea mar (el)
seafood marisco (el)
season, epoch época (la)
  season (to) condimentar
seat asiento (el)
  seat belt cinturón (el)
secondhand de segunda mano
sedative calmante (el)
see, look at (to) ver
seem (to) parecer
self-service autoservicio (el)
sell (to) vender
send, order (to) mandar
serious serio(a)
  seriously en serio
serve, help (to) servir (i)
several, various varios(as)
sharp (*exact time*) en punto
shirt camisa (la)
shock (to) chocar
shoe store zapatería (la)
shopping: to go ~ ir de compras
short corto(a)
  short, brief breve
  in short en fin, por fin
shot inyección (la)
shoulder hombro (el)
show (to) mostrar (ue)
shower ducha (la)
shrimp camarón (el)
sick, ill enfermo(a)
  get sick (to) enfermarse
sickness enfermedad (la)

sideburn patilla (la)
sight, view vista (la)
sign (to) firmar
single soltero(a)
   single; simple sencillo(a);
   single (*room*), one-way
   (*ticket*) sencillo(a)
sir señor
sirloin solomillo (el)
sister hermana (la)
sit down (to) sentarse (ie)
sleep (to) dormir (ue)
sleeping car coche cama (el)
sleepy: to be ~ tener sueño
slip (to) resbalar
slippery resbaladizo(a)
slow lento(a)
   slowly despacio
small pequeño(a)
smell (to) oler (hue)
   smell fishy (to) olerle mal a
   uno
smile (to): Smile in the face of
   adversity. A mal tiempo,
   buena cara.
smoke (to) fumar
snack merienda (la)
   snack (to) merendar (ie);
   snack (*Mexico*) botana (la)
snow nieve (la)
   snow (to) nevar (ie)
so así que
soap jabón (el)
   soap opera telenovela (la)
something algo
sometimes a veces
son hijo (el)
soup sopa (la)
south sur (el)
speak (to) hablar
specialize (to) especializar
speed rapidez (la), velocidad (la)
speedometer velocímetro (el)
spend (to) gastar
spontaneous espontáneo(a)
sports deportes (los)
spouse esposo(a) (el/la)
square plaza (la)

stainless inoxidable
staircase escalera (la)
stairs escalera (la)
standard shift manual
standard transmission
   transmisión manual, de
   cambios (la)
start (to) comenzar (ie)
start, root (to) arrancar
starter arranque (el)
station; season estación (la)
stay away (to) quitarse
stay in bed (to) guardar cama
steak, fillet filete (el), bisté (el)
steel acero (el)
steering wheel volante (el)
stewardess azafata (la)
still, yet todavía
stomach estómago (el)
stop parada (la)
   stop (sign) stop (el), alto (el);
   stop (to) dejar, dejar de,
   parar, pararse; stop, detain
   (people) (to) detener
store tienda (la)
straight recto(a)
street calle (la)
strict, severe estricto(a)
strong fuerte
study (to) estudiar
successful: to be ~ tener éxito
suffer (to) padecer (c)
sugar azúcar (el/la)
suit (to) convenir (ie)
suitcase maleta (la)
sun sol (el)
Sunday domingo (el)
sunny: to be ~ hacer sol
supper cena (la)
swallow (to) tragar
sweet dulce
swim (to) nadar
symptom síntoma (el)
syrup jarabe (el)

T

table mesa (la)
tablet pastilla (la)

taco taco (el)
tailor sastre(a) (el/la)
   tailor's shop sastrería (la)
take, drink (to) tomar
   take a seat (to) tomar asiento;
   take away (to) quitar; take
   care (to) cuidar, ocuparse;
   take charge of (to) encargarse
   de; take out (to) sacar
tank tanque (el)
tariff, fee tarifa (la)
taste, flavor sabor (el)
   taste like (to) saber a
tasty, delicious sabroso(a)
tax impuesto (el)
taxi driver taxista (el/la)
tea té (el)
telephone teléfono (el)
temperature temperatura (la)
tender, soft blando(a), tierno(a)
terrain terreno (el)
terrible terrible
terrific estupendo(a)
Texan texano(a)
thank (to) agradecer
thankful agradecido(a)
that que
theme tema (el)
then entonces
there, over there allí
thigh muslo (el)
thin, skinny delgado(a), flaco(a)
think (to) pensar (ie)
third tercero(a)
thirsty: to be ~ tener sed
this este (*m.*)
throat garganta (la)
Thursday jueves (el)
ticket billete (el), pasaje (el),
   boleto (el)
   one-way ticket ida (la);
   round-trip ida y vuelta (la);
   ticket agent, clerk
   taquillero(a) (el/la); ticket
   window taquilla (la)
time tiempo (el)
   time (*in a series*) vez (la);
   ahead of time con antici-

pación; **on time** a tiempo
tip, gratuity propina (la)
tire llanta (la), neumático (el)
   spare tire llanta de respuesto (la)
to, in order to; for para
today hoy
tomato tomate (el)
tomorrow: See you tomorrow. Hasta mañana.
tonight esta noche
tooth diente (el)
toothpaste crema dental (la)
touch (to) tocar
tourism turismo (el)
towel toalla (la)
trademark marca (la)
train tren (el)
translate (to) traducir
travel, trip viaje (el)
   travel (to) viajar
traveler viajero(a) (el/la)
tree árbol (el)
trolley tranvía (el)
truck, bus camión (el)
trunk baúl (el), cajuela (la)
   trunk (*of a car*) maletero (el)
truth verdad (la)
try to (to) tratar de
Tuesday martes (el)
tuna atún (el)
turkey pavo (el)
turn, bend (to) doblar
   turn (**+ adjective**) **(to)** ponerse (+ adjective); **to turn off** apagar
twist, sprain (to) torcer (ue)
twisted, bent torcido(a)
two dos
typical típico(a)

U

ugly feo(a)
ulcer úlcera (la)
umbrella paraguas (el)
unable: to be ~ to stand no poder ver
uncle tío (el)

undershirt camiseta (la)
understand (to) comprender, entender (ie)
undo, melt (to) deshacer
unexpected imprevisto(a)
unhappy descontento(a)
unlucky: to be ~ tener mala estrella, tener mala pata
unpack the suitcase (to) deshacer la maleta
unpleasant (*people*) antipático(a)
until, to hasta
up-to-date: to be ~ estar en onda
use (to) usar

V

vacation vacaciones (las)
   be on vacation (to) estar de vacaciones
vaccine vacuna (la)
valuable valioso(a)
value, stock valor (el)
variety variedad (la)
veal ternera (la)
vegetable verdura (la)
   vegetables legumbres (las), vegetales (los)
vermouth vermut (el), vermú (el)
visit (to) visitar
vitamin vitamina (la)

W

waist cintura (la)
wait on (to) atender (ie)
waiter, waitress camarero(a) (el/la), mesero(a) (el/la), mozo(a) (el/la)
walk (to) andar
wall pared (la)
wallet, purse cartera (la)
want, wish (to) desear
warn, inform (to) avisar
wash (to) lavar
waste time (to) perder el tiempo
water agua (*f.*) (el)
wave onda (la)
wavy, hilly ondulado(a)

way: by the ~ a proposito; **No ~!** ¡Ni modo!
weak débil
weather: What's the ~? ¿Qué tiempo hace?
Wednesday miércoles (el)
week semana (la)
welcome bienvenida (la)
   welcome (to) dar la bienvenida
well pozo (el)
wheel rueda (la)
while rato (el)
white blanco(a)
wide ancho(a)
win, earn (to) ganar
window ventana (la)
   small window ventanilla (la)
windshield parabrisas (el)
   windshield wiper limpiaparabrisas (el)
windy: to be ~ hacer viento
wine vino (el)
   red wine tinto(a); **wine cooler** sangría (la)
wish, want (to) querer (ie)
woman mujer (la)
wool lana (la)
word palabra (la)
work (to) funcionar, trabajar
world mundo (el)
worn-out gastado(a)
worry (to) preocuparse
worth: to be ~ valer
worthwhile: to be ~ valer la pena
wrist, doll muñeca (la)
write (to) escribir

X

X ray radiografía (la)

Y

yellow amarillo(a)
yesterday ayer
yogurt yogur (el)
young joven
your tu, tus